Psychosomatic Disorders

Psychosomatic Disorders

Benjamin B. Wolman

Editor-in-Chief
International Encyclopedia of Psychiatry, Psychology,
Psychoanalysis, and Neurology

PLENUM MEDICAL BOOK COMPANY
NEW YORK AND LONDON

Library of Congress Cataloging in Publication Data

Wolman, Benjamin B.
  Psychosomatic disorders / Benjamin B. Wolman.
     p.   cm.
  Includes bibliographies and index.
  ISBN 0-306-42945-4
  1. Medicine, Psychosomatic. I. Title.
  [DNLM: 1. Psychophysiologic Disorders. WM 90 W865p]
RC49.W65   1988
616.08—dc19
DNLM/DLC   88-22555
for Library of Congress   CIP

© 1988 Plenum Publishing Corporation
233 Spring Street, New York, N.Y. 10013

Plenum Medical Book Company is an imprint of Plenum Publishing Corporation

Printed in the United States of America

Preface

This volume is an encyclopedic book on psychosomatic disorders, written for neurologists, psychiatrists, psychologists, psychiatric social workers, and other mental and physical health professionals. It could be used as a textbook in advanced training programs for the above-mentioned professions. It covers the entire field of mind–body issues in psychology and psychiatry and related areas of clinical medicine.

The mind–body relationship is a two-way street. Anxiety, fear, anger, and other emotional states can produce physiological changes such as tears, elevated heart rate, and diarrhea. When these changes affect one's health, they belong to the province of *psychosomatic medicine*. On the other hand, the intake of alcohol and other substances can affect such psychological processes as thinking and mood. When the intake of substances is helpful, they belong to the province of *psychopharmacology*. The substances that are hurtful and adversely affect one's mental health belong to the category of addictions and drug abuse. All these issues are *somatopsychic*.

The present volume does not deal with somatopsychic phenomena no matter what effect they may have. It deals with the physical effects of psychological issues, and only with those that cause harm to the human body. Thus, it describes and analyzes psychosomatic disorders.

It is divided into four major parts: theoretical viewpoints, etiological considerations, the psychosomatic diseases, and treatment methods.

I am greatly indebted to my two research assistants, Mahala Buckingham-Clark and Susan Friedman, for their most efficient cooperation. I am also grateful to the editorial and production staff of Plenum Publishing for their cordial and most encouraging attitude.

Benjamin B. Wolman

Contents

.

I
Foundations

1

Conceptual Framework

Defining Psychosomatics

Psychomatic disorders are diseases of the body. They are physicochemical, anatomical, or physiological disorders of living organisms. The term *psychosomatic* is quite ambiguous, for there are usually certain psychological factors in the etiology of many nonpsychosomatic diseases and in the treatment of patients, irrespective of the nature of their sickness (Knapp, 1985).

There are at least three different approaches to the field of psychosomatics. Psychosomatics can be regarded as: (1) a theory of mind–body relationships; (2) a theory of certain illnesses; and (3) a therapeutic technique that includes both the medical and the psychological devices. As mentioned in the preface, this volume is comprised of four parts: theories, etiology, diseases, and treatment methods.

Lipowski (1985) stressed the need to distinguish between psychosomatics as a science and psychomatics as an approach to the practice of medicine and consulting activities. Psychosomatic *science* studies the relationship between psychological and biological phenomena in human beings, whereas the practice of medicine and health-consulting activities is different and is not necessarily a theoretically oriented field. Lipowski emphasized the role of "liason-psychiatry" as a particular branch of psychiatry concerned with the diagnosis, treatment, and prevention of psychiatric aspects of physical illness. Grinker and Robbins (1953) defined psychosomatics as a conceptual approach to relationships and not necessarily as any new physiological or psychological theory or new therapeutic approach to illness.

Psychosomatic medicine has often been criticized for not providing an answer to the question of how "social experiences and/or psychological conflicts and induced emotions could be possibly translated (transduced) into bodily physiology leading to illness" (Weiner, 1980, p. 223). Does the brain "translate" psychological experience into a physiological experience?

Or, following Pavlov, how can "nonmaterial" anxiety or depression cause "material" physiological phenomena in the gastrointestinal or cardiovascular systems?

Furthermore, Weiner (1980) wrote that:

> One of the major reasons for the failure to solve this problem is that we have had only *one hypothesis* that the emotional response is the mediator of stress and the physiological responses . . . however, the problem is again complicated by the fact that we do not know how impulses arriving over sympathetic or vagal afferent pathways can be perceived and acquire conscious meanings. (p. 226)

Two years later, Weiner (1982) wrote:

> Psychosomatic medicine is concerned with the social and psychobiological factors that antecede disease or are associated with its onset rather than with the pathophysiology and pathological anatomy of diseased organs (and their cells) or bodily systems after onset. Yet even this claim is overstated, because the impact and meaning of disease or of being ill on individuals, their families, and their social groups have also been a vital and major concern of those interested in the psychosomatic approach. In short, it is believed by those who hold to this approach that social and psychological factors play some role in the predisposition to, initiation of, response to, and maintenance of every disease. (p. 31)

HOMEOSTATIC APPROACH

Several psychosomatic researchers (Engel, 1980; Hofer, 1984; Weiner, 1982) have applied the general systems theory and the cybernetic concepts of self-regulation and feedback. They have followed, to a certain degree, Claude Bernard's (1878) and Cannon's (1932) principles of homeostasis. Contemporary concepts of homeostatic systems are quite different from Bernard's formulation. They incorporate the knowledge that the composition of the interior environment is only partly determined by regulatory processes within cellular and subcellular units. The individual's exterior environment also plays a significant role in maintaining physiological homeostasis. Disturbances in regulation can arise anywhere within the system, from the social to the cellular level, and can cause altered physiology that may contribute to one's susceptibility to disease. Certain psychosomatic diseases have been conceptualized as disorders of regulation, including essential hypertension, bronchial asthma, and peptic ulcer disease (Taylor, 1987).

Undoubtedly, a child's interaction with the mother or any other social relations and the interpersonal regulatory system affects the functioning of the individual's self-regulatory system:

> The development of an attachment bond between mother and infant and the experience of tolerance levels of disengagement permit a gradual transition from interactional regulatory processes which use sensorimotor pathways, to regulatory interactions that are primarily psychological.

Weiner (1982) and Hofer (1984) have suggested that some individuals fail to achieve the usual and proper levels of self-regulation. Like the infant, they continue to rely excessively on another person to maintain their psycho-biological equilibrium. Such a developmental arrest is consistent with the observations made by Alexander (1950) and other early psychosomaticists, that people who are prone to developing classical psychosomatic diseases are excessively dependent. However, this dependency cannot be attributed simply to the repeated frustration of oral instinctual needs in early life. Dependent people have suffered deficiencies in their earliest object relationships; their inner worlds lack adequate representation of a well-functioning self-selfobject unit that normally would substitute for the external mother and provide self-regulatory functions. To compensate for this, many of these people retain a symbiotic involvement with the mother or form a substitute symbiotic selfobject relationship with a "key figure." According to Hofer's model (1984), because of the "withdrawal of specific sensorimotor regulators hidden within the many complex interactions of the relationship" (p. 188), they are at greater risk for developing physical disease following separation and object loss. (Taylor, 1987, pp. 283–287)

CONSCIOUS AND UNCONSCIOUS

Early theoreticians and practitioners of psychosomatic medicine were not concerned with the how or why of psychosomatic disorders. Freud (1933/1964) was satisfied with knowing that there was a relationship between the conscious and unconscious states and bodily functions. It was enough for him to observe, for example, a connection between emotion and blushing. Today, however, the practitioner seeks to find the mental patterns by which blushing is determined, as well as how it is generated from the blood vessels.

Over the years, the types of psychosomatic diseases themselves have changed. Today, one can rarely find a classic case of hysteria; this disease has evolved into new patterns of a vegetative type. A disease of this vegetative type, such as eczema, is classified as psychosomatic as it begins concurrently with mental conflicts and ends with a resolution of these conflicts. In the face of these vegetative disorders, classic medicine is at a loss, most often attempting to treat the physical symptoms while denying the psychological causes (Schaefer, 1966).

The somatic connections between mental states and physical well-being can be both conscious and unconscious. Quite often, they shift from conscious to unconscious or stay in between, in the protoconscious (Wolman, 1986). Some psychosomatic phenomena originate in consecutive emotional reactions. Consider the origin of eczema in a child suffering from lack of mother love: the mother's love is withheld; the child turns to self-satisfaction; caressing is satisfying, and a variant of caressing is scratching; this leads to itching; which finally leads to skin damage (Schaefer, 1966). Other psychosomatic phenomena do not have such a clear, consecutive organization.

Shaefer (1966) proposed that what we do know, in any case, is that mental and physical events are both inseparable in one unit, the human being, which cannot be divided into a somatic half and a physical half. Both the conscious and the unconscious affect the physical. Further, somatic events are mainly influenced by emotions, which are mental and physical simultaneously. The split between mind and body has resulted from methodological abstractions, not from any reality of being. According to Schaefer, in order to assess and treat psychosomatic disorders, these two concepts must be joined.

Ullman (1986, p. 566) goes even further in pointing to unconscious processes of psychosomatic disorders and views psychosomatic phenomena as physical analogies to telepathic messages. Ullman quotes extraordinary circumstances that led to the simultaneous deaths of 32-year-old schizophrenic twins who were under observation on different wards in a psychiatric hospital.

Psychology and Physiology

According to some scientists, psychological and physiological issues are merely two different sides of a coin. However, the interpretation of how both come about is subject to frequent misinterpretation. Being two sides of the same coin, they could be the product of a third variable: "For example, the behavioral and psychological changes seen in primary anorexia nervosa, and the correlated immaturity of circadian pattern of luteinizing hormone secretion, may simply be the 'read out' of a defect in the anterior hypothalamus" (Weiner, 1980, p. 227). Moreover, it is possible that the psychological and physiological phenomena belong to unrelated realms of events, and that they have nothing to do with each other and proceed independently. In this view, a bereavement may produce grief in the bereaved, but the physiological changes of weeping, or of rheumatoid arthritis, are independent of his or her loss. The distinction between physiology and psychology continues (Wolman, 1981).

In 1935, Moritz Schlick, a leading member of the neopositivistic philosophical "Viennese Circle" wrote: "The adjectives 'physical' and 'mental' formulate only two different representational modes by which the data of experience are ordered: they are different ways of describing reality" (Schlick, 1949, p. 403).

Ayer (1948) wrote that:

> The problem with which philosophers have vexed themselves in the past concerning the possibility of bridging the "gulf" between mind and matter in knowledge or action, are all fictitious problems arising out of senseless metaphysical conceptions of mind and matter or minds and material things as "substances." (p. 124)

In a way, Pavlov (1928) echoed the theories of philosophers who advocated radical materialistic views. Karl Vogt wrote, in *Vorlesungen über den Menschen* (1863), that thinking is related to the human brain as gall is related to liver, and that consciousness is merely one of the functions of the brain. More or less at the same time, Moleschott wrote, in *Der Kreislauf des Lebens* (1852), that division between body and mind is hopeless, for the body and the material world are real, whereas the concepts of the mind and the spiritual deal with the imaginary.

According to Irani (1980), the mind–body problem is not much discussed nor successfully banished. Apparently, nature crosses the mind–body bridge, but scientific research is still far from finding an adequate answer to this perennial problem. The field of psychosomatic disorders offers valuable insights, but the final answer is still a controversial issue.

REFERENCES

Alexander, F. *Psychosomatic medicine.* New York: Norton, 1950.

Ayer, A. J. *Language, truth and logic* (2nd ed.). London: Victor Golancz, 1948.

Bernard, C. *Leçons sur les phénomes de la vie commune aux animaux et aux vegetaux.* Paris: Balliére, 1878.

Cannon, W. B. *Bodily changes in pain, hunger, fear and rage.* New York: Appleton-Century-Crofts, 1932.

Engel, G. L. The clinical application of the biopsychosocial model. *American Journal of Psychiatry*, 1980, *137*, 535–544.

Freud, S. New introductory lectures on psychoanalysis. *Standard Editions* (Vol. 2, pp. 3–184). London: Hogarth Press, 1964. (Originally published, 1933.)

Grinker, R. R., & Robbins, F. P. *Psychosomatic case book.* New York: Blakiston, 1953.

Hofer, M. A. Relationships as regulators: A psychobiologic perspective on bereavement. *Psychosomatic Medicine*, 1984, *46*, 183–197.

Irani, K. D. Conceptual changes in the problem of mind-body relation. In R. W. Rieber (Ed.), *Body and mind* (pp. 57–77). New York: Academic Press, 1980.

Knapp, P. H. Current theoretical concepts in psychosomatic medicine. In H. I. Kaplan & B. J. Sadock (Eds.), *Comprehensive textbook of psychiatry* (4th ed.), (pp. 1113–1121). Baltimore: Williams & Wilkins, 1985.

Lipowski, Z. J. *Psychosomatic medicine and liason psychiatry.* New York: Plenum Press, 1985.

Moleschott, H. *Der Kreislauf des Lebens.* Breslau, 1852.

Pavlov, I. P. *Lectures on conditioned reflexes.* New York: Liveright, 1928.

Rieber, R. W. (Ed.). *Body and mind: Past, present and future.* New York: Academic Press, 1980.

Schaefer, H. Psychosomatic problems of vegetative regulatory functions. In J. C. Eccles (Ed.), *Brain and conscious experience* (pp. 522–535). New York: Springer, 1966.

Schlick, M. On the relation between psychological and physical concepts. In H. Feigl & W. Sellars (Eds.), *Readings in philosophical analysis.* New York: Appleton-Century-Crofts, 1949.

Taylor, G. J. *Psychosomatic medicine and contemporary psychoanalysis.* New York: International Universities Press, 1987.

Ullman, M. Psychopathology and psi-phenomena. In B. B. Wolman (Ed.), *Handbook of parapsychology* (pp. 557–575). Jefferson, NC: McFarland, 1986.

Vogt, K. *Vorlesungen über den Menschen.* Breslau: 1863.

2

Historical Overview

ANCIENT IDEAS

The idea that mental states can affect the functions of the human body is not new. Centuries ago, several thinkers pointed to the impact of the mind on the body.

Plato (428–347 B.C.), in the book *Charmides*, quoted Socrates as follows:

> As it is not proper to try to cure the eyes without the head nor the head without the body, so neither is it proper to cure the body without the soul, and this is the reason why so many diseases escape Greek physicians who are ignorant of the whole. (Plato, 1942)

According to Hippocrates (460–377 B.C.), psychosomatic disorders are abnormal physical reactions to stressful emotions, incidents, and situations. Hippocrates noticed that strong emotional experiences, especially fear and anger, could produce disturbances in bodily functions (Rieber, 1980).

A. Galen (A.D. 129–199) maintained that mental processes are produced by interaction between the cortical and the subcortical matter. Fear, anger, grief, and other emotions are "diseases of the soul." Galen's theory was supported by a detailed anatomical research conducted by Vesalius in 1800 (Heilman & Valenstein, 1979).

MODERN TIMES

In 1637, Descartes advocated dualism and drew a clear distinction between the mind, called "thinking entity," and the body called "non-thinking entity" (Descartes, 1956; Wilson, 1978).

Benjamin Rush (1745–1813) advocated the unity of mind and body. According to Rush (1811), the division of mind and body is appropriate for religion, but in the eyes of a physician, humans are indivisible beings, united in mind and body. Mental actions influence the function of the body, and they can be the causes of many diseases.

At the same time, F. J. Gall (1835) theorized that cognitive processes are a product of interaction of the two cerebral hemispheres. He also suggested that the subcortical centers are in charge of life-sustaining functions. He believed that the frontal lobes are the site of intelligence and introduced a theory of phrenology relating cognitive processes to brain asymmetrics. A. R. Luria (1980) maintained that Gall's ideas of phrenology were so "fantastic" that the scientific community could not accept them.

However, Gall's theory of functional localization was supported by Ernest Auburtin, who maintained that speech ability is related to the anterior region of the brain (Hynd & Willis, 1985). Pierre Paul Broca (1861) performed an autopsy on a patient who suffered right-side paralysis and speech disorder. The autopsy uncovered a lesion of the left side of the temporal gyrus, the corpus striatum, and the insular cortex. Thus, the motorspeech center, called after Broca, was discovered.

In 1830, Charles Bell published a book on *The Nervous System of the Human Body*. Bell had proved that the ventral roots of the spinal cord are composed of motor nerves only, whereas the sensory nerve fibers compose the dorsal roots and the spinal ganglia. The distinction between motor and sensory functions had been made much earlier, but Bell (and simultaneously and independently François Magendie) discovered that these functions are performed by different nerve fibers. In addition, Bell and Magendie demonstrated that conduction goes only one way, the stimulus being conducted from the sensory organ to the center of the nervous system. The response goes from the center to the muscle, never from the muscle to the center. This Bell–Magendie "law of forward conduction" paved the way for the later concept of the *reflex* as a stimulus–response phenomenon.

Bell's work was continued by Johannes Müller and Ernst Heinrich Weber. Müller's experiments on frogs led to a division of the neural activity of a reflex into three stages: (1) centripetal conduction, (2) connections within the center, and (3) response to the proper muscles.

Müller (1838–1842) concluded that, as perception depends on sensory nerves, the content of perception cannot depend only on stimulus but is affected by the nature of the sensory nerve. This conclusion led to the law of "specific energies of sensory nerves," which states that "external agencies give rise to no kind of sensation which cannot also be produced by internal causes exciting changes in the condition of our nerves" (p. 29). For example, sensations of vision are:

> . . . perceived independently of all external exciting causes. . . . The excited condition of the nerve is manifested even while the eyes are closed, by the appearance of light or luminous flashes which merely are sensations of the nerve, and not owing to the presence of any surrounding objects. (p. 30)

The same external stimulus may give rise to different sensations in the various senses: "The mechanical influence of a blow, concussion, or pressure excites, for example, in the eye, the sensation of light and colors" (p. 30).

In France, Pierre Flourens extirpated parts of the pigeon brain and observed the psychological impact of the extirpation. Flourens's studies led to discoveries of the localization of brain functions. Flourens found that the cerebral lobes perform the functions of perceiving, understanding, memorizing, and willing, and that the cerebellum coordinates movements; thus, the relationship between memory, understanding, and the functions of the nervous system was established. The next step was to conclude that psychology and physiology were mutually related and complementary disciplines (Flourens, 1824).

PSYCHOPHYSICAL PARALLELISM

E. H. Weber's findings (1834) proved that the discrimination of weight is finer when the weight is perceived by several senses. The division into the five traditional senses was replaced by a new concept of a larger number of senses. In Weber's experiments, the differences in weight were better determined when the subjects lifted the weights instead of just holding them, for in lifting, the muscular sense was added to the senses that perceive weight. Weber found that the ability to discriminate small differences in a stimulus depends not on the intensity of the stimulus alone but on a certain ratio between the difference and the standard weight used in the experiment.

This important discovery led to the formulation by Gustav Theodore Fechner of the so-called Weber's law. Weber's study was a milestone in the experimental research on sensation, and it encouraged more general concepts regarding the nature of perception.

In 1860, Fechner published a volume entitled *Elements of Psychophysics.* Fechner believed that he had found the bridge connecting physical and mental phenomena: all stimuli belong to the physical world; all sensations belong to the mental. A definite relation between mental and physical was discovered by Fechner and was presented in a mathematical formula.

Fechner elaborated on the concept of threshold. The *initial threshold* was the minimal intensity of a stimulus necessary for the stimulus to be perceived. The *differential threshold* was the minimum of increase or decrease in intensity of the stimulus necessary for the perception of these decreases or increases.

The impact of Fechner's work was tremendous. His study of the sensory processes became the generally accepted frame of reference in psychology for at least half a century. "Even Fechner's critics," wrote William

James (1890), "should always feel bound, after smiting his theories hip and thigh and leaving not a stick of them standing, to wind up by saying that nevertheless to him belongs the imperishable glory, of first formulating them and thereby turning psychology into an *exact science*" (p. 549).

James felt that Fechner's method was arid and futile, but one should not forget that Fechner introduced a quantitative method into the study of sensation and developed a system of experimentation in psychology.

Another outstanding scientist, Hermann von Helmhotz, studied the speed of neural conduction in both motor and sensory nerves. He found that the speed of conduction in the motor nerve was 30 meters per second. Although his estimate was much below today's estimate, his experiments gave impetus to the very popular studies of "reaction time." Of even greater importance to the growing psychological science was his monumental work in vision and hearing. Helmholtz (1856–1866) applied Müller's law of specific energies and developed a thoroughly experimental method for the study of sensory reactions.

Karl Wernicke (1874) demonstrated that damage to the posterior part of the left temporal lobe adversely affects one's ability to comprehend verbal communication; thus, he discovered the auditory-linguistic center. Moreover, Wernicke correctly hypothesized that Broca's region, which is responsible for motor–speech images, and the audiolinguistic region (now called the Wernicke lobe) are connected by intrahemispheric fibers.

In 1874, J. H. Jackson observed that the left hemisphere is the center for the automatic revival of images, whereas the right side of the brain is the center for recognition. He maintained that the left hemisphere functioned automatically, but that the functions of the right hemisphere were based on cognitive processes.

In 1925, O. Schwarz published a collective volume that advocated mind–body unity. The book stressed the need to include the role of psychological factors in all diseases and in medical practice.

THE BEGINNINGS OF PSYCHOSOMATIC MEDICINE

In 1935, Flanders Dunbar published a comprehensive review of psychosomatic literature stressing the conviction that psyche and soma are "two aspects of a fundamental unity".

The American Psychosomatic Society was founded in 1939. Dunbar was the first editor of its journal, which emphasized psychiatry and psychoanalysis. In 1939, the first issue of the journal, *Psychosomatic Medicine,* included an introductory statement that read: "[The journal's] object is to study in their interrelation the psychological and physiological aspects of normal and abnormal bodily functions and thus to integrate somatic therapy and psychotherapy" (quoted in Lipowski, 1985, p. 122). The statement encompassed the psychosomatic field both as a science and as a clinical practice, and it emphasized a monistic approach to the mind/body dichotomy.

In 1943, Dunbar published the comprehensive volume *Psychosomatic Diagnosis*. Dunbar related particular psychosomatic disorders to distinct personality traits. Dunbar maintained that people who are self-controlled perfectionists tend to develop essential hypertension when faced with an acute conflict with people in authority. All other psychosomatic disorders are similarly typical for individuals with consistent attitudes and personality traits.

In 1953, the Academy of Psychosomatic Medicine was founded and began to broaden the concept of psychosomatic disorders to include all fields of medicine. At the same time, leading psychoanalysts embarked on research related to psychosomatic symptoms (Alexander, 1950; Alexander & Flagg, 1965; Alexander, French, & Pollack, 1968). The psychoanalytic theories of psychosomatic disorders will be described in this volume in a separate chapter. A historical overview of psychoanalytic contributions follows:

> One of the major figures in psychosomatic medicine in the last 50 years was Alexander (1950). (In fact, the psychosomatic approach to disease and his name are virtually synonymous in the minds of most people). In Alexander's work, we find the point of view that specific, dynamic, unconscious constellations of conflicts characterized patients with the diseases he studied. These constellations were not, in his view, unique to those with these diseases, but they differed in individuals with different diseases and were, therefore, specific to the disease. The patient with a peptic duodenal ulcer has an unconscious wish to be fed and to receive. Being ashamed of this wish, he or she becomes excessively independent. Patients with essential hypertension fear their own aggressive assertiveness, which they inhibit or repress, often from fear of retaliation. The child with bronchial asthma wishes to be enveloped and protected by the mother. In some children that wish is expressed in a cry for the mother's protection, but the cry is inhibited for fear that the mother will repudiate the child. In other children, the wish to be protected and enveloped can be averted by separating the child from its mother.
>
> Much controversy has surrounded Alexander's formulations about specific psychological conflicts. While this controversy was raging, his other statements were forgotten. His concept of these diseases was actually tripartite: (1) the specific conflict predisposed patients to certain diseases, but only in the presence of other (at his time, undetermined) genetic, biochemical, and physiologic X factors; (2) in certain specific life situations to which the patient was sensitized by virtue of his or her key conflict, the conflict was activated and enhanced; (3) strong emotions accompanied the activated conflict; through autonomic, hormonal, or neuromuscular channels, they produced changes in structure and function.
>
> Alexander made the most comprehensive statements about the several factors that play a role in the etiology and pathogenesis of disease. His concepts contain statements about the (multiple) predisposition to, onset, and initiation of a finite number of diseases (incorrectly called the only "psychosomatic"

ones). Furthermore, Alexander also specified the developmental-experimental origins of the psychological conflicts and how they were habitually handled. When not handled, they aroused strong emotions.

His concepts are heuristically powerful because they separate the predisposition to disease from the context in which it began and the (presumed) mechanisms that produced it.

By specifying different psychological conflicts in different bodily diseases, Alexander abjured studying the psychological characteristics that patients with these and other diseases shared. Reusch, in particular, stressed the age-inappropriate behavioral and psychological features of adult patients that made them particularly unadapted to and unable to cope with their environments. He listed features such as impaired or arrested social learning, a reliance on imitating others, a tendency to express thought and feeling in direct physical action, dependency on others, passivity, childlike ways of thinking, lofty and unrealistic aspirations, difficulties in assimilating and integrating life experiences, a reliance on securing love and affection from others, and—above all—an inability to master changes in their lives or to learn new techniques for overcoming the frustration of their wishes. The other writers describe features, which they call *alexithymic*, whose central aspects are (1) a failure of such patients to be aware of their own emotions (which serve as signals of personal distress) and to resort to constructive imagination in solving problems and (2) a preoccupation with the concrete specifics rather than the meaning of events in their lives.

Many writers have stressed their patients' adaptive incapacities and the reliance on others. This notable shift from a preoccupation with intrapsychic conflicts, stressed by Alexander, to maladaptive psychological features is further supported by and implicit in the work of Engel (1968), Greene (1954), and Schmale (1958), who have stressed that many diseases begin in a setting of separation or bereavement for people who are particularly reliant on others and cannot cope without their support and help. The consequence of such separations and bereavements ("losses") is a state of adaptive failure, signaled by helplessness, hopelessness, and giving up. Conversely, the consequences of "losses" can be averted by making available to the stricken person supportive measures that are usually provided by by families, friends, nurses, physicians, or other health workers.

This brief summary of the history of some of the concepts of psychosomatic medicine is designed to highlight a shift away from a preoccupation with intrapsychic conflict to a study of psychological adaptation and the key role that personal relationships between patients and others play in health and disease. (Weiner, 1982, pp. 33–34)

REFERENCES

Alexander, F. *Psychosomatic medicine.* New York: Norton, 1950.

Alexander, F., & Flagg, W. N. The psychosomatic approach. In B. B. Wolman (Ed.), *Handbook of clinical psychology* (pp. 855–947). New York: McGraw-Hill, 1965.

Alexander, F., French, T. M., & Pollack, G. H. *Psychosomatic specificity: Experimental study and results.* Chicago: Chicago University Press, 1968.

Bell, C. *The nervous system of the human body.* Edinburgh, 1830.

Broca, P. P. Nouvelle observation d'aphemie produite par une lesion de la moite posterieure des deuxième et troisième circonvolution frontale. *Bulletin de la Societé Anatomique de Paris,* 1861, *36,* 398–407.

Descartes, R. *Discours on method.* New York: Bobbs-Merrill, 1956.

Dunbar, F. *Emotions and bodily change: A survey of literature of psychosomatic relationships: 1910–1933.* New York: Columbia University Press, 1935.

Dunbar, F. *Psychosomatic diagnosis.* New York: Hoeber, 1943.

Engel, G. L. A life setting conducive to illness: The giving up, given up complex. *Annals of Internal Medicine,* 1968, *69,* 293–300.

Fechner, G. T. *Elemente der psychophysik.* Leipzig, 1860.

Flourens, M. J. P. *Recherches expérimentales sur les propriétés et les functions du système nerveux dans les animaux vertébrés.* Paris: Creyot, 1824.

Gall, F. J. *Critical review of some anatomico-physiological works, with an explanation of a new philosophy of moral qualities and intellectual faculties.* Boston: Marsh Copen & Lyon, 1835.

Greene, W. A., Jr. Psychological factors and reticuloendothelial disease: 1. Preliminary observations on a group of males with lymphomas and leukemias. *Psychosomatic Medicine,* 1954, *16,* 220–230.

Heilman, K. M. & Valenstein E. (Eds.). *Clinical neuropsychology.* New York: Oxford University Press, 1979.

Helmholtz, H. von *Handbuch der physiologischen optik.* Leipzig: 1856–1866.

Hynd, G. W., & Willis, W. G. Neurological foundations of intelligence. In B. B. Wolman (Ed.), *Handbook of intelligence.* New York: Wiley, 1985.

Jackson, J. H. On the nature of the duality of the brain. *Medical Press Circulator,* 1874, *1,* 41–46.

James, W. *Principles of psychology.* New York: Holt, 1890.

Lipowski, Z. J. *Psychosomatic medicine and liason psychiatry.* New York: Plenum Press, 1985.

Luria, A. R. *Higher cortical functions in man.* New York: Basic Books, 1980.

Miller, N. E. Behavioral medicine: Symbiosis between laboratory and clinic. *Annual Review of Psychology,* 1983, *34,* 1–32.

Müller, J. *Handbook of physiology.* Breslau, 1838–1842.

Plato, *Charmides: The best known works of Plato.* Garden City, NY: Ribbon Books, 1942.

Plato, *Republic.* Indianapolis: Hacket, 1974.

Rieber, R. W. (Ed.). *Body and mind: Past, present and future.* New York: Academic Press, 1980.

Rush, B. *Seven introductory lectures.* Philadelphia: Bradford & Innkeep, 1811.

Schmale, A. H., Jr. Relation of separation and depression to disease: 1. A report on hospitalized medical population. *Psychosomatic Medicine,* 1958, *20,* 259–277.

Schwartz, O. (Ed.). *Psychogenese und Psychotherapie körperlicher Symptome.* Vienna: Springer, 1925.

Weber, E. H. *De tactu: Annotattiones anatomicae et physiologicae.* Breslau: 1834.

Weiner, H. Psychobiological factors in bodily disease. In T. Millon, C. Green, & R. Meagher (Eds.), *Handbook of clinical health psychology* (pp. 31–52). New York: Plenum Press, 1982.

Wernicke, K. *Lehrbuch der Gehirnkrankheiten.* Breslau, 1874.

Wilson, M. D. *Descartes.* London: Routledge & Keegan Paul, 1978.

3

Psychoanalysis

SIGMUND FREUD

Psychosomatic medicine as a study of physical illnesses caused by emotional disorders was, in a way, an outgrowth of psychoanalysis. Freud (1905/1953) related the etiology of hysteria to both mental and physical factors. He wrote: "As far as I can see, every hysterical symptom involves the participation of both sides. It cannot occur without a certain degree of somatic compliance" (1905/1953, p. 40).

Fenichel (1945) drew a distinction between conversations and organ neuroses. Organ neuroses are related to inappropriate physiological functions; conversions are reflections of unconscious fantasies. Organic neuroses are psychosomatic: "One of them is physical in nature and consists of physiological changes caused by inappropriate use of the function in question" (p. 236). These symptoms are organ-neurotic. The conversion symptoms have "a specific unconscious meaning and are expressions of a fantasy in body language and are directly accessible to psychoanalysis in the same way as dreams" (p. 236).

Groddeck (1961) maintained that physical illnesses reflect an inner, emotional conflict. Illnesses can serve various purposes, either repressing the conflict and keeping it repressed or helping to resolve it.

Deutsch (1953, 1959) related psychosomatic disorders to an inadequate or missing emotional gratification in childhood. Lack of maternal affection, separation anxiety, and abandonment trigger the somatization of emotion: "The biologic expression of the unconscious is due to a preformed functional pattern of the past . . . a fusion and interaction of psychic and somatic phenomena which begins at a very early age, becomes solidified and persists throughout life" (1953, pp. 175–176).

Freud (1895/1966) defined conversion as a process "whereby an unbearable idea is rendered innocuous by the quantity of excitation attached to it being transmitted into some bodily form of expression." Repression of unconscious wishes leads to transformation of conversion into somatic symptoms.

Freud was faithful to the monistic philosophy and conception of the unity of the human and nature, and his entire system was guided by the monistic and materialistic concepts of the human organism.

Freud never gave up the search for an organic equivalent of mental disturbance. It is not surprising that Freud's model of personality was influenced by physics, that his theory of libido was modeled on electrical concepts, and that human actions were represented by him as discharges of energy.

In 1895, Freud wrote that it is "scarcely possible to avoid picturing these processes as being in the last resort of a chemical nature" (p. 61). He never gave up this belief; even when he introduced several nonreductionistic concepts, he kept referring to the future research that would probably close the gap between physicochemical and mental facts.

Among the first principles that he postulated was the concept of energy. All mental activities and everything that psychology deals with are discharges of mental energy analogous to, or in some cases derivative of, physicochemical energy. However, Freud did not try to close the gap between physical and mental processes by a simple reductionism that overlooked the differences between these two realms. He was very much against such a naive reductionism (Wolman, 1965, 1981).

In his last work, Freud (1938/1949) tried to bring together the doctrines of psychoanalysis and to state them in the most positive terms:

> We know two things concerning what we call our psyche or mental life: firstly, its bodily organ and scene of action, the brain (or nervous system), and secondly, our acts of consciousness, which are immediate data and cannot be more fully explained by any kind of description. Everything that lies between these two terminal points is unknown to us and, so far as we are aware, there is no direct relation between them. If it existed, it would at the most afford an exact localization of the processes of consciousness and could give us no help toward understanding them. (pp. 13–14)

Freud did not reject the organic foundations of the mental life. "Id," he said, "contains everything that is inherited, that is present at birth, that is fixed in constitution" (p. 104). But he never ran into shallow reductionism. At best, he believed, one can assume, and never more than assume, that mental processes utilize some kind of energy that is at the disposal of the living organism. This energy is analagous to any other energy, and that is all we know: "We assume, as the other natural sciences have taught us to expect, that in mental life some kind of energy is at work; but we have no data which enable us to come nearer to a knowledge of it by analogy with other forms of energy" (Freud, 1923/1962, p. 104).

Freud never gave up the hope of a monistic interpretation that would combine both physical and mental processes. But as things stand now, one has to reject reductionism for methodological reasons and has to develop some new hypothetical constructs independent of the physical sciences.

This is what Freud actually did. He was fully aware that the new constructs were nonreductionistic and nonreducible to any of the constructs of physics or chemistry. He felt that the future might prove that some chemical substances were influencing the amount of energy and its distribution in the human mind. Such an assumption today would be, to say the least, useless. Today, psychology must develop its own hypotheses and concepts.

The processes with which psychology is concerned:

> . . . are in themselves just as unknowable as those dealt with by the other sciences, by chemistry or physics, for example; but it is possible to establish the laws which those processes obey and follow over long and unbroken stretches their mutual relations and interdependences. . . . This cannot be effected without framing fresh hypotheses and creating fresh concepts. . . . We can claim for them the sense value as approximations as belongs to the corresponding intellectual scaffolding found in the other natural sciences, and we look forward to their being modified, corrected and more precisely determined as more experience is accumulated and sifted. So too it will be entirely in accordance with our expectations if the basic concepts and principles of the new science (instinct, nervous energy, etc.) remain for a considerable time no less indeterminate than those of the old sciences (force, mass attraction, etc.). (Freud, 1938/1949, p. 30)

Fenichel (1945), one of the leading thinkers in psychoanalysis, summarized the scientific task of psychoanalysis as follows:

> Scientific psychology explains mental phenomena as a result of interplay of primitive physical needs . . . and the influences of the environment on these needs. . . . Mental phenomena occur only in living organisms; mental phenomena are a special instance of life phenomena. The general laws that are valid for life phenomena are also valid for mental phenomena; special laws that are valid only for the level of mental phenomena must be added. . . . Scientific psychology investigates, as does any science, general laws. It is not satisfied with a mere description of individual psychic processes. . . . Its subject is not the individual but the comprehension of general laws governing mental function. (p. 5)

ALEXANDER'S THEORY

The psychosomatic approach is based on certain basic postulates:

1. Psychological processes must be subjected to the same scientific scrutiny as is customary in the study of physiological processes. Therefore, instead of referring to emotions by such general terms as *anxiety* or *tension*, the actual psychological content of an emotion must be defined so that it may then be studied with the advanced methods of dynamic psychology and may correlated with bodily responses.

2. Psychological processes are fundamentally not different from other processes that take place in the organism. They are at the same time physiological processes and differ from other body processes only in that they

are perceived subjectively and can be communicated verbally and nonverbally to others. Therefore, they can be studied by psychological methods, verbal communication being the principle one. Bodily processes are directly or indirectly influenced by psychological stimuli because the whole organism constitutes a unit in which all the parts are directly or indirectly connected with the seat of psychological processes, the highest integrating center of the nervous system (the brain). The psychosomatic approach can therefore be applied to most phenomena that take place in the living organism.

3. Psychological observations should be correlated with their physiological concomitants whenever possible by standardized objective methods.

4. Some psychophysiological interactions can be best studied according to a psychosomatic model, and others according to a somatopsychic model. The influence of grief, for example, on gastrointestinal or circulatory functions requires the psychosomatic model; the influence of alcohol on ideation requires the somatopsychic model. This statement does not imply that they are two fundamentally different processes, for psychologically induced elation or grief, as well as alcohol-induced elation or grief, has its physiological correlate. The two models, the somatopsychic and the psychosomatic, are simply methodological choices of approach dictated by the specific phenomenon under investigation (Alexander, 1950; Wolman, 1984).

The psychosomatic approach is basically an attempt to place medical art or the psychological effect of the physician on the patient on a scientific basis and to make it an integral part of treatment. The modern psychosomatic approach in medicine tries to span the gulf that, until the present time, separated psychiatry, the "art of medicine," from scientific medicine. This separation occurred as a result of the rapid advancements that medicine had made by successfully applying the principles of physics and chemistry during the nineteenth century. A psychosomatic approach in medicine based on sound scientific principles rather than on intuition would have been impossible without the discovery of the psychoanalytic method of Freud, which gave clinicians the first reliable method for the systematic study of the human personality. Personality research or motivational psychology as a science began with Freud. He was the first to apply consistently the postulate of the strict determinism of psychological processes (psychological causality).

By discovering that a great part of human behavior is determined by unconscious motivation, and by developing a technique by which unconscious motivations could be made conscious, Freud was able to demonstrate for the first time the psychogenic factors in psychopathological processes. The view emerged that the personality is an expression of the unity of the organism. Just as a machine can be understood only from its function and purpose, the synthetic unit that we call the living organism can be fully understood only from the point of view of the personality, the needs of which are served, in the last analysis, by all parts of the body in an intelligible coordination (Alexander & Flagg, 1965).

According to Alexander, psychoanalysis has introduced a synthetic point of view, building a bridge between the psychological and the physiological approaches to diseases. Alexander followed Freud in accepting some of Fechner's and Weber's ideas related to the psychological aspects of sensory experiences in vision, hearing, and others. However, whereas the experimental psychologists did not try to understand the interrelationship of "mental faculties" and did not integrate them into "human personality," Gestalt psychologists did develop a holistic system that combined the psychological and physiological orientations. Without such an approach, the functions of the human organism could not be understood. According to Alexander, the two aspects of human personality could be thoroughly understood only after the meaning of the whole had been discovered (Köhler, 1940; Wolman, 1981; Yacorzynski, 1965):

> The work of Hughlings-Jackson, and Sherrington in neurology demonstrated the hierarchical organization of the central nervous system. Thus, the unity of the organism is clearly expressed in the function of the central nervous system, which regulates the internal vegetative processes in the organism (internal affairs of the organism) and its interaction with the environment (external affairs). The central government is represented by the highest center of the nervous system, the psychological aspects of which in human beings are called the "personality." In fact, it became obvious that psychological studies of the highest centers of the central nervous system and psychological studies of the personality deal with different aspects of one and the same thing. As physiology approaches the function of the central nervous system in terms of space and time, psychology approaches them in terms of the various subjective phenomena which are the subjective reflections of physiological processes.
>
> An added stimulus for the synthetic point of view came from the discovery of the ductless (endocrine) glands; this furthered the understanding of the many complicated interactions between the different vegetative functions of the organism with one another and with the environment. The endocrine glands also were found to be arranged in a hierarchical order, with the anterior pituitary functioning as the master gland. Present-day research findings indicate that the regulation of the ductless glands is ultimately subjected to the highest level of brain function, that is, to psychological stimuli. Thus, the mechanisms of how "the mind rules the body" and how peripheral functions of the body in turn influence the central functions of the nervous system became established on anatomical, neurophysiological, and endocrinological principles. Our whole life consists in carrying out voluntary movements aimed at the realization of ideas and wishes and the satisfactions of subjective feelings and needs, such as anxiety, love, hate, thirst, hunger, etc., which are all accompanied by physiological processes.
>
> The application of all these considerations to certain morbid processes of the body gradually led to the psychosomatic approach, which involved a new and more sophisticated multidisciplinary study of the causation of disease. Knowl-

edge of the influence of acute emotions on body functions belongs to everyday experience. However, the specific syndrome of physical change corresponding to a particular emotional situation, that is, the specific psychosomatic response (for example, laughter and weeping), was considered of little medical interest since these bodily reactions to acute emotions were felt to be of passing nature. However, psychoanalytic studies of hysterical patients by Freud revealed unmistakably that the influence of prolonged emotional conflicts could contribute to chronic physical disturbances of the body (conversion hysteria). These changes were noted in muscles, controlled by will, and in sense perceptions. Thus Freud demonstrated that ego-alien emotions which become repressed and which cannot be expressed and relieved through normal channels by voluntary activity may become the source of chronic psychic and physical dysfunction. Physiologically viewed, hysterical conversion symptoms resemble any usual voluntary or expressive innervations or perceptions, but in hysteria the motivating psychological impulse is unconscious. In a conversion symptom the leap from the psychic to the somatic is similar to that which takes place in any common voluntary motor innervation except that the motivating psychological content is unconscious, and hysterical symptoms are to a high degree individual, sometimes unique, creations of the patient, invented by him to express his particular repressed psychological content. Expressive movements like laughter are, in contrast, standardized and universal.

A fundamentally different group of psychogenic bodily disturbances are those of internal vegetative organs innervated by the autonomic nervous system. Early psychoanalytic investigators repeatedly erred in attempting to extend the original concept of hysterical conversion to all forms of psychogenic disturbances of the body, including even those occurring in the visceral organs. They ignored the fact that the vegetative organs, since they are controlled by the autonomic nervous system (and thus are not directly connected with ideational processes), could not express ideational content. Such symbolic expression of psychological content exists only in the field of voluntary innervations, such as speech, and expressive innervations (a possible exception is blushing). Though several organs, such as the liver and the kidney, cannot express ideas, they can be influenced by emotional tensions which are conducted to any part of the body via corticothalamic and autonomic pathways. This type of chronic emotional stimulation or inhibition of a vegetative function, once it becomes chronic and excessive, has been called an "organ neurosis" or a "vegetative disturbance of psychogenic origin." These are disturbances of the vegetative organs which are caused, at least partially, by nervous impulses, originating in the cortical and subcortical areas of the brain. (Alexander & Flagg, 1965, pp. 858–859)

Alexander (1950) drew a distinction between conversions that he believed were a symbolic expression of psychological problems, on one side, and "vegetative" or "organ" neuroses reflecting chronic emotional states.

Alexander believed that there are seven psychosomatic diseases: bronchial asthma, essential hypertension, neurodermatitis, peptic ulcer, rheumatoid arthritis, thyrotoxicosis, and ulcerative colitis. He viewed psychosomatic disorders as physiological concomitants of particular emotional tensions.

The difference between a conversion symptom and a vegetative neurosis (an organ neurosis) can be defined as follows: A conversion symptom is a symbolic expression of an emotionally charged psychological conflict that attempts to find discharge for the emotional tension that led to the conflict. Thus, conversion symptoms occur in the voluntary, neuromuscular, or sensory-perceptive systems whose original functions are to register, express, and relieve emotional tension. In contrast, a vegetative neurosis is not an attempt to express an emotion but a physiological adaptive response of the vegetative organs to constant or periodically recurring emotional states. Blood pressure can be elevated under the influence of rage, but it does not necessarily relieve the emotional state of rage. The main similarity between hysterical conversion symptoms and vegetative responses to emotions is that both are responses to psychological stimuli (Ammon, 1979).

In functional disturbances of vegetative processes, the personality of the patient becomes one important object of therapy, and the emotional influence of the doctor on the patient (medical art) has been recognized in scientific medicine as a most important therapeutic factor. However, the role of psychotherapy is rather limited to mild functional disturbances, as opposed to genuine and severe organic diseases. Although the emotional state of the patient definitely has a considerable influence on the course of an organic disorder, the causal connection between psychological conflict and chronic organic disease is still not very clear. The traditional distinction between the organic and the nonorganic disturbances is gradually disappearing as evidence is accumulated to show that nonorganic disorders of long duration can lead, and have led, to serious organic disorders associated with definite and distinct morphological changes; for example, a hysterical paralysis of a limb might lead to degenerative changes in the muscles and joints, or emotional conflicts causing continued fluctuations of blood pressure could result, sooner or later, in chronic elevated blood pressure, with vascular changes and irreversible forms of kidney damage.

The concept of "psychogenic organic disorder" was formuated by Alexander, recognizing two phases in the development of these disorders: first, a functional disturbance of a vegetative organ, caused by chronic and excessive emotional stimulation, and second, the gradual transition from a chronic functional disorder to tissue changes and finally to an irreversible organic disease (Alexander, French, & Pollock, 1968).

The etiological concepts were expanded when it was recognized that disturbed function might be the cause of altered mental structure. This was a most basic revision of medical thinking because it opposed the medical dictum based on Rudolph Virchow's principle that disease is caused by disturbed structure. The concept that disturbed function can cause disturbed structure met with strong resistance because the classical concept of pathology viewed disturbed function as always resulting from disturbed structure. However, many chronic diseases of unknown origin might be proved ultimately to be instances of diseases in which prolonged disturbed function has led to structural changes. An outstanding example is toxic goiter, the onset of which is often due to emotional trauma, followed eventually by pronounced structural changes within the thyroid and the cardiovascular system. Essentially, the functional theory of organic disorders amounts to a recognition of the existence not only of acute external causative factors but also of chronic internal causes of disease.

Stated more simply, many chronic disturbances are not caused primarily by external mechanical or chemical factors or bacteria, but by the continuous functional stress arising during the everyday life of the individual in her or his struggle for existence. Fear, aggression, guilt, and sexual tension, if repressed, result in permanent chronic emotional tensions that disturb the functions of the vegetative organs. Just as certain bacteria have a special affinity for certain organs, so also there is strong evidence that certain specific emotional conflicts tend to afflict certain internal organs. Inhibited rage, for example, seems to have a specific relationship to the cardiovascular system. Dependent, help-seeking tendencies seem to have a specific relationship to the functions of nutrition. A conflict pertaining to communication with others seems to have a specific influence on respiratory functions. The psychosomatic approach brings internal physiological processes into synthesis with the individual's relations to his or her social environment (Reiser, 1966).

The term *psychosomatic* does not imply a dichotomy between mind and body. It should be understood that psychic phenomena are the subjective aspect of certain physiological or central nervous system processes. The term *psychosomatic* designates merely a method of approach, both in research and in therapy, that is aimed toward the simultaneous and coordinated use of somatic and psychological methods and concepts. Some scientists view the psychosomatic approach as a transitory phase in medicine that will be abandoned when improved physiological or electronic techniques are developed for studying those processes that today yield only to psychological methods (for example, grief). This contention is often held by those who interpret psychological processes as merely "epiphenomena." It is indeed possible that, in the future, a biochemical or electronic formula may be used to describe a receptive longing that takes place somewhere in the cortex, but such a formula could describe only the processes within the organism itself. It could never explain or describe satisfactorily the transactional aspects of the organism with its environment, that is, its social or interpersonal relations.

Alexander *et al.* (1968) related the seven psychosomatic disorders to seven distinct personality types and specific emotional conflicts. For example, bronchial asthma is related to the child's fear of losing the mother. Hypertension is believed to be associated with difficulties in controlling one's own aggressiveness. Arthritis in females is a protest against parental tyranny and restriction of muscular reactions. Peptic ulcers reflect an inner conflict over the need to be dependent and the craving for independence.

Dermatological disorders convey a conflict over physical closeness. The fear of death causes thyrotoxicosis, and hostile feelings lead to colitis.

OTHER PSYCHOANALYTIC APPROACHES

Other psychoanalysts have continued Alexander's work. Let us mention Schur, Greene, Engel, and Schmale.

Schur (1955) maintained that the newborn's initial reactions to stimuli are somatic, and that, only gradually, an infant learns to control himself or herself. The child's reaction becomes *desomatized* as the child learns affective, cognitive, and behavioral self-control in reacting to stress. Psychosomatic reactions, which Schur preferred to call *somatic,* are regressions to an early developmental stage: they are *resomatizations.* Regressions could be caused by endocrine changes, by a change in sleep–wake patterns, or by traumatic experiences.

Greene (1954) studied cancer patients with Hodgkins disease, leukemia, and lymphomas and related the diseases to severe depression caused by the real or anticipated loss of a beloved person.

Engel (1962) related cerebrovascular accidents, myocardial infarctions, and duodenal ulcers to depression. Loss of self-esteem and failure of ego mechanisms can create a state of helplessness and hopelessness. When the depressive feelings fall on the fertile soil of an organ vulnerability created by constitutional or genetic factors, they may cause a severe psychosomatic illness. According to Engel, grief is as important as bacteria in producing diseases, for grief created by a real or a threatened object-loss affects the functions of the limbic and the reticular activating systems.

Schmale (1972) reported that 41 out of 42 patients hospitalized reported that, before the onset of their physical diseases, they had suffered object loss and had experienced feelings of helplessness and hopelessness. Schmale maintained that giving up is the common pathway to changes in health.

Reiser (1966) tried to relate psychoanalytic concept to physiological data. He stressed the role of the amygdala, the limbic system, the hypothalamus, and the endocrine system:

> In suggesting an approach toward an integrated theory it was hypothesized that those physiological states of the brain which permit pathways for peripheral discharge to dormant medically pathogenic central nervous systems circuits, may be the same as the ones which are defined psychologically as altered ego (consciousness) states. (p. 579)

According to Weil (1974), emotion consists of combinations of behavioral and perceptual reactions related to the upper limbic-hypothalamic-reticular (UHR) system. They can be expressed in several ways, such as, for example, excitement, movement, and psychosomatic reactions.

It is quite possible that psychosomatic symptoms indicate structural ego disturbances. Children who have been prevented from developing an ordered world of inner representation and from forming adequate id, ego, and superego macrostructures tend to become severely maladjusted and to have a variety of psychosomatic symptoms.

Taylor (1987) stressed that psychosomatic disorders are not a product of psychodynamic conflicts, as psychoneuroses are defects in *ego functioning* are the basis of psychosomatic disorders.

Taylor described the evolution of psychosomatics and its relationship to psychoanalysis as follows:

> In my opinion, psychosomatic medicine has failed to advance its understanding of the psychological states that play a role in health and illness because of its rejection of the psychoanalytic method of investigation. Although there have been occasional pleas for a "new and active involvement of psychoanalysis with psychosomatic medicine" (L. Deutsch, 1980, p. 699), there has been little response to this challenge. The lack of response may be attributed partly to the disillusionment with psychoanalytic approaches during the 1950's, an attitude transmitted to the current generation of psychosomaticists. Like most of their surviving teachers, they have ignored the recent developments in psychoanalysis and have failed to investigate the relevance of contemporary psychoanalytic concepts for patients with physical diseases. (p. 4)

Further on, Taylor wrote:

> As psychoanalysis expanded beyond the neuroses to include patients with more primitive mental states, several new models of psychopathology have evolved. However, the majority of contemporary psychoanalysts have given little attention to psychosomatic phenomena and have overlooked the psychobiological significance of several of the newer psychoanalytic concepts. The alternative models of normal development and psychopathology provided by object relations theory and self psychology shift the emphasis away from the drives and defenses to the vicissitudes of interpersonal relationships. In so doing, they have focused greater attention on the early mother-infant relationship and its importance for the development of both psychosomatic unity and a healthy personality. Psychobiological research and observational studies of infants are confirming that deficiencies in early object relationships result in developmental defects which reduce an individual's capacity to self-regulate essential psychobiological functions, thereby predisposing the individual to bodily disease. (p. 6)

REFERENCES

Alexander, F. *Psychosomatic medicine.* New York: Norton, 1950.
Alexander, F., & Flagg, G. W. The psychosomatic approach. In B. B. Wolman (Ed.), *Handbook of clinical psychology* (pp. 855–947). New York: McGraw-Hill, 1965.
Alexander, F., French, T. M., & Pollock, G. H. *Psychosomatic specificity: Experimental study and results.* Chicago: University of Chicago Press, 1968.
Ammon, G. *Psychoanalysis and psychosomatics.* New York: Springer, 1979.
Deutsch, F. (Ed.). *On the mysterious leap from the mind to the body.* New York: International Universities Press, 1953.

Deutsch, F. (Ed.). *The psychosomatic concept in psychoanalysis.* New York: International Universities Press, 1959.

Engel, G. L. *Psychological development in health and disease.* Philadelphia: Saunders, 1962.

Fenichel, O. *The psychoanalytic theory of neurosis.* New York: Norton, 1945.

Freud, S. *An outline of psychoanalysis.* New York: Norton, 1949. (Originally published, 1938.)

Freud, S. Psychical (or mental) treatment. *Standard Edition,* (Vol. 1, 283–302). London: Hogarth Press, 1953. (Originally published, 1905.)

Freud, S. The ego and the id. *Standard Edition* (Vol. 1, pp. 3–63). London: Hogarth Press, 1962. (Originally published, 1923.)

Freud, S. Project for a scientific psychology. *Standard Edition* (Vol. 1, pp. 281–397). London: Hogarth Press, 1966. (Originally published, 1895.)

Greene, W. A. Psychological factors and reticuloendothelial disease: Preliminary observations on a group of males with lymphomas and leukemias. *Psychosomatic Medicine,* 1954, *16,* 220–230.

Groddeck, G. *The book of the id.* New York: Vintage Books, 1961.

Heigl-Evers, A. Zur Bedutung des therapeutischen Prinzips der Interaktion. In H. J. Haase (Ed.), *Psychotherapie.* Erlangen: Perimed, 1980.

Köhler, W. *Dynamics in psychology.* New York: Liveright, 1940.

Reiser, M. F. Toward an integrated psychoanalytic-physiological theory of psychosomatic disorders. In R. Loewenstein (Ed.), *Psychoanalysis: A general psychology* (pp. 570–582). New York: International Universities Press, 1966.

Schmale, A. H., Jr. Giving up as a final common pathway to changes in health. *Advances in Psychosomatic Medicine,* 1972, *8,* 20–40.

Schur, M. Comments on metapsychology of somatization. *Psychoanalytic Study of the Child,* 1955, *10,* 67–103.

Taylor, G. J. *Psychosomatic medicine and contemporary psychoanalysis.* Madison, CN: International Universities Press, 1987.

Weil, J. L. *A neurophysiological model of emotional and intentional behavior.* Springfield, IL: Thomas, 1974.

Wolman, B. B. *Handbook of clinical psychology.* New York: McGraw-Hill, 1965.

Wolman, B. B. *Contemporary theories and systems in psychology* (rev. ed.). New York: Plenum Press, 1981.

Wolman, B. B. *The logic of science in psychoanalysis.* New York: Columbia University Press, 1984.

Yacorzynski, G. K. Organic mental disorders. In B. B. Wolman (Ed.), *Handbook of clinical psychology* (pp. 653–688). New York: McGraw Hill, 1965.

4

Neurophysiological Approach

Some researchers maintain that conversion symptoms are produced by the central nervous system, whereas psychosomatic symptoms are usually produced by the autonomic and neuroendocrine systems. According to Cannon (1920), animals react to pain, fear, hunger, and rage by changes in gland secretion, as well as by disturbances in muscle tone and in the cardiovascular and gastrointestinal systems, all under the control of the autonomic nervous system.

According to Sherrington and Cannon, diseases of the CNS can result in regression of the CNS to earlier levels of function. Sherrington (1941) demonstrated that a simple reflex-arc undergoes continuous change and can even be reversed under the influence of the central nervous system. According to Cannon's *thalamic theory*, a discharge of excitation in the thalamus, if it is communicated to the cortex, can give rise to profound emotions. The sympathetic part of the autonomic nervous system plays a distinct role in the preparation of the organism for emergency situations. In situations that evoke fear and/or rage, significant changes take place in the body, such as the inhibition of salivation, gastric motility, the secretion of gastric juices and peristalsis, an acceleration of heartbeat, a redistribution of the blood to the musculature, and an increase in blood pressure, preparing the body for vigorous muscular activity. Cannon's elaboration (1920, 1942) of the interaction between the endocrine glands and the vegetative functions helped to elaborate how emotional tension could be conducted to any part of the body via corticothalamic and autonomic pathways.

According to Cannon's theory of *homeostasis*, an excitation of the sympathetic nervous system, combined with an increased adrenaline secretion, is an emergency reaction of the organism. Cannon pointed out the interlocking mechanisms by which the organism maintains a dynamic equilibrium. He discovered that the sympathetic nervous system resists environmental pressures, whereas the main function of the parasympathetic system is to build up the organism's resources. The physical changes that are associated with strong emotions, as well as with the organism's reactions to heat and cold, are produced by the sympathetic nervous system and serve the bodily balance as homeostatic mechanisms. Fear and anger indicate a certain level of disturbance and serve as signals that equilibrium has to be restored.

Cannon's theory of homeostasis was further elaborated on by Selye (1956). Selye pointed out that the pituitary adrenocortical system responds to both physical and emotional stress by a release of ACTH into the bloodstream. Animals exposed to stress secrete not only more adrenalin, but also larger quantities of cortical hormones in order to counteract the damage of stress. He introduced the term *general adaptation syndrome* (Selye, 1946, 1956).

ALEXANDER

According to Alexander, disorders of long duration tend to lead to serious organic disorders associated with definite and distinct morphological changes; for example, a hysterical paralysis of a limb might lead to degenerative changes in the muscles and joints, or emotional conflicts causing continued fluctuations of blood pressure could, sooner or later, result in chronic elevated blood pressure, with vascular changes and irreversible forms of kidney damage. Apparently, many chronic diseases of unknown origin are instances of diseases in which prolonged disturbed function has led to structural changes. Another example is toxic goiter, the onset of which is often due to emotional trauma, followed eventually by pronounced structural changes within the thyroid and the cardiovascular system. Repressed fear, aggression, guilt, and sexual tension result in permanent chronic emotional tensions that disturb the functions of the vegetative organs. Dependent, help-seeking tendencies have a specific relationship to the functions of nutrition. A conflict pertaining to communication with others has a specific influence on respiratory functions (Alexander & Flagg, 1965).

The main function of the sympathetic nervous system is the regulation of internal vegetative functions in relation to external activity, particularly emergency situations. During the preparation for, and the performance of, such activities, it inhibits anabolic processes, such as gastrointestinal activity, and it stimulates heart and lung action and changes the distribution of the blood. To a high degree, the sympathetic and parasympathetic actions are antagonistic. Under parasympathetic preponderance, the individual withdraws into a merely vegetative state, whereas under sympathetic stimulation, he or she inhibits the peaceful functions and turns his or her attention to the external environment. In neurotic disturbances of the vegetative functions, this harmony between the external situation and the internal vegetative processes is disturbed (Cannon, 1920).

The inhibition of self-assertive hostile impulses blocks appropriate adaptive behavior (fight or flight), and if this inhibition is chronic, the organism remains in a state of preparedness, which is normally needed only in emergency situations. These bodily changes are usually temporary, lasting only as long as the need for increased effort persists, and rapidly returning to a normal baseline on the cessation of action. However, when activation of the vegetative processes involves no action, and when repeated stimulation of these adaptive physiological responses occurs, they eventually become chronically elevated. For example, in essential hypertension, the blood pressure is sustained pent-up and is never fully relieved.

Specificity of Emotional Factors in Psychosomatic Disturbances

The theory of specificity states that both normal and morbid physiological responses to emotional stimuli vary according to the nature of the precipitating emotional state. Thus, laughter is a response to merriment, and weeping is a response to sorrow. The vegetative responses to different emotional stimuli also vary according to the quality of emotions, and every emotional state has its own physiological response. Thus, increased blood pressure and accelerated heart action are constituent parts of rage and fear. Alexander's specific theory differentiates between the two attitudes mentioned above:

> 1) a preparation to deal with the anxiety-producing situation by meeting it actively, and 2) a retreat from it to a dependent, child-like appeal for help. In accord with Cannon's concepts, the first type of emotional attitude goes with increased sympathetic, and the second with increased parasympathetic excitation. . . . The theory of emotional specificity does not imply that nonemotional factors such as the constitution and history of the organ system involved are unimportant influences in its specific susceptibility to emotional stimuli. . . . The physiological response depends upon the manner in which the psychological motivating force may express itself; for instance, hostility can be expressed in physical attack, whether this is via the extremities, by spitting, by verbal invectives, by destructive fantasies, or by other less direct modes of attack. The physiological responses will vary accordingly. Thus, the psychological content, together with the dynamic configuration of these motivating forces determines, at least partially, the physiological functions that will be activated or inhibited. (Alexander & Flagg, 1965, pp. 863–864)

CORTICOVISCERAL MEDICINE

In the USSR the psychosomatic attitude is usually represented by corticovisceral medicine. Soviet researchers have stressed the role of corticovisceral discharge, and they have conducted detailed research on interoceptive conditioned reflexes and their impact on disturbed psychosomatic functioning. A considerable part of the research has been devoted to work on animals, and the theoretical conclusions derived from animal experiments have been applied to human behavior. Russian scientists (e.g., Ayrapetyants, 1959; Bykov, 1957; Pavlov, 1927, 1955) have stressed the role of corticovisceral interactivity in hypertension, peptic ulcers, and bronchial asthma (Brozek, 1977; Corson & Corson, 1976; Razran, 1958; Wolman, 1968).

Soviet scientists have applied exteroceptive conditioning to humans in the production of psychosomatic "neurosis." Pshonik (1961) (as quoted by Bykov) produced a vascular neurosis by the disruption of a conditioned pattern of an interoceptive conditioned stimulus and by the disruption of verbal conditioning. Corticovisceral medicine differs from psychosomatic medicine in proposing a unitary etiological concept of neurosis and psychosomatic diseases. The importance of constitution and predisposition is accepted as basis for the choice of organ in the development of disease. According to Bykov (1957), interoceptive impulses are even more important than exteroceptive stimulation for organ choice and explain more convincingly, by their ubiquitous, unconscious, and readily conditionable nature, the chronic character of corticovisceral illness.

According to Wittkower and Solyom (1967):

> Three discernable tendencies in cortico-visceral medicine are: 1) to demonstrate the relevance of temperamental types (choleric, sanguinic, phlegmatic, melancholic) to the nature and course of psychophysiological disturbance; 2) to show that the pathophysiology of nervous breakdown, i.e. forced collision or overstraining of excitation and/or inhibition, is responsible for malfunctioning of internal organs; and 3) to stress the role of peripheral factors. The protective, compensatory influence of the cortex is not disputed, but a concomitant "locus minoris resistantiae" is implicated in the choice of organ pathology. (p. 229)

CURRENT RESEARCH

Current research is going on in more than one direction. For instance, sleep research points to the role of the abducent nuclei in initiating the rapid eye movements (REM) of desynchronized sleep, the role of the spinal cord in mediating the phasic muscle twitches of REM sleep, and the role of the medulla oblongata in initiating muscle atoxia and other symptoms (Carley & Hobson, 1979). Apparently, research in biological rhythm, the sleep–dream cycle, hypnosis, and the altered states of consciousness has opened new vistas in the understanding of psychosomatic phenomena (Wolman & Ullman, 1986).

Another theory was forwarded by Nemiah (1982), who related psychosomatic disorders to defects in neural mechanisms. He maintained that perception of traumatic events could affect the functions of the hypothalamic autonomic centers.

It is apparent that the brain can affect the functions of the cardiovascular and gastrointestinal systems (Green, 1954). Increases in blood pressure can stimulate, via a low brain center, a reflex that slows the heart rate, but in anger, fear, and other instances of strong emotional arousal, these reflexes are inhibited by higher brain centers, and the blood pressure is free to rise (Bartrop, Luckhurst, Lazarus, & Kiloh, 1977).

Conflict situations may produce high levels of plasma corticosterone, a depletion of brain norepinephrine, and stomach lesions. According to Miller (1983, p. 18), there are certain patients who, when told that they have inoperable cancer, turn their faces to the wall and die in a few days from no ascertainable physical cause.

It seems, therefore, that psychosomatic symptoms can have more than one cause and can be interpreted in more than one way.

REFERENCES

Alexander, F., & Flagg, G. W. The psychosomatic approach. In B. B. Wolman (Ed.), *Handbook of clinical psychology* (pp. 855–947). New York: McGraw Hill, 1965.

Ayrapetyants, E. Sh. *Higher nervous activity and the receptors of internal organs* (Russian). Moscow: Soviet Academy of Sciences, 1959.

Bartrop, R. W., Luckhurst, E., Lazarus, L., & Kiloh, L. G. Depressed lymphocyte function after bereavement. *Lancet*, 1977, *1*, 834–836.

Brozek, J. Union of Soviet Socialist Republics: Psychology. In B. B. Wolman (Ed.), *International encyclopedia of psychiatry, psychology, psychoanalysis and neurology* (Vol. 11, pp. 328–330). New York: Aesculapius Publishers, 1977.

Bykov, W. H. *The cerebral cortex and the inner organs*. New York: Chemical Publishers, 1957.

Cannon, W. B. *Bodily changes in pain, hunger, fear and rage*. New York: Appleton, 1920.

Cannon, W. B. Voodoo death. *American Anthropologist*, 1942, *44*, 169–181.

Carley, R. W., & Hobson, J. A. The form of dreams and the biology of sleep. In B. B. Wolman (Ed.), *Handbook of dreams* (pp. 76–130). New York: Van Nostrand Reinhold, 1979.

Corson, A. S., & Corson, E. G. (Eds.). *Psychiatry and psychology in the USSR*. New York: Plenum Press, 1976.

Greene, W. A. Psychological factors and reticuloendothelial disease: Preliminary observations on a group of males with lymphomas and leukemias. *Psychosomatic Medicine*, 1954, *16*, 220–230.

Miller, N. E. Behavioral medicine: Symbiosis between laboratory and clinic. *Annual Review of Psychology*, 1983, *34*, 1–32.

Nemiah, J. C. A reconsideration of psychological specificity in psychosomatic disorders. *Psychotherapy and Psychosomatics*, 1982, *38*, 39–45.

Pavlov, I. P. *Conditioned reflexes.* London: Oxford University Press, 1927.

Pavlov, I. P. *Selected works.* Moscow: Foreign Languages Publishing House, 1955.

Razran, G. Soviet psychology and psychophysiology. *Science,* 1958, *128,* 1187–1194.

Selye, H. The general adaptation syndrome and the disease of adaptation. *Journal of Clinical Endocrinology,* 1946, *6,* 117–127.

Selye, H. *The stress of life.* New York: McGraw-Hill, 1956.

Sherrington, C. S. *Man on his nature.* New York: Macmillan, 1941.

Simonton, D. C., & Simonton, S. *Getting well again.* New York: Prentice-Hall, 1978.

Solomon, G. F., & Amkraut, A. A. Emotions, immunity, and disease. In L. Temoshok, C. Van Dyke, & L. Zegans (Eds.), *Emotions in health and illness.* New York: Grune & Stratton, 1983.

Wittkower, E. D., & Solyom, L. Models of mind-body interaction. *International Journal of Psychiatry,* 1967, *4,* 225–233.

Wolman, B. B. (Ed.). *Historical roots of contemporary psychology.* New York: Harper & Row, 1968.

Wolman, B. B., & Ullman, M. *Handbook of states of consciousness.* New York: Van Nostrand Reinhold, 1986.

5

The Immune System

ANATOMY AND PHYSIOLOGY OF THE IMMUNE SYSTEM

The immune system is a guardian apparatus that defends the living organism against foreign bodies and, especially, disease-causing micro-organisms such as germs and viruses:

> The principal cells of the immune system are lymphocytes, plasma cells, and macrophages which are parts of the lymphoid tissue. The thymus, lymph nodes and spleen are examples of highly developed lymphoid tissues. The gastrointestinal tract, the tonsils, the Peyer's patches and the appendix also have lymphoid tissue. . . .
>
> There are two distinct types of lymphocytes. These two types were first demonstrated in chickens by removal of the thymus or by removal of the bursa of Fabricius (a lymphoid organ near the cloaca) during the neonatal period. Excision of the bursa resulted in low immunoglobulin levels and impaired antibody synthesis. Lymphoid nodules did not develop in lymph nodes and spleen. . . . The cell-mediated immunity remained intact as proven by delayed hypersensitivity and allograft rejection. Evidence for two types of immunocompetent cells in humans has largely come from the study of congenital and acquired defects of immunity as well as from the identification of populations of lymphocytes. The two types of immunocompetent lymphocytes are referred to as B cells and T cells. (Gilliland, 1980, p. 315)

It is estimated that the B cells compose close to 20% of the peripheral blood lymphocytes. They also form about 50% of the splenic lymphocytes, and about 75% of the lymphocytes in the bone marrow. Undoubtedly, they are the main cells in the cortical germinal centers and medullary cords of the lymph nodes. They carry membrane-bound immunoglobulins and produce antibodies.

The T cells form close to 80% of the peripheral blood lymphocytes and 90% of the lymphocytes in the thoracic duct fluid. Some T cells are helpers, and some are suppressors of the immune response; thus, they play opposite roles in immune and self-immune disorders.

The macrophages are released into the circulation as monocytes that comprise 5%–8% of the circulating leukocytes. As soon as they enter tissues, the monocytes turn into macrophages; the main tissue sites are the liver, the peritoneum, the lung, the spleen, and the lymph nodes. Macrophages have surface receptors for IgG1 and IgG3, as well as a receptor for C3b. The macrophages can bind antigen–antibody complexes consisting of IgG antibodies or immune complexes that contain C3. The main task of the macrophages is to kill bacteria, viruses, tumor cells, and fungi. The macrophages also induce the immune response by processing and presenting immunogenic material to lymphocytes (Gilliland, 1980, pp. 315–317).

The basic biochemical structure of the immune system, as well as its physiological predispositions, is *genetically determined*. However, the level and efficiency of its disease-combating cells depend on a combination of genetic and somatopsychic environmental elements, for even the strongest biological structure can be affected by psychosocial lifetime experiences. It is the *hammer-and-anvil* scenario, and how the immune system facilitates or fights psychosomatic disorders is a highly complex issue.

The function of the immune system can be divided into two types of processes, those mediated by T lymphocytes (cell-mediated immune functions) and those mediated by B lymphocytes (humoral immune processes). The monocytes, macrophages, mast cells, and neutrophils have accessory processing and effector functions in many immune responses. Antigens attach to particular lymphocytes that are programmed to recognize that antigen, inducing lymphocyte proliferation:

> Antibodies are immunoglobulins, of which there are five classes in man. The IgM and IgG immunoglobulins are produced in response to a wide variety of antigens, with initial production of IgM after antigenic stimulation, followed by higher levels of IgG. IgA appears to be specifically localized to secretory fluids, such as saliva and milk. The role of IgD is unclear at present. IgE binds to mast cells that actively release mediators of immediate hypersensitivity on reexposure to specific antigen. These mediators include histamine, kinins, and slow-reacting substance (leukotrienes). The primary protective function of humoral immunity is against bacterial infections. At times, however, the response can be pathological, such as in anaphylaxis and asthma and, occasionally in response to the organism's own tissue in an autoimmune disorder, such as systemic lupus erythematosus (SLE). (Stein, Schleifer, & Keller, 1985, p. 1206)

AUTOIMMUNE AND ANTIAUTOIMMUNE DISEASES

It is my conviction that cancer is an autoimmune disease and that AIDS is an antiautoimmune disease. The immune system mediates between the pathophysiological, biochemical, and endocrinological processes and the psychosocial events processed by the central nervous system. The immunocompetent lymphocytes are divided into two groups: the B cells, which carry immunoglobin and produce antibodies, and the T cells. The helper T cells cooperate with the B cells in inducing and producing antibodies. In most cases of viral infections, the B cells and the helper T cells join forces in containing the virus replication. They release effector molecules, such as interferon, cytotoxin, and lymphocyte-transforming factors, in considerable quantity, protecting the organism against the invading disease-producing bodies, as well as against future invasions. The suppressor T cells control the immune response and prevent overreaction.

The immune system may or may not respond to the antigens. Whether there is or is not an immune response on exposure to invading foreign bodies depends on several factors, some related to the nature of the antigens, and some related to the biochemical and some to psychological functions of the immune system. The unresponsiveness ("tolerance") can be caused by the antibodies, which can produce changes in the antigens and prevent their recognition by and interaction with the lymphocytes or, in some instances, by suppression of the immune response. It is my hypothesis that AIDS is a case of *grave overreaction of the suppressor T cells* that reduces the proliferation of B cells and the production of antibodies, and that *prevents* the immune response. In AIDS, the suppressor T cells overreact and paralyze the immune system, leaving it the mercy of the invading LHTV-III viruses. The hyperfunction of suppressor T cells suppresses the cell-mediated and humoral immunity and turns the organism into a defenseless territory open to the invading opportunistic infections.

In cancer, the opposite takes place: *the suppressor T cells fail to act.* Let us use pictorial language. The human organism has an army of lymphocytes, plasma cells, and macrophages that defends it against the antigen invaders. The two main protective armies are the B cells and the helper T cells, divided into several types and units stationed in various organs and parts of the body. The T cells are divided into helper T cells and suppressor T cells. The suppressor T cells are a sort of military police, called in wherever the B cells and the helper T cells overreact. The normal ratio of T helpers to T suppressors is 1.7±5 (that is, there are about twice as many soldiers as military police). An overreaction of the suppressor T cells paralyses the immune response. In cancer, the suppressor T-cell "military police" fail to act, and some units of the defensive army go on a rampage, killing friend and foe. They fail to recognize the healthy cells from the invading antigens and destroy the organs they are supposed to defend. In metastasis, they cross the borders and spread destruction to other parts of the organism, while the military police, the suppressor T-cells, do nothing to prevent the catastrophe.

A few additional facts will support the hypothesis that an *overfunction* of the immune system (of the B and T helper cells) causes cancer. Old age brings a decline in the immune system, and elderly people are less capable of fighting diseases. The fact is that pneumonia and other diseases kill older people, whereas younger people have a better chance in their fight against disease.

According to this hypothesis, cancer is caused by an overreaction of the immune system; thus, the old-age decline of the immune system should cause a decline in the incidence of cancer. And this is precisely the truth. The peak increase in cancer incidence and mortality occurs between the ages 45 and 65 and afterward goes down. At ages 65 to 69, cancer accounts for no more than 30% of the deaths, and it causes death in only 12% of people over the age of 80 (Silverberg, 1984).

The incidence of cancer compared to the incidence of the acquired immunodeficiency syndrome (AIDS) supports the hypothesis that AIDS and cancer are opposite diseases. Cancer patients may develop all kinds of diseases, but so far, there are no cancer patients afflicted by AIDS nor AIDS patients suffering from cancer. Only *after* AIDS has played havoc with the organism may a cancerous disease (Kaposi sarcoma) finish the destructive job.

Systemic lupus erythematosus (SLE) deserves to be mentioned here, for SLE is related to the immune system. The outstanding feature of SLE is the presence in the serum of the patients of antibodies to nuclear antigens, such as deoxyribonucleic acid (DNA), nucleoprotein, and other nuclear antigens (ANA). Probably, SLE is caused by a viral infection in genetically predisposed individuals (there is a high concordance of clinical SLE in monozygotic twins), and it is related to a reduced control of the T-cell suppressors over the B cells (Levy, 1982). One can put it in a figurative way: The T-cell suppressors that should play the role of military police fail to prevent and/or to suppress the riotous behavior of the B cells, the armed forces. The failure of the suppressor T cells is the main factor in autoimmune diseases. Apparently, cancer belongs to the category of *autoimmune* diseases, and AIDS belongs to the opposite category: it is an *antiautoimmune disease.*

PSYCHOLOGICAL ASPECTS

The immune system is quite sensitive to psychological influences. There is abundant evidence that psychological factors, and especially one's attitude about oneself and one's outlook on life, can slow down or accelerate the proliferation of malignant cells and the growth of cancer (Goldberg, 1981; Simonton & Simonton, 1975; Solomon & Amkraut, 1981): Stressful experiences, profound states of tension and anxiety, severe frustrations, prolonged depression, frequent sleep deprivation, bereavement, mourning, and other negative emotional states can cause a temporary or lasting reduction in the responsiveness of the immune system and can make the organism fall prey to diseases (Lipowski, 1985).

The central nervous system exercises a significant influence on the functions of the immune system:

> There is an increasingly solid experimental evidence that the brain plays an important role in modulating and responding to changes in immune status. These changes seem to be mediated by the hypothalamus and by pituitary hormones. Many factors can alter the body's immune responses: time of the day, age of the individual, pregnancy, and of course, stress. High doses of exogenous steroids are known to have immuno-suppressive effects on both humoral and cellular immune responses. . . . Any stressful process that alters the normal physiology of hormones will naturally have an impact on immunological behavior. (Zegans, 1982, p. 149)

Psychoimmunology is a branch of the immunological science that studies the relationship between the endocrine nervous systems and the psychological processes, as well as their impact on the functions of the immune system. A deficiency or dysfunction of the immune system can produce a variety of physical and/or psychosomatic disorders.

Stressors have been applied in several instances of animal research; the stressors have decreased the responsiveness of the immune system. In many cases, corticosteroids and other stress-responsive hormones have affected the components of the immune responses. According to Lipowski (1985):

> Current knowledge of immune mechanisms allows one to hypothesize that events at man's symbolic level of organization and their emotional correlates may modify, i.e., enhance or inhibit, the body's immune defenses whose role in the genesis of neoplasms is postulated. (p. 82)

Moreover, an inadequate vigilance of the immunocompetent lymphocytes encourages the development of a variety of psychosomatic symptoms.

Mason (1975) reported that stressful experience may cause endocrine changes that can seriously affect the functions of the immune system and can thus increase the organism's vulnerability to diseases. Stressful events can influence the functions of the biogenic amines in the central nervous system, reduce the organism's resilience, and foster psychosomatic disorders. Dorian, Keystone, Garfinkel, and Brown (1982) reported stress-related changes in the number of lymphocytes and their responsiveness. According to Jermott and Locke (1984), stressful experiences can cause a decline in the reactions of the immune system to infectious diseases.

Bartrop, Luckhurst, Lazarus, and Kiloh (1977) found that bereavement depresses the function of the T cells; they found a 1:10 difference between bereaved spouses and controls. The activity of the T cells was found to be considerably decreased in college students under stress (Stein, Schiavi, & Camerino, 1976; Stein *et al.*, 1985). In almost all reported cases, the stress adversely affected the functions of the T cells.

It is quite apparent that psychological stress reduces the defensive powers of the organism and increases the susceptibility to disease. For instance, the incidence of diarrhea and stomach lesions has been related to one's feelings of defeat and helplessness (Miller, 1983). One of the effects of frustration and of unpredictable, uncontrollable stressors is depression. Even a minor depression can lead to an abandonment of rational and hygienic behavior. A major depression may lead to a catastrophic neglect of one's health and, in some cases, to suicide: "Some patients, when told that they may have inoperable cancer, turned to the wall and died in a few days from no ascertainable physical cause" (Miller, 1983, p. 18). Apparently, their immune system ceased to function.

How stress affects the immune system is not always clear. The fact is that corticosteroids released during stress can suppress immune reactions. They interfere with the actions of white blood cells, suppress the formation of gamma globulin, produce the involution of lymphoid tissue, and reduce the eosinophil count (Levy, 1982). The macrophages and the T-helper and T-suppressor cells are involved in the cellular reactions of the immune system, and these cells are receptors for certain hormones and peptides controlled by the brain. It seems, therefore, that stress not only releases corticosteroids but also activates catecholamines that have a rapid onset and rapid decay and affect the functions of the immune system (Ader, 1981). There is, however, no conclusive evidence of a stress-induced immunosuppression.

Current research has demonstrated that conditioning can affect the functions of the immune system (Ader & Cohen, 1984). It may reduce immunocompetence, produce "learned helplessness," and gradually decrease the antibody responses.

Kimball (1978) described the impact of a child's separation from its parents. The separations worthy of note are the absences of parents, of mothers for repeated childbirth, and of fathers for war and/or business service. Regressive behaviors are frequently observed at such times, and it may be pertinent to learn through which organ systems they are manifested (e.g., thumbsucking, hair pulling, enuresis, encopresis, tics, stuttering, school phobias, tantrums, asthma, eczema, and cough). According to Kimball (1978), not enough attention has been focused on childhood behavior, including illness, during the first full-time separation from mother, which occurs with entrance into the first grade at age 6. Frequently, these illnesses are explained in epidemiological terms of exposure to strains of bacteria and viruses different from those to which the individual has developed *immunity:*

> We are less likely to consider whether the work of separation may relate to a reduction of *immunological defenses* as it may to the ego defenses around the transient loss of mother and home and the stresses of the alien environment of the classroom. We might consider the childhood illnesses and their manifestations as the illnesses of stress, at once reducing immunological defenses and giving stimulus to a rebuilding of these. (Kimball, 1978, p. 697)

The musculoskeletal and cardiovascular systems are most affected in a speculative review of Kimball's work on lymphomas. Greene (1954) has hypothesized an "umbilical phase" of development that when traumatized, reaction to stress at these times would need to be addressed in a broad sense along the continuum of health and illness, including social, psychological, and physiological reactions. Whereas each one of these reactions will always be present, the explanation that fits best at one time or another may be predominantly of one approach. These reactions need not be addressed only in terms of pathology or *decompensation* but should also be looked at in terms of their stimulus for growth and differentiation.

In this discussion of children and their subsequent growth as affected by stress, specifically the stress of loss, extensive studies report the incidence:

> . . . of somatic, social, and psychological distress in the later life of children suffering the loss of a parent under the age of 15 as compared with controls. When this loss occurred prior to the age of 8 and/or included the loss of both parents, the resulting pathology was much greater than for controls as well as for losses between age 8 and 15. (Kimball, 1978, p. 697)

According to Ader and Cohen (1984), despite a common exposure to pathogenic stimuli, only a *relatively small proportion* of infected individuals actually manifest disease. Moreover, psychosocial factors may influence the development and the course of disease. In a study of infectious mononucleosis in more than 1,000 cadets, two thirds were found to be immune to infectious mononucleosis, approximately 20% became infected, and one quarter of those infected developed clinical infectious mononucleosis. The psychosocial factors that increased risk of infection included having fathers who were "overachievers," high motivation, and relatively poor academic performance. Further studies in nonhumans indicate that "a stressful stimulus at a critical time could alter the host's defense mechanisms, allowing an otherwise inconsequential exposure to a pathogenic organism to develop into a clinical disease" (Ader & Cohen, 1984, p. 125).

The relationship between psychosocial factors and immunological reactivity indicates that lymphocytes from the members of a bereaved group showed a significantly suppressed mitogenic reactivity, although other factors of the immune system did not appear to be affected by bereavement. In general, high stress or high life-change-scale scores, with low ego strength or presumably unsuccessful coping response, was associated with depressed immunological defenses (Ader & Cohen, 1984, p. 131). One must also consider nutritional state and sleep deprivation in assessing the immunological effects of "stress." For example, morbidity in infectious diseases and the prevalence of infectious disease as the cause of death is increased in overweight people.

Ader and Cohen also reported that, like the data on disease susceptibility, the effects of experimental factors capable of modifying immune responses seem to depend on the quality and the quantity of the environmental situation, a variety of host factors, the nature of the immunogenic stimulus, and the parameters of immunological reactivity that are chosen for measurement. Consequently, the results of the effects of experimental factors on immunological reactivity are small and inconsistent.

Ader and Cohen (1984) claimed that the effect of psychosocial factors on immune competence, as reflected by studies of clinical disease or immunological reactivity, is determined by several major variables:

1. The quality or quantity of naturally occurring or experimentally imposed alterations in the psychosocial environment.
2. The quality and quantity of immunogenic or pathogenic stimulation.
3. Myriad host factors on which the environmental and immunogenic stimuli are superimposed.
4. The temporal relationship between psychosocial and immunological events.
5. Procedural factors, such as the nature of the dependent variables and the sampling parameters.
6. The interaction among any or all of the above.

According to Simonton and Simonton (1978), undue stress interferes with the immune system, thus allowing the growth and proliferation of the cancer cells that are ever-present in the body. Good feelings, coincident with a lessening of stress, increase the efficiency of the immune system and enable the body to destroy cancer cells. The Simontons provided cancer patients with a cassette tape that guided them through a meditation procedure that included encouraging the cancer patient to visualize the cancer being destroyed by the body's defenses.

The contribution of imagery to health is not yet as well substantiated, though there are many anecdotal reports and observations of changes in the direction of health as the apparent result of creating mental images. Examples are a chemotherapy patient who believed that she had avoided losing her hair through systematic imagery of her hair remaining full and a woman who created the image of herself reacting with distaste toward sweets, and who lost a good deal of weight as a result (Goldberg, 1981).

Highly motivated, persistent, and self-confident cancer patients do better and live longer than passive, insecure, depressed, and giving-up patients.

According to Bilick and Nuland (1981), it is the cancer patient who is assumed to be weak, whereas the deficit lies in the factors that are interfering with the *immune* system's normal functioning. Without the alleviation of his or her psychological stresses, the patient must rely solely on medical treatment, which not only overlooks the importance of psychological stresses on the disease process but often further suppresses the immune system, thus increasing the probability of additional medical complications.

Bilick and Nuland hypothesized that the immune system's functioning can be influenced by specific psychological techniques, such as autogenic techniques, relaxation techniques, biofeedback techniques, and hypnosis. In this model, it is assumed that patients who take responsibility for participating in their own recovery by actively involving themselves in their fight against cancer do better than those patients who experience themselves as helpless victims of their disease.

Bilick and Nuland further discuss the relationship between positive belief systems and illness expectations. In this approach, unlike in the medical model, cancer patients have the use of *visual imagery*. The patients have the opportunity to examine their underlying beliefs and attitudes, to develop a positive belief system about their immune system and medical treatment, and to acquire a self-help method that fosters confidence and self-reliance. These patients are taught to activate meditative processes, and to visualize white blood cells, the immune system, and the current medical treatment. The patients visualize that they are *destroying* cancer cells while leaving healthy tissue unharmed. Thus, they can focus on symbolic images that represent positive beliefs in the potency of their immune system.

REFERENCES

Ader, R. (Ed.). *Psychoneuroimmunology*. New York: Academic Press, 1981.

Ader, R., & Cohen, N. Behavior and the immune system. In W. D. Gentry (Ed.), *Handbook of behavioral medicine* (pp. 117–173). New York, London: Guilford Press, 1984.

Bartrop, R. W., Luckhurst, E., Lazarus, L., & Kiloh, L. G. Depressed lymphocyte function after bereavement. *Lancet*, 1977, *1*, 834–836.

Bilick, H. A., & Nuland, W. A. Psychosocial model in the treatment of cancer patients. In J. G. Goldberg (Ed.), *Psychotherapeutic treatment of cancer patients* (pp. 58–70). New York: Free Press, 1981.

Dorian, B. J., Keystone, E., Garfinkel, P. E., & Brown, G. M. Aberrations in lymphocytes subpopulations and functions during psychological stress. *Clinical-Experimental Immunology*, 1982, *50*, 132–138.

Franz, M. L. von. Der Traum des Descartes. In C. A. Meyer (Ed.), *Zeitlose Dokumente der Seele*. Zurich: Rascher, 1952.

Gilliland, B. C. Introduction to clinical immunology. In T. R. Harrison (Ed.), *Principles of internal medicine* (9th ed., pp. 315–325). New York: McGraw-Hill, 1980.

Goldberg, J. G. (Ed.). *Psychotherapeutic treatment of cancer patients*. New York: Free Press, 1981.

Jermott, J. B., & Locke, S. E. Psychosocial factors, immunologic meditation, and human susceptibility to infectious diseases. *Psychological Bulletin*, 1984, *95*, 52–77.

Kimball, C. P. Diagnosing psychosomatic situations. In B. B. Wolman (Ed.), *Clinical diagnosis of mental disorders: A handbook* (pp. 677–708). New York: Plenum Press, 1978.

Levy, S. (Ed.). *Biological mediator of stress and disease: Neoplasms*. New York: Elsevier-North Holland, 1982.

Lipowski, Z. J. *Psychosomatic medicine and liason psychiatry.* New York: Plenum Press, 1985.
Mason, J. W. Psychologic stress and endocrine function. In F. J. Sachar (Ed.), *Topics in endocrinology.* New York: Grune & Stratton, 1975.
Miller, N. E. Behavioral medicine: Symbiosis between laboratory and clinic. *Annual Review of Psychology,* 1983, *34,* 1–32.
Silverberg, E. *Cancer statistics.* New York: American Cancer Society, 1984.
Simonton, O. C., & Simonton, S. Belief systems and management of the emotional aspects of malignancy. *Journal of Transpersonal Psychology,* 1975, *7,* 29–47.
Simonton, D. C., & Simonton, S. *Getting well again.* New York: Prentice-Hall, 1978.
Solomon, G. E., & Amkraut, A. A. Psychoneuroendocrinological effects of the immune response. *Annual Review of Microbiology,* 1981, 35, 155–184.
Stein, M., Schiavi, R., & Camerino, M. Influence of brain and behavior on the immune system. *Science,* 1976, *191,* 435–440.
Stein, M., Schleifer, S. J., & Keller, S. E. Immune disorders. In H. I. Kaplan & B. J. Sadock (Eds.), *Comprehensive textbook of psychiatry* (4th ed.), pp. 1206–1212). Baltimore, Maryland: Williams & Wilkins, 1985.
Zegans, L. S. Stress and the development of somatic disorders. In L. Goldberger & S. Bresnitz (Eds.), *Handbook of stress* (pp. 134–152). New York: Free Press, 1982.

6

Monistic Transitionism

The difference between psychology and physiology, as J. B. Watson saw it, was that physiology studied separate physiological functions, whereas psychology dealt with the functions of the organism as a whole: "The findings of psychology become the functional correlates of structure and lend themselves to explanation in physico-chemical terms" (Watson, 1913, p. 166). V. M. Bekhterev (1913, p. 156) believed that consciousness is a state of physical energy related to central inhibition and resistance in cortical processes. D. O. Hebb (1949) wrote about "the kind of activity *throughout the cerebrum* which we call consciousness" (p. 129). He also believed that "interest or motivation" can be "provisionally translated into the stability and persistence of the phase sequence" in nerve cells (p. 233).

Some psychologists vigorously rejected any sort of theoretical reductionism. According to B. F. Skinner (1953):

> Modern science has attempted to put forth an ordered and integrated conception of nature. . . . The picture which emerges is almost always dualistic. The scientist humbly admits that he is describing only half of the universe, and he defers to another world—a world of mind or consciousness—for which another mode of inquiry is assumed to be required. (p. 126)

According to Skinner (1950), there is no valid reason to reduce psychological data to physiology, physics, or chemistry. Also, Kurt Lewin (1951) saw no advantage in reducing psychology to physiology and objected to the Gestaltists' isomorphic theory of mind and body.

Most psychological theorists have neither accepted nor rejected reductionism but have professed a hoped-for reductionism. For instance, C. L. Hull (1943) maintained that there is no adequate neuropsychology to which psychology could be reduced at the present time. Also, Freud (1938/1949) believed that the "future may teach us how to exercise a direct influence, by means of particular chemical substances, upon the amount of energy and their distribution in the apparatus of mind" (p. 79).

45

THE CONCEPT OF CHANGE

Change does not imply discontinuity. A fertilized egg becomes a zygote, and the zygote becomes an embryo, a fetus, a neonate, an infant, a toddler, a little child, an adolescent, a college student, and eventually, for example, a famous pediatrician. Is the pediatrician "the same" as or "identical" with the nursery child he or she was 40 or 50 years ago? *The answer is yes, in the sense of continuity, but no, in the sense of identity.*

In order to tackle this question, one must start by clarifying the terms *same*, *identical*, and so on. Let us start with the mathematical sign = (equals). Consider the equation:

$$a + b = 0$$

This equation does not imply identity. The sign a and the sign b have the same numerical value, one of them positive, and the other negative. The sign symbol zero is not necessarily identical with the composite sign "$a + b$." The equation merely represents a mathematical operation, but not an identity relationship. Translated into simple English, it reads as follows: "*a added to b equals 0*, but they are a and b, and they are *not* zero."

The philosophy of science is full of concepts uncritically borrowed from mathematics. Such a state of affairs was perhaps justified in the times of Spinoza or Kant, when philosophers believed in the alleged superiority of the newer mathematical systems. Riemann's and Lobachevki's geometry, Boyle's system, matrix algebra, and topology have challenged the axiomatic nature of the mathematical systems and have made mathematics into a systematic aggregate of symbolic signs and operations, a sort of language or game.

This change in the role of mathematics permits a far-reaching revision of several concepts. Consider the equation:

$$a = a$$

This equation seems to be self-evident, but this alleged self-evidence can be questioned. For instance, in traditional algebra:

$$a + b = b + a$$

but in matrix algebra:

$$\{a + b \neq b + a\}$$

In topological mathematics, the equation $a + b = b + a$ can become meaningless, as the relative position of the elements in regard to each other is the relevant issue in topology.

Furthermore, consider the chemical equation:

$$C + C + O = C_2O$$

Is C_2O identical with $C + C + O$? The empirical evidence militates against such an assumption, for the *quality* of C_2O is different from two unbound C's and an O. Thus, the equation $C + C + O = C_2O$ does not represent an identity but merely describes a complex process by which C and C and O can become C_2O. Moreover, this description is far from being accurate, which may undermine one's belief in the applicability of simple mathematical signs to the description of complex phenomena.

The development of thermodynamics should have aroused serious doubts concerning the possibility of anything's ever being identical with anything, including itself. In thermodynamics, heat *changes* into kinetic energy. Does this mean that heat is kinetic energy? Is fuel identical with energy? Is water identical with vapor and ice? Empirical speaking, ice $\neq$ water $\neq$ vapor. Are they, therefore, the same? Or are they not?

Heraclitus said that no one can bathe twice in the *same* river. It also seems obvious, however, that no one could ever remain the same person. A person P at time t and m environment e is not exactly the same as the "same" person a while later at time t_2 and in an environment e_2. Thus:

$$P_{t1e_1} \neq P_{t2e_2}$$

Kurt Lewin, Harry Stack Sullivan, Benjamin B. Wolman, and several others have pointed to the *field-theoretical* nature of human personality. Prognosis of mental or physical diseases can be, at best, a statistical approximation. In order to predict an individual case, a clinician must possess a complete knowledge of *all* the relevant factors affecting the patient, and the prediction, if any, must be field-theoretical. The "same" patient reacts differently to the "same" disease in different environments and under different treatments.

It is an undeniable fact that, under certain conditions, certain bodies change, merge, split, grow, shrink, move, stop, fall apart, and so on. Indians in Montana used to squeeze the skulls of their newborn infants to make them look prettier by the standards of the prevailing fashion. Contemporary women starve themselves to meet the standards set by the garment center's fashion designers. When a woman has lost 20 pounds, is she still the same woman or not? When a child has grown up, when an attic has been added to a house, when a man has shaved his beard: Are these all still the same?

There are degrees of change. When a pot of water is put on a stove, the temperature of the water changes. When the water reaches a boiling point, further changes take place. Logically speaking, as long as at least one element of A_1 persists in A_2, we can speak of *continuity*.

There are a great many types and degrees of change, and there is no reason to prescribe to them one path and one pattern. The fact of continuity in change is evident in many, if not all, phenomena and events in the universe. Water evaporates and turns into clouds, and clouds give rain and fill rivers with water. Lava erupts and turns into fertile soil, and some fertile soil is eroded or covered by dunes. Species develop and perish, and new worlds develop out of old ones.

This continuous change is expressed in a theory of *monistic transitionism*. Monistic transitionism: (1) takes into account the diversity and variability of nature, (2) unites this empirical diversity into an overall continuous *unity*, and (3) introduces the general idea of the continuous changeability of things. Transitionism does not assume uniformity of the universe; it assumes only its continuity (Wolman and Nagel, 1965).

Transitionism views the universe in a continuity of changes and transitions from one phase of existence into another. It presents the evolution of matter in three recognizable phases: (1) the inanimate or inorganic matter at a certain point of evolution undergoes changes and becomes (2) organic, as described in the experimental studies by A. I. Oparin (1957). Then, at a certain phase in evolution, matter turns into (3) psychological processes (which can also be called behavioral). Transitionism links all three phases into one process of change and continuity. This process is also reversible, for, as the inorganic matter may become organic matter and the organic matter may become psychological, the psychological elements can turn organic, and organic elements may turn inorganic. For example, under the impact of alcohol, human feelings can change; under the impact of human feelings, bodily chemistry can change. Nature crosses this bridge from mind to body and from body to mind every day in a series of psychosomatic and somatopsychic phenomena. Mind and body represent two levels of transition; the mind is a higher level of transition.

Psychosomatic and somatopsychic phenomena are daily occurrences. Emotions affect the circulatory and gastrointestinal systems, and an intake of food and liquids affects mental functions. In certain instances, psychological factors affect physical health and cause damage to the human body. These instances are the subject matter of psychosomatic medicine.

PSYCHOSOMATIC SYMPTOMS

Psychosomatic symptoms always carry a message. All of them serve the same purpose: *escape* from a difficult, embarrassing, or painful situation. Headaches, bellyaches, skin rashes, and diarrhea are frequent and easily diagnosed psychosomatic symptoms. They usually serve a discernible purpose and require a mild, if any, therapeutic intervention. Should they continue, they could cause considerable harm to behavior and to the body.

More serious cardiovascular, respiratory, and gastrointestinal psychosomatic disorders can cause grave biochemical damage.

As mentioned above, an escape from a minor trouble into a major one is like the proverbial escape from a frying pan into a fire.

Quite often, patients themselves give verbal clues to their problems. They may say, "I don't have the heart to . . ." explaining their psychosomatic heart troubles. "I can't stomach it," said a throwing-up young woman talking about her marital difficulties.

A Few Cases

Psychosomatic Pseudopregnancy

A 28-year-old divorced woman was anxious to remarry. When she met a 30-year-old bachelor, she described him as her "Prince Charming." He was bright, successful, attractive, and polite and liked her very much, but how could she make him marry her?

One day, she came to my office with good news: she was pregnant. She had all the symptoms: her breasts and so on. I sent her to a gynecologist. The gynecologist called me and explained that the symptoms were indeed striking, but she was not pregnant. I asked her, "Did you have sex with your boyfriend?" She answered, "Yes, oral sex only."

Psychosomatic Heart Trouble

A 40-year-old businessman complained about pain in the chest, shortness of breath, and a series of other symptoms that could have been associated with heart disease. His business was not in good shape, and he was losing money. Once a week, he held sales meetings, which were rather discouraging. Usually, after such a meeting, but also on other occasions, he withdrew to a back room behind his executive office. He told his secretary not to give him any telephone calls and called his wife on a private, unlisted phone. His wife was supposed always to be available to come over and console her husband. She would rush to his office to find him in grave chest pain on the couch. She was supposed to sit down next to him, caress his head, and prevent the oncoming heart attack.

I sent the man to a university hospital for a thorough examination by a leading professor of cardiology. After a few days, the cardiologist sent me a totally negative report, with a warning that should these symptoms continue, the prognosis was unpredictable. Psychogenic diseases are diseases, and heart trouble resulting from psychological causes can be as real and as dangerous as any other heart trouble.

Encopresis

Many psychosomatic symptoms start in early years but may persist and outlast their original purpose. I had once in treatment a young man who was not incontinent but suffered from almost uncontrollable diarrhea.

At the age of 2, he had already achieved complete control of bowels and bladder, but when he was 3 year old, he became incontinent. He was the only child of a mild-mannered father and a forceful aggressive mother. His mother looked down on her husband and did not pay much attention to the boy.

When the boy was 10 years old, his mother gave birth to a girl. Life in the house underwent a radical change: the house turned into a pattern of lower- and upper-class social strata. The father and the boy slept in just a small room from then on. A private sleep-in nurse received the neighboring room. The mother and the nurse catered to the little princess, and a part-time maid took care of the boy's and father's lodging.

Every morning, the 10-year-old boy went on a school bus to a private school. He was a fourth- or fifth-grade student, but he was made to stay for too long. By around 10 or 11 o'clock in the morning, he was losing his bowel control and was sent home in a cab. The baby nurse refused to take care of the "smelly kid," and the mother had no choice but to throw him in a tub and wash him. She was furious and did not spare blows and verbal insults. The 20-year-old man described the tub scene with nostalgic feelings.

Pubic Area Skin Rash

An angry young woman came to my office. Her dermatologist had referred her to me with a case of frequent recurrence of rash in her pubic area. "Do you want me to undress so you can see what I am going through?" she asked me angrily.

"No," I replied. "I have a detailed report from your doctor. Shrinks don't ask people to undress." The dermatologist reported that he had treated the woman unsuccessfully for over 2 years, soon after she got married.

It took a while before I could unravel the truth. Years before, someone had told her that her pelvic bones were very narrow and that she might not be able to survive childbirth. Her husband wanted children, and every month after her period, she developed a rash.

Throwing Up

When this patient entered my consultation room, she suggested that I remove the carpet. "I can't control nausea," she said, "I throw up frequently."

She did not throw up in my office. She told me that her parents had forced her to marry an old, "very rich man." She couldn't "stomach" that kind of life. She felt like throwing up.

It is rather rare or even impossible to develop psychosomatic disorders that do not serve a purpose. On several occasions, my patients have maintained that their ailments were psychosomatic, but on a thorough examination, their hypotheses had been dismissed unless the symptoms represented a clear escape from a difficult situation.

REFERENCES

Bekhterev, V. M. *Objective Psychologie-Reflexologie*. Liepzig: Teubner, 1913.
Freud, S. *An outline of psychoanalysis*. New York: Norton, 1949, p. 79. (Originally published, 1938.)
Hebb, D. O. *The organization of behavior*. New York: Wiley, 1949.
Hull, C. L. *Principles of behavior: An introduction to behavior therapy*. New York: Appleton-Century-Crofts, 1943.
Lewin, K. *Field theory in social science*. New York: Harper, 1951.
Oparin, A. I. *The origins of life on earth*. New York: Academic Press, 1957.
Skinner, B. F. Are theories of learning necessary? *Psychological Review*, 1950, *57*, 193–216.
Skinner, B. F. *Science and human behavior*. New York: Macmillan, 1953.
Watson, J. B. Psychology as the behaviorist sees it. *Psychological Review*, 1913, *20*, 158–177.
Wolman, B. B., & Nagel, E. (Eds.) *Scientific psychology*. New York: Basic Books, 1965.

II

Etiological Considerations

7

Stress

DEFINING STRESS

Webster's Collegiate Dictionary defines stress as pressure or strain. Wolman's *Dictionary of Behavioral Science* (1973) defines stress as a condition of physical or mental strain that produces changes in the autonomic nervous system. Stress is a state of pressure that puts enormous demands on the organism. Sometimes, the stress may be more than the organism can cope with.

Selye (1956, 1976) developed a theory of reactions of an organism to stress. According to this theory, called *general adaptation syndrome,* the organism reacts to stress in three phases, usually alarm reaction, resistance, and finally exhaustion. In Selye's experiments, animals were subjected to a variety of stressful conditions, including starvation, infections, poisoning, extreme cold, extreme heat, and surgical hemorrhage. The animals' reactions were not specific to the stress but consisted of a general pattern of change that was much the same for all stimulus situations. The alarm reactions followed the application of physical injury but could be provoked by stimuli of a symbolic nature.

STRESSORS

When an intense stress-provoking stimulus, called by Selye "stressor," acts on an organism, the organism responds by a series of biochemical and physiological changes in the glands of inner secretion, called the "alarm reaction." The alarm reaction is followed by an increased hormonal secretion of the pituitary gland, which activates the cortex of the adrenal glands. The hormone produced by the anterior part of the pituitary gland is called *corticotropin,* or *ACTH;* the hormone secreted by the adrenal cortex is called *cortin.* Cortin and corticotropin mobilize, as it were, the latent resources of the organism and enable it to withstand the harm caused to it or to compensate for that harm.

The adaptation to one stressor may be paid for by a reduction of resistance to the other stressor. The adaptation may also fail if the stress is too severe or lasts for too long a time. For instance, during periods of famine in Nigeria and Bangladesh, many people managed to survive on what is normally believed to be an inadequate supply of food, but they were exceedingly vulnerable to diseases and had little resistance to infections, and more people died from diseases than from starvation.

However, every human organism has a breaking point beyond which it cannot go. Sooner or later, every organism reaches the phase of exhaustion. A further exposure to stress may cause a total collapse of functioning, and death will eventually follow (Goldberger & Bresnitz, 1982).

PROLONGED STRESS

A similar principle applies to mental stress. Every human being can withstand some degree of stress, but no human being can be indefinitely exposed to unlimited stress. People do not "get used" to stress; on the contrary, stress has a cumulative effect. Continuous stress reduces one's work efficiency, produces states of anxiety and irritability, and lowers one's ability to adapt to new situations. Lazarus (1966) observed that people exposed to prolonged stress situations tend to become rigid and unable to react spontaneously to new situations.

Lazarus distinguished between *stimulus* and *response* definitions of stress. The stimulus definition describes the stress-producing situations, such as military combat, floods, tornadoes, and grave illness or injury. The stimulus definition describes the circumstances that are conducive to disturbed reactions (Lazarus & Folkman, 1984).

RESPONSE TO STRESS

The response definition describes the stress reactions to a disturbing situation, such as panic in the face of a mortal threat or anxiety as a product of conflict.

One may distinguish two kinds of responses to severe stress: the *denial set* and the *intrusion set*. Denial includes the unrealistic avoidance of an appraisal of the meaning of the stressful event, such as the death of a beloved one, injury, or rape. The intrusion set is the opposite of the denial set and includes recurrent thoughts and images of the past traumas. Several years ago, I worked with people who had lived through the terrors of the Nazi concentration camps. Some of them had repressed their past experiences and were somewhat emotionally numb. The others almost continuously recalled the horrors of their past.

The same stress may evoke different reactions in different people— and even different reactions in the same person at different times. For instance, it has been noticed that graduate students did not experience much anxiety 3 months before an exam, although the results of the exam were of utmost importance and could determine whether they would be allowed to continue their doctoral studies. However, as the time of the exam approached:

> Stomachaches, asthma, and a general feeling of weariness became common complaints, and other psychosomatic symptoms appeared. The use of tranquilizers and sleeping pills became more frequent. When the examinations are nearly upon the student, anxiety is very high. (Mechanic, 1980, p. 142)

Selye's concepts have undergone considerable modifications. In 1978, Tache and Selye wrote that stress is a nonspecific response of the body to the demands made on it. It is a sort of call to arms of the body defenses (a triphanic response). There are three phases in the reaction to stress: (1) the alarm reaction; (2) the state of resistance, during which the initial symptoms are reduced or disappear; and (3) the stage of exhaustion. The demands are mediated through a corticotrophic releasing factor (CRF) produced by the hypothalamus. The hypothalamic-pituitary-adrenal system organizes the defensive action that precipitates psychosomatic diseases.

There is no unanimous agreement on this issue. For instance, Lazarus (1966) maintained that stress is an *internal state* of an individual who perceives physical or mental threats. Stress is communicated symbolically, and it conveys a confrontation with a harmful condition.

In a more recent development, Lazarus and his associates (Coyne & Lazarus, 1980; Lazarus, 1980) have maintained that psychological stress can be conceptualized in terms of person–environment transactions that exceed the resources of the person. Stress is neither an environmental stimulus nor a response; it is a relationship between demands and the power to deal with them without unreasonable or destructive costs. Two processes mediate the person's contribution to this relationship: *appraisal* and *coping*.

APPRAISAL AND COPING

The concept *appraisal* is related to the person's continually reevaluated judgments about the demands and constraints in the interaction process with the environment. The degree to which a person experiences psychological stress greatly depends on what is at stake (primary appraisal) and what coping resources are available (secondary appraisal). The distinction between primary appraisal and secondary appraisal serves a useful purpose when it draws attention to the different sets of variables affecting cognition, coping, and adaptational outcome. A firm sense of self-efficacy (secondary appraisal) can lead one to appraise transactions as benign or irrelevant (primary appraisal); alternatively, a sense that one's coping resources are limited can lead to appraisals of potential threat (Coyne & Holroyd, 1982).

According to Kasl (1984), stress is a complex process of a series of multilevel responses related to physical and mental health. This process may cause a decline in the levels of norepinephrine and serotonin and an increase in the levels of plasma corticosterone and in the activity of the anterior pituitary hormones (Anisman, 1978; Anisman, Pizzion, & Sklar, 1980).

CONCEPTUAL EVOLUTION

Zegans (1982) summarized the evolution of the concepts of stress as follows:

> The stress as stimulus concept has triggered very active research on possible connections between stress and bodily illness. Many years ago, Meyer (1958) argued that certain alterations of life circumstances, such as changes of habitat, births, deaths, and new jobs, have a potent influence on the balance between health and illness. Holmes and Rane (1967), Rahe (1976), and their collaborators examined this perception in a series of studies geared to determine whether changes in a person's life could be statistically correlated with onset of illness. The *psychosomatic medicine movement* had long before associated certain internal psychological conflicts with predispositions to particular diseases (e.g., asthma, ulcers, ulcerative colitis). The *life events research model* hypothesized that it is possible to make predictions about stress and susceptibility to a much wider array of diseases (infectious, neoplastic, autoimmune) by determining the magnitude of critical life changes taking place within a limited span of time. (p. 138)

Zegans went on to say:

> Stress appears to be an altered state of the individual that arises as a consequence of adaptive failure and not adaptive challenge. Illness is the outcome of multiple characteristics of the organism, which interact with a variety of interdependent factors, including social context and disease agents. As Cleary (1974) and Rabkin and Streuning (1976) have pointed out, the life events research, while calling attention to an important source of stress, has focused only on linear relationships between independent and dependent variables. The task of new investigation and theory is to go beyond the linkage of stimulus and probability of illness to illuminate those internal mechanisms through which life events are believed to have their pathological impact. (p. 139)

Stress is a reaction of the organism to noxious or threatening stimuli. Noxious or threatening stimuli may come from within in a physical or a mental disorder, but most often, these stimuli come from without, from one's physical or social environment (Wolman, 1984).

Human beings react in different ways to noxious and/or threatening stimuli. Some individuals escape into psychosomatic symptoms, whereas others can adequately cope with ongoing adverse stimuli.

Needless to say, one must take into consideration several aspects of the role of stress in the etiology of psychosomatic disorders, while not overlooking the role of the immune system. Psychological stress can reduce the functions of the immune system, thus increasing the organism's susceptibility to a variety of diseases (Miller, 1983; Rogers, Dabey, & Reich, 1979). Feelings of defeat and helplessness can affect the organism's resilience and can cause a variety of psychosomatic disorders.

REFERENCES

Anisman, H. Neurochemical changes elicited by stress. In H. Anisman & G. Bignami (Eds.), *Psychopharmacology of adversively motivated behavior.* New York: Plenum Press, 1978.

Anisman, H., Pizzion, A., & Sklar, L. S. Coping with stress, norepinephrine depletion and escape performance. *Brain research,* 1980, *191,* 583–588.

Cleary, P. J. Life events and disease: A review of methodology and findings. *Reports from the Laboratory for Clinical Stress Research, Stockholm,* 1974, *3,* 1–50.

Coyne, J. C., & Holroyd, K. A transactional perspective. In T. Millon, C. Greene, & R. Meagher (Eds.), *Handbook of clinical health psychology* (pp. 103–128). New York: Plenum Press, 1982.

Coyne, J. C., & Lazarus, R. S. Cognitive style, stress perception and coping. In J. L. Kutash & B. Schlesinger (Eds.), *Handbook on stress and anxiety: Contemporary knowledge, theory and treatment.* San Francisco: Jossey-Bass, 1980.

Goldberger, L., & Breznitz, S. (Eds.). *Handbook of stress.* New York: Macmillan-Free Press, 1982.

Holmes, T. H., & Rahe, R. H. The social readjustment rating scale. *Journal of Psychosomatic Research,* 1967, *2,* 213–218.

Kasl, S. V. Stress and health. *Annual Review of Public Health,* 1984, *5,* 319–342.

Lazarus, R. S. *Psychological stress and the coping process.* New York: McGraw-Hill, 1966.

Lazarus, R. S. The stress and coping paradigm. In L. A. Bond & J. C. Rosen (Eds.), *Competence and coping during adulthood.* Hanover, NH: University Press of New England, 1980.

Lazarus, R. S., & Folkman, S. Coping and adaptation. In W. Gentry (Ed.), *Handbook of behavioral medicine* (pp. 282–325). New York: Guilford Press, 1984.

Mechanic, D. The experience and reporting of common physical complaints. *Social Behavior,* 1980, *21,* 146–155.

Meyer, A. *Psychobiology: A science of man.* Springfield, IL: Thomas, 1958.

Miller, N. E. Behavioral medicine: Symbiosis between laboratory and clinic. *Annual Review of Psychology,* 1983, *34,* 1–32.

Rabkin, J. G., & Streuning, E. L. Life events, stress, and illness. *Science,* 1976, *194,* 1013–1020.

Rahe, R. H. Stress and strain in coronary heart disease. *Journal of South Carolina Medical Association,* 1976, *72,* 7–14.

Rogers, M., Dabey, D., & Reich, P. The influence of the psyche and the brain on immunity and direct susceptibility: A critical review. *Psychosomatic Medicine,* 1979, *41,* 147–164.

Selye, H. *The story of the adaptation syndrome.* Montreal: Actra, 1952.

Selye, H. *The stress of life*. New York: McGraw-Hill, 1956.

Selye, H. *The stress of life* (2nd ed.). New York: McGraw-Hill, 1976.

Tache, J., & Selye, H. On stress and oping mechanisms. In C. D. Spielberger & I. G. Sarason (Eds.), *Stress and anxiety* (Vol. 5). Washington, DC: Hemisphere, 1978.

Wolman, B. B. *Dictionary of behavioral science*. New York: Van Nostrand Reinhold, 1973.

Wolman, B. B. *Problems of modern living: Psychology of adjustment*. Boston: American Press, 1984.

Zegans, L. S. Stress and the development of somatic disorders. In L. Goldberger & S. Breznitz (Eds.), *Handbook of stress: Theoretical and clinical aspects* (pp. 135–152). New York: Macmillan-Free Press, 1982.

8

Conditioned Reflexes

PAVLOV'S THEORY

Pavlov used two unconditioned stimuli: a food stimulus, which produced a positive reflex, and an acid stimulus, which produced a negative one. In several experiments, the salivary secretion was conditioned to metronome beats, to the sight of geometrical figures and letters, to cutaneous stimuli, and to the odor of camphor. A conditioned reflex occurs when an object is placed in the mouth of the dog and its properties excite the simple reflex apparatus of the salivary glands.

In Pavlov's experiments, the duct of the parotid gland in the dog was diverted by a small surgical operation. The saliva then flowed through an opening in the dog's cheek into a small glass funnel. A tuning fork was sounded, and 8 seconds later, meat powder was given to the dog. After 10 times of presenting the food and the sound, some slight salivation came after the sound, and after 30 tests, the saliva appeared in greater quantities (Pavlov, 1927).

Pavlov believed that conditioning takes place in the cerebral cortex; in experiments in which both hemispheres were removed, no conditioning took place. In later experiments by Pavlov and his associates, auditory salivary conditioned reflexes were reestablished after the removal of both temporal lobes. Several other experiments have proved that conditioning in decorticated dogs is possible.

Pavlov manipulated the temporal relationships between the unconditioned and the conditioned stimuli. In most experiments, the conditioned stimulus was administered from a fraction of a second to 5 seconds before the unconditioned stimulus and was continued simultaneously. In these experiments, the conditioned response followed immediately. In other experiments, the conditioned stimulus started earlier and continued until the start of the unconditioned stimulus. In such cases, when a simultaneous conditioned response was already established, a delayed conditioned response occurred.

In other experiments, conditioned and unconditioned stimuli did not overlap but were separated by a time interval. As a rule, the longer the interval, the more difficult it was to condition, but always, the conditioned stimulus was administered before the unconditioned stimulus.

Pavlov believed that some trace of the stimulus persisted in the organism after the conditioned stimulus was discontinued. When the conditioned stimulus was administered ahead of time, its trace persisted until the unconditioned stimulus was administered. Thus, the traces of the conditioned stimulus and the unconditioned stimulus were simultaneous, and a reinforcement could take place in this trace reflex. Obviously, this is one of the mechanisms of conditioning in psychosomatic symptoms. Conditioned responses can serve as unconditioned ones in "higher-order" conditioning. Once the sound of the metronome evoked salivation, a black square was held before the eyes of the dog for 10 seconds, and after an interval of 15 seconds, the metronome was sounded again for another 30 seconds. Now, the metronome was used as an unconditioned stimulus and the black square as the conditioned one.

The conditioned response is not identical with the unconditioned one, although they may be very much alike. The conditioned stimuli are divided into positive stimuli (i.e., provoking excitation) and negative stimuli (i.e., provoking inhibition). The conditioned stimuli are related, like the unconditioned ones, to the various functions of the organism, such as food, sex, and defense, and can serve as a bridge between psychological and somatic phenomena.

Pavlov never believed in an independent psychological science. Although he did not suggest substituting physiology for psychology, he doubted whether psychology could ever develop into an autonomous discipline capable of objective and scientific research. Pavlov maintained that psychology must be rooted in and related to physiology: he believed that physiology builds the "foundations," while psychology should build the "superstructure." However, because physiological concepts are "necessarily spatial" and psychology is limited to subjective states, Pavlov (1928) felt that the position of psychology as a science was "completely hopeless."

Pavlov avoided mentalistic terms. He pursued his research empirically, inductively, and experimentally. Pavlov (1928) emphasized that his study was "absolutely excluding psychological conceptions, and that his study of the activity of the central nervous systems had to do always with only objective facts—facts existing in time and space.

Some of Pavlov's experiments have shown that psychosomatic neurotic symptoms can be experimentally produced. Pavlov gradually intensified the pitch of the soft and low tones, making them quite similar to the high ones. At a certain point, the difference became so small that the dog was no longer able to distinguish between them. In some cases, the dog broke down and started to bark and bite, apparently exposed to conflicting stimuli of excitation and inhibition. This state was called by Pavlov "experimental neurosis." He described a case in which a light circle used as a conditioned stimulus had to be distinguished from an ellipse. These two stimuli became undistinguishable when the semiaxes of the ellipse reached the ratio of 9 to 8. At that time, Pavlov (1927) reported, that the whole behavior of the animal underwent an abrupt change: "The hitherto quiet dog began to squeal in its stand, kept wriggling about, tore off with its teeth the apparatus for mechanical stimulation of the skin. . . . On being taken into the experimental room the dog now barked violently. . . . In short it presented all the symptoms of a condition of acute neurosis" (p. 291).

Some animals seemed to succumb easily to stress, whereas others showed more resistance. The different types of disorder developed under stress were related to the already existing differences in the behavior of the animals. Some dogs easily formed positive reflexes, but it was difficult to produce in them inhibitory reflexes. The same dogs were characterized by the prevalence of excitatory reflexes and were usually very aggressive. When exposed to two opposite processes of excitation and inhibition in an experiment that called for a differentiation that overtaxed their abilities, they broke down with a neurasthenia in which the inhibitory processes disappeared. Dogs that easily formed inhibitory reflexes were characterized by a quiet, timid, and submissive behavior. When exposed to the above-mentioned experiment, they faced a nervous breakdown of a hysterical type in which the inhibitory processes prevailed. The third type, the *central* or equilibrated animals, took strain well. In a way, Pavlov introduced a theory of susceptibility to mental disorder based on differences in personality makeup. Pavlov (1928) continued the study of personality disposition to illness. He attempted to classify temperamental differences in relation to excitation and inhibition. His classification included the excitatory, the inhibitory, and the central or equilibrated type, the last of which could be divided into quiet and lively types. Accordingly, Pavlov divided all his experimental dogs into four categories and believed that humans could be classified in the same way. His division followed the four types suggested in ancient times by Hippocrates; choleric and melancholic, which were the two extreme types, and sanguinic and phlegmatic, which were the two equilibrated types.

The excitable dog—that is, the *choleric* type—responded quickly to positive stimuli, became easily conditioned, and was not easily inhibited. It was "pugnacious, passionate, and easily and quickly irritated" (p. 377). The choleric type corresponded to neurasthenia.

The inhibitory type was the *melancholic*. To this dog, "every event of life becomes an inhibitory agent; he believes in nothing, hopes for nothing, in everything he sees the dark side" (p. 378). The melancholic type corresponds to the hysterical.

Between these two extreme and pathological types, there were the two equilibrated or central or healthy types, the *phlegmatic* and the *sanguinic*. The phlegmatic was "self-contained and quiet; persistent and steadfast." The sanguinic is "energic and very productive" but, without constantly new stimulations, got bored and fell asleep easily (Pavlov, 1928, p. 377).

Schizophrenia is, according to Pavlov, a severe hysteria. Pavlov (1928) believed that the inhibitory hysterical dogs "have very weak cortical cells easily passing over into various degrees of a chronic inhibitory condition," and that:

> The basic features of human hysteria are also a weakness of the cortex. Schizophrenia is an extreme weakness of the cortex, as a marked degree of hysteria. . . . In our inhibitory, hysterical dogs, by applying the functional difficulties presented by our experiments, we can make completely isolated pathologic points and foci in the cortex; in schizophrenia, in the same manner, under the influence of certain experiences of life, acting perhaps on the already organically pathological condition, gradually and constantly there appear a larger and larger number of such weak points and foci, and by degrees there occurs a breaking up of the cerebral cortex, a splitting up of its normally unified function. (p. 378)

Cyclic psychosis represents an extreme case of neurasthenia. Neurasthenics have periods of intense activity and then times of deep depression with curtailment of their activities and abilities.

Pavlov's research has opened new vistas in the development of psychomatic concepts, as will be described in the following chapters. According to Pavlov, personality traits depend on innate qualities of the nervous cells. However, environmental influences may cause substantial modifications. Pavlov maintained that all animals are subjected to the various effects produced by the environment. Thus, the final nervous activity present in an animal is an alloy of the features peculiar to the type and of the changes wrought by the environment. In other words, the symptoms are related both to genetic factors and to one's interaction with the environment.

In Pavlov's footsteps, Soviet scientists applied Pavlov's classical conditioning method in their study of physical diseases and psychosomatic symptoms. They adduced empirical evidence of the possibility of conditioning the autonomic nervous system and producing psychosomatic disorders (Bykov, 1957). Using Pavlov's experimental methods, they pointed to the role of psychological factors in the etiology of physical disease, and they proved that subjecting animals to severe stress can facilitate the development of malignant tumors (Schmale, Morrow, & Ader, 1977).

Razran (1961) reported Soviet experiments in interoceptive condition-

ing. He quoted Pshonik's work with conditioned vasodilation and vasoconstriction. Razran described Lisina's experiments as demonstrating
that, when the subject has become aware of the connection between the
reinforcement and his or her own response, the stress-induced vasoconstriction turns into vasodilation.

Unconscious Motivation

Apparently, unconscious motivation and interoceptive conditioning
play a significant role in the etiology of psychosomatic disorders. Several
studies that have correlated conscious and unconscious anxiety with autonomic response (Lacey, Smith, & Green, 1955) have shown very different
physiological patterns in subjects who were aware of the conditioning
procedures, as opposed to subjects who were unaware and presumably
developed "unconscious anxiety" following the experimenters' successful
manipulation of the conditioning procedures. The spread of anxiety appeared to be greater in the subjects functioning under unconscious anxiety.
The subjects who were aware of the experimental design before the experiment developed a strong emergency response following the designated
stimulus words, and this response showed a gradual adaptation. Lisina (in
Razran, 1961) also demonstrated that, if a subject is made fully conscious of
the conditioned connection, this connection can be radically altered.

Experiments on inhibition versus expression of affect as a factor in
physiological response under stress were conducted by Oken (1962). The
author measured two groups of subjects on the basis of free expression of
affect versus low expression of affect. The findings contradicted the hypothesis that emotionally expressive subjects would give lower physiological responses for heart rate, systolic blood pressure, skin resistance, calf-
muscle blood flow, and respiratory rate. The only variables that showed
greater physiological response in the inhibited group of subjects were
skin temperature and diastolic and finger blood flow. The author interpreted the findings as meaning that a suppression of feelings is linked to
the development of essential hypertension. However, it was impossible
to determine whether the feelings were inhibited unconsciously or were
of a low order of response for other reasons, such as defective or initially
low hypothalamic excitability (Wittkower & Dudek, 1973). The Soviet research on interoceptive conditioning suggests that autonomic responses
condition readily and are more "fixed" than skeletal responses once they
have been established. Apparently, more unconscious conditioning of the
autonomic nervous system occurs in infancy and adulthood than has
been suspected. This may help to explain the idiosyncrasies in physiological patterning either when the expected stimulus specifically does not

occur or when it cannot be explained by an external S-R connection (Wolman, 1981).

According to Lacey (1967), psychophysiological experiments demonstrate that different stimulus situations produce different patterns of somatic response (e.g., anger directed outward and anger directed inward). Another pattern is that attentive observation of the external environment produces cardiac deceleration, cardiac stabilization, and either blood pressure decrease or a marked diminution of pressure increase. These results occur simultaneously with other procedures, such as vasocostriction and palmar conductance increase: "We heuristically interpreted these results to mean that depression-decelerative processes facilitated environmental intake and that pressor-accelerative responses tended to filter out irrelevant stimuli that have distraction value for the performance of internalized cognitive elaboration" (pp. 33–34).

The conclusion that can be drawn is that there are physiological patterns of response for general classes of behavioral function (e.g., cognitive or externalized attending) that impose a specific behavior. To the extent that cognitive or attentional factors are involved, they "can diminish, cancel, or convert cardiac acceleration and blood pressure increases 'caused' by suitable behaviors," (Lacey, 1967, p. 35), and cardiac activity, in turn, exercises considerable control over the bulbar inhibitory areas, which have a capacity to decrease cortical electrical activity. Thus, at early stages in the transmission process, cortical and subcortical systems and peripheral mechanisms can control the very nature and kind of signals that are allowed to be transmitted and can even determine the variable nature of the transmission process itself (Lacey, 1967, p. 33). It has also become obvious that there are different patterns within the sympathetic nervous system, and that these are related to the stimulus characteristic.

Research points out the importance of both the environmental and the physiological factors to which the organism is responding. Although the physiological patterns follow a stereotype, the cognitive factors play a large part in determining which stereotype will take over and why. Intention and direction are important factors in the explanation of symptom choice in psychosomatic medicine (Wittkower & Dudek, 1973).

In experiments with curarized rats, DiCara and Miller (1968), showed that heart rate, peripheral vasomotor responses, gastrointestinal motility, and urine production can be modified by brain stimulations or by the effect of painful electric shock used as reinforcement. In order to rule out the mediation of visceral responses by respiratory change and/or overt skeletal responses, the rats were paralyzed.

Moreover, the experimental research in instrumental conditioning reported by DiCara and Miller demonstrated that physical and chemical pathological methanisms can be conditioned and extinguished. This finding led to wide applications of the behavioral treatment of psychosomatic disorders.

HEART RATE AND CONDITIONING

Shapiro (1970) demonstrated significant heart-rate conditioning in humans in a single session without concomitant effects on systolic blood pressure. He concluded that the data demonstrated that "instrumental fractionation of closely related visceral behavior is possible for man, and support the possibility of a behavioral therapy for autonomically-mediated disorders" (p. 423). Weiss and Engel (1971) reported the long-term control of heart rate in patients with premature ventricular contractions by means of operant conditioning.

Belanger and Feldman (1962) demonstrated that animals showed heart rate increase when they found themselves before a dish containing water. The subsequent experiments with water-deprived rats, in which these authors found no heart rate changes when the animals were presented with an empty dish, served to demonstrate that an interaction between an internal condition (organic need) and an appropriate environmental cue was required for a measurable physiological change to manifest itself. Ducharme (1962) demonstrated "that cues other than those of adequate unconditioned reinforcement can produce heart rate acceleration in the animal 'sensitized' by deprivation" (p. 298). Ducharme made it clear that the "conditioned cues" can be even more effective than the "unconditioned cues" in effecting behavioral change. The interoceptive experiments of the Soviet scientists arrived at the same conclusions (Razran, 1961).

According to Pavlov (1928), the presentation of the bell stimulus resulted in salivation in the dog. Analogously, in psychosomatic disorders, a neutral stimulus may elicit an anxiety response. This process is exemplified by cancer patients who get nauseated and begin vomiting at the sight or smell of the hospital in which they have previously received chemotherapy that has reliably induced vomiting chemically during the course of their treatment. Such responses involve various kinds of autonomic processes rather than voluntary motor and sensory pathways. The overactivity of selected organ systems in vulnerable individuals produces changes in physiology. The objective in classical behavioral therapy is the training of the individual to alter the undesired physiological response. Because it is hypothesized that anxiety and other aversive emotions trigger the undesired response, teaching the individual to use a response that is incompatible with anxiety results in its alleviation. Relaxation responses made in the presence of a conditioned, anxiety-inducing stimulus seek to replace the undesired conditioned response (Wolpe, 1980).

Operant Conditioning

The operant conditioning concept is associated with B. F. Skinner (1938, 1953; Wolman, 1981). The focus of control in this system is on the consequences of behavior. Skinner was rather undecided about what really takes place in conditioning. Skinner (1953) believed that the connection between reinforcement and satiation must be sought in the process of evolution:

> We can scarcely overlook great biological significance of the primary reinforcers. Food, water, and sexual contact, as well as escape from injurious conditions are obviously connected with the well-being of the organism. . . . It is tempting to suppose that other forms of stimulation produced by behavior are similarly related to biologically important events. . . . A biological explanation of reinforcing power is perhaps as far as we can go in saying why an event is reinforcing. Such explanation is probably of little help in a functional analysis, for it does not provide us with any way of identifying a reinforcing stimulus as such before we have tested its reinforcing power upon a given organism. (pp. 81–84)

Although Skinner felt unable to explain the nature of reinforcement, his experimental studies made a significant contribution toward the understanding of the problem. He could not find the answer to the problem of why reinforcement reinforced, but he did offer a detailed and precise description of reinforcement.

In a series of experiments with pigeons, Skinner studied interval and ratio reinforcement; these two types of reinforcement are included in the category of intermittent reinforcement. In experiments related to interval or periodic reinforcement, reinforcements were given at more-or-less fixed intervals, a definite number of times per hour. The results of this interval reinforcement were rather stable and constant and were highly resistant to extinction.

In experiments with ratio reinforcement, the reinforcement was administered not at certain time intervals, but after a certain number of responses. The less frequent the reinforcement, the quicker the response. The ratio of unreinforced responses to reinforced ones, called the *extinction ratio*, was 20 to 1 in the interval reinforcement and 200 to 1 in the ratio reinforcement. The implications for education are quite obvious.

An originally neutral stimulus can become reinforcing through its repeated association with a reinforcing stimulus. The neutral stimulus acquires a reinforcing value of its own and may be called a *conditioned, secondary,* or *derived reinforcement*. A secondary reinforcement can be extinguished when repeatedly applied to a response for which there is no ultimate primary reinforcement (Skinner, 1969).

The reflex reserve was originally defined by Skinner (1938) as the "available activity, which is exhausted during the process of repeated elicitation of which the strength of the reflex is at any moment a function" (p.

26). In operant reflexes, the reflex reserve is related to the "strength of reflex," which is proportional to the reserve:

> All operations that involve elicitation affect the reserve directly, either to increase or to decrease it. Conditioning increases it; extinction and fatigue decrease it. . . . Facilitation and certain kinds of emotion increase the strength, while inhibition and certain kinds of emotion decrease it without modifying the reserve. The operations that control the drive also affect the proportionality factor. Without altering the total number of available responses, a change in drive may alter the rate of elicitation of an operant from a minimal to a maximal value. (pp. 26–27)

N. E. Miller (1969) conducted several experiments that proved that heart rate, intestinal contractions, and salivation are subject to instrumental conditioning. Moreover, blood pressure and the rate of urine formation in the kidney can also be modified by instrumental conditioning. In another study, Miller (1966) used the example of two children who fear a forthcoming examination in school and develop psychosomatic symptoms. Suppose the mother of the first child, who has developed a pallor, a faint feeling, and other cardiovascular symptoms, tells the child to stay home. The child would feel rewarded by staying home and would become apt to develop similar symptoms in the future. Suppose the mother of the second child ignores the cardiovascular psychosomatic symptoms but takes care of the child when the child develops gastrointestinal symptoms; the second child would learn to develop this kind of symptom on future occasions. In other words, psychosomatic disorders can be produced by instrumental conditioning as practiced by parents in regard to their children.

References

Belanger, D., & Feldman, S. M. Effects of water deprivation upon heart rate and instrumental activity in the rat. *Journal of Comparative and Physiological Psychology*, 1962, 55, 220–225.

Bykov, M. *The cerebral cortex and the internal organs.* New York: Chemical Publishing, 1957.

DiCara, L. V., & Miller, N. E. Instrumental learning of systolic blood pressure responses by curarized rats: Dissociation of cardiac and vascular changes. *Psychosomatic Medicine*, 1968, 30, 484–494.

Ducharme, R. *Inanition et activation: Leur influence sur l'activité intrumentale.* Montréal: Université de Montréal, 1962.

Lacey, J. I. Somatic response patterning and stress: Some revisions of activation theory. In M. H. Appley & R. Trumbull (Eds.), *Psychological stress.* New York: Appleton-Century-Crofts, 1967.

Lacey, J. I., Smith, R., & Green, A. Use of conditioned autonomic responses in the stury of anxiety. *Psychosomatic Medicine*, 1955, 17, 208–217.

Miller, N. E. Experiments relevant to learning theory and psychopathology. *Proceedings of the 18th International Congress of Psychology.* Moscow, 1966.

Miller, N. E. Psychosomatic effects of specific types of training. *Annals of the New York Academy of Sciences*, 1969, 159, 1025–1039.

Oken, D. Relation of physiological response to affect expression including studies of autonomic response specificity. *Archives of General Psychiatry*, 1962, *6*, 336–351.

Pavlov, I. P. *Conditioned reflexes*. London: Oxford University Press, 1927.

Pavlov, I. P. *Lectures on conditioned reflexes*. New York: Liveright, 1928.

Razran, G. The observable unconscious and the inferable conscious in current soviet psychophysiology. *Psychological Review*, 1961, *68*, 81–147.

Schmale, A., Morrow, G., & Ader, R. Cancer, leukemia, and related diseases: Psychosomatic aspects. In B. B. Wolman (Ed.), *International encyclopedia of psychiatry, psychology, neurology and psychoanalysis* (Vol. 3, pp. 11–16). New York: Aesculapius Publishers, 1977.

Shapiro, D. Differentiation of heart rate and systolic blood pressure in man by operant conditioning. *Psychosomatic Medicine*, 1970, *32*, 417–423.

Skinner, B. F. *The behavior of organisms: An experimental analysis*. New York: Appleton-Century-Crofts, 1938.

Skinner, B. F. *The behavior of organisms*. New York: Appleton-Century-Crofts, 1953.

Skinner, B. F. *Contingencies of reinforcement: A theoretical analysis*. New York: Appleton-Century-Crofts, 1969.

Weiss, T., & Engel, B. T. Operant conditioning on heart rate in patients with premature ventrical contractions. *Psychosomatic Medicine*, 1971, *33*, 301–321.

Wittkower, E. P., & Dudek, S. Z. Psychosomatic medicine: The mind-body-society interaction. In B. B. Wolman (Ed.), *Handbook of general psychology* (pp. 242–274). Englewood Cliffs, NJ: Prentice-Hall, 1973.

Wolman, B. B. *Contemporary theories and systems in psychology* (rev. ed.). New York: Plenum Press, 1981.

Wolpe, J. Behavior therapy for psychosomatic disorders. *Psychosomatics*, 1980, *21*, 379.

9
Sociocultural Determinants

THE BASIC DRIVES

From the beginning of life until its last moments, all living organisms do whatever they can in order to stay alive. *Lust for life* is the basic drive of all living organisms. All organisms fight to eat and not to be eaten, thus Ares, the Greek god of war, is the aboriginal symbol of survival. The basic biochemical energy of all living organisms is directed toward survival, but at a certain evolutionary level, part of this energy became invested in procreation or the preservation of the life of the species, as if the life of one individual continued through its offspring. From that time on, the lust-for-life drive split into Ares and Eros, the war and the love drives, respectively (Wolman, 1984).

An organism can be forceful, full of energy, most capable of providing food for itself, and well prepared for self-defense, or it may be sick, declining, and dwindling to nothing. When the vital energies become exhausted and vitality reaches the zero point, the organism dies. As long as the organism is alive, its energies can be used in two directions, either toward the promotion of life or toward its destruction. The instinctual force, lust for life, divided into two arms, serves the promotion of life as Eros or Ares. Eros, or love, can be directed toward oneself or toward others. Ares serves destruction, and it, too, can be directed toward oneself or toward others. Ares is an earlier and stronger drive than Eros. In the case of inner conflict, Ares prevails; no animal can copulate when its skin is burned or its bones are broken (Pavlov, 1928).

When one is hungry, thirsty, or sick, one is hardly in a mood for love. Hurt people are likely to be irritable, hostile, and agressive. The libido seems to be sort of a "higher" energy, the destrudo a "lower" one; when there is no threat to life, a balanced love for oneself and for others suffices for survival. In emergencies, people act as if they had a new supply of energy; the more basic energy, destrudo, is put to use (Gedo & Goldberg, 1973; Wolman, 1973).

Eros and Ares are the two channels for the general drive for life; they "release" mental energy. Ares, like Eros, has an impetus, a source, an object, and an aim. The impetus is the amount of destructive energy (destrudo) that Ares activates; its source is threat to one's own life; the aim of Ares is a complete or partial destruction of enemies; and the object of Ares' hostility can be anything, including oneself.

Hostile, aretic behavior originates in threat to life. No one hates unless he or she fears. Immortals do not have to fight for survival, and an omnipotent being does not fight with anyone. Only a god can forgive all enemies, because the god does not fear them; animals and human beings fear death and hate their enemies because enemies inflict injury and may kill. The ultimate fear is the mortal fear, the fear of perishing.

Unless exposed to a particular stimulus, human beings are in a state of relative balance. Whenever human beings are exposed to pressure that affects the inner balance, they tend to react. The reaction can be somatopsychic or psychosomatic. It is important to state at this point that, in most situations, the reactions are life-protecting and are aimed at restoration of the balance. In some situations, the reactions are self-defeating, and this volume describes the self-defeating psychosomatic defenses. But let us briefly describe the issue of inner balance.

EQUILIBRIUM AND CONSTANCY

An organism is in a state of equilibrium when its distribution of energies is such that all energies are kept constant. A perfect equilibrium cannot be accomplished in organic matter; it is possible only in an inorganic world, and even there, the existence of a perfect astronomic peace or a perfect motion is questionable. However, organic matter constantly changes its chemical composition by the process of growth and decline, composition and decomposition.

Several scientists have followed in Cannon's footsteps (1932) in believing that "Organisms composed of material which is characterized by the utmost inconstancy and unsteadiness have somehow learned the methods of maintaining constancy and keeping steady in the presence of conditions which might reasonably be expected to be profoundly disturbing" (p. 282).

Freud initially ascribed this tendency to restore the balance to the nervous system and, later on, to the entire universe. The *constancy principle* was one of the earliest concepts formulated by Breuer and Freud in 1895: "The nervous system endeavors to keep constant something in its functional condition that may be described as the 'sum of excitation.' It seeks to establish the necessary precondition of health by dealing with every sensible increase of appropriate motor reaction" (p. 30).

The principle of constancy served as the general framework of Freud's theory of motivation. It represents a tension–relief continuum and explains the compulsion to repeat first experience. According to the constancy principle, all living organisms are capable of responding or reacting to inner and outer stimuli. When an organism is stimulated, a state of disequilibrium is created, and every living organism tends to restore its former balance. It is a universal tendency to keep the quantity of excitation as low as possible, for an increase in excitation disrupts the inner balance of the organism:

> The attributes of life were evoked in inanimate matter by the action of a force of whose nature we can form no conception. . . . The tension which then arose in what had hitherto been an inanimate substance endeavored to equalize its potential. In this way the first instinct came into being: the instinct to return to the inanimate state. . . . For a long time perhaps, living substance was thus being constantly created afresh and easily dying, till decisive external influences altered in such a way as to oblige the still surviving substance to diverge ever more widely from its original course of life and to make ever more complicated detours before reaching its goal in death. (Freud, 1920/1962, p. 50)

Freud made two assumptions. He assumed, first, that there is a universal and *phylogenetic conservative tendency* and, second, that the entirety of organic nature has the *regressive tendency* to go back to its *inorganic origin.*

There is little reason to believe in the tendency toward *phylogenetic* conservatism, for such an assumption would contradict evolution. Were it true that organic nature tends to restore the former state of things, human beings would turn into anthropoids, mammals into fish, vertebrates into invertebrates, and so on; but the idea of conservatism in *ontogenetic evolution* points to regressive tendencies that are pathological, and it might explain hypochondriasis and several psychosomatic phenomena in terms of fixation on an earlier developmental stage and/or a regression to it. *Social pressures*, and interactional hardships are a distinct etiological factor in psychosomatic diseases, to be described later in this chapter.

THE PSYCHOPHYSIOLOGICAL LINK

As mentioned above, the tendency to restore balance can go wrong, and psychosomatic disorders tend to remove a minor imbalance by creating another one, usually more damaging than the initial disturbance. In higher biological species, the neuroendocrine system is the bridge that nature uses in going from organic to mental processes and vice versa. The neuroendocrine system, as it were, translates emotions into biochemical processes and translates chemistry into psychology.

Selye (1956) looked for the disease-producing hormones. He pointed to the extreme sensitivity of the neuroendocrine system to stress. There is no question that neurological, endocrinological, and other pathophysiological mechanisms mediate between psychological variables and diseases; but psychological factors can produce a variety of morbid physiological phenomena (Feuerstein, Labbe, & Kuczmierczyk, 1986; Kimball, 1978).

The third edition of the *Diagnostic and Statistical Manual of Mental Disorders* of the American Psychiatric Association (DSM-III; APA, 1980) deemphasized the role of one-cause–one-effect etiology in psychosomatic disorders. Following the current research, it points to the complexity of psychosomatic issues in interaction with physiological regulatory mechanisms and psychological and environmental factors (Garrick & Kimball, 1983; Pinsker, 1983).

According to the DSM-III, psychological factors are etiologically involved in somatic symptoms whenever:

1. There is a temporal relationship between an environmental stimulus that is apparently related to a psychological conflict.
2. The symptom enables the individual to avoid some activity that is noxious to him or her.
3. The symptom enables the individual to get support from the environment that otherwise might not be forthcoming.

Stressful Situations

Psychosomatic studies must take into consideration the impact of social environment (Lipowski, 1985; Syme, 1984). Stressful occupations, harassing situations, the loss of a job, the experience of living in an overcrowded environment, exposure to changes in family life or marital ties, prejudice, and persecution may cause grave emotional reactions that can seriously affect reticular activation and endocrine secretion. An increase in population density, migration, poverty, family discords, and a decline in the quality of social interactions can elicit immunological-physiological responses that can reduce one's resistance to diseases. Overstimulation may cause "excessive autonomic and cortical arousal leading to cognitive and/or motor performance . . . such repeated or sustained arousal may lead to physiological changes as well as behavior, enhancing the subject's general *susceptibility to illness* " (Lipowski, 1985, pp. 38–39).

Environmental changes can profoundly affect the hormonal balance of the body, and a host of socioeconomic and sociocultural factors play a significant role in the etiology of psychosomatic disorders (Rosenberg, 1969; Vance, 1982).

Socially stressful situations, such as fear of enemies, economic depression, prolonged unemployment, a hostile environment, prejudice, and persecution can cause a variety of psychosomatic symptoms. For example, a policeofficer or a prison guard who lives in a barren physical environment, exposed to a hostile attitude from prison inmates, may develop psychosomatic symptoms such as ulcers, muscle spasms, and tension headaches (U.S. Department of Justice, 1968).

During World War II, I was assigned to psychological services and had the opportunity to work with soldiers afflicted with psychosomatic disorders caused by their combat experiences. Every war causes overwhelming fear reactions. Blank (1982) described psychosomatic symptoms related to the Vietnam War, especially acute reactions leading to a variety of psychosomatic symptoms, among them trembling, vomiting, and diarrhea (Blank, 1982, p. 638).

Inadequate social relations greatly contribute to the development of a variety of physical and mental disorders. Berkman and Syme (1979) conducted a 9-year study of the population of Alameda County, California. Their sample included 6,928 adults. The study covered social relationships, marital status, close ties with relatives and friends, and membership in religious, political and other organizations. The Berkman and Syme study indicated that the people with more social ties had a lower mortality rate. Almost identical results were reported by House, Robbins, and Metzner (1982) in a study of 2,754 adults in Michigan.

The incidence of coronary heart disease (CHD) is higher in urban and industrialized areas than in other areas, and it is higher among individuals in stressful occupations than among those in less stressful occupations. In general, married individuals, in practically all countries, have a lower rate of psychosomatic diseases than widowed, divorced, or single individuals. Apparently, sociocultural influences are a relevant etiological factor (Cacioppo & Petty, 1983).

MIGRATION

Changing one's place of living and the resulting breaking off of personal relationships with neighbors, along with its ensuing need to develop new contacts, can be traumatic. In many instances, migration has contributed to psychosomatic symptoms. The loss of old relationships, the moving away from a familiar environment, and the need to adjust to a new environment and new ways of life are highly significant factors in the etiology of several psychosomatic disorders (Dorfman & Cristofar, 1985; Gentry, 1984). In a comparison of the frequencies of coronary heart disease and subsequent mortality, the lowest incidence was found among Japanese in Japan, a higher incidence among Japanese in Hawaii, and the highest among Japanese in California. Moreover, the Japanese who retained their own customs and cultural tradition had a lower incidence of coronary heart disease than those who tried to adjust speedily to their new country (Syme, 1984).

Experimental studies on environmental changes that used animals offer significant support to the role of environment in psychosomatic disorders. Henry, Meehan, and Stephens (1962) simulated real-life stressor conditions in experimental animals by playing on their inborn drives for territory, survival, and reproduction. Four techniques were used: (1) mixing adult males that had never met previously; (2) submitting male and female mice to threats from a predator; (3) reducing the floor space available until animals were closely aggregated; and (4) exposing males and females to an interconnecting box system, leading to chronic territorial conflict. The experiments were continued for 6–12 months. The experimenters summarized their findings as follows:

> (1) All methods resulted in a sustained elevation of systolic arterial pressure of the order of 160 mg Hg in the males. There was elevation to 140–150 mg Hg in the females, and the aggregation of male castrates showed only minimal blood pressure effects.
>
> (2) Histologic examination of the kidneys in controls and in the less affected experimental groups showed no abnormality which would account for the blood pressure changes, but interstitial nephritis was found in the severely hypertensive group.
>
> (3) On returning mice to a less stimulating situation, the pressures usually subsided toward the baseline control value of 126 ± 12 mm Hg.
>
> (4) Early experience proved to be important. If the aggregated animals or those in the interconnected boxes were kept together from birth, the pressure elevations were less severe, while isolation from weaning to maturity exacerbated the blood pressure effects of the conflict for territory.
>
> (5) The sustained blood pressure elevations persisted despite ether anesthesia but fell to normal with reserpine administration.
>
> (6) The results support current hypotheses that in a constant external environment the systemic arteriolar pressure of a group is a measure of the symbolic stimuli received during social interaction and that early experience plays a role in determining the arousal value of the stimuli received. (Meredith, 1973, p. 254)

REFERENCES

American Psychiatric Association. *Diagnostic and Statistical Manual of Mental Disorders* (3rd ed.). Washington, DC: American Psychiatric Association, 1980.

Berkman, L. F., & Syme, S. L. Social networks, host resistance and mortality. *American Journal of Epidemiology*, 1979, *109*, 186–204.

Blank, A. S., Jr. Stresses of wars: The example of Vietnam. In L. G. Goldberger & S. Breznitz (Eds.), *Handbook of stress* (pp. 631–643). New York: Macmillan–Free Press, 1982.

Breuer, J., & Freud, F. (1895). Studies on hysteria. *Standard Edition* (Vol. 2). London: Hogarth Press, 1962.

Cacioppo, J. T., & Petty, R. E. *Social psychophysiology*. New York: Guilford Press, 1983.

Cannon, W. B. *Bodily changes in pain, hunger, fear, and rage*. New York: Appleton-Century-Crofts, 1932.

Dorfman, W., & Cristofar, L. (Eds.). *Psychosomatic illness review*. New York: Macmillan, 1985.

Feuerstein, M., Labbe, E. E., & Kuczmierczyk, A. R. *Health psychology: A psychobiological perspective*. New York: Plenum Press, 1986.

Freud, S. Beyond the pleasure principle. *Standard Edition* (Vol. 18, pp. 7–65). London: Hogarth, 1962. (Originally published, 1920.)

Garrick, T. R., & Kimball, C. P. Recent developments in psychosomatic disorders. In B. B. Wolman (Ed.), *The therapist's handbook* (2nd ed.), pp. 514–528). New York: Van Nostrand Reinhold, 1983.

Gedo, E., & Goldberg, A. *Models of mind*. Chicago: University of Chicago Press, 1973.

Gentry, W. D. (Ed.). *Handbook of behavioral medicine*. New York: Guilford Press, 1984.

Henry, J. P., Meehan, J. P., & Stephens, P. M. Use of psychological stimuli to induce prolonged systolic hypertension in mice. *Psychosomatic Medicine*, 1967, *29*, 408–432.

House, J. S., Robbins, C., & Metzner, H. L. The association of social relationships and activities with mortality. *American Journal of Epidemiology*, 1982, *116*, 123–140.

Kimball, C. P. Diagnosing psychosomatic situations. In B. B. Wolman (Ed.), *Clinical diagnosis of mental disorders: A handbook* (pp. 677–708). New York: Plenum Press, 1978.

Lipowski, Z. J. *Psychosomatic medicine and liason psychiatry*. New York: Plenum Press, 1985.

Meredith, H. V. Somatological development. In B. B. Wolman (Ed.), *Handbook of general psychology* (pp. 230–272). Englewood Cliffs, NJ: Prentice-Hall, 1973.

Pavlov, I. P. *Lectures on conditioned reflexes*. New York: Liveright, 1928.

Pinsker, H. Diagnostic and Statistical Manual of the American Psychiatric Association. In B. B. Wolman (Ed.), *International encyclopedia of psychiatry, psychology, psychoanalysis and neurology* (Progress Vol. 1, pp. 97–100). New York: Aesculapius Publishers, 1983.

Rosenberg, C. M. Determinants of psychiatric illness in young people. *British Journal of Psychiatry*, 1969, *115*, 907–915.

Selye, H. *Physiology and pathology of exposure to stress*. Montreal: Acte Press, 1956.

Syme, S. L. Sociocultural factors and disease etiology. In W. D. Gentry (Ed.), *Handbook of behavioral medicine*. New York: Guilford Press, 1984.

U.S. Department of Justice. *A handbook of correctional psychiatry*. Washington, DC: U.S. Government Printing Office, 1968.

Vance, E. T. Social disability and stress. In L. Goldgerger & S. Breznitz (Eds.), *Handbook of stress* (pp. 506–514). New York: Macmillan–Free Press, 1982.

Wolman, B. B. *Call no man normal*. New York: International Universities Press, 1973.

Wolman, B. B. *The logic of science in psychoanalysis*. New York: Columbia University Press, 1984.

10

Parents and Children

Several studies stress the role of parent–child interaction in the etiology of psychosomatic diseases. Interparental discord, parental rejection, separation, divorce, and abandonment of the child or the adolescent are frequent causes of psychosomatic disorders (Baker, Minuchin, & Roman, 1978; Bowlby, 1980; Joffe & Vaughn, 1982).

Human beings derive their feeling of security from two sources: (1) their own power and (2) support by their powerful allies. A child's own power is very limited, and the child's feeling of security depends on the child's belief that the parents are very strong and are determined to use their power for the child's protection. The fear of abandonment is the worst of all other fears, and many children develop psychosomatic symptoms hoping to gain parental support.

Parental approval and affection give the child the feeling of security. It is not enough for a child to be fed now: The child's security depends on his or her confidence that the food and the protection will continue. The newborn is endowed with the ability to perceive nonverbal signals and to feel whether or not it is loved by the feeding mother or the maternal substitute. This ability, called *empathy*, imbues the infant with feelings of security and euphoria, or of fear and anxiety. Infants need to be loved, and they are blissfully happy when the feeding mother hugs and kisses them and speaks affectionately to them. When the feeding mother resents the child and thinks how great her life could be without the baby, the child empathizes her feelings and becomes anxiety-ridden. It clings to its mother because it does not trust her and fears she will abandon it.

A mother's working outside the home does not necessarily harm the child's mental health. A mother may go to work every day and leave the child with a trusted person, provided the child is sure that the mother will come back at a certain time. Infants do not need clocks; they follow their own biological time clock. Parental dependability reduces the displeasure of temporary separation, and as long as the child can trust its mother's love, it can accept her absence and relate well to the grandmother, the nurse, or the baby-sitter who substitutes for her.

It cannot be stressed often enough that, though parents may occasionally disapprove of their child's behavior, they should *never disapprove of the child himself or herself* or threaten him or her with abandonment. They may say, even harshly, "I don't like your messing up the living room," or (to an older child), "You are not allowed to eat with your fingers; here are the fork and knife," but they must convey with words and deeds that they are both strong and friendly. The child who receives this message will love and trust his or her parents and will grow into a secure and self-assured adult.

A child threatened with abandonment—"I will give you up for adoption," "I will go away and leave you alone," or, worst of all, "I will kill myself"—is likely to develop severe anxiety (Wolman, 1978, p. 111).

Some parents are quite critical of their children and make them feel guilty for committed or even uncommitted sins. Many a guilt-ridden child wishes to punish himself or herself, and in a way, the wish comes true in psychosomatic disorders. It is quite natural for school-aged children to become aware of their family's problems and to worry their parents. As long as parents do not impose their anxieties and worries on the children, the children's fears will remain within normal limits. Unfortunately, some parents overcommunicate with their children or tell each other things that they should not say in the presence of a child. The father's loss of a job may not necessarily be a catastrophe, but if it is communicated in a manner that implies immediate starvation, it will seem to be one. Parents who occasionally disagree and exchange harsh words in front of a child may leave the child terrified and expecting violence and divorce.

Some parents, wittingly or unwittingly, make their children feel guilty for *their* true or imaginary misfortunes. A sensitive 8- or 9-year-old may come to believe it is his fault that his father did not get an expected raise or suffered business losses. Guilt feelings may give rise to a disturbing state of anxiety that interferes with the normal process of child development (Wolman, 1978, p. 71). Moreover:

> The loss through death, separation, or divorce of one or more parents or their surrogates will characterize the past of more than a third of our patients. . . . Other separations worthy of note are those around absences of parents, of mothers for repeated childbirth, of fathers for war and/or business service. Regressive behaviors are frequently observed at such times, and it may be pertinent to learn through which organ systems they are manifested, e.g., thumb-sucking, hair pulling, enuresis, encopresis, tics, stuttering, school phobias, tantrums, asthma, eczema, coughs, and other illnesses. (Kimball, 1978, pp. 696–697)

During World War II, when London was undergoing air raids and bombardment by the Nazis (in the Blitz), many parents sent their children away to remote and peaceful areas. However, the separation from their family was more stressful and produced more psychosomatic symptoms in these children than in those who remained with their parents under the Blitz (A. Freud & Burlingham, 1944).

Changing the place of living and the resultant breaking up of personal friendships are quite traumatic for children and adolescents. Whereas adults may occasionally like a change, provided it leads to a better job, more income, or a better neighborhood, most children prefer to stay in the same environment and in the same place. Many years ago, when I was director of a mental health clinic for children and adolescents, I had to treat some of them for psychosomatic symptoms related to a change to a not-too-distant location.

Many children, afraid of an unknown future, develop psychosomatic disorders as if trying to prevent the dislocation. Some of them fear that the parents will not be with them, and the fear of abandonment makes their condition more severe.

Separation from parents may be a cause of regressive behaviors, such as enuresis, encopresis, thumbsucking, hair pulling, stuttering, and other psychologically determined dysfunctions (Weininger, 1972). It may also cause psychosomatic disorders, such as asthma and dermatological diseases. There are various types of separation, such as divorce, a mother's absence caused by business or military service, or a loss caused by the death of one or both parents. The earlier the separation, the more severe the disorder. For instance, the loss of parents before the age of 8 causes more damage to a child's health than a loss that occurs when the child is between the ages of 8 and 15 (Brown, 1966; Cherlin, 1979).

According to Lipsitt (1985), parental lack of concern may cause somatic preoccupation in children. When the mother does not respond to the child's bodily needs, the child's frustration may lead to a variety of psychosomatic disorders. Clinical experience and observation support the belief that psychosomatic pathology is often a result of some developmental failure that may include a combination of intrauterine factors, constitutional predisposition, mother–infant relationship, language and communication development, and other factors.

Spitz (1945) described severe mental and physical symptoms in institutionalized children. The children were taken care of by competent nurses, but they received no attention, affection, or love. The lack of emotional support was responsible for the children's physical deterioration and, in some instances, even led to death. Horney (1950) described an experiment with neonates on a nursing ward. Infants who were picked up, cuddled, and affectionately treated by the nurses thrived and gained weight, whereas infants who received the same care but no affection did not.

Goode (1956) gathered data from 400 divorced women and arrived at the conclusion that divorce affects children's adjustment. There is still a question about whether it is the divorce or the marital conflict that causes the damage to the child's mental health. Moreover, one may ask whether the different types of parent–child relationships could create more damage than the divorce or the marital conflict (Levinger & Moles, 1979).

Nye (1957) studied the level of adjustment of high-school youths from unhappy but intact homes and compared it to the level of adjustment of youths from happy but broken homes. He analyzed their school relationships, their religious life, their delinquent tendencies, and their psychosomatic disorders. Adolescents from broken homes showed significantly better adjustment than those from unbroken but unhappy homes in relation to psychosomatic illnesses and delinquency behavior. Children living in mother-only households scored higher than those who lived with both parents in an atmosphere of conflict and rejection (Nye, 1957, pp. 236–357).

THE IMPACT OF DIVORCE

Children of divorced parents often develop psychosomatic disorders, especially asthma (French & Alexander, 1941; Fritz, 1985; Kelly, 1982; Wallerstein & Kelly, 1980). Purcell (1969) studied chronically asthmatic children on a daily basis during periods in which they lived with their own families and during a period in which they had no contact with their family but were cared for in their own home by a substitute mother. A total of 25 children were evaluated. On the basis of the selection instrument (a detailed, structured interview for assessing parental and child perceptions of the precipitants of asthma attacks), it was predicted that 13 of these children would respond positively to this experimental separation, whereas 12 would show no improvement in asthma. For the 13 predicted positives, all measures of asthma, including expiratory peak flow rates, amount of medication required, daily history of asthma, and daily clinical examination, indicated significant improvement during the period of family separation for the group as a whole. For the group of 12 predicted nonresponders, only the daily history suggested improvement during separation. None of the other measures showed any difference between the separation and the nonseparation periods (Purcell, Weiss, & Hahn, 1972, p. 718).

The ability of a child to deal with separation and divorce is greatly influenced by the age of the child. Children between the ages of approximately 2 and 8 do not understand as well as older children, and they have a harder time expressing their feelings. They are particularly vulnerable at the impact stage of divorce. Wallerstein and Kelly (1980) found that short-term responses could be broken down into four distinct patterns based on age level and developmental level. The *preschoolers* (ages 3–5) were frightened and confused by the departure of one parent. Bed-wetting and crying, examples of temporary regression, were common. These children could not comprehend the separation and were very fearful that the remaining parent would also leave them. The *younger school-agers* (ages 6–8) could understand the situation only slightly better than the preschoolers. They showed considerable fear and sadness and had fantasies of rejection and deprivation. Many mourned for the departed parent and felt anger at the custodial parent. They felt pressured to reject one parent or the other and expressed conflict about which one to support and which one to reject.

The *older school-agers* (ages 9–12) were more realistically aware of the separation and divorce. They often tried to reconcile their parents, but they were also likely to become more involved in hobbies and sports. These children were able to articulate their anger at the parents. They often felt that the divorce had disturbed the moral order, and petty theft was not uncommon.

The *adolescents* (ages 13–18) had established well-developed relationships with their parents before the divorce, but these relationships were subsequently threatened. The separation or divorce often accelerated the progress of these children toward maturity, but this progress often had undesirable side effects. Because the divorce occurred at a time when they were questioning their self-identity, the experience prompted questions about prospects for a happy life and marriage. Anger and a pervasive sense of loss were common (Chiriboga, 1983, pp. 104–105).

THE MOTHER–CHILD RELATIONSHIP

One of the classic psychosomatic disorders that commonly begins in childhood is ulcerative colitis, a disease of the large intestine. This disease tends to be associated with feelings of rage, grief, or fear. Quite often, children with ulcerative colitis belong to a constricted personality type resulting from psychopathological family dynamics such, as a dominating mother or an ineffectual father. There is a high correlation between specific emotional stress and specific disorders, although most literature surrounding ulcerative colitis has been unable to pinpoint a reason for the psychological choice of the gastrointestinal tract to express rage, anger, grief, or fear.

Vandersall (1982) maintained that his clinical experience had not offered clear-cut proof that psychological problems are either necessary or sufficient to produce ulcerative colitis in childhood. He felt that the therapist must take care to approach every patient with ulcerative colitis as an individual, without letting preconceived causal theories cloud a fact-finding approach.

Possibly, ulcerative colitis and other psychosomatic disorders in childhood are a product of several causes, but the mother–child relationship plays a significant role in wholesome or disturbed child development. The way in which the mother relates to the child and the way in which the child reacts to it, consciously or unconsciously, greatly influence how the child perceives herself or himself (Field & Widmayer, 1982). Many psychosomatic symptoms are a child's reaction to the mother's attitude. The fact that not all children react the same way to maternal rejection does not allow us to dismiss its role. For instance, Engel (1954) stressed that ulcerative colitis is a disease of the lining surface of the bowel, a surface continuous with the outside of the body, a kind of inner skin and part of the individual's contact with the environment. Engel described a distinctive mother–child relationship in children with ulcerative colitis that, when disturbed or ruptured, leads to the tissue reaction of the disease. The disturbance in the relationship may be real or fantasy; onset or relapse of the disorder results when the affect associated with the loss of the relationship is one of hopelessness and despair.

Prugh (1951) found children with ulcerative colitis to be passive, rigid, quite dependent on parent figures (particularly the mother), inhibited, often narcissistic, and emotionally immature. Although there was a suggestion of a correlation between emotional stress and exacerbations of the disease, it was not possible to establish such relationships in all cases. The parents in Prugh's study were characterized as rigid, at times overindulgent, and often inconsistent. In play therapy, the children were stereotyped, unimaginative, and reluctant to express any aggression toward adult figures.

THE CHOICE OF SYMPTOMS

According to Alexander and Flagg (1965), the choice of psychosomatic symptoms depends on the psychodynamic constellation and on early predispositions. Migraine and hypertension, for example, involve pent-up destructive, hostile impulses, and the coincidence of migraine and hypertension is fairly common. In the above disorders, the specificity of the precipitating psychodynamic factors (i.e., the nature of the hostile impulses) must be considered. A full aggressive attack has three phases: the preparation of the attack in fantasy (the conceptual phase); the circulatory and metabolic changes that prepare the body for concentrated activity (the vegetative phase); and the consummation of the aggressive act through muscular activity (the neuromuscular phase) (Alexander & Flagg, 1965, p. 896).

Alexander and Flagg's hypothesis need not be taken in a dogmatic manner. As mentioned above, psychosomatic disorders in childhood are definitely related to parent–child interaction. This interaction is a highly relevant, but not the sole, determinant of the ensuing psychosomatic disorder.

Socioeconomic Factors

There is no evidence that low socioeconomic status as such can cause psychosomatic symptoms, although it has been correlated with emotional disorders; some researchers view low socioeconomic status as a cause and others as an effect of emotional disorders. However, when family conflict is added to socioeconomic hardship, the possibility of psychosomatic symptoms is increased. Interparental conflict and an inadequate parent–child relationship are factors that contribute to psychosomatic symptoms in the child who, consciously or unconsciously, uses sickness as a defense mechanism.

Moreover, rhythmicity and orderliness in an infant's immediate environment, as well as levels of stimulation, affect the development of the brain (Levine, 1961; Rosenzweig, 1966). The family, the child's close environment, has a definite impact on cortical excitability in the child's growth and development (Vance, 1982). Apparently, early stimulation may exercise considerable influence on the child's predisposition to develop psychosomatic symptoms in childhood and in later years.

Adolescent is a period of increased sensitivity and, in some cases, emotional vulnerability. The parental attitude and the peer group may cause severe emotional problems that lead to a variety of psychosomatic symptoms. Many adolescent girls develop anorexia nervosa, and many adolescent boys develop acne and increased physiological reaction and neuroendocrine arousal (Hamburg, Hamburg, & Barchas, 1975; Petersen, 1984).

One may refer here to two comments, the first is by Mahler, Pine, and Bergman (1975):

> It is necessary to realize that every individual born into a society is from birth—and in all probability from before birth—subjected to a progressive moulding by the culture, mediated through all those with whom he comes into contact, so that the temper tantrums, the tightened muscles, the change in the manufacture of blood sugar, and the verbal insults hurled at the offending parent, all become patterned and integrated. Then we see that every individual, and not merely every patient, may be viewed from the psychosomatic point of view, within which individuals who show definite organ neuroses are merely extreme and special developments of one potentiality of the total personality. And we further see that there is no basic "human" personality but that every individual must be seen against the cultural base line, that he is a special idiosyncratic variant of one of many culturally unique ways in which human personality is developed. (p. 68)

According to the second comment, by Wittkower (1977), disease can be viewed from various angles—from the genetic, biological, psychological, social, and cultural viewpoints. To gain a wider perspective on the patient, one must view him or her as a person acting within and interacting with his or her total sociocultural environment. Transcultural psychosomatics interprets the observed phenomena in cultural terms. The questions that are asked are aimed at an evaluation of the differences in value orientation, family structure, the role and status of women, urbanization, political change, social institutions, and so on as these relate to and influence the frequency and incidence of psychosomatic disorders. Wittkower indicated that there are two approaches to cultural and transcultural psychosomatics: the clinical (psychiatric) and the social science approaches.

The methodologies of transcultural psychosomatic research apply the same investigative technique to persons and situations in constrasting cultures either by the same observers or by different observers. Wittkower's approach (1977) resembles that of Alexander. However, he placed much greater emphasis on the contribution that culture makes to the choice and the symbolic elaboration of the symptom. Wittkower's basic assumption is that certain sociocultural systems make people susceptible to certain psychosomatic disorders.

References

Alexander, F. *Psychosomatic medicine*. New York: Norton, 1950.

Alexander, F., & Flagg, G. W. The psychosomatic approach. In B. B. Wolman (Ed.), *Handbook of clinical psychology*. New York: McGraw-Hill, 1965.

Baker, L., Minuchin, S., & Roman, B. L. *Psychosomatic families*. Cambridge: Harvard University Press, 1978.

Bowlby, J. *Attachment and loss*. New York: Basic Books, 1980.

Brown, F. Childhood bereavement and subsequent psychiatric disorder. *British Journal of Psychiatry*, 1966, 112, 1035–1041.

Cherlin, A. Work life and marital dissolution. In G. Levinger & D. Moles (Eds.), *Divorce and separation: Context, causes and consequences*. New York: Basic Books, 1979.

Chiriboga, D. A. Divorce: Psychological aspects. In B. B. Wolman (Ed.), *International encyclopedia of psychiatry, psychology, psychoanalysis and neurology* (Progress Vol. 1, pp. 101–106). New York: Aesculapius Publishers, 1983.

Engel, G. L. Studies of ulcerative colitis: 2. The nature of the somatic processes and the adequacy of psychosomatic hypotheses. *American Journal of Medicine*, 1954, 16, 415–433.

Field, T. M., & Widmayer, S. M. Motherhood. In B. B. Wolman (Ed.), *Handbook of developmental psychology*. Englewood Cliffs, NJ: Prentice-Hall, 1982.

French, T. M., & Alexander, F. Psychological factors in bronchial asthma. *Psychosomatic Medicine Monographs*, 1941, 4(1).

Freud, A., & Burlingham, D. *Infants without families*. New York: International Universities Press, 1944.

Fritz, G. K. Childhood asthma. In W. Dorfman & L. Cristofar (Eds.), *Psychosomatic illness review* (pp. 135–145). New York: Macmillan, 1985.

Goode, W. J. *After divorce*. New York: Free Press, 1956.

Hamburg, D., Hamburg, B. A., & Barchas, J. D. Anger and depression in perspective of behavioral biology. In L. Levi (Ed.), *Emotions: Their parameters and measurement*. New York: Raven, 1975.

Horney, K. *Neurosis and human growth*. New York: Norton, 1950.

Joffe, L. S., & Vaughn, B. E. Infant-mother attachment. In B. B. Wolman (Ed.), *Handbook of developmental psychology*. Englewood Cliffs, NJ: Prentice-Hall, 1982.

Kelly, J. B. Divorce: An adult perspective. In B. B. Wolman (Ed.), *Handbook of developmental psychology*. Englewood Cliffs, NJ: Prentice-Hall, 1982.

Kimball, C. P. Diagnosing psychosomatic situations. In B. B. Wolman (Ed.), *Clinical diagnosis of mental disorders* (pp. 677–708). New York: Plenum Press, 1978.

Levine, S. Psychophysiological effects of early stimulation. In E. L. Bliss (Ed.), *Roots of behavior*. New York: Hoeber, 1961.

Levinger, G., & Moles D. (Eds.). *Divorce and separation: Context, causes and consequences*. New York: Basic Books, 1979.

Lipsitt, D. R. The somatization process and its relation to psychosomatic pathology. In P. Pichot, P. Berner, R. Wolf, & K. Thou (Eds.), *Psychiatry: The state of the art: 4. Psychotherapy and psychosomatic medicine* (pp. 375–380). New York: Plenum Press, 1985.

Mahler, M. S., Pine, F., & Bergman, A. *Psychological birth of the human infant*. New York: Basic Books, 1975.

Nye, F. I. Child adjustment in broken and unhappy homes. *Marriage and Family Living*, 1957, *19*, 356–361.

Petersen, A. C. Adolescent health: Developmental issues. In T. J. Coates, A. C. Petersen, & C. Perry (Eds.), *Adolescent health: Crossing the barriers*. New York: Academic Press, 1984.

Prugh, D. G. The influence of emotional factors on the clinical course of ulcerative colitis in children. *Gastroentirology*, 1951, *18*, 339–354.

Purcell, K. The effect on asthma in children of experimental separation from the family. *Psychosomatic Medicine*, 1969, *31*, 144–164.

Purcell, K., Weiss, J., & Hahn, W. Certain psychosomatic disorders. In B. B. Wolman (Ed.), *Manual of child psychopathology* (pp. 706–741). New York: McGraw-Hill, 1972.

Rosenzweig, M. R. Environmental complexity, cerebral change and behavior. *American Psychologist*, 1966, *21*, 321–332.

Spitz, R. Hospitalism: An inquiry into the genesis of psychiatric conditions in early childhood. *The Psychoanalytic Study of the Child* (Vol. 1). New York: International Universities Press, 1945.

Vance, E. T. Social disability and stress. In L. G. Goldberger & S. Breznitz (Eds.), *Handbook of stress* (pp. 506–514). New York: Macmillan–Free Press, 1982.

Vandersall, T. Psychophysiological disorders in childhood. In J. B. Lachenmeyer & M. S. Gibbs (Eds.), *Psychopathology in childhood* (pp. 109–119). New York: Gardner Press, 1982.

Wallerstein, J. S., & Kelly, J. B. *Surviving a breakup: How children and parents cope with divorce*. New York: Basic Books, 1980.

Weininger, O. Effects of parental deprivation: An overview of literature and report on some current research. *Psychological Reports*, 1972, *30*, 591–612.

Wittkower, E. D. Transcultural psychiatry. In B. B. Wolman (Ed.), *International encyclopedia of psychiatry, psychology, psychoanalysis and neurology* (Progress Vol. 1, pp. 244–247). New York: Aesculapius Publishers, 1977.

Wolman, B. B. *Children's fears*. New York: Grosset & Dunlap, 1978.

11

Personality Types

Several researchers have assumed that personality traits play a significant role in the *etiology* of physical diseases via neurological or neuroendocrine responses. As early as 1942, Cannon, in an article on voodoo death, excluded the possibility of any organic causes and related the cause of death to sympathetic adrenal reaction to fear. Thirty-two years later, Angoff and Barth (1974) quoted several death cases related to psychological factors with no organic causes.

In 1943, Dunbar established statistical correlations between personality types and psychosomatic diseases. She related eight physical diseases (angina pectoris, cardiac arrhythmia, coronary occlusion, diabetes, fractures, hypertension, rheumatoid arthritis, and rheumatic fever) to eight distinct personality types.

There have been several approaches to the problem of psychological predispositions to psychosomatic disorders.

According to Horney (1950), psychosomatic illnesses relieve tensions caused by inner conflicting drives of self-hatred and self-destruction. Neurotic individuals, driven by a false feeling of pride, strive for unattainable perfection. The inevitable failure leads to self-hatred. Self-hatred and neurotic pride are two steps in the same process of striving for perfection and self-punishment for failure. Psychosomatic symptoms are an unconscious, self-inflicted punishment for not being able to attain the unattainable.

A and B Types

The cardiologists Friedman and Rosenman (1959) observed that rapid-speaking, competitive, impatient, hard-driving, aggressive, angry, and hostile men and women are much more "coronary-prone" than people who do not have these psychological traits. The behavioral patterns of the people who had these traits were called *Type A*. Those who did not have these psychological traits were called *Type B*. Several researchers have confirmed that rapid speech, impatience, anger, and hostility are often related to coronary heart disease (Krantz, Grunberg, & Baum, 1985). Researchers have studied how the autonomic nervous system reacts to stressful situations as well as the patterns of speech and anger. The incidence of coronary atherosclerosis was found to be quite high in aggressive, competitive, and hostile individuals. It was also found that Type A people are twice as likely as Type B people to develop angina pectoris and myocardial infarction. In women, the relationship between the A and B types was 3.32 for angina and 2.14 for infarction (Rosenman & Chesney, 1982).

A study of 3,524 men in the Western Collaborative Group Study (WCGS) reported by Dembroski (1977) found that ambitious, assertive men with Type A behavior experience twice as many cases of coronary heart disease than men of Type B. At ages 39–49, Type A men had 10.5 cases of coronary heart disease per population of 1,000 compared to men of Type B, who had 5 cases per 1,000 population. At the age of 50–59, men of Type A had 18.7 cases of coronary heart disease per 1,000 population, compared to 8.9 cases of the disease among Type B men. According to Krantz and Glass (1984), Type A behavior meets the most stringent etiological criteria established by epidemiologists, namely, that the Type A personality precedes the onset of coronary heart disease, that it definitely contributes to the etiology of the disease, that it is at least involved in precipitating the clinical complications. Moreover, the Type A person is less inclined to develop meaningful social contacts that Type B, and it is believed that inadequate social relations are a factor contributing to the etiology of psychosomatic disorders, especially of the cardiovascular system.

Studies of executives and other people in leadership positions (McClelland, 1979) found, in two different samples, that individuals with the leadership motive pattern had higher blood pressure, indicating a strain on the cardiovascular system. A study that sampled the power imagery of men at the age of 30 and that measured their diastolic blood pressure at the ages of 51 to 53 showed that inhibited power is conducive to hypersensitivity. Men high in the need for power who reported an above-median number of power stresses also reported more severe illnesses.

Further research stressed the role of the sympathetic nervous system. Type A individuals showed elevations in their arousal level in stressful situations. Under stress, they showed a considerable elevation of plasma levels of catecholamines, epinephrine, and norepinephrine, which may contribute to the pathogenesis of coronary heart disease. Patients who display symptoms of ischemic heart disease (myocardial infarction and angina pectoris) have definitely elevated neuroendocrine and hemodynamic responses to stressful situations, as Type A people do (Krantz & Glass, 1984).

Genetic Predisposition

Undoubtedly, there are considerable individual differences in physiological responses to stress. These differences may be related to genetic predisposition and to the individual's ability to cope with or master the adverse conditions that cause or represent a challenge (Krantz *et al.*, 1985, p. 355). The etiological data are far from being conclusive, and the question of why one organism under stress responds with psychosomatic mechanisms, whereas another one with similar organ involvement under similar stress is able to choose between fight or flight and a third develops neurotic or psychotic adjustment patterns, is not at all clear. There is a body of research that indicates the importance of genetic and immunological factors, on the one hand, and of early experience or conditioning, on the other hand, in the predisposition to diseases. This reaction to stress can take the form of somatic breakdown, thus affecting the maladaptive pattern of physiological as well as psychological adaptation. Psychotic breakdown or medical intervention may cause serious changes in the patterns of both physiological and psychological adaptation processes (Farber, 1982).

Graham and Kunish (1965) related psychosomatic disorders to an individual's attitudes. For instance, people who are apprehensive of dangers and tend to be on guard are assumed to be prone to develop hypertension.

Some etiological studies have related the origin of psychosomatic diseases to a "vulnerable organ concept" that suggests a *genetic* predisposing factor in the development of certain psychosomatic diseases. When a particular organ is exposed to certain environmental stimuli, psychosomatic disorders develop out of a combination of genetic, intrauterine, and extra-uterine influences (Gellhorn, 1967).

Some researchers maintain that certain definite psychological traits, such as feelings of helplessness and hopelessness, predispose people not to a particular psychosomatic disease but to a variety of diseases (Schmale, 1972). In most instances, however, an individual *is* predisposed to a certain disease, and her or his "giving-up" attitude contributes to that disease.

The theory of a specific personality or a specific environment as the sole cause of a psychosomatic disorder has often been criticized. As Kimball (1978) put it, "A passive-dependent personality does not cause peptic ulcer disease although it may be related to it. Nor does a specific social situation cause a specific psychological reaction, although in a specific culture there may be a high correlation between the two" (p. 681).

One also needs to draw a distinction between various types of stress and how people perceive them. Cold and heat can be stressful, but unless one perceives them this way, they are not stressful (Rahe, 1974). In other words, a lot depends on how people experience particular events and situations.

Vulnerability to stress that affects one's health could be related to several factors, mainly to physiological predisposition and specific psychological attitudes. Physiological and immunological vulnerability is most often genetically determined, but it may also be produced by serious physical or mental traumatic events. Specific psychological attitudes, perceptions, and sensitivities are most often acquired, but one need not dismiss the role of a particular personality predisposition that affects the development of certain attitudes and perceptions (Leigh & Reiser, 1980).

Adverse life experience can adversely affect one's resilience and can increase his or her vulnerability. Stressful experiences may cause *endocrine changes* and may thus enhance one's susceptibility to illness. Severe and/or chronic stressors, such as war, prolonged unemployment, imprisonment, repeated threats, and fear for one's life may cause lasting physical and/or mental harm (Gleser, Singer, & Winget, 1981).

Apparently, human vulnerability to stress cannot be reduced to a single cause. Nor can susceptibility to psychosomatic disorders be viewed as a product of one clearly determined condition. However, one's predispositions are highly relevant factors in the etiology of psychosomatic disorders. In other words:

> Patients with certain psychological predispositions may unconsciously seek out life situations which complement their predispositions. For example, hypertensives who are characterized by the tendency to carry on their work dutifully . . . such a "beast of burden" type of patient may subtly invite heavier and heavier loads just because he so patiently submits to indignities. (Alexander, French, & Pollock, 1968, p. 111)

The same reasoning can be applied to almost all psychosomatic symptoms.

REFERENCES

Alexander, F., French, T. M., & Pollock, G. H. *Psychosomatic specificity: Experimental study and results.* Chicago: University of Chicago Press, 1968.

Angoff, A., & Barth, D. (Eds.), *Parapsychology and anthropology.* New York: Parapsychology Foundation, 1974.

Cannon, W. B. Voodoo death. *American Anthropologist.* 1942, 44, 169–181.

Dembroski, T. M. (Ed.). *Proceedings of the Forum on Coronary Prone Behavior.* Washington, DC: U.S. Government Printing Office, 1977.

Dunbar, F. *Psychosomatic diagnosis.* New York: Hoeber, 1943.

Farber, S. L. Genetic diversity and differing reactions to stress. In L. Goldberger' S. Breznitz (Eds.), *Handbook of stress* (pp. 123–133). New York: Macmillan–Free Press, 1982.

Friedman, M., & Rosenman, R. H. Association of specific overt behavior patterns with blood and cardiovascular findings—Blood cholesterol level, blood clotting time, incidence of arcus senilis, and clinical coronary artery disease. *Journal of American Medical Association,* 1959, 162, 1286–1296.

Gellhorn, F. The turning of the nervous system: Physiological foundations and implications for behavior. *Perspectives in Biology and Medicine*, 1967, *10*, 559–591.

Gleser, G. C., Singer, J. E., & Winget, C. *Prolonged psychological effects of disaster*. New York: Academic Press, 1981.

Graham, D. T., & Kunish, N. O. Physiological responses of unhypnotized patients to attitude suggestions. *Psychosomatic Medicine*, 1965, *27*, 317–329.

Horney, K. *Neurosis and human growth*. New York: Norton, 1950.

Kimball, C. P. Diagnosing psychosomatic situations. *In B. B. Wolman (Ed.), Clinical diagnosis of mental disorders: A handbook* (pp. 677–708). New York: Plenum Press, 1978.

Krantz, D. S., & Glass, D. C. Personality, behavior patterns, and physical illness: Conceptual and methodological issues. In W. D. Gentry (Ed.), *Handbook of behavioral medicine* (pp. 38–86). New York: Guilford Press, 1984.

Krantz, D. S., Grunberg, N. E., & Baum, A. Health psychology. *Annual Reviews of Psychology*, 1985, *36*, 349–383.

Leigh, H. Evaluation and management of stress in general medicine: The psychosomatic approach. In L. Goldberger & S. Breznitz (Eds.), *Handbook of stress* (pp. 733–744). New York: Macmillan–Free Press, 1982.

Leigh, H., & Reiser, M. F. *The patient: Biological, psychological and social dimensions of medical practice*. New York: Plenum Press, 1980.

McClelland, D. C. Inhibited power motivation and high blood pressure in men. *Journal of Abnormal Psychology*, 1979, *88*, 182–190.

Rahe, R. H. Life change and subsequent illness reports. In K. E. Gunderson & R. H. Rahe (Eds.), *Life stress and illness*. Springfield, IL: Thomas, 1974.

Rosenman, R. H., & Chesney, M. A. Stress, type A behavior, and coronary disease. In L. Goldberger & S. Breznitz (Eds.), *Handbook of stress* (pp. 546–565). New York: Macmillan–Free Press, 1982.

Schmale, A. H., Jr. Giving up as final common pathway to changes in health. *Advances in Psychosomatic Medicine*, 1972, *8*, 20–40.

III
The Disorders

12

Hypochondriasis

Definitions

The second edition of *The Diagnostic and Statistical Manual of Mental Disorders* of the American Psychiatric Association (DSM-II; APA, 1965), defined the hypochondriacal neurosis as follows:

> The hypochondriacal neurosis is dominated by preoccupation with the body and with fear of presumed diseases of various organs. Though the fears are not of delusional quality, as in psychotic depression, they persist despite reassurance. The condition differs from hysterical neurosis in that there are no actual losses or dislocations of function.

A few years later, the third edition of *The Diagnostic and Statistical Manual* (DSM-III; APA, 1980), defined hypochondriasis as a condition in which:

> The predominant disturbance is an unrealistic interpretation of physical signs or sensations as abnormal, leading to the preoccupation with the fear or belief of having a serious disease . . . the disturbance is not due to any mental disorder, such as schizophrenia, affective disorder, or somatization disorder. (p. 249)

According to the DSM-III, the unrealistic fear or conviction of having a serious disorder persists in hypochondriachal patients despite medical examinations and reassurances, and it may adversely affect these patients' behavior.

Etiology

All psychosomatic disorders serve a purpose, be it gaining attention, soliciting sympathy and help, avoiding responsibility, or any other hoped-for gain. Hypochondriasis can serve manifold purposes, especially gaining attention and care, avoidance of responsibilities, and escape into parasitic ways of life.

97

Hypocondriasis is always related to childhood experience, especially to parental rejection. The need to be loved is a basic need of childhood. Lack of affection may adversely affect the child's mental and physical health and may even disrupt the natural processes of physical growth and maturation (Horney, 1939, 1945; D. R. Lipsitt, 1974; 1982; L. Lipsitt, 1980; Spitz, 1945; Wolman, 1972, 1978). People deprived of affection tend to regress to infantile modes of behavior.

Some parents pay little attention to their children, but the child's sickness forces them to take care of the child. In many instances, the parents show the sick child their true or untrue concern, and the child perceives parental care as a compensation or even a reward for being ill. The escape into physical illness becomes a device for gaining attention and affection and is the first step toward hypochondriasis in adulthood.

Hypochondriasis is a combination of fear of being sick and a wish to be sick. Hypochondriachal and psychosomatic symptoms are an expression of a conscious fear of sickness and an unconscious regressive wish to be sick and to be taken care of. The gastrointestinal tract is the choice site of illness in old age, as the ailment offers a justification for reduced activity and lack of responsibility. The regressive overconcern about bodily functions represents a call for the help and care that the hypochondriac did not receive in childhood.

In younger people, the choice of hypochondrial fears is often related to the type of illness or fear of illness that did attract parental attention. One patient often complained about his nonexisting imaginary heart troubles, because his father suffered angina pectoris and both parents believed in its genetic transmission.

Hypochondriasis and Depression

Several researchers and mental health practitioners who treat depressed patients have reported the frequency of psychosomatic symptoms. Even mild cases of depression and fleeting depressive moods of hysterics may cause a variety of somatic symptoms: the affected patients tend to believe that they are physically ill (Katon, Kleinman, & Rosen, 1982; Roy, 1982).

Not all depressed individuals develop hypochondriasis, and not all hypochondriacs are depressed, but depressed patients tend to be preoccupied with minute somatic symptoms. Hypochondriacs are always preoccupied with somatic symptoms, as if the mildest discomfort is an indication of a serious disease. According to Stoudemire and Blazer (1985), physical symptoms may exist, but the "patient may develop an obsessive fear that the symptoms represent something terribly serious and even life threatening . . . patients who are depressed may also have prominent somatic symptoms and interpret them unrealistically" (Stoudemire & Blazer, 1985, p. 568).

Depression is a feeling of helpless anger directed against oneself, usually associated with guilt feelings and with blaming oneself for being weak and helpless. Depressed individuals are accident-prone and often wish to be sick, as if believing that their suffering will elicit attention, affection, and care. They are "love addicts" who need unlimited signs of attention and love, and their psychosomatic symptoms serve this purpose (Wolman, 1984).

Hypochondriasis often serves as a defense against feelings of guilt and inferiority (Barsky & Klerman, 1983; Brown & Vaillant, 1981). Depressed individuals can be tortured by feelings of guilt and inadequacy, and in many cases, psychosomatic symptoms are experienced by depressive individuals as well-deserved punishment. In some instances, the psychosomatic symptoms serve to cover up and mask depression (Lesse, 1967).

HYPOCHONDRIASIS AND PERSONALITY TYPE

According to Kenyon (1964), hypochondriasis is always related to affective disorders. Kenyon received the records of 512 patients. Of these, 301 patients were diagnosed as being afflicted by "primary" hypochondriasis, and 211 were diagnosed as "secondary" hypochondriacs. Almost all of the 211 patients had initially been diagnosed as having affective disorder, and only about one third of the primary hypochondriacs had been diagnosed as being afflicted with affective disorders. However, nearly all 512 patients were anxiety-ridden and depressed.

In Kenyon's cases, the highest incidence of hypochondriasis occurred during the fourth decade in males and the fifth decade in females. Some authors believe that hypochondriasis most frequently occurs in old age, but apparently, it may start at any age (Ladee, 1966).

Hypochondriasis can be associated with any mental disorder, but it seems to be a quite frequent symptom in sociopaths. A study of sociopathic individuals (Wolman, 1987) described their hypochondriasis as follows:

> Being exceedingly selfish and overconcerned with their own wellbeing, the sociopaths tend to worry about their health and appearance. They tend to seek medical help whenever there is a tiniest or even non-existing threat to their health. A mild cold, a tiny blemish, indigestion, or a slight feeling of discomfort drives them to the doctor's office. All the sociopathic patients I have seen in forty years of my clinical practice were hypochondriacs, and most of them were referred to my office by physicians who could not discover any physical ailment, and told the complaining sociopaths their problem must be psychogenic. (p. 44)

Lipsitt (1974) described hypochondriachal adults who, having been deprived of adequate mothering in childhood, nursed and mothered themselves and lived in a state of constant somatic preoccupation.

Nemiah (1985) emphasized two personality features of hypochondriachal patients: narcissistic personality and obsessive-compulsive traits. Hypochondriacs are "egocentric, excessively concerned with themselves and their bodies, and unduly sensitive to criticism or slight or as treating their bodies as libidinal objects" (p. 941).

Nemiah described the behavioral patterns of hypochondriacs as follows:

1. They are verbose, tending to present their complaints in length and in detail.
2. They like to display their symptoms, no matter how minute or insignificant they are.
3. They tend to use medical terms borrowed from their compulsive reading of medical books and articles.
4. They make frequent visits to doctors and clinics.

Hypochondriacs tend to exaggerate, as well as to complain about, their true and imaginary discomforts. They are prone to developing psychosomatic disorders, making their morbid wishes come true. Hypochondriasis may continue throughout one's life span: once a hypochondriac, perhaps always a hypochondriac.

REFERENCES

American Psychiatric Association. *Diagnostic and Statistical Manual of Mental Disorders* (2nd ed.—DSM-II). Washington, DC: Author, 1965.

American Psychiatric Association. *Diagnostic and Statistical Manual of Mental Disorders* (3rd ed.—DSM-III). Washington, DC: Author, 1980.

Barsky, A. J., & Klerman, G. L. Overview: Hypochondriasis, bodily complaints and somatic styles. *American Journal of Psychiatry,* 1983, *140,* 273–283.

Brown, H. N., & Vaillant, G. E. Hypochondriasis. *Archives of Internal Medicine,* 1981, *141,* 723–726.

Horney, K. *New ways in psychoanalysis.* New York: Norton, 1939.

Horney, K. *Our inner conflicts.* New York: Norton, 1945.

Katon, W., Kleinman, A., & Rosen, G. Depression and somatization: A review. *American Journal of Medicine,* 1982, *72,* 127–135.

Kenyon, F. E. Hypocondriasis: A clinical study. *British Journal of Psychiatry,* 1964, *110,* 478–488.

Ladee, G. A. *Hypochondriachal syndromes.* Amsterdam and New York: Elsevier, 1966.

Lesse, S. Hypochondriasis and psychosomatic disorders masking depression. *American Journal of Psychotherapy,* 1967, *21,* 607–620.

Lipsitt, D. R. Psychodynamic considerations of hypochondriasis. *Psychotherapy and Psychodynamics,* 1974, *23,* 132–141.

Lipsitt, D. R. The painful woman: Complaints, symptoms, and illness. In M. Notman & C. Nadelson (Eds.), *The woman patient* (pp. 147–171). New York: Plenum Press, 1982.

Lipsitt, L. (Ed.) *Advances in infant development.* Hillsdale, NJ: Erlbaum, 1980.

Nemiah, J. C. Somatoform disorders. In H. I. Kaplan & B. J. Sadock (Eds.), *Comprehensive textbook of psychiatry* (4th ed.). Baltimore, MD: Williams & Wilkins, 1985.

Roy, A. *Hysteria*. New York: Wiley, 1982.

Spitz, R. A. Hospitalism: An inquiry into the genesis of psychiatric conditions in early childhood. *Psychoanalytic Study of the Child*, 1945, *1*, 53–74.

Stoudemire, A., & Blazer, D. G. Depression in the elderly. In E. E. Beckham & W. R. Leber (Eds.), *Handbook of depression: Treatment, assessment and research* (pp. 556–586). Homeward, IL: Dorsey Press, 1985.

Wolman, B. B. *Manual of child psychopathology*. New York: McGraw-Hill, 1972.

Wolman, B. B. *Interational psychotherapy*. Van Nostrand Reinhold, 1984.

Wolman, B. B. *Children's fears*. New York: Grosset & Dunlop, 1978.

Wolman, B. B. *The sociopathic personality*. New York: Brunner/Mazel, 1987.

13

Asthma

DEFINING ASTHMA

Asthma is a disease of the respiratory system. It is manifested by a sudden narrowing of the air passages and paroxysms of wheezing, coughing, and dyspnea. The asthmatic attacks do not last long, and they are following by long symptom-free periods.

Asthma represents a reduced sensitivity to the beta adrenergic receptors of the bronchial smooth muscle, the mucosal blood vessels, and the mucous glands. This diminished sensitivity can be genetic or acquired, and when the catecholamine-sensitive receptors are blocked, the asthmatic symptoms occur.

Asthma is related to enzyme deficiencies. When the activity of adenyl cyclase is substantially reduced, there is a decline in catecholamine responsiveness and an increase in asthmatic bronchial constriction (Jacobs, 1977). Asthma is related to adrenergic blockage and to a deficient mobilization of epinephrine, which indicates an inadequate functioning of the sympathetic nervous system and the dominance of the parasympathetic nervous system (Boushey, 1981).

Asthma is related to dysbalance of the autonomic nervous system. The sympathetic nervous system controls dilations in the lungs, and the parasympathetic nervous system controls constrictions in the lungs. As mentioned above, in asthma the parasympathetic system dominates.

Asthmatic attacks are caused by an edema of the bronchial wall, bronchospasm, and the formation of plugs in the bronchial lumina. An attack can be provoked by a variety of physical, chemical, and psychological factors, including temperature changes, infections, allergens, chemical irritants, dust, overexertion, bad news, frustrations, and any other emotional disturbance (Dorfman & Cristofar, 1985; Harrison, 1980).

Incidence

Asthma afflicts 4%–7% of the U.S. population and causes close to 5,000 deaths every year; similar numbers are reported from other countries, but asthma is a rather rare occurrence among American Indians, Eskimos, West Africans, and New Zealand highlanders. Over 50% of all asthma cases start before the age of 40. The male–female ratio in childhood is 2 to 1, but this difference is gradually reduced, and around the age of 30, the incidence of asthma is the same for males and females (McFadden & Austen, 1980; Purcell, Weiss, & Hahn, 1972).

Etiological Studies

One may draw a distinction between *allergic asthma* and *idiosyncratic asthma*. Allergic asthma seems to be related to a failure of immunological defenses and to a variety of allergic diseases, such as eczema, rhinitis, and urticaria (Seleznick & Sperber, 1965). Allergic asthma is often seasonal and occurs frequently in children, teenagers, and young adults. Nonseasonal allergic asthma may be related to a variety of allergies, such as feathers and molds. Idiosyncratic asthma can develop out of a common cold and/or a variety of psychological factors to be described later on.

Fritz (1985) distinguished between *intrinsic* and *extrinsic* cases of asthma. Intrinsic asthma is believed to be a reaction to abandonment by one or both parents (parentectomy). Extrinsic asthma is related to allergies.

Masuda, Notske, and Holmes (1966) studied the biochemical factors in asthma. Of 17 patients interviewed, 7 showed a gradual increase in asthmatic symptoms. The reactors were differentiated from the nonreactors by their lower levels of excretion of metadrenaline in the interview, reflecting a nonresponsive adrenal medulla. During an asthmatic attack, whether naturally occurring or induced, there was an increase in the normetadrenaline–metadrenaline ratio, indicating a disproportionate increase in sympathetic nervous activity. The investigators suggested that the adrenal medulla functions at a lower level in asthmatics and fails to respond in stimulus situations tending to evoke attacks of asthma.

Dudley, Masuda, Martin, and Holmes (1965) focused on the experimental induction of changes in the pulmonary ventilation of normal subjects as well as of some suffering from pulmonary tuberculosis or obstructive-airways disease. The respiratory changes, such as ventilation, carbon dioxide production, oxygen uptake, and alveolar ventilation occurring during anger or anxiety, were similar to those occurring during real or suggested exercise, and the changes occurring during depression were similar to those occurring during real or suggested sleep.

"Conditioned" Asthma

French and Alexander (1941) concluded that asthma attacks may be precipitated by a conditioned-reflex mechanism. The famous example given by MacKenzie in 1886 of a woman who was supposedly allergic to roses and who developed asthma when an artificial rose was held before her has been cited many times in the literature.

Kinsman, Spector, Shugard, and Luparello (1974) maintained that the combination of physiological and psychological elements is responsible for 97% of all asthma cases. The original precipitants are infections and/or allergens, but the emotional ones become *conditioning stimuli* and cause airway obstructions. Excessive fatigue, fear, irritability, and other emotional upsets can cause bronchial constrictions. There is, however, no conclusive evidence concerning the hypothesis that asthma can be a product of conditioning.

Emotional Factors

A considerable body of empirical evidence points to the role of emotional factors in the etiology of asthma, especially in childhood. Some researchers provoked asthma attacks: Enclosing people in a whole-body plethysmograph caused severe emotional stress and, in some individuals, precipitated an asthma attack (Stein, 1962).

In their study of 406 attacks in nine severely asthmatic patients Knapp and Nemetz (1960) found that feelings and fantasies of physical illness tended to accompany asthmatic attacks. These fantastes protected these patients against obvious psychological problems, although after the asthma had become established, there were emotional concomitants of a depressive character, such as sadness, helplessness, hopelessness, and, at times, ideas of dangerous or poisonous inner substances. Usually, within 48 hours before an attack, some event had caused the arousal and excitement of a drive or impulse, and the arousal had been inhibited because of a fear of loss of love. Thus, events that lead to the frustration of powerful impulses may activate a vulnerable respiratory pattern having both intake and expulsion functions (Knapp & Nemetz, 1957).

Parental Attitudes

The Child Study Center at Mount Sinai Hospital, Los Angeles, has studied eczema and asthma in preschool children (Alexander & Flagg, 1965). Based on their observations of the interfamilial dynamics in early eczema and asthma that precipitated and/or reinforced the symptoms, they proposed a developmental communicative scheme in regard to these illnesses. They maintained that the eczematous child is infantilized by its parents. The asthmatic child feels that the mother thinks she is inadequate in attending to the child's needs. The child develops a pseudomature character structure, which is perpetuated as long as he or she has a modicum of support forthcoming from the mother or her surrogate. The child fears estrangement from the mother, the pseudomature defense structure collapses, and this collapse leads to an asthmatic wheeze.

French and Alexander (1941) hypothesized that asthma represents a suppressed cry, with the implication that asthmatic children cry less than nonasthmatics, especially in critical periods of separation conflict. Some researchers have noted a tendency for crying to be distorted in a silent, awkward way in certain asthmatics. Some patients reported that crying, laughing, and coughing can trigger attacks of asthma; these patients sometimes deliberately seek to avoid crying and laughing. The occasionally observed inability to cry or the silent, suppressed manner of crying may reflect an attempt to prevent an asthmatic attack.

Purcell established two subgroups on the basis of whether or not a spontaneous remission of symptoms occurred within a short time after admission to the Children's Asthma Research Institute and Hospital. Certain psychological differences were found between the groups, particularly between the rapidly remitting group (those who remained virtually symptom-free and required no medication during the 18–24 months of residency) and the steroid-dependent group (those requiring continuous maintenance doses of corticosteroid drugs). For example, in response to a structured interview technique, the rapidly remitting children reported, significantly more often than did the steroid-dependent children, that emotions such as anger, anxiety, and depression triggered asthma. Furthermore, the results of a questionnaire devised to assess parental child-rearing attitudes indicated that both the mothers and the fathers of the rapidly remitting children showed authoritarian and punitive attitudes to a greater degree than the parents of the steroid-dependent children (Purcell et al., 1972, p. 717).

INNER CONFLICTS

The Chicago Institute for Psychoanalysis outlined a nuclear psychodynamic conflict: The asthma patient shows repressed dependence on the mother. The patient may be aggressive and ambitious, or he or she may be hypersensitive. The asthma patient wants to be accepted and protected by the mother or her surrogate. The patient's fantasies and dreams reflect this wish, expressing a high frequency of intrauterine fantasies in the form of water symbolism. Separation from the protective mother image precedes an asthmatic attack. The precipitating factor in the attacks of the illness could be: (1) the birth of a sibling, or sibling rivalry that develops later; (2) (in a girl) the menarche, which may separate the girl symbolically from her mother because she now sees herself as the mother's competitor instead of her child; (3) (in a boy) oedipal wishes that threaten the dependent relationship with the mother (The mothers of asthmatics are often physically attracted to their sons and, as a defense, react to them with rejection, which the boy perceives as a separation trauma); or (4) any aggressive or defiant impulse directed against the mother or any surge of independent behavior. Maternal rejection is found as a leading motif in the lives of asthma patients, and the child who needs maternal care and acceptance responds to it with an increase in insecurity and clinging to the mother (Alexander & Flagg, 1965; Jackson, 1985).

Ago, Nagata, Teshima, Miyata, Nakagawa, Sugita, and Ikemi (1985) studied 209 asthmatic patients (105 males and 104 females) in the Department of Psychosomatic Medicine at the Kyushy University Hospital in Japan. The patients who had developed asthma in childhood showed more allergic factors, whereas those who had developed asthma in their 20s showed more psychosocial factors. Those who had developed bronchial asthma before the age of 10 showed that parental discord and separation had played a significant etiological role. First asthma attacks in the teens had usually occurred at the time of high school or college entrance examinations.

Many women had had their first asthma attack in their 20s as a result of conflicts with their parents and/or marital difficulties. Young men had had their first asthma attacks related to their first job. Many men and women had had their first asthma attack in their 30s or 40s, related to their jobs and/or difficulties with their spouses and/or their growing children.

The most severe cases of asthma were those of childhood involving rejection by the parents or the loss of one or both parents by death or divorce. Some of these patients had never had a chance to relieve their tension by being listened to by the parents or by receiving parental sympathy and guidance (Moore, 1965).

Several authors have stressed the child's ambivalent attitude toward the mother. The child fears separation and is overdependent on the mother and, at the same time, resents the mother's domineering qualities and overprotectiveness and tries to suppress this resentment. In many instances, asthma in children is related to paternal rejection and/or abandonment. Asthmatic female children and asthmatic adult females tend to be self-punitive. Their anger, originally directed at the rejecting father, is repressed and is redirected at themselves in a classic psychosomatic pattern.

According to Weiner (1977, 1985), children whose asthmatic attacks had to be controlled by a continuous use of steroid medication instantly remitted when they were removed from their home environment. Some asthmatic children do not have attacks when they are in school, even when they are exposed to the same allergic stimulants as in their homes. Thus, Weiner concluded, "Such observations provide powerful support to the idea that psychological factors within the children and the social context in which they find themselves do play a role in precipitating asthmatic attacks and in altering the course of asthma" (Weiner, 1985, p. 1161).

References

Ago, Y., Nagata, S., Teshima, H., Miyata, M., Nakagawa, T., Sugita, M., & Ikemi, Y. Environmental stress factors and bronchial asthma. In P. Pichot, P. Berner, R. Wolf, & K. Thau (Eds.), *Psychiatry: The state of the art: Vol. 4. Psychotherapy and psychosomatic medicine.* New York: Plenum Press, 1985.

Alexander, F. *Psychosomatic medicine.* New York: Norton, 1950.

Alexander, F., & Flagg, G. W. The psychosomatic approach. In B. B. Wolman (Ed.), *Handbook of clinical psychology* (pp. 855–947). New York: McGraw-Hill, 1965.

Boushey, H. A. Neural mechanisms in bronchial asthma. In H. Weiner, M. A. Hofer, & A. J. Stunkard (Eds.), *Brain, behavior and bodily disease.* New York: Raven Press, 1981.

Dorfman, W., & Cristofar, L. (Eds.) *Psychosomatic illness review.* New York: Macmillan, 1985.

Dudley, D. L., Masuda, M., Martin, C. J., & Holmes, T. H. Psychophysiological studies of experimentally induced action directed behavior. *Journal of Psychosomatic Research,* 1965, *9,* 209–221.

French, T. M., & Alexander, F. Psychogenic factors in bronchial asthma. *Psychosomatic Medicine Monographs,* 1941, *2,* 4.

Fritz, G. K. Childhood asthma. In W. Dorfman & L. Cristofar (Eds.), *Psychosomatic illness review.* New York: Macmillan, 1985.

Harrison, T. R. (Ed.). *Principles of internal medicine* (9th ed.). New York: McGraw-Hill, 1980.

Jackson, M. Psychosomatic pathology as developmental failure: A model for research. In P. Pichot, P. Berner, R. Wolf, & K. Thau (Eds.), *Psychiatry: The state of the art: Vol. 4. Psychotherapy and psychosomatic medicine.* New York: Plenum Press, 1985.

Jacobs, M. A. Psychosomatic aspects of allergic respiratory diseases with special focus on bronchial asthma. In B. B. Wolman (Ed.), *International encyclopedia of psychiatry, psychology, psychoanalysis and neurology* (Vol. 9, pp. 293–297). New York: Aesculapius Publishers, 1977.

Kinsman, R. A., Spector, S. L., Shugard, D. W., & Luparello, T. J. Observations on patterns of subjective symptomatology of acute asthma. *Psychosomatic Medicine,* 1974, *36,* 129–143.

Knapp, P. H., & Nemetz, S. J. Personality variations in bronchial asthma. *Psychosomatic Medicine,* 1957, *19,* 443–465.

Knapp, P. H., & Nemetz, S. J. Acute bronchial asthma: Concomitant depression with excitement and varied antecedent patterns in 406 attacks. *Psychosomatic Medicine,* 1960, *22,* 42–50.

Masuda, M., Notske, R. N., & Holmes, T. H. Catecholamine excretion and asthmatic behavior. *Journal of Psychosomatic Research,* 1966, *10,* 255–262.

McFadden, E. R., & Austen, K. F. Lung diseases caused by immunologic and environmental injury. In T. R. Harrison (Ed.), *Principles of internal medicine* (9th ed., pp. 1203–1210). New York: McGraw-Hill, 1980.

Moore, N. Behavior therapy in bronchial asthma: A controlled study. *Journal of Psychosomatic Research*, 1965, *9*, 257–262.

Purcell, K., Weiss, J., & Hahn, W. Certain psychosomatic disorders. In B. B. Wolman (Ed.), *Manual of child psychopathology* (pp. 706–742). New York: McGraw-Hill, 1972.

Seleznick, S. T., & Sperber, Z. The problem of eczema-asthma complex: A developmental approach. In N. S. Greenfield & W. C. Lewis (Eds.), *Psychoanalysis and current biological thought*. Madison: University of Wisconsin Press, 1965.

Stein, M. Etiology and mechanism in thedevelopment of asthma. In J. H. Nodine & J. H. Moyer (Eds.), *Psychosomatic medicine*. Philadelphia: Lee & Febiger, 1962.

Weiner, H. *Psychobiology and human disease*. New York: Elsevier, 1977.

Weiner, H. Respiratory disorders. In H. I. Kaplan & B. J. Sadock (Eds.), *Comprehensive textbook of psychiatry* (4th ed.). Baltimore, MD: Williams & Wilkins, 1985.

14

Gastrointestinal Diseases

The gastrointestinal system is very sensitive to emotional disturbances. From the earliest days of life, the alimentary process is the main source of pleasure and displeasure. Hunger, the intake of food, saturation, and elimination are the leading and most frequent factors of emotional reactions of fear, anger, relief, and joy (Feuerstein, Labbé, & Kuczmierczyk, 1986).

Gastrointestinal diseases demonstrate the frequent transition from mind to body and vice versa (see Part I, Chapter 4). The intake of food, the loss or gain of weight, poor or good appetite, and diarrhea or constipation can control one's emotional well-being and can be controlled by emotions. The psychosomatic disorders of the gastrointestinal system include a great many different pathological patterns, such as anorexia, bulimia, gastric neuroses, peptic ulcers, ulcerative colitis, irritable bowel syndrome, and encopresis. Experimental research on animals has shown that stressful stimuli can produce gastrointestinal lesions (Weiss, 1984). Apparently, the same reaction appears in human beings, as will be described later on in this chapter.

The infant's emotional security is associated with being fed. The satisfaction of hunger is essential not only to physical survival but also for normal emotional development. To be fed means to be loved and secure. The nucleus of insecurity is fear of starvation (fear of the future), which may be openly expressed in pronounced depressive states. The child's feeling of utter dependence on adults for food and security is linked with eating and hunger, and it may produce greed and envy. To the child, possession is equivalent to oral incorporation, and frustration of this possessive tendency leads to aggressive impulses. Biting becomes the first manifestation of hostility and aggressive impulses that center on oral incorporation (Wolman, 1970, 1978).

Possessiveness, greed, envy, and the striving for security in disorders of the alimentary function are closely linked with oral incorporation. The pleasurable physical sensations connected with the early forms of nutrition (sucking) explain the frequency of emotional disturbances of the nutritional function when the mature genital functions are inhibited by conflicts. Then a regression to an early pregenital phase may take place (Alexander & Flagg, 1965).

Anorexia Nervosa

Occasional or even lasting loss of appetite is typical of depression, and it may occur in states of pain and discomfort associated with a variety of physical and/or mental disorders. When a loss of appetite is the main or only symptom and serves a distinct psychological purpose, it is anorexia nervosa. Extreme cases of anorectic starvation represent a threat to life (Bruch, 1982; Garfinkel & Garner, 1982; Selvini-Palazzoli, 1978).

Current research has led to several hypothetical statements concerning the etiology of anorexia nervosa. Whereas no one questions the psychological causes of anorexia, there is a considerable amount of evidence linking anorexia to endocrinological disorders and other organic factors. According to Halmi (1985), tyrosine (Tu) levels are in a low-normal range, and the serum triodothyronine (T_3) levels are quite decreased in anorectic patients. Moreover, in anorectic patients, the hypothalamic-pituitary-ovarian system is disturbed. Emaciated anorexics suffer from hypoplasia in bone marrow, low levels of plasma fibrinogen, low erythrocyte sedimentation rates (ESR), and, in many instances, hypercarotenemia and hypokalemic alkalosis. To what extent the endocrine and related symptoms are causes of anorexia is an open question (Beaumont, 1984; Hamburg, Elliott, & Parron, 1982; McKerns, & Pantić, 1985).

Weiner (1977) reported that close to 50% of all cases of anorexia begin with *amenorrhea*, and amenorrhea is associated with an immature onset of secretory patterns of the pituitary luteinizing hormone (LH) and the follicle-stimulating hormone (FSH). Again, it is not absolutely clear that amenorrhea causes anorexia, although amenorrhea antecedes the excessive dieting of anorectic patients.

King (1963) studied 21 cases and differentiated a primary from a secondary syndrome of anorexia nervosa. In the primary form, the abstinence from food was a positive pleasure; in secondary cases, the cause was phobia, delusions, and/or depression. King viewed primary anorexia nervosa as an organic disorder that is influenced secondarily by psychological factors. In severe anorexia, secondary manifestations of impaired endocrine function appear, such as loss of axillary hair, cessation of menstruation, disappearance of sexual desire, and cessation of growth. Abnormalities in behavior that resemble anorexia nervosa can be produced by starvation. Anorexia nervosa is caused by psychological conflict, but diminished activity of the endocrine glands and an increase in blood ketones reinforce the loss of appetite on an organic basis (Darby, Garfinkel, Garner, & Coscino, 1983).

Psychoanalytic studies of anorexia patients reveal as outstanding factors unconscious conflicts over aggressive impulses such as envy and jealousy. The patient inhibits these aggressive impulses because of guilt and expiates the guilt by denying himself or herself the pleasure of eating. Anorexia is an unconscious spite reaction in which the patient, like an angry, pouting child, extorts special favor from his or her environment. Bruch (1966; 1977) pointed to two areas of functionally disordered psychological experiences in anorexia patients:

> 1. Disturbance of *body image* of delusional proportions and lack of concern over emaciation.
> 2. A disturbance in the perception of stimuli arising in the body which causes an inability accurately to perceive nutritional needs. Coddington, Dean, Bruch, and Keller (1963) tested the ability to perceive gastric stimuli in patients with eating disorders and normal persons by administering known amounts of fluid to their stomachs. They found that the lower the subject's ability to perceive the gastric stimuli, the greater the abnormality. (1963, p. 7)

Some cases of anorexia are associated with impulsive behavior, kleptomania, self-mutilation, and suicidal attempts. In many instances, anorexia is associated with *bulimia,* a morbid craving for food and getting rid of food by purging (Leon, 1982).

Bulimia

The main symptoms of bulimia are compulsive overeating followed by self-induced purging. Prolonged bulimic behavior may cause a chronic irritation of the mouth, the throat, and the esophagus. Bulimic patients tend to deny having personality difficulties, and some of them prefer not to admit to their eating binges and self-induced vomiting.

Bulimia is a quite frequent phenomenon among adolescent and young adult women afflicted by anorexia nervosa (Halmi, 1983). It is usually associated with an overambitious and perfectionist personality type. Some female college students, driven by guilt feelings when their college marks fail to meet their mothers' approval, develop anorectic behavior combined with periods of overeating followed by self-induced vomiting.

One of my anorectic-bulimic patients went on reassuring me that she was constantly getting better and becoming more efficient and self-assured. She was symbiotically tied up to her domineering mother, who was presenting herself as a self-sacrificing martyr and was making her daughter feel guilty for not being able to solve her mother's real and imaginary troubles.

Alexander and Flagg (1965) maintained that voracious bulimic-type eating results from an intense craving for love mixed with aggressive tendencies to devour or possess the love object. Unconscious feminine sexual fantasies, pregnancy fantasies, and castrative wishes may play an important role. In two cases analyzed by Alexander and Flagg (1965), obesity was a defense against the feminine role, sort of a "protective coat" covering the feminine body, which both patients rejected because of its masochistic connotation. Gottsfeld (1962) compared the body self-cathexes of "super-obese" patients and neurotic patients by using a questionnaire and body drawings and found that the superobese group had a more negative body cathexis than the neurotic group, but not a more negative self-cathexis.

ANORECTIC FAMILIES

Minuchin, Roman, and Baker (1978) related anorexia nervosa and other disorders of the gastrointestinal system to a particular family constellation that stimulates the child to escape into psychosomatic symptoms.

Anorectic families tend to overemphasize achievement, drive, the importance of food, and, above all, self-sacrifice (Selvini-Palazzoli, 1978). Anorectic patients view themselves as strong-willed and as self-sacrificing martyrs who make heroic efforts to achieve, no matter what the price. Quite often, they start starving themselves when facing a threat to their parents and embark on what they believe is a self-sacrificing task of saving the family.

One of my anorexic patients kept telling me again and again about her self-sacrificing mother and her uninterested father. She was an attractive young woman, bright and conscientious. Her life was one of continuous service and submissiveness to her mother's whims. She would occasionally overeat, but not to the excessive level of bulimia, and she frequently practiced self-induced vomiting. She felt inefficient and inadequate, and she tried to be ambitious. In her job, she tried to outdo her co-workers and "prove" herself. She maintained that she was in a process of continuous progress, and she believed that every day she would become a "better person and a more successful co-worker."

Poor outcomes in anorexia are associated with longer duration of illness, older age of onset, lower weight during illness, the presence of symptoms such as bulimia, frequent vomiting, inadequate social adjustment in childhood, an overdemanding attitude on the part of the mother, and lack of affection on the part of the patient's father. An early onset of anorexia, a friendly relationship with peers, good achievements in high school, and employment in skilled occupations or professions are usually correlated with a better prognosis (Touyz, Beamont, & Glaun, 1985).

GASTRIC NEUROSIS

The secretory and motor functions of the stomach and the duodenum can be affected by emotional factors. Faulty eating habits related to emotional conflicts can produce organic disturbances. The causes of faulty eating habits, such as incomplete mastication, rapid eating and overeating, and poor food selection, are usually emotional. The psychosomatic symptoms range from slight heartburn to intractable vomiting or to a chronic gastric neurosis such as "rejection dyspepsia," which occurs in people who complain of abdominal distension, chronic eructation of air, and small amounts of gastric juice (Alexander, French, & Pollock, 1968; Drossman, 1983).

Psychosomatic gastric disturbances represent a conflict due to the frustration of the infantile need to be taken care of, that is, the dependent tendencies. These infantile dependency fixations present a conflict with one's mature need for independence and may give rise to psychosomatic symptoms (Alexander & Flagg, 1965).

Ulcers

Ulcers occur in the stomach and in the duodenum. They are chronic lesions that extend into the wall of the gastrointestinal tract.

According to Mirsky (1958), emotional needs do not cause ulcers but aggravate an already existing condition. Mirsky maintained that the gastric hypersecretion may be present at birth and that psychological factors may reinforce and aggravate the existing allergic predispositions. Moreover, several studies using primates as experimental subjects have proved that emotional problems, and especially conflict situations, can produce increased gastric acid secretion and thus cause gastric duodenal ulceration (Purcell, Weiss, & Hahn, 1972).

Duodenal ulcers can be caused by a variety of physical and emotional factors. They may be a product of severe emotional stress as well as of brain injury. They may cause bleeding. If the lesion perforates the walls of the gastrointestinal tract, the content of the tract that enters the peritoneal cavity may cause *peritonitis*. Duodenal ulcers are often related to heavy drinking of alcohol caused by severe emotional disturbances (Oken, 1985; Pilot, Rubin, Schafer, & Spiro, 1963).

Peptic ulcer is perhaps the most widely recognized condition in which chronic functional disturbance leads to organic tissue changes. Peptic ulcers may develop after a long history of gastritis; they may also develop acutely, with no significant history of gastrointestinal distress.

Peptic ulcers are usually caused by enlarged and/or prolonged gastric acid secretions and may cause bleeding. They may be related to (1) an excessive activity of the gastrin-producing cells; (2) excessive vagal drive; and (3) mucuous protection of the living epithelium (Wolf, 1985).

Alexander (1950) maintained that peptic ulcers are produced by gastric hypersecretion and cause an increased stimulation of the hypothalamus as a response to unfulfilled emotional oral needs. Alexander stressed the role of *conflict* between hunger and aversive psychological stimuli, as well as between the childlike need to depend on others and the adult craving for independence.

Studies conducted at the Chicago Institute for Psychoanalysis have shown that ulcer occurs more often in a certain personality type. These studies represent a *typical conflict* situation in which a patient may develop an ulcer. The crucial factor in the pathogenesis of ulcers is the frustration of help-seeking demands for love. When the wish to receive love is rejected or frustrated, it is converted into a wish to be fed. This longing to receive love becomes a chronic stimulus that activates gastric hyperfunction. In response to these emotional needs, the stomach reacts with hypersecretion and hypermotility (Alexander *et al.*, 1968).

Pilot *et al.* (1963) described the onset of peptic ulcer in identical twins. Both had very similar character structures (both were passive, shy, and dependent), and both had high blood-pepsin levels. A peptic ulcer developed when each individual found himself in a typical, specific precipitating conflict situation. Twin A developed an ulcer when his wife had a near psychotic breakdown and threatened violence to their children. The second twin, married to a protective, maternal woman, developed an ulcer when his wife lost her job and thought she was pregnant.

ULCERS IN CHILDREN

It seems that the incidence of childhood ulcers is increasing. Several surveys indicate that this increase could be due to improved diagnostic aids, such as the use of radiological equipment, rather than to a real increase in incidence. At present, approximately 10% of children are found to have peptic ulcers (Wolf, 1985).

A study of 109 patients at the Mayo Clinic showed that there is a 50% chance that a duodenal ulcer in childhood will persist or will recur in adolescence or adulthood if medical treatment alone is administered. Peptic ulcers occur with a fairly even distribution over the age range of birth to 16 years; duodenal ulcers are 17 times as frequent as gastric ulcers, and there is a slightly greater incidence of ulcers in male than in female children—a ratio of 1.6 to 1 (Wolf, 1985).

Ulcers occur with high frequency in neonates, possibly because of fluctuations in gastric acid during the neonatal period. Elevated levels of acid are obtained during the first 40 hours after birth, a substantially suppressed level for the next 4–10 days, and normalization at adult levels around the third week of life.

At birth, all the glandular elements of the adult gastrointestinal mucosa are present. The body and base of the stomach contain cells that secrete hydrochloric acid and pepsin. In the newborn child, the first stimulus for gastric secretion is the intake of food; conditioning soon occurs; the sight, odor, or taste of food can stimulate the "cephalic" or "psychic" stage of digestion, and gastric secretion is set in motion. When food reaches the antrum of the stomach, the second (or gastric) phase begins, and secretions of the hormone gastrin take place. Gastrin itself, released into the bloodstream, causes further acid secretion. The release of pepsin and gastrin are controlled by vagal stimulation, as well as by pH levels and by the distension of the antrum of the stomach.

It is a balance of chemical, mechanical, neural, and humoral processes that is responsible for obtaining optimal and efficient levels of gastric juices. However, there is evidence that these functions can be disrupted by psychological as well as physiological stimuli, as experimental studies with animals have shown. In one of these studies, for 47 out of every 48 hours, rats were forced to cross an electrically charged grid in order to obtain food and water; for the last hour, they were allowed free access to the food and water. This treatment continued for 30 days, and a control group was subjected to a 47-hour deprivation schedule for the same amount of time. With high shock levels, 76% of the experimental animals developed gastric ulcers, whereas none of the control animals had ulcers. Obviously, ulceration was caused by a conflict: the experimental animals could sense the food and water but could not obtain it without pain. In other studies establishing a conflict situation, a significant level of ulceration was obtained. It was also shown that rats separated from their mothers at 15 days of age were significantly more susceptible to ulcers than controls weaned at 21 days (Oken, 1985; Rosenbaum, 1985; Weiner, 1977).

Ulcers have been produced in monkeys. The experimental subjects were required to press a bar every 20 seconds for a period of 6 hours in order to avoid being shocked. Yoked control monkeys were subjected to exactly the same experience, including equal frequency and intensity of shock, but did not have the option of pressing a button to avoid shock. Under these conditions, the two experimental monkeys developed ulcers, whereas their controls did not (described by Purcell *et al.*, 1972, p. 728).

Case-history reports provide a useful source of data for the psychogenic aspects of ulcer. In one report described by Purcell the patient had experienced recurring abdominal pain since age 3. Following a panic reaction to a fireworks display at age 5, he became constantly ill, and X-ray examination showed a definite ulcer crater. The author described the child as having "a sense of inferiority and insecurity" and as being in a "mental and emotional no-man's land" and suggested that these factors, plus the fear inspired by the fireworks display, were psychogenic clues that aided in the diagnosis of peptic ulcer. At the same time, it was observed that the father had a chronic duodenal ulcer and the mother had frequent gastric symptoms. From the data available, there is no way of ascertaining whether the panic reaction actually led to a flare-up of the ulcer condition or whether this was only a natural worsening of the condition, which had been present for 2 years. The personality traits of inferiority and insecurity could have been a result of the environment and/or the fact that the child was ill and "undersized."

Another study (Purcell, Weiss, & Hahn, 1972), which reported five cases of peptic ulcer in children, noted that these children were reluctant to attend school. Apparently, the parents' failure to set limits for the children and the conflict over mother–child separation were related to the ulcers. It is possible that the children wished to stay home near their mothers because the mothers gave them medicine to alleviate stomach pains. Apparently, acute stress situations elicit feelings of resentment and stimulate high levels of gastric secretion, which increases the parietal-cell hydrochloric acid output and leads to an ulcer.

Early observations report an apparent relationship between the onset of ulcerative colitis and the occurrence of traumatic emotional events. Prugh (1951) related the onset of the disease in 12 out of 16 cases to such "firsts" as going away to school, being severely punished by the father, or having sex play with another child. The threat of separation from the mother or the mother substitute in a setting of mutual dependence, or "toilet symbiosis," established during the first 3 years of life seems to be an important factor. Preoccupation with bowel functions on the part of the parents of ulcerative colitis patients before the onset of the disease may foster specific anxieties capable of triggering or perpetuating the disease process.

Prugh (1951) reported an inverse relationship between premorbid adjustment and the rapidity of development of the disease, with more adequately adjusted patients showing slower development. A similar relationship has been reported between assessed adjustment and prognosis (Langford, 1964). Of 24 patients who came from severely disturbed environments, 75% died or required surgical intervention, whereas of 12 patients who came from relatively good homes, 66% improved and 33% died or required surgery. Grace, Wolf, and Wolff (1951) observed that induced fear and dejection were associated with hypofunction of the bowel, whereas anger, resentment, and hostility were associated with hyperfunction. A number of observations have suggested that severity varies, at least in part, with emotional upset. Prugh (1951) described a case in which the sight of another child soiling induced an attack. Langford (1964) reported remission in 45 cases within 4–6 weeks following hospitalization, regardless of whether the patient was on medication. Parental visits to the hospital were said to produce short-lived symptom recurrences. The histories of these patients revealed that other separations (e.g., going to camp) had, in a number of instances, produced similar good results and that the return home had resulted in relapse. Apparently, parent–child interaction may contribute heavily to the etiology of ulcerative colitis.

ULCERATIVE COLITIS

Ulcerative colitis is an inflammatory, chronic disorder of the colon and/or the rectum with stools containing blood or pus. Ulcerative colitis is associated with distinct bowel pathology, and it affects the mucosa of the large intestine. It is a disease of the lining surface of the bowel. The mortality rate for ulcerative colitis in the United States is 0.5% of the population. About 10% of patients die of the disease. It is possible that the etiology of ulcerative colitis can be related to a genetic predisposition combined with consecutive postnatal unwholesome psychological experiences. The parents of children affected by ulcerative colitis are usually ambivalent, and they practice alternate overprotection and rejection. The mothers tend to be domineering and the fathers passive and nonparticipatory. Children affected by this disease are passive, somewhat rigid, and most often narcissistic and overdependent on their parents. Small wonder that family therapy seems to be the method of treatment of choice for children afflicted by ulcerative colitis (Karush, Daniels, Flood, & O'Connor, 1977; Vandersall, 1978).

Ulcerative colitis affects predominantly a young population (15–20 years old), and especially the Jewish population. It is associated with a high degree of chronic disability and a high incidence of carcinoma of the colon. Ulcerative colitis causes rectal bleeding, diarrhea, weight loss, malnutrition, hypoalbuminemia, and anemia, and it may affect other bodily areas, such as the liver and the spine. More recent research centers on autoimmune and infectious factors (Feuerstein et al., 1986; Gentry, 1984; Locke, Ader, Besedovsky, Hall, Solomon, & Strom, 1984).

According to Langford (1964), the parents of people afflicted by ulcerative colitis were preoccupied with their children's bowel movements before the onset of the disease. Tudor (1967) also related peptic ulcers to morbid parental attitudes.

IRRITABLE BOWEL SYNDROME

The irritable bowel syndrome is quite frequently a gastrointestinal disorder. It usually starts in late adolescence or in young adults, male and female. The ratio of males to females is 1 to 2 (Latimer, 1985).

There are frequent changes in bowel movement habits; abdominal pain is the main symptom of the irritable bowel syndrome. Usually, the abdominal pain follows bowel movements, as well as the intake of food, but in some instances, there is no pain at all or only a mild discomfort. There is no persistency nor continuity in the irritable bowel syndrome, and there are occasional periods of aggravation and improvement, even relapses and remission, vaguely related to the patient's moods. Stressful events and situations usually provoke relapses. The irritable bowel syndrome is a chronic condition that flucuates irregularly but does not disappear completely (Karush *et al.*, 1977).

The irritable bowel syndrome is not related to any organic disease, or to any anatomical defects. It is clearly a psychosomatic disorder, but its frequent occurrence over a period of years can cause harm to the human body.

The irritable bowel syndrome is associated with distinct psychological features. People affected by this syndrome are highly conscientious and hypersensitive. They strive for perfection in whatever they do. They are superbly organized, meticulous, and hyperloyal and overcommitted to their parents, family members, and friends. They are never late to their appointments, and they and their garments are spotless. They tend to experience feelings of guilt for uncommitted sins, and they are inclined to punish themselves for true or imaginary imperfections. Most probably, the irritable colon syndrome is a fulfillment of their unconscious wish to be punished for not being perfect.

I have had in psychotherapy a few women patients afflicted by the irritable bowel syndrome. They had strict and overdemanding mothers who made their daughters feel guilty no matter how obedient the girls were. My patients felt that they were not good daughters, for they could never please their mothers. They were overdependent, hyperconscientious, and unable to assert themselves.

ENCOPRESIS

Encopresis is an involuntary defecation not related to any organic disease. Most children attain continence at the age of 2 or 3, and when incontinence continues for years, one must assume that there are some physical or mental reasons (Roy, Silverman, & Corretto, 1975).

Incontinence can be associated with old-age diseases, such as senile dementia and Alzheimer's dementia. In these cases, the inability to control bodily functions is a product of widely spread or total physical and mental deterioration, but encopresis is a disorder that starts in childhood and may continue in the adult years. It is, however, not a sign of a total physical or mental deterioration (Pierce, 1985).

Encopresis is often related to mental retardation and sometimes to minimal brain dysfunction. Some children react to fear and stress by an instant bowel movement; encopresive children, on the other hand, are continuously or at least frequently depressed, angry, irritable, and asocial. Baird (1974) related the etiology of encopresis to parent–child interaction. The main features of encopretic families are infantilization of the child, interparental miscommunication and mishandling of anger, and lack of rational parent–child guidance and encouragement. Bemporad (1978) noted that chronic encopretics did not progress psychologically much beyond the 2-year-old level or had regressed to that level as a result of intrafamilial tension. Parent–parent conflicts often lead to using the child as a scapegoat for the parents' disappointment in each other. Many parents of encopretic children maintain that they would divorce their spouses if not for "that unhappy kid," and they are angry at the encopretic child who "forces" them to stay in the unhappy marriage. Encopretic children grow up in families where the father is depressed and is emotionally absent from his family. The intramarital relationship is full of conflicts, and many of these marriages break down. The mothers are cold and unemotional, oscillating between hostile rejection and infantilizing overprotection of their children (Cavanaugh, 1983).

Many encopretic children soil only at home and usually in the presence of the mother, probably intending to embarrass her, to punish her, or to force her to take care of them. The encopretic's willful regression forces the mother to take care of the 6-, 8-, or 10-year-old child, who regresses to the toilet training age.

DIARRHEA

Diarrhea is one of the frequent reactions to emotional tension. It is also a frequent reaction to fear or anger. It may lead to *mucous colitis.* In some instances, the tendency toward diarrhea is an overstayed encopretic reaction (Oken, 1985).

According to Alexander (1950), the gastrointestinal system can be divided into the three basic mechanisms (vectors) of reception, elimination, and retention, and psychosomatic disorders can affect one or all of the three mechanisms. As described above, gastrointestinal disorders, such as anorexia, ulcers, and encopresis, may affect one bodily area but are related to the entire emotional system of an individual.

OBESITY

Obesity can present a serious threat to health and, in extreme cases, even to human life. Heart troubles are a common occurrence.

With the exception of clearly organic cases related to glandular dysfunction, faulty metabolism, and so on, obesity belongs to the category of psychosomatic disorders, for the bodily disorders are caused by psychological factors; and in many instances, to psychopathology (Powers, 1985; Schachter & Rodiu, 1974).

However, obesity is not always produced by a distinct type of mental disorder. In my years of clinical practice, I have treated obese individuals who suffered from a variety of emotional problems. Some obese patients I treated were mildly neurotic, whereas others were manic-depressive and schizophrenic psychotics.

Bruch (1977) noticed that the "absence of uniform psychological features is often cited as evidence against the etiological importance of psychological factors" (p. 97). The fact is that even thyroid dysfunction and the resulting obesity could be related to emotional disorder (Alexander & Flagg, 1965), and that psychological factors, especially depression, are the most frequent causes of obesity.

Some researchers have pointed to the connection between low socioeconomic status and obesity. Stunkard (1980, 1985) compared the socioeconomic level of 1,000 people with the socioeconomic level of their parents. The evidence of the connection between obesity and the level of income was overwhelming; the lower the socioeconomic status of an individual and her or his parents was, the greater was the likelihood of their being overweight. The hypothesis that low socioeconomic status gives rise to frustration and depression—and consequently, to obesity—has been supported by several research workers. A higher percentage of obesity in women of lower socioeconomic class has been found, compared to a lower percentage of obesity in upper-class women. However, low socioeconomic status becomes a significant factor only if it is associated with depression.

Depression is self-directed helpless anger; it is an angry feeling of one's own weakness and helplessness. Depressed people are angry at the whole world for not helping them. They are most angry at themselves for being weak. They hate themselves for being weak and often act in a self-destructive manner, as if trying to punish themselves. Obesity is one of the choice self-punitive devices.

Depressed people are starved for love. They are hungry and insatiable. The more they get, the more they crave, and when they do not get enough—and there is never enough for them—they are angry at those who fail to give them enough and angry at themselves for being unable to get what they want (Stunkard & Koch, 1964). Depressed individuals are irritable and prone to anger and, at the same time, overflow with overdone love and affection. Their hostile or friendly, overdemanding, and exaggerated behavior usually discourages other people from associating with them and makes the depressed individuals still more depressed.

Even a success in social relations leads to self-defeating maneuvers. In their innermost thoughts, they do not believe that they deserve love; they feel that those who love them must be wrong, stupid, or worthless. At any rate, this is never the "great love" they dreamed of, and certainly, there must be something wrong with the person who loves them because they do not deserve love.

Quite often, a patient of mine says, "I feel miserable. I know I have no reason to feel unhappy. Everything I can think of is just fine. I have nothing to complain about, but why do I feel so miserable?"

A decrease in self-esteem and a low estimate of one's power are the common denominators of all depressive states.

Affiliation Motive and Depression

No human being is capable of satisfying all his or her needs, and every human life starts in a state of total dependence on support from without. As children grow, the degree of dependence is gradually reduced, but no human being can ever attain full independence. Adulthood is not independence but *interdependence*, and even the most powerful individuals need allies.

The need to be accepted is one of the fundamental needs of nearly all organic nature. Comparative psychologists names it the *herd instinct* because a great many species group together for hunting and protection against predators. Affiliation, cooperation, and acceptance are the various names for a behavior of helping one another, that is, in getting food and whatever else the organisms need, and in mutual protection against enemies. Loneliness implies weakness; having no allies makes one vulnerable and is therefore conducive to exogenous depression.

Adults' security depends on their own power first and, second, on acceptance; children's security depends first on acceptance by others and then on their own power. Power is the ability to satisfy one's needs, and survival is certainly the arch need. Acceptance has been defined as a willingness to satisfy the needs of other people, that is, to help, protect, and defend them (Wolman, 1978).

Children have no say in choosing their environment or in influencing their opportunities. Adults have some degree of mobility; they can change their jobs, their place of residence, their marital relations, their religion, their business, and their social and political affiliations. Children are born to and are brought up by people they did not choose, and for several years, they are a captive audience in their parents' home.

In most instances, adults can create a more-or-less stable environment; they can live in a certain neighborhood, practice a certain occupation, develop friendly relations with neighbors and relatives, and establish daily routines of their own choice. Children do not have these options; they must move to a new neighborhood and attend a new school; they may feel uprooted whenever their parents decide to change their place of residence, their family relationships, or any other social interactions.

Adults remain adult as long as they live, whether they are young or middle-aged or old, and their behavioral patterns are more-or-less circumscribed by their sex, their age, their occupation, their religion, and so on. Children's behavioral patterns are in a continuous flux, for children need not remain children.

All children wish to please their parents. This wish, conscious or unconscious, is related to the basic drive for survival. Parental approval means food and protection and the feeling of safety.

The worst childhood fear is the fear of abandonment (Wolman, 1978). All human beings derive their feeling of security from two sources: their own power and the loyalty and power of their allies. The child's own power is negligible; the younger the child is, the less power she or he has. The child's feeling of security depends on the power of her or his parents and their willingness to use it to protect her or him. Abandonment is therefore the worst thing that can happen to a child, for the supply of food and survival itself depend on parental care.

It is not enough for a child to get food. His or her security depends on the belief that the food and the protection will be forthcoming in the future. The newborn child is endowed with empathy, that is, the ability to perceive nonverbal signals and to feel whether or not it is loved by the feeding mother or maternal substitute. This ability imbues the infant with feelings of security and euphoria, or of fear and anxiety. Infants need to be loved, and they are happy when the feeding mother hugs them, kisses them, and speaks affectionately. When the feeding mother resents the child and thinks how great her life could be without the baby, the child empathizes with her feelings and becomes anxiety-ridden (Wolman, 1970).

Parent–Child Relationship

Almost all cases of obesity start in childhood, and the parent–child relationship plays a highly significant role in children's eating habits and obesity. Atkinson and Ringuette (1967) studied individuals whose weight was 100% over the average. Of these, 81% had started to gain weight at the age of 12 or earlier, and they had become obese in adolescence or somewhat later. The authors pointed to depression, frustrations, and boredom as the causes of obesity. Of these obese individuals, 86% had at least one obese family member. In her numerous publications, Bruch (1969, 1971, 1973, 1977) reported the role of parental attitudes in children's obesity.

Many obese people dissociate their craving for food from the normal feeling of hunger. They are preoccupied with thoughts of food all the time, and they are unaware whether they are hungry. Stunkard and Koch (1964) measured the contractions of the stomach in obese individuals. The contractions recorded on the gastric balloon used by the investigators were not at all related to the craving for food of the obese individuals, who frequently reported hunger irrespective of the stomach contractions.

   Some authors believe that people affected with obesity have somehow failed to learn to discriminate the contractions of the stomach related to food deprivation. The dissociation between hunger and the intake of food is related to childhood experiences. Parental feeding supplies children with more than food, for giving food implies giving love. Loving parents feed their children, and well-fed children feel loved and thus secure. Receiving food is reassuring, and children derive a triple satisfaction from eating, for in addition to satisfying hunger and providing gustatory pleasure, it is also a sign of being cared for and loved. Thus, feeding provides nutrition, pleasure, and security.

   Quite often, parents overplay and/or misdirect the feeding process. Some parents praise children who overeat and criticize poor eaters. Normally, the amount of food taken in by an infant corresponds, more or less, to the physiological needs of the infant organism. Some parents give their children the impression that overeating is a sign of good health, and many a mother praises the infant for finishing the bottle. The infant is rewarded for eating without hunger.

   Some children are made to believe that the more they eat, the more their parents will love them, and losing weight makes them feel anxious and guilty (Stunkard, 1980).

   Some insecure and guilt-ridden parents try to overcome their own emotional shortcomings by an overzealous and overprotective attitude in feeding. It is worthwhile to mention that rejecting-accepting parents (parents who basically reject their children but who, once in a while, when they are guilt-ridden, shower their child with food and affection) most often have obese offspring.

   When the obese child reaches adolescence and is criticized by classmates and neighbors, the insecure mother often joins the critics. The obese child is torn between an already established desire to overeat in order to please the mother of yesterday and the fear of malicious criticism and ridicule by his or her peers and by the mother of today.

   Bruch (1977) noticed that overprotecting mothers are quite ambivalent toward their children and alternate their overprotectiveness with outbursts of hostility that produce in the child a feeling of low self-esteem, a conviction of helplessness, and a clinging to the overprotecting mother, who is really a rejecting mother.

   Emotionally balanced individuals tend to eat when they are hungry and also when they are calm and in a good mood, and they do not feel like eating when they are worried, upset, or frightened. Depressed people act in a different way. Food deprivation has little effect on the amount of food they eat, and their craving for food is the same, irrespective of the amount of their previous food intake and the time that has since elapsed. Anxiety and depression do not reduce their appetite; on the contrary, the more they are depressed, the more frequently they eat. They seem to be unsatisfied by food, in a close resemblance to their emotional makeup: they are love hungry and food hungry.

Schachter and Rodin (1974) experimented with normal and obese people and found that the obese people ate the same amount of food whether they had been deprived of food or not and whether they felt secure or frightened. Normal people ate more when they had been deprived of food and less when frightened. Apparently, food deprivation does not affect the desire for food in overweight individuals. For obese people, eating does not appear to be related to any physiological condition, and it is stimulated by emotional factors, such as anxiety, depression, fear, and frustration.

Body Image

The body-image concept that an individual internalizes has been studied through perceptual, cognitive-evaluative, and interview procedures. The evidence concerning the permanence with which obese persons who have lost weight maintain an image of themselves as fat and unattractive has varied. According to cognitive-evaluative indices of body image, obese people exhibit a more positive evaluation of their body as weight loss progresses and their physical appearance is less deviant. Both moderately and massively obese persons were more negative in the various evaluations of their body before, as compared with after, weight loss.

Adolescents and adults who are obese often verbalize the feeling that their bodies are grotesque and loathsome, and they often exhibit low self-esteem and a generalized negative self-concept. The onset of this evaluation of one's body as extremely ugly and unattractive was found to have occurred during adolescence. Stunkard and Mendelson (1967) reported that some adults, even after weight loss, continued to think of their bodies in an extremely negative manner and became anxious whenever they gained just a pound or two. The investigators concluded from their research and their clinical experience that body-image disturbances occur in neurotic obese persons whose obesity began before they became adults.

Body-image disturbance in adult persons of normal weight with a history of juvenile-onset obesity is consonant with Bruch's formulation (1977) of the "fat-thin syndrome." This syndrome is seen in formerly obese individuals who, even after having attained a normal weight level and maintaining it for a significant number of years, continue to think of themselves as fat and unattractive. These individuals are described as intensely preoccupied with thoughts of food, engaging in a detailed planning of every eating situation, and becoming extremely anxious if they gain even a small amount of weight. Bruch felt that the psychodynamic reasons for this particular syndrome were similar to the dynamics of developmental obesity, which she considered a serious psychopathological disorder.

However, because of some type of environmental influence, these "fat-thin" individuals are able to exert control over their eating behavior. None-theless, Bruch felt that the psychodynamic conflicts are still those of a fat person, and that the only way this control over their eating behavior can be achieved is through the constant vigilance over the preoccupation with food and dieting that these persons manifest. Individuals manifesting this syndrome, however, retain the lack of body identity and the other features of the distorted body image of the developmentally obese (Bruch, 1977; Wolman, 1982).

In evaluating the issue of body-image distortions in obese individuals, it is extremely important to bear in mind the particular subject population that has been sampled. Clearly, persons who are seeking short-term or extended psychotherapeutic help for their obesity problem and who are desperately unhappy about their weight status are different in a number of ways from persons who are overweight and would like to lose weight, but whose weight status has not become an overriding issue in their lives. Some persons manifest serious psychological problems that may be exacer-bated by their obese state, although these problems have not necessarily caused their obesity. Furthermore, one can question whether an extremely obese person who feels that he or she is unattractive and extremely large is indeed manifesting a body-image disturbance, or a fairly accurate evalua-tion of his or her appearance with respect to current societal standards of ideal body weight.

In adolescence, a serious deviation from the accepted norms of ap-pearance may be viewed with alarm by youngsters. Many adolescents are preoccupied with a skin blemish or other bodily imperfections that may be only barely visible to another person. Juvenile-onset obesity can be concep-tualized as an extremely visible physical deviation. The ramifications of this deviation may include teasing by peers and family members and an inadequate opportunity to learn appropriate social skills. Obese young-sters develop an extremely poor self-concept and body image. These pain-ful experiences can exert a continuing negative psychological influence (Leon, 1982). Depressed individuals often develop devious and morbid methods of coping with their feeling of depression. Some of them turn to alcohol; a frequent and generous intake of alcohol gives them the illusion of power. When intoxicated, they believe themselves to be attractive, socia-ble, ready to embrace the entire world, and able to bring about an easy solution to all ills. They become elated and hyperoptimistic. Some of them turn to drugs that give them feelings of profound euphoria and omnipo-tence. Some depressed individuals turn to food; they become overeating addicts (Wolman, 1973, 1984).

Staying obese is one of the choices in the self-defeating behavior of depressed people. Being obese invites dislike, criticism, ridicule, and even ostracism. Children call an obese child disparaging names. Friends and relatives are usually eager to offer unkind remarks about overweight, sugar-coated as advice and guidance.

Many obese people tend to withdraw from social contacts, to lose their friends, and to lead a lonely life. Eating becomes their main source of consolation and comfort. A vicious circle evolves; being overweight, they invite criticism and rejection, which induces them to avoid unpleasant encounters and to seek comfort in food, which then makes them more obese, more rejected, more isolated, and so they eat more. Obesity leads to alienation, and alienation may contribute to obesity (Wolman, 1978).

The obese show defects of adaptation and an overall immaturity. They frequently show defects characterized by such words as *withdrawn* or *seclusive*. Associated with these defects is a sense of helplessness, a conviction of inadequacy and inner ugliness, and derogatory and self-destructive attitudes, which are compensated for by flights of fancy and daydreams (Bruch, 1973).

My obese patients often tell me the following story of their dieting: They have tried to lose weight and have gone on all kinds of diets, with or without medications. Sometimes, they have lost weight in a short time but have regained it as fast as they lost it or even faster, for indeed, they did not want to lose weight. In most instances, they wished to lose weight and feared getting slim; consciously, they liked the idea of losing weight, but their unconscious fear prevailed. Their obesity served as a sort of an alibi for passivity and failure, and getting slim would have deprived them of the excuse of being passive. Some of my patients feared sexual relations and used their obesity as a convenient excuse; dieting would have eliminated this defense mechanism and would have forced them to face their problem.

Failure in dieting further contributes to one's feeling of helplessness. Quite often, my patients complain about their lack of willpower and their inability to control their eating habits. This failure represents a self-fulfilling prophecy, for they wish to fail.

Obesity and Schizophrenia

Depressive mood can be associated with various clinical entities. In my books and papers on schizophrenia, I have related the etiology of schizophrenia to peculiar intrafamilial dynamics. When two parents, disappointed and displeased with one another, expect their child to compensate for their misery and to meet their emotional needs, they create a reversal of social roles and a displacement of libido cathexes. The child is forced to give more love than he or she receives from the parents. Instead of the normal, instrumental child–parent attitude, the child is forced to assume a precocious vectorial attitude and to become, as it were, the parent of his or her parents. Thus, I have called schizophrenia *vectoriasis praecox* (1966), and my book on schizophrenia in childhood is entitled *Children without Childhood* (1970). The child doomed to become schizophrenic is supposed to be a model child; he or she is constantly exposed to exaggerated parental expectations and demands (the "overdemanded" child). However, because no child can satisfy these morbid parental demands, the efforts of the schizophrenic-to-be are doomed to fail, and a profound feeling of frustration and helplessness ensues. Schizophrenics are usually more depressed than manic-depressive psychotics; they hate themselves for hating their parents. Some of them—the paranoid schizophrenics—project their hatred onto others; catatonics, out of fear of their own anger, paralyze themselves. When the defenses collapse, schizophrenics act in uncontrollable fury. In my book *Call No Man Normal* (1973), I referred to them as "fallen angels." Obesity facilitates withdrawal from social relations.

Bruch (1958) moved away from a classical psychoanalytic interpretation of eating disorders to a psychodynamic formulation based on a distinction between what she termed "developmental" and "reactive" types of obesity. She regarded the former as a deep-seated disturbance resembling preschizophrenic development. Developmental obesity is conceptualized as beginning in infancy and as being caused by a fundamental feeling of rejection by the mother toward her child. Because of these strong feelings of rejection, the mother attempts to compensate by overprotective behaviors toward her child, including excessive feeding. Specifically, the mother is perceived as responding to all of the child's needs by the giving of food. Therefore, as the child develops, he or she is unable to distinguish between the various bodily urges and sensations. The result of the mother's food-giving behavior is that the child develops a disturbed body image and a lack of body identity (i.e., a feeling of not owning one's own body). Reactive obesity, on the other hand, is viewed as occurring primarily in adults in response to traumatic environmental circumstances. This type of obesity is not seen as being so integrally involved in fundamental life relationships. However, in both types of obesity, symptom removal without dealing with the underlying causes of the disorder may be expected to result in a deterioration of functioning.

REFERENCES

Alexander, F. *Psychosomatic medicine.* New York: Norton, 1950.

Alexander, F., & Flagg, G. W. The psychosomatic approach. In B. B. Wolman (Ed.), *Handbook of clinical psychology* (pp. 855–947). New York: McGraw-Hill, 1965.

Alexander, F., French, T. M., & Pollock, G. H. *Psychosomatic specificity: Experimental study and research.* Chicago: University of Chicago Press, 1968.

Atkinson, R. M., & Ringuette, E. A survey of biographical and psychological features in extraordinary fatness. *Psychosomatic medicine,* 1967, *29,* 121–133.

Baird, M. Characteristic interaction patterns in families of encoprectic children. *Bulletin of Menninger Clinic,* 1974, *38,* 144–153.

Beaumont, J. G. *Introduction to neuropsychology*. New York: Guilford, 1984.

Bemporad, J. R. Encopresis. In B. B. Wolman, J. Egan, & A. O. Ross (Eds.), *Handbook of treatment of mental disorders in childhood and adolescence* (pp. 161–178). Englewood Cliffs, NJ: Prentice-Hall, 1978.

Bruch, H. *The importance of overweight*. New York: Norton, 1958.

Bruch, H. Anorexia nervosa and its differential diagnosis. *Journal of Nervous Diseases*, 1966, *141*, 155–170.

Bruch, H. Obesity and orality. *Contemporary Psychoanalysis*, 1969, *5*, 129–144.

Bruch, H. Family transactions in eating disorders. *Comprehensive Psychiatry*, 1971, *12*, 238–248.

Bruch, H. *Eating disorders: Obesity, anorexia nervosa, and the person within*. New York: Basic Books, 1973.

Bruch, H. Obesity and its treatment. In B. B. Wolman (Eds.), *International encyclopedia of psychiatry, psychology, psychoanalysis and neurology* (Vol. 8, pp. 95–106). New York: Aescuplapius Publishers, 1977.

Bruch, H. Anorexia nervosa: Therapy and theory. *American Journal of Psychiatry*, 1982, *12*, 139–145.

Cavanaugh, R. M., Jr. Encopresis in children and adolescents. *American Family Physician*, 1983, *27*, 107–114.

Coddington, R. D., Bruch, H., & Keller, J. Gastric perceptivity in normal, obese and schizophrenic subjects. Quoted in B. B. Wolman (Ed.), *Handbook of clinical psychology*. New York: McGraw-Hill, 1965.

Darby, P. L., Garfinkel, P. E., Garner, D. M., & Coscino, D. W. *Anorexia nervosa: Recent developments in research*. New York: Liss, 1983.

Drossman, D. A. The physician and the patient. In M. H. Slesenger & J. S. Fordtran (Eds.), *Gastrointestinal disease: Pathophysiology, diagnosis and management*. Philadelphia: Saunders, 1983.

Feuerstein, M., Labbé, E. E., & Kuczmierczyk, A. R. *Health psychology: A psychobiological perspective*. New York: Plenum Press, 1986.

Garfinkel, P. E., & Garner, D. M. *Anorexia nervosa: A multidimensional perspective*. New York: Brunner/Mazel, 1982.

Gentry, W. D. (Ed.). *Handbook of behavioral medicine*. New York: Guilford, 1984.

Gottsfeld, H. Body and self-cathexis of super-obese patients. *Journal of Psychosomatic Research*, 1962, *6*, 177–183.

Grace, W. J., Wolf, S., & Wolf, H. G. *The human colon*. New York: Hoeber-Harper, 1951.

Halmi, K. A. The state of research in anorexia nervosa and bulimia. *Psychiatric Developments*, 1983, *1*, 247–257.

Halmi, K. A. Anorexia nervosa and bulimia. In W. Dorfman & L. Cristofar (Eds.), *Psychosomatic illness review* (pp. 37–51). New York: Macmillan, 1985.

Hamburg, D. A., Elliot, G. R., & Parron, D. L. (Eds.). *Health and behavior: Frontiers of research in the biobehavioral sciences*. Washington, DC: National Academy Press, 1982.

Karush, A., Daniels, G. E., Flood, C., & O'Connor, J. F. *Psychotherapy in chronic ulceratice colitis*. Philadelphia: Saunders, 1977.

King, A. Primary and secondary anorexia nervosa syndromes. *British Journal of Psychiatry*, 1963, *109*, 470–479.

Langford, W. S. Psychological aspects of ulcerative colitis. *Clinical Proceedings of the Children's Hospital*, Washington, 1964, *30*, 89–97.

Latimer, P. R. Irritable bowel syndrome. In W. Dorfman & L. Cristofar (Eds.), *Psychosomatic illness review* (pp. 61–75). New York: Macmillan, 1985.

Leon, G. R. Personality and behavioral correlates of obesity. In B. B. Wolman (Ed.), *Psychological aspects of obesity* (pp. 15–29). New York: Van Nostrand Reinhold, 1982.

Locke, S., Ader, R., Besedovsky, H., Hall, N., Solomon, G., & Strom, T. (Eds.). *Foundations of psychoneuroimmunology*. Hawthorne, NY: Aldine, 1984.

McKerns, K. W., & Pantić, V. *Neuroendocrine correlates*. New York: Plenum Press, 1985.

Minuchin, S., Roman, B., & Baker, L. *Psychosomatic families: Anorexia nervosa in context.* Cambridge: Harvard University Press, 1978.

Mirsky, I. A. Psychoanalysis and the biological sciences. In F. Alexander & H. Ross (Eds.), *Twenty years of psychoanalysis.* New York: Norton, 1958.

Oken, D. Gastrointestinal disorders. In H. I. Kaplan & B. J. Sadock (Eds.), *Comprehensive handbook of psychiatry* (4th ed., pp. 1121–1132). Baltimore: Williams & Wilkins, 1985.

Pierce, C. M. Encopresis. In H. I. Kaplan & B. J. Sadock (Eds.), *Comprehensive handbook of psychiatry* (pp. 1847–1850). Baltimore: Williams & Wilkins, 1985.

Pilot, M., Rubin, J., Schafer, R., & Spiro, H. M. Duodenal ulcer in one of identical twins. *Psychosomatic Medicine,* 1963, *25*(3).

Powers, P. S. Obesity. In W. Dorfman & L. Cristofar (Eds.), *Psychosomatic illness review* (pp. 23–36). New York: Macmillan, 1985.

Prugh, D. G. The influence of emotional factors on the clinical course of ulcerative colitis in children. *Gastroenterology,* 1951, *18*, 339–354.

Purcell, K., Weiss, J., & Hahn, W. Certain psychosomatic disorders. In B. B. Wolman (Ed.), *Manual of child psychopathology* (pp. 706–749). New York: McGraw-Hill, 1972.

Rosenbaum, M. Ulcerative colitis. In W. Dorfman & L. Cristofar (Eds.), *Psychosomatic illness review* (pp. 76–89). New York: Macmillan, 1985.

Roy, C. C., Silverman, A., & Corretto, F. *Pediatric clinical gastroenterology.* St. Louis: Mosby, 1975.

Schachter, S., & Rodin, J. *Obese humans and rats.* New York: Halstead Press, 1974.

Selvini-Palazzoli, M. *Self-starvation.* New York: Jason Aronson, 1978.

Sperling, M. Psychoanalytic study of ulcerative colitis in children. *Psychoanalytic Quarterly,* 1946, *15*, 302–329.

Stunkard, A. J. (Ed.). *Obesity.* Philadelphia: Saunders, 1980.

Stunkard, A. J. Obesity. In H. J. Kaplan & B. J. Sadock (Eds.), *Comprehensive handbook of psychiatry* (4th ed.), (pp. 1133–1142). Baltimore: Williams & Wilkins, 1985.

Stunkard, A. J., & Koch, C. The interpretation of gastric motility: Apparent bias in the reports of hunger by obese persons. *Archives of General Psychiatry,* 1964, *11*, 74–85.

Stunkard, A. J., & Mendelson, M. Obesity and body image: Characteristics of disturbances in the body image of some obese persons. *American Journal of Psychiatry,* 1967, *10*, 123–130.

Touyz, S. W., Beamont, P. J. V., & Glaun, D. Refeeding patients with anorexia nervosa. In P. Pichot, P. Berner, R. Wolf, & K. Thau (Eds.), *Psychiatry: The state of the art: Vol. 4. Psychotherapy and psychosomatic medicine.* New York: Plenum Press, 1985.

Tudor, R. R. Peptic ulcerations in childhood. *Pediatric Clinics in North America,* 1967, *14*, 109–139.

Vandersall, T. A. Ulcerative colitis. In B. B. Wolman, J. Egan, & A. O. Ross (Eds.), *Handbook of treatment of mental disorders in childhood and adolescence* (pp. 144–152). Englewood Cliffs, NJ: Prentice-Hall, 1978.

Weiner, H. M. *Psychobiology and human disease.* New York: Elsevier, 1977.

Weiss, J. H. Behavioral and psychological influences on gastrointestinal pathology: Experimental techniques and findings. In W. D. Gentry (Ed.), *Handbook of behavioral medicine* (pp. 174–221). New York: Guilford Press, 1984.

Wolf, S. Peptic ulcer. In W. Dorfman & L. Cristofar (Eds.), *Psychosomatic illness review* (pp. 52–60). New York: Macmillan, 1985.

Wolman, B. B. *Vectoriasis praecox or the group of schizophrenics.* Springfield, IL: Thomas, 1966.

Wolman, B. B. *Children without childhood: A study of childhood schizophrenia.* New York: Grune & Stratton, 1970.

Wolman, B. B. *Call no man normal.* New York: International Universities Press, 1973.

Wolman, B. B. *Children's fears.* New York: Grosset & Dunlop, 1978.

Wolman, B. B. Obesity and depression. In B. B. Wolman (Ed.), *Psychological aspects of obesity: A handbook* (pp. 88–103). New York: Van Nostrand Reinhold, 1982.

Wolman, B. B. *Interactional psychotherapy.* New York: Van Nostrand Reinhold, 1984.

15

Cardiovascular Diseases

ETIOLOGY

Coronary heart disease, essential hypertension (EH), and other cardiovascular diseases account for one of every two deaths in the United States (Krantz & Manuck, 1984). According to the *Mortality and Morbidity Weekly Report* of December 19, 1986 (published by the Center for Disease Control, U.S. Department of Health and Human Services), in 1984, in the United States, 1,563,000 people died of heart disease and 290,000 of cerebrovascular disease.

There are many causes of cardiovascular diseases; some are related to genetic predisposition, and some are related to other physical diseases. However, exposure to stressful events, occupational pressure, repeated failures and frustrations, marital discord, improper parent–child relationships, and poor social relations increase the risk of cardiovascular diseases (Elliott & Eisdorfer, 1982; Hamburg, Elliott, & Parron, 1982). In some instances, these psychological stressors cause cardiovascular diseases, but when they are not the causes, they are definitely contributing factors to the onset, the continuation, and the grave deterioration caused by existing incipient cardiovascular disease.

One need not, however, overlook the role of elevated norepinephrine and cholesterol levels, inappropriate nutrition, lack of exercise, and other physical and chemical factors (Kaplan & Kimball, 1982).

As has already been discussed, the mind–body and body–mind transition is continuous. The central nervous system serves as a bridge for the transition, and it links psychological factors to cardiac dysfunction. Cardiac death is most often related to myocardial disease and especially to coronary atherosclerosis, but it greatly depends on a variety of physiological and psychological factors mediated by the central nervous system (Feuerstein, Labbé, & Kuczmierczyk, 1986).

Behavioral tension can cause a rise in arterial blood pressure and a reduction in renal blood flow. Even a moderate irritation or a sudden anger or fear can instantly and temporarily affect cardiovascular functions. An elevation in blood pressure and an acceleration in the heartbeat are frequent and are not necessarily morbid phenomena. However, frequent and severe psychological stress mediated by the central nervous system can cause a precipitous release of chemical mediators that could lead to acute myocardial infarction (AMI) and even to sudden coronary death.

An individual who tends to react to stress through the cardiovascular system, and thus to affect its regular functions, may be inclined to develop a pathophysiological decompensation that could lead to myocardial infarction.

Coronary Heart Disease

Coronary heart disease (CHD) remains the primary cause of premature death in the United States. Coronary heart disease, as well as atherosclerotic heart disease and ischemic heart disease, is a condition in which atherosclerosis is the primary characteristic. The clinical complications include angina pectoris, sudden arrhythmic death, and myocardial infarction (MI).

There is little evidence concerning the genetic origins of coronary heart disease; the main risk factors are elevated serum cholesterol, hypertension, smoking, physical inactivity, obesity, age, sex, diabetes mellitus, and familial history. Rosenman and Chesney (1982) have added a highly relevant psychological risk factor: the *Type A personality*. Type A is characterized by expressive facial and body gestures, rapidity and explosiveness of speech, restlessness, time urgency, irritability, lack of patience, overdriven ambition, overassertiveness, and highly competitive, intolerant and hostile attitudes toward others. The Type A personality is by far more frequent and more pronounced in males than in females.

In 1963, serum lipids and lipoproteins were determined on 20 men in a "blind study" by Rosenman and associates (Chesney & Rosenman, 1982). Of these men, 10 exhibited the overt behavior Type A, which in earlier work was associated with a high prevalence of clinical coronary heart disease, and 10 showed a converse overt behavior pattern (Type B). The men exhibiting Type A behavior were found to have high serum levels of triglycerides, phospholipids, cholesterol, serum beta, and other low-density lipoprotein lipids, as well as significantly lower a/b lipoprotein cholesterol ratios, which were not ascribable to differences in diet, weight, or physical activity. They displayed an overt behavior pattern important in the pathogenesis of coronary heart disease occurring in young and middle-aged men, characterized notably by enhanced drive, competitiveness, ambitiousness, and an excessive sense of urgency of time, which appeared to stem from their involvement in multiple vocational and avocational pursuits subject to "deadline" time pressures.

The occupations in the Type B group demanded neither competitive activity nor preoccupation with deadlines, such as municipal employment in clerical or accounting duties, embalming, and routine bookkeeping.

Physiological studies of people afflicted by coronary heart disease point to increased serum triglyceride activity before and after the digestion of a fast meal and elevated norepinephrine levels during a contest.

Psychophysiological studies have found that most CHD patients exhibit elevations in systolic blood pressure but not in diastolic blood pressure or heart rate, and that they exhibit considerable decreases in pulse transmit time when confronted with a difficult, stressful condition. Coronary heart disease seems to be more related to suppressed anger and hostile feelings than to other emotions. As a rule, CHD patients tend to hide and suppress their symptoms (Feuerstein *et al.*, 1986; Krantz & Manuck, 1984).

Type A individuals have been distinguished from Type B by their psychological and physiological sensitivity to challenge. Type A individuals have high autonomic and neuroendocrine responses under challenge and slower recovery rates. These findings are related to sympathetic arousal and the associated endocrine activity in the development of atherosclerosis.

Middle-aged men who have high blood pressure, and high serum cholesterol and who smoke have more than a 6-to-1 chance of developing a first major coronary attack over men of the same age with none of these risk factors. Men with two of the three risk factors have a 4.5-to-1 chance; men with one of the risk factors have a 2.5-to-1 chance of contracting coronary heart disease.

However, during 10 years of observation, 14% of men with all three above-mentioned risk factors developed coronary heart disease, 9% did not, and 5% with one risk factor had a coronary attack (Marmot & Winkelstein, 1975). Apparently, there are other risk factors than those mentioned.

It seems that there are at least two additional possibilities (i.e., genetic and sociocultural factors) that predispose one to coronary heart disease. When people of a certain ethnic and probably of a common genetic background migrate from a low-CHD area to a high CHD-area, their incidence of coronary heart disease increases (Syme, Marmor, Kougan, Kato, & Rhoads, 1975). A study among Japanese migrants found the lowest rates in Japan proper, medium rates in Hawaii, and the highest rate in California of morbidity and mortality from coronary heart disease. As mentioned in Part II of this book, those Japanese migrants who adopted the Western way of life, acculturating quickly, had a much higher rate of coronary heart disease than those who maintained the traditional Japanese ways (Marmot & Syme, 1976).

Minc, Sinclair, and Taft (1963) related the efficiency of cardiovascular adaptation to an adequate arousal of the autonomic nervous system. Individuals who exercise more intellectual control are prone to cardiocoronary disturbances. Thus, coronary disease may be caused by socially imposed pressures that lead to an intellectually controlled mode of activity and to an insufficient integration of emotional with rational activity. Coronary patients seem to be more inhibited in both behavior and cerebral cortical functioning. In many instances, the level of cortical alertness has been environmentally determined. However, Minc *et al.* (1963) cited evidence that subjects with high serum cholesterol have a constitutional temperament incompatible with inhibited behavior. Apparently, in most cases, coronary heart disease is caused by a combination of physiological and psychological elements. Which element represents the cause and which the effect has been neither consistently nor clearly established.

Cleveland and Johnson (1962) studied 25 males hospitalized with myocardial infarction. The research controls were males awaiting serious surgery and 25 males with benign skin disorders. The coronary patients showed a great deal of anxiety concerning physical harm, decline, and death; they also experienced, but did not express, feelings of hostility. The anxiety level for the group with skin disorders was significantly below that in both the coronary and the presurgery groups because they were obviously not in an immediately life-threatening situation. The coronary patients were frightened and felt shattered, as though their lives hung by a thread.

The coronary patients were significantly less achievement-oriented than the controls. They felt a hopeless, "what's-the-use" attitude and showed nostalgia for the past. Some of them tried to find religious salvation. The precoronary patients were unable to relax. They tried to control their anxiety and to behave in a conventional manner, to give the impression of being controlled and cautious individuals.

Many cardiac patients have a close relationship with their fathers and perceive their mothers to be cold, distant people, most of the time depressed and dissatisfied (reported by Alexander & Flagg, 1965).

FAMILY BACKGROUND

Thomas (1961) investigated the precursors of hypertension and coronary disease, including genetic, physiological, metabolic, and psychological characteristics in young and healthy individuals. Her observations could be summarized as follows:

1. Children with two parents affected with hypertension and/or coronary disease are quite different from the children of two unaffected

parents. They are, on the average, 10 pounds heavier, have hypo-
cholesteremia and higher resting systolic blood pressure, and are
likely to be smokers.
2. Children of two obese parents are distinguished by their own excessive weight and higher cholesterol levels.
3. Children of two parents unaffected by hypertension, coronary artery disease, obesity, or diabetes tend to weigh less. Most of them
have lower cholesterol levels and lower systolic blood pressure,
and fewer of them smoke.
4. Children with at least one parent affected by hypertension and/or
coronary heart disease tend to react with anger and tremulousness
when under stress. They tend to have a strong need to eat and an
urge to confide and seek advice.

Parental approval or disapproval contingent on improved performance in children who are predisposed to a heightened response to "loss
of control" or "disapproval" and who tend toward social comparisons
explains the tendency for these individuals to show overdriven, ambitious
behavior; striving for perfection; excessive self-assertion; impatience; and
proneness to develop coronary heart disease. The tendency to develop
coronary heart disease is somewhat associated socially and economically
with the occupational and other pressures of the middle class (Cleveland &
Johnson, 1962; Kaplan & Kimball, 1982; Weiner, 1977).

Parents' pressures and their overdemanding attitude serve as a modeling and conditioning pattern in the offspring. In many instances, these
characteristics lead to the development of competitive and aggressive behavior and Type A personality patterns (Feuerstein *et al.*, 1986).

THE WORK ENVIRONMENT

There seems to be an etiological relationship between emotional,
work-related tension (especially suppressed anger) and angina pectoris,
coronary artery disease, hypertension, and stroke (cerebrovascular acci-
dent). The expressions "Don't have a stroke," "Don't have a coronary,"
and "Don't get your blood pressure up" are not chance remarks.

Warren (1963) studied cases of myocardial infarction in a large industrial utility. He found that 79.4% of the attacks were experienced in the 46-
to 60-year age group and that the place where the coronary occlusion
occurred was related to the time spent in that specific activity. Hypertension, obesity, diabetes, peptic ulcer, renal disease, and smoking were related to an increased incidence of myocardial infarction.

Pell and D'Alonzo (1963) studied 1,356 employed patients from 25 to
64 years of age. These authors found that the risk of infarction appeared to

be inversely related to job level. An increase of attacks occurred during the waking hours in persons with hypertension and/or diabetes and in overweight men under 45.

The *person–environment fit theory* hypothesizes that an incompatibility, or "poor fit," between the job's demand and the worker's skills and abilities and/or the job's not fulfilling a worker's personal needs results in occupational stress. According to this theory, the lack of fit results in job stress, psychological distress, and/or negative health outcomes, and it could contribute to the development of coronary heart disease (Feuerstein *et al.*, 1986). Apparently, there is a correlation between work load and anxiety in Type A's in varying occupations. Moreover, Type A workers tend to indicate dissatisfaction with their subordinates, to feel misunderstood by their supervisors, and to wish to work alone when under threat. Type A individuals tend to become overinvolved in their jobs and unwillingly and unwittingly to create more stress for themselves.

ESSENTIAL HYPERTENSION: SYMPTOMS

Essential hypertention, a disorder of the cardiovascular system, is an abnormally high blood pressure. Essential hypertension may lead to myocardial infarction or stroke, and it is responsible for over 15% of all deaths in people over 50 years old. It is caused by constriction of the smaller blood vessels. Several studies (e.g., Herd, 1984) point to a multiplicity of etiological factors related to essential hypertension: Essential hypertension can be a product of neuroendocrine or psychological factors, or a combination of both. Essential hypertension can be related to stresses of modern life as well as to overweight and increased salt consumption. It is interesting to note that many hypertension patients still prefer diets high in salt (Weiner, 1980), which could indicate their self-defeating attitude.

The symptoms of essential hypertension include heart palpitation, dizziness, headaches, and excessive fatigue. The following are the pathophysiological effects of essential hypertension (Taylor & Fortman, 1985, p. 92):

1. Fibrinoid necrosis.
2. Hyperplasia in the intima of the arterioles.
3. Atherosclerosis.
4. Necrosis of the tunica media of the ascending portion of the aorta (aneurysms).

There have been two main approaches to describing the physiology of blood pressure:

1. The *renin–angiotensin system*. The renin–angiotensin–aldosterone axis is the basic control system for simultaneously regulating arterial pressure and the sodium balance (Laragh, 1980).

2. *Blood-volume control in the kidneys.* There is a good deal of evidence of a powerful effect of the kidneys on blood pressure regulation (Guyton, 1980).

As mentioned above, the incidence of essential hypertension increases with age, and under age 50, it is more frequent in men than in women.

PSYCHOLOGICAL FACTORS

There is some evidence that a certain psychological personality type could be particularly prone to developing essential hypertension, but probably, some individuals are genetically predisposed to increased cardiovascular responsiveness. Adverse psychological stimuli, stress, acute anxiety, resentment, and anger can cause an increase in sodium retention in the kidneys and can cause cardiovascular dysfunction (Krantz & Manuck, 1984). A complication in the essential hypertension and hypertensive fibrinoid arteritis may cause rupture of the vessels and may produce a massive cerebral hemorrhage. Hypertensive individuals are prone to renal vasoconstriction and may develop a variety of lethal complications related to dysfunctions of the sympathetic nervous system and its impact on the kidneys. Moreover, the brain of hypertensive individuals tends to become edematous and is predisposed to focal lesions, such as hemorrhage or infarcts (Cassem, 1984; Goldstein, 1981; McKerns & Pantiĉ, 1985).

As mentioned above, several researchers (e.g., Alexander, 1950; Shapiro, 1977) have maintained that hypertension is most often related to suppressed hostile feelings that cause an increase in norepinephrine and elevated blood pressure. The hypothesis of suppressed hostility has had considerable follow-up (Gentry, 1984).

ESSENTIAL HYPERTENSION: THE NERVOUS SYSTEM

In the early phase of the disease, the blood pressure is labile and fluctuates markedly, but in later stages, it becomes stabilized at a high level and may cause secondary kidney and heart damage. The elevated arterial pressure is attributed to a widespread constriction of the arterioles throughout the vascular system. The pressor responses in early hypertension (such as reactions to external stimuli, such as immersion of the hand in ice water, to physical work, and to emotional conflicts) increase blood pressure (Goldstein, 1981; Gottschalk, 1979).

According to Katz (1962), the involvement of the nervous system in essential hypertension includes (1) afferent nerves from many external and internal sensors and (2) the complex CNS cybernetic apparatus (the hypothalamus, the thalamus, the limbic areas, and the cerebral cortex). These hypertension impulses reach their final common paths in the efferent nerves to the systemic arterioles, the venules, and the heart and through the efferent nerves, to the kidney vasculature, the excretory apparatus, and/or its secretory portion (the juxtaglomerular apparatus), where renin is formed. In addition, some afferent impulses probably act on the endocrine glands, notably the adrenal medulla and cortex and the anterior and posterior pituitary (Goldstein, 1981; Herd, 1984; McKerns & Pantiĉ, 1985; Weiner, 1977).

Often, people show a high blood-pressure elevation in response to stressful stimuli. In one individual, the stressors may cause a temporary rise in blood pressure, whereas in another person, the same stimuli may cause an excessive rise in blood pressure for a protracted time and may cause hypertension. Katz (1962) assumed that the continuation of hypertensive episodes leads to an anatomical change in the arterioles, and hypertension develops. It seem apparent that the autonomic nervous system is involved in hypertension.

Many studies have related psychogenic factors to the aggravation of symptoms in essential hypertension. Stressing the role of inhibited hostile tendencies in chronic hypertension follows Cannon's observation (1932) that fear and rage produce increased blood pressure because of activation of the sympathetic nervous system and the secretion of epinephrine (Heilman & Satz, 1983; McKerns & Pantiĉ, 1985).

Alexander (1950) commented that the chronic inhibited aggressive impulses associated with anxiety influence blood-pressure levels. Alexander's studies at the Chicago Institute for Psychoanalysis outlined certain characteristics of the hypertensive patient. Hypertensive patients have in common the inability to express aggressive impulses freely, and they maintain a remarkable degree of self-control. They usually give the impression of being well-adjusted and mature individuals. They are compliant and tend to please, and although they are ambitious, they limit their competition to their fantasy lives. The more they are compliant, the greater is their reactive hostility to those to whom they submit. There is pronounced conflict between passive-dependent or feminine tendencies and compensatory, aggressive-hostile impulses. Sexual inhibitions are common in these people, and illicit relationships produce a great amount of guilt. Even rebellion against their own submissiveness produces anxiety and forces a retreat from competition to a passive-dependent attitude. A vicious circle ensues because the passive dependency stirs up more inferiority feelings and hostilities. An emotional paralysis results from the opposing tendencies of submission and aggression.

MITRAL VALVE PROLAPSE

The mitral valve prolapse (MVP) is a cardiovascular disorder closely associated with anxiety and states of panic. The main symptoms of the mitral valve prolapse are arrhythmias, ballooning of the valve, and systolic murmur. The psychological symptoms are severe anxiety, feelings of fatigue, dizziness, and chest pain. Most patients afflicted by mitral valve prolapse have been diagnosed as exceedingly prone to anxiety states, having frequent symptoms of discomfort and cardiac arrhythmias (Cassem, 1984; Weiss & Engel, 1971). It seems that stress and the feelings of insecurity and inadequacy are the blows of a hammer that fall on the morbid physiological anvil, and that, together, they cause the psychological states of anxiety and/or panic that lead to pathophysiological coronary arrhythmia and the disease of mitral valve prolapse, which can be fatal.

VARIOUS CARDIOVASCULAR DISEASES

In nearly all cardiovascular diseases, the physical symptoms are concomitant with psychological symptoms, such as depression, feelings of discomfort, hypochondriacal fears, and acute anxiety. In many instances, the cardiac symptoms are followed by or are associated with panic states that may lead to paroxysmal coronary attacks (Dohrenwend & Dohrenwend, 1981; Weiner, 1977).

Obviously, not all cardiovascular diseases are caused by psychological conditions, nor do all states of anxiety or panic lead to cardiovascular disorders. However, morbid psychological states can cause cardiological diseases, and people afflicted by prolonged and grave anxiety states are more prone to developing cardiovascular disorders. In many instances, severe attacks of panic can lead to serious and life-threatening heart troubles. Coronary artery disease, heart block, congestive heart failure, and so on are physical, pathophysiological phenomena, but in many instances, emotional disorders are a quite important contributing factor, acting on an existing physical coronary predisposition (Weiner, 1977). The various cardiac arrhythmias, such as atrial fibrillation, paroxysmal atrial tachycardia, and ventricular fibrillation, which are serious and often fatal conditions, are at least partially related to psychological factors. Quite often, emotional stress and anxiety precede cardiac failure and sudden death.

Many cardiac patients have a history of depression and of hypochondriacal attitudes: "Patients suffering generalized anxiety may complain of palpitations, tremulousness and tachycardia . . . weakness and fatigue may accompany depression, cardiac ailments, congestive heart failure, and cardiac therapy" (Hackett, Rosenbaum, & Cassem, 1985, p. 1150). "About 20 percent of patients with acute, life threatening ventricular arrhythmias had experienced a sudden emotional event as precipitant" (Hackett et al., 1985, p. 1153).

Herd (1984) summarized the impact of social, psychological, and behavioral factors on the physiological and biochemical processes related to the pathogenesis of cardiovascular disease. According to Herd, there are several lines of evidence that prove the following:

1. Behavioral factors are related to cardiovascular diseases.
2. There is a definitely proven association between Type A personality type and several kinds of heart diseases, including myocardial infarction and sudden cardiac death.
3. There is a clear association between inadequate social interaction and missing or weak social support and coronary heart disease.
4. Mental disorders, and especially cases of severe depression, are associated with angina pectoris, myocardial infarction, and some instances of cardiac death.

Apparently, psychosomatic disorders, including coronary diseases, are precipitated by environmental stressors such as moving, unemployment, the breaking up of close relationships, and bereavement. In many instances, the essential hypertension is related to crowded living conditions, poor neighborhoods, family tension, job pressures, loss of a job, unemployment, and other psychosocial tensions.

Exaggerated cardiovascular reactions to situational or behavioral stressors are linked to the incidence and prevalence of coronary arrhythmias, hypertension, coronary heart disease, and sudden cardiac death.

REFERENCES

Alexander, F. *Psychosomatic medicine*. New York: Norton, 1950.

Alexander, F., & Flagg, W. N. The psychosomatic approach. In B. B. Wolman (Ed.), *Handbook of clinical psychology* (pp. 855–947). New York: McGraw-Hill, 1965.

Cassem, N. H. Critical care psychiatry. In W. C. Shoemaker, W. I. Thompson, & P. H. Holbrook (Eds.), *Textbook of critical care*. Philadelphia: Saunders, 1984.

Cannon, W. B. *The wisdom of the body*. New York: Norton, 1932.

Center for Disease Control. *Morbidity and Mortality Weekly Report*, December 19, 1986.

Chesney, M. A., & Rosenman, R. H. Strategies for modifying type A behavior. *Consultant*, 1980, *20*, 216–222.

Cleveland, S. E., & Johnson, D. L. Personality patterns in young males with coronary disease. *Psychosomatic medicine*, 1962, *26*, 6–10.

Dohrenwend, B. S., & Dohrenwend, B. P. (Eds.), *Stressful life events and their contexts*. New York: Watson, 1981.

Elliott, G. R., & Eisdorfer, C. *Stress and human health: Analysis and implications of research*. New York: Springer, 1982.

Feuerstein, M., Labbé, E. E., & Kuczmierczyk, A. R. *Health psychology: A psychobiological perspective*. New York: Plenum Press, 1986.

Gentry, W. D. (Ed.). *Handbook of behavioral medicine*. New York: Guilford, 1984.

Goldstein, D. S. Plasma norepinephrine during stress in essential hypertension. *Hypertension*, 1981, *3*, 551–556.

Gottschalk, C. W. Renal nerves and sodium excretion. *Annual Review of Physiology*, 1979, *41*, 229–244.

Guyton, A. C. *Arterial pressure and hypertension*. Philadelphia: Saunders, 1980.

Hackett, T. P., Rosenbaum, J. F., & Cassem, N. H. Cardiovascular disorders. In H. I. Kaplan & B. J. Sadock (Eds.), *Comprehensive textbook of psychiatry* (4th ed., pp. 1148). Baltimore: Williams & Wilkins, 1985.

Hamburg, D. A., Elliott, G. R., & Parron, D. L. (Eds.). *Health and behavior: Frontiers of research in bio-behavioral sciences*. Washington, DC: National Academy Press, 1982.

Heilman, K. M., & Satz, P. (Eds.). *Neuropsychology of human emotions*. New York: Guilford, 1983.

Herd, J. A. Cardiovascular disease and hypertension. In W. D. Gentry (Ed.), *Handbook of behavioral medicine* (pp. 222–281). New York: Guilford Press, 1984.

Kaplan, W., & Kimball, C. The risk and course of coronary heart disease: A biopsychosocial perspective. In T. Millon, C. Green, & R. Meagher (Eds.), *Handbook of clinical health*. New York: Plenum Press, 1982.

Katz, L. N. Newer concepts in relation to hypertension. *California Medical Association Journal*, 1962, *97*, 4.

Krantz, D. S., & Manuck, S. B. Acute psychophysiologic reactivity and risk of cardiovascular disease: A review and methodologic critique. *Psychological Bulletin*, 1984, *96*, 435–464.

Laragh, J. H. Hypertension. *Drug Therapy*, 1980, *10*, 71–80.

Marmot, M., & Winkelstein, W., Jr. Epidemiologic observations on intervention trials for prevention of coronary heart disease. *American Journal of Epidemiology*, 1975, *101*, 177–181.

Marmot, M. G., & Syme, S. L. Acculturation and coronary heart disease in Japanese-Americans. *American Journal of Epidemiology*, 1976, *104*, 225–247.

McKerns, K. W., & Pantić, V. (Eds.). *Neuroendocrine correlates*. New York: Plenum Press. 1985.

Minc, S., Sinclair, G., & Taft, R. Some psychological factors in coronary heart disease. *Psychosomatic Medicine*, 1963, *25*, 2–12.

Pell, S., & D'Alonzo, C. A. Acute myocardial infarction in a large industrial population. *Journal of the American Medical Association*, 1963, *185*, 21–28.

Rosenman, R. H., & Chesney, M. A. Stress, type A behavior, and coronary disease. In L. Goldberger & S. Breznitz (Eds.), *Handbook of stress* (pp. 546–565). New York: Macmillan–Free Press, 1982.

Shapiro, A. P. Cardiovascular diseases: Psychosomatic aspects. In B. B. Wolman (Ed.), *International encyclopedia of psychiatry, psychology, psychoanalysis and neurology* (Vol. 3, pp. 22–27). New York: Aesculapius Publishers, 1977.

Syme, S. L., Marmor, M. G., Kougan, A., Kato, H., & Rhoads, G. Epidemiologic studies of coronary heart disease and stroke in Japanese men living in Japan, Hawaii and California: Introduction. *American Journal of Epidemiology*, 1975, *102*, 477–480.

Taylor, C. B., & Fortman, S. P. Essential hypertension. In W. Dorfman & L. Cristofar (Eds.), *Psychosomatic illness review* (pp. 90–106). New York: Macmillan, 1985.

Thomas, C. B. Pathogenic interrelations in hypertension and coronary artery disease. *Systematic Monographs Supplement*, 1961, *22*, 39–45.

Warren, J. E. Myocardial infarction in an industrial population. *Archives of Environmental Health*, 1963, *7*, 210–220.

Weiner, H. *Psychobiology and human disease*. New York: Elsevier, 1977.

Weiner, H., Hofer, M., & Stunkard, A. J. (Eds.). *Brain, behavior and bodily disease*. New York: Raven Press, 1980.

Weiss, T., & Engel, B. T. Operant conditioning on heart rate in patients with premature ventrical contractions. *Psychosomatic Medicine*, 1971, *33*, 301–321.

16

Skin Diseases

THE VITAL FUNCTIONS

The skin covers the entire body with a protective surface; it is the largest and the most exposed bodily organ. The skin performs numerous vital functions: it regulates the body's temperature and serves the sensory functions of reacting to touch, heat, and cold.

The human skin is quite sensitive to external influences, such as heat and cold, pressure, and blows. Physical harm to the human body often starts with the skin, and most accidents begin with damage to this protective cover. Small wonder that the skin is also sensitive to harmful influences coming from within the organism, both physical and mental (Medausky, 1980).

The weight of the skin of an average-sized adult is between 6 and 7½ pounds, and it has a surface area measuring approximately 2 square yards. The thickness of skin can vary from ⅟₃₂ of an inch to ⅛ of an inch. The composition of the skin includes numerous glands, nerves, skin cells (which are specialized), hair and hair follicles, and blood vessels (Katch & Katch, 1980).

ANATOMY AND PHYSIOLOGY

The skin is composed of three layers: the epidermis, the dermis, and the subdermis. The *epidermis* is the outer portion of the skin, which normally contains no blood vessels or nerves. The dead cells that are sloughed off are contained in the outer layer of the epidermis, called the *cornified layer,* or the *stratum corneum.* The epidermis is generally tough because it contains *keratin,* a hornlike material. The lighter layer, below the cornified layer, is called the *stratum lucidum.*

The skin that is visible on the surface of the body is made up mostly of dead cells. This surface skin is renewed slowly, as the dead cells are constantly being cast off, and smoother, healthier skin remains. Healthy skin has many *pores,* which are the openings of glands. The *sebaceous glands* secrete an oily fluid that causes the skin to appear either waxy or greasy. Hair, which is found nearly all over the body, grows from *follicles,* which are pits within the skin.

Just below the epidermis, which includes the cornified layer, the stratum lucidum, and the stratum mucosum, is the *dermis.* Hair follicles and a system of blood vessels are found throughout the dermis, along with the elastic fibers that are responsible for the elasticity of the skin. Nerves and nerve endings are found in the dermis, allowing sensations to be experienced. These nerve endings are responsible for keeping the skin out of danger by modifying conditions in emergencies such as cold or heat. The nerve endings alert the body to external dangers. The nerve endings for touch sensation exist in greater number than those for cold and heat. The dermis extends into the epidermis; therefore, the two layers interweave.

The third layer of the skin, called the *subdermis,* is located below the dermis. This layer is made up of fatty tissues that have the ability to insulate (Clark & Cumley, 1973).

Melanin, a brown to black pigment, influences the color of the skin. The production of melanin is caused by a sequence of biochemical reactions. This series begins with the oxidation of *tyrosine* and is catalyzed by *tyrosinase.* Tyrosine is an amino acid and tyrosinase is an enzyme. Heriditary factors determine how much melanin is produced. However, melanin can be present in greater amounts than normal, may be missing entirely, or may be distributed unevenly. When there is a small amount of melanin in the skin, the skin has a pink color. When the skin appears yellowish, this may be due to the presence of the pigment *carotene.* This pigment is often found in many vegetables and is related to vitamin A. When there is an excessive consumption of foods with vitamin A, the skin may become abnormally yellow. This condition is known as *carotenemia.* Other unnatural causes can create discoloration of the skin. Jaundice causes the skin to appear more yellow as the result of internal organs that are afflicted with some form of disease. Skin changes with age, irritation, or excessive exposure to sunlight or wind.

SKIN AND PSYCHOSOMATICS

The skin, being the protective surface of the body, is exposed to numerous harmful influences, and the nerve endings in the skin are recipients of a great variety of antigens. The skin is highly sensitive to pain, which can be elicited by physical and psychological factors. Most skin diseases are not lethal, but they are usually quite painful and may seriously affect the physical and mental functioning of an individual (Medansky, 1980).

Psychological factors and especially emotions exert considerable influences on the skin. Blushing is usually an expression of shame, and itching is a sign of impatience. The body surface is also the somatic locus of exhibitionism. Reflex changes in the skin, such as pallor and flushing, are constituent parts of the emotional states of rage and fear. The skin functions as an important sensory organ and is affected by conversion symptoms such as anesthesia and paresthesia. Clinical studies of skin manifestations as a part of neurotic symptomatology have been conducted on neurodermatitis, eczema, angioneurotic edema, uticaria, and pruritis. In eczema and neurodermatitis, sadomasochistic and exhibitionistic trends have been claimed to be correlated with the skin symptoms (Alexander & Flagg, 1965; Engels, 1983, 1985; Torch & Bishop, 1981).

All psychosomatic disorders serve a purpose, such as gaining affection or escaping from responsibilities. Psychosomatic disorders require visibility, and the skin is a choice location for visibility. The need to be seen and to get attention is well served by skin diseases, and with the exception of clearly organic cases, most skin diseases are psychosomatic.

Psychosomatic disorders are often associated with self-directed harmful behavior. Self-induced pain and accident-proneness are usually of psychosomatic origin. In skin diseases, scratching is of considerable etiological significance. Psychoanalytic studies imply that scratching is due to inhibited hostile impulses, which, because of guilt feelings, are deflected from their original target and are turned against oneself. Craving for physical signs of affection, such as being held, cuddled, stroked, and soothed, is involved in skin reactions to the feelings of guilt for being overdemanding. Scratching is used as a self-punishing defense mechanism (Alexander, 1950; Musaph, 1964, 1977).

ALLERGIES

Allergies have been defined as an "overreaction" of the organism's defense system. Usually, the body fights antigens (the foreign invading bodies) by producing antibodies, but in allergies, the development of antibodies in reaction to allergens is excessive and definitely out of proportion to the threat.

Allergies represent a combination of physicochemical and psychological determinants. The invading allergens can affect the gastrointestinal system, the respiratory system, and the skin. Allergic disorders vary from mild to very severe, and even lethal. Well over 10% of the U.S. population has some allergy, and one need not exclude the possibility of there being certain genetic predispositions to allergies.

Most probably, the "hammer-and-anvil" scheme mentioned in Chapter 15 applies to allergies. The genetic predisposition of the *immune system* is the anvil, and the *two hammers* are the allergens and the stressors. Parental rejection is a highly relevant emotional "hammer" in asthma; frustrations and the loss of a beloved person are relevant "hammers" in neurodermatitis; and the emotional inconsistency of a child's parents plays the role of "hammer" in infantile eczema.

DERMATITIS

Dermatitis is an inflammation of the skin. The inflammation can be caused by either physical or psychological factors or by both. Obsessive-compulsive neurotics, perfectionists, and anxiety- and guilt-ridden individuals often suffer from various skin ailments, especially dermatitis.

The main symptoms of dermatitis are reddening of the skin, erythema, crusting, blisters, scaling, cracking, oozing of fluids, and intense itching. The severity of the symptoms is usually related to an emotional disorder: disturbed individuals develop facial and genital lesions; the least disturbed have blisters on their hands (Whitlock, 1976).

Infantile dermatitis is most often a product of maternal rejection. The rejected child resents the rejecting mother, and the skin eruption may represent outbursts of anger and hostile feelings. Some children resent themselves for resenting the rejecting parents; they blame themselves for being the cause of maternal rejection and punish themselves for being "bad children".

Adult dermatitis is often caused by sexual conflicts, lack of self-esteem, and sexual problems.

A Case Report

A few years ago a young married woman was referred to me by a dermatologist. He had treated her unsuccessfully for two years for a recurring severe skin rash in the pubic area.

This very attractive 28-year-old woman came reluctantly to my office. She told me in a most angry and belligerent manner, that she is not a mental case, does not need any psychotherapy, and despises shrinks. I replied calmly that she was under no obligation to talk to me, but that her doctor had given up on treating her; he had told me that her problems must be psychogenic and had requested my help.

The young woman decided "to give me a chance." She asked, "Should I undress to show you the mess I am in?" When I told her that no psychoanalytic or other psychotherapeutic methods require undressing, she replied sarcastically, "How can you cure it if you refuse to look at it?" I explained to her that her doctor had given me, in writing, a detailed description of the symptoms and his diagnostic evaluation.

It took a while before we discovered the truth. Four years before, the woman had married a man 10 years her senior. Her husband was anxious to have children, but she had asked him "not to rush her." Two years before, the husband had made it clear that he did not intend to wait much longer. His words had sounded like an ultimatum and the young woman went off the birth control pill. However, something strange happened. She developed a pubic skin rash with intense itching. Sexual relations had become most uncomfortable, and quite often painful. The woman offered oral, manual, and any other sexual gratification to her husband, always with apologies and excuses, but the husband was quite annoyed about her skin rash.

She went for help. The kind and competent dermatologist tried his best. He treated her for almost two years. Finally, he gave up and referred the woman to me. She did not tell him about her husband, nor did she tell me. She talked in my office about everything else except about her husband's wish to have children. She loved her husband and praised him and felt guilty for depriving him of genital sex relations.

This had been going on for a while when she had a strange dream that offered the right clues. In the dream, her belly was getting big, and her pelvic bones were shrinking. After the dream, she asked me, "Why don't you want to see me naked? How can you help me if you don't see the skin rash? I know that my lower part, the pelvic bone, is abnormally narrow. I am fat on the top and skinny at the bottom!"

I explained that the dermatologist had described her skin condition, and her concern about the shape of her body offered an important clue.

She admitted her fear of pregnancy. She felt she had no chance to give birth to a child, and she feared that, in labor, either she or the infant would die.

I sent her to a gynecologist-obstetrician for a thorough examination. Her fears were irrational, and the rash disappeared.

Recently, I received a letter from her. She has three children.

NEURODERMATITIS

Some people tend to develop a skin disease called *neurodermatitis*, often referred to as *atopic dermatitis*. The main symptoms are dry and flaky skin, scaly hyperkeratosis, crusting, vesicles and papules, and exudation of serum. The disease may disappear for several years and come back, in either a mild or a severe form. It may affect children, adolescents, and adults, and in most cases, the symptoms appear on the face and spread to other parts of the body, especially the knees and elbows.

The etiology is not clearly determined; there is a possibility of multiple causation (Rajka, 1975), but emotional factors are always present. Frustration and loss of a loved one have often been observed at the onset of the disease. Lack of maternal affection and physical closeness with the mother are relevant etiological determinants (Wittkower & Hunt, 1958), as well as irritability and repressed hostility.

Cleveland and Fisher (1956) compared 25 male patients suffering from neurodermatitis with a group of 22 males with industrial and accidental skin lesions. The dermatitis patients showed a high degree of masochism and a highly depreciated self-concept. The dermatitis patients conceive of their bodies in terms of dirt and repulsion. They also tended to cover and hide the body because of their negative body image. Although repressed hostility toward both parental figures was found, they showed an "armor-plate" defense in that their bodies were conceived of as being surrounded by an impermeable barrier. They viewed their fathers as powerful and distant and attempted to placate them in a masochistic manner. Even more anxiety and conflict existed in their relationships with their mothers, toward whom they held great resentment because of never having received love and attention.

PRURITUS ANOGENITALIS

In pruritus anogenitalis, the itching occurs on the testicles (pruritus scroti) or on the vulva (pruritus vulvae), and sometimes on the anus (pruritus ani). It could be related to physical factors, such as diabetes mellitus, jaundice, or lice, but in a vast majority of cases, it is caused by emotional conflict. The nature of the conflict varies: It can be suppressed anger, boredom, or sexual frustration or guilt feelings and an unconscious wish for self-punishment. Sometimes, it starts quite early and can be related to a child's resentment of toilet training, where the intense itching is an expression of suppressed anger, frustration, and anxiety (Hill, 1976).

According to Alexander and Flagg (1965), pruritus scroti and pruritus vulvae are related to inhibited sexual excitement, and scratching is a source of conscious erotic pleasure and a masturbatory equivalent. According to Engels (1985), pruritus is caused by an early conflict between the child and his or her mother. Pruritus patients did not receive adequate maternal affection in childhood and therefore crave affection in later life. Their repressed feelings of frustration and anger lead to scratching, which represents both gratification and self-imposed punishment for being angry. Pruritus ani often represents rebellion against toilet training. Pruritus vulvae often serves a pleasurable masturbatory function and as a self-imposed punishment for masturbation.

INFANTILE ECZEMA

Infantile eczema seems to be a product of emotional inconsistency in parental care. When one parent offers too much gratifying physical body contact and the other deprives the child of physical and psychological expressions of affection, some children develop infantile eczema.

A restrictive, overprotective atmosphere, compensating for destructive attitudes in the mother, has commonly been observed as conducive to infantilization of the child. The eczematous child is involved in an intense infantile relationship with the mother. Sexual impulses occurring in the oedipal situation threaten the child with estrangement from the infantilizing mother, now experienced as a sexual mother. Initial attacks of asthma in some eczematous children occur when they are confronted with the conflicts characteristic of the anal or the oedipal developmental phase (Alexander & Flagg, 1965).

Several studies indicate that the face and the genitals are commonly the most highly cathected parts of the body (Engels, 1985; Whitlock, 1976).

Bergman and Aldrich (1963) conducted a follow-up study on 28 adolescents who had been treated for infantile eczema between 1940 and 1946. They included the parents, covered the psychiatric history, and appraised the subjects' current adaptation. Of these 28 subjects, 14 still suffered from active atopic eczema, and 6 of the 14 who no longer had evidence of active eczema had asthma or hay fever. Eighteen of the subjects were afflicted by a definite psychosis or personality-trait disturbance, and 11 of these 18 subjects with specific psychiatric disorders still had eczema, including 3 of the subjects with the most severe eczema and most of those with severe psychiatric disturbance. Sixteen mothers showed rejection or overprotection. Evidence of passivity and pronounced skin cathexis was frequently found. Exacerbations of eczema were usually associated with threats to the patients' dependent relationships, and remissions were related to periods of increased security.

URTICARIA (HIVES)

The main symptoms of urticaria are skin rashes or blotches of different sizes. The blotches may be localized or may spread over the entire body. The swelling often includes the lips and the face. In some cases, it may spread to the throat. Urticaria is associated with intense itching and if it affects the throat, it may become life-threatening (Whitlock, 1976).

Urticaria is believed to be related to an allergy. As explained above, allergies are an overreaction of the immune system by an overproduction of antibodies, totally out of proportion to threat to the organism (Medansky, 1980).

Some researchers have related urticaria to suppressed weeping. According to Alexander (1950), in patients with urticaria (as in those with asthma, to which urticaria has an intrinsic relationship), inhibited dependent longings for a parental object are a conspicuous finding. The fact that in many urticaria patients who inhibit weeping the urticarial attacks are often terminated by weeping indicates an intimate relationship between weeping and urticaria.

Shoemaker (1963) studied the determinants of chronic urticaria. He evaluated 40 cases to determine whether they manifested any psychosomatic specificity. He compared cross-sectional psychiatric studies of patients suffering from hives with longitudinal studies. He found that all patients had been more active before the onset of urticaria, and that they had experienced events and circumstances that had caused a breakdown of various activities that, before the hives, had served as defenses. There was also a quite consistent history of some form of parental rejection. Physical violence had played a significant role in the psychodynamics of chronic urticaria. Anxiety was always present, and hostility appeared as an important factor in the etiology of urticaria. At the onset of the urticarial reaction, the patients appeared to be caught between abject dependency and destructive rage.

According to Graham, Graham, and Kabler (1962), individuals who develop urticaria feel that they are mistreated and are unable to defend themselves. The feeling of helplessness and unfair treatment leads to the development of hives.

ACNE

Acne is an inflammation of the skin due to an overfunction of the oil (sebaceous) glands. The main symptoms are red pimples, blackheads, and whiteheads.

Acne usually occurs in adolescence and is relative to endocrinological changes, but not all adolescents develop acne. Depressed, anxious, and insecure adolescents are prone to developing acne. According to Graham *et al.* (1962), adolescents who feel "picked on" by peers or adults wish to be alone and tend to develop acne. In nearly all cases, acne is a product of emotional conflicts between adolescents and their parents (Minuchin *et al.*, 1975).

HYPERHYDROSIS

Hyperhydrosis, or excessive sweating, can be caused by physicothermal factors or by psychological factors such as anxiety, hypochondriasis, and/or depression. Most hyperhydrosis patients tend to feel embarrassed by their condition, and they fear that other people may smell or see their perspiration. Their embarrassment makes them sweat more profusely and contributes to a growing tension. Some hyperhydrosis patients develop delusional fears of causing harm by their bad odors of perspiration, and they may withdraw from all social relations. In some cases, individuals affected by hyperhydrosis develop paranoid ideas and believe that other people avoid them (Lerer, 1979; Lerer, Jacobowitz, & Wahba, 1980).

Rosacea

Rosacea is more common in females than in males and occurs in the fourth or fifth decade of women's lives. The main symptoms are red and shiny skiny, excessive blushing, increased vascularity, and the formation of papules and pustules on the face and the upper chest. Quite often, rosacea causes red deformity of the nose and inflammation of the eyes.

Individuals affected by rosacea are perfectionistic. They usually display the need to please others and are predisposed to guilty and shameful feelings. They tend to feel guilty for uncommitted sins and often suffer a self-imposed feeling of embarrassment and shame for not being as perfect as they wish to appear. Their excessive blushing seems to be the physiological expression of their feelings, and it may cause a variety of skin problems, such as dilated blood vessels in the upper dermis and edema. In some instance, the skin is affected by leukocytic infiltration and the formation of granuloma (Engels, 1985).

Psoriasis

The main symptoms of psoriasis are large red plaques with thick white or gray scales. The red plaques are rough and produce a burning sensation rather than an itching sensation. These plaques are white or gray scales and are quite dry and hard. The plaques may cover various parts of the body, and they appear on the scalp, the face, the arms, the legs, the back, and the behind. Sometimes, they affect the eyebrow and the fingernails. Psoriasis may occasionally disappear for a while, but it usually comes back again and again (Engels, 1983, 1985).

The etiology of psoriasis is unknown, but its occurrence is frequently seen in stressful situations. One of my patients afflicted with psoriasis experienced frequent and severe recurrences of the red lesions whenever she was exposed to emotional upheavals such as her child's diseases and fights with her husband.

Delusional Parasitosis

Delusional parasitosis is a hypochondriacal psychosomatic disease. It occurs in elderly individuals, most of them females, who have the delusion that their skin is being invaded by small insects. The main symptoms are skin detritus and itching.

The delusionary symptoms are often related to paranoia and senile psychoses (Torch & Bishop, 1981). Several European researchers have tended to include delusional parisitosis in the class of *monosymptomatic hypochondriachal psychoses* typical of aged people.

SELF-IMPOSED SKIN DISEASES

Some individuals, motivated by unconscious or conscious feelings of guilt, inflict damage on their skin (Engels, 1983; Musaph, 1964). They experience an almost uncontrollable urge to "dig" into their skin, and even a mild instance of itching stimulates forceful scratching that may lead to serious damage to the skin.

Some depressed individuals practice compulsive hair-pulling, or *trichotillomania*. Trichotillomania can occur at any age, and it is more common in females than in males. It is usually related to guilt feelings and to self-punitive inclinations.

REFERENCES

Alexander, F. *Psychosomatic medicine.* New York: Norton, 1950.

Alexander, F., & Flagg, G. W. The psychosomatic approach. In B. B. Wolman (Ed.), *Handbook of clinical psychology* (pp. 855–947). New York: McGraw-Hill, 1965.

Bergman, R., & Aldrich, C. K. The natural history of infantile eczema: A follow-up study. *Psychosomatic Medicine,* 1963, *25,* 495.

Clark, R. L., & Cumley, R. W. (Eds.). *The book of health.* New York: Van Nostrand Reinhold, 1973.

Cleveland, S. E., & Fisher, F. Psychological factors in neurodermatitis. *Psychosomatic Medicine,* 1956, *18,* 13–31.

Engels, W. D. Dermatologic disorders: Psychosomatic illness review. *Psychosomatics,* 1983, *23,* 1209–1216.

Engels, W. D. Dermatologic disorders. In W. Dorfman & L. Cristofar (Eds.), *Psychosomatic illness review* (pp. 146–161). New York: Macmillan, 1985.

Graham, D. T., Graham, F., & Kabler, J. B. Physiological response to the suggestion of attitudes specific for hives and hypertension. *Psychosomatic Medicine,* 1962, *24,* 220–228.

Hill, D. (Ed.). *Modern trends in psychosomatic medicine.* London: Butterworth, 1976.

Katch, F. L., & Katch, V. I. Measurement and prediction errors in body composition assessment and the search for the perfect prediction equation. *Research Quarterly for Exercise and Sport,* 1980, *51,* 249–260.

Lerer, B. Hyperhydrosis: A review of its psychological aspects. *Psychosomatics,* 1979, *20,* 28–31.

Lerer, B., Jacobowitz, J., & Wahba, A. Personality features in essential hyperhydrosis. *International Journal of Psychiatry,* 1980, *10,* 59–67.

Medansky, R. S. Dermatopsychosomatics: An overview. *Psychosomatics,* 1980, *21,* 195–200.

Minuchin, S., et al. A conceptual model of psychosomatic illness in children. *Archives of General Psychiatry,* 1975, *32,* 1031–1038.

Musaph, H. *Itching and Scratching: Psychodynamics in dermatology.* Philadelphia: Davis, 1964.

Musaph, H. Dermatology and psychiatry. In B. B. Wolman (Ed.), *International Encyclopedia of Psychiatry, Psychology, Psychoanalysis and Neurology* (Vol. 4, pp. 75–78). New York: Aesculapius Publishers, 1977.

Rajka, G. *Atopic dermatitis.* Philadelphia: Saunders, 1975.

Shoemaker, R. J. A search for the affective determinants of chronic urticaria. *Psychosomatics,* 1963, *4,* 125–132.

Torch, E. M., & Bishop, E. R. Delusions of parasitosis: Psychotherapeutic engagement. *American Journal of Psychotherapy,* 1981, *35,* 101–106.

Whitlock, F. A. *Psychophysiological aspects of skin disease.* Philadelphia: Saunders, 1976.

Wittkower, E. D., & Hunt, R. O. Psychological aspects of atopic dermatitis in children. *Canadian Medical Association Journal,* 1958, *79,* 810–817.

17

Psychosomatic Aspects of Cancer

The term *cancer* covers over 100 different diseases. Their common denominator is an unrestrained proliferation of abnormal cells that form malignant tumors. Cancer can be defined as a hyperplasia of glandular or
epithelial cells that infiltrates and inevitably destroys. When cancer starts
in the epithelial tissues, it is a *carcinoma;* when it starts in connective
tissues, it is a *sarcoma.*

Cancer is not a psychosomatic disease. There is no evidence that psychological factors such as pain, frustration, defeat, depression, grief, or
any other type of stress can produce any one of the various types of cancer.
So far, there is no uniform and generally accepted etiological interpretation
of malignant tumors, and no one knows for sure what causes cancer (see,
e.g., Bammer & Newberry, 1982; Gengerelli & Kirkner, 1954; Harrison,
1980; Silverberg, 1984).

SYMPTOMATOLOGY

The main symptoms of all 100 types of cancer are cellular growth and
proliferation. The cancerous cells multiply rapidly, destroy healthy cells
and tissues, and, in many instances, invade any tissue and any organ
outside the original cancer site. When a piece of a malignant tumor breaks
off and is carried by the lymph or blood current to other parts of the body
or to some remote lymph nodes, the process is called *metastasis.* Most often
the metastasis cells attack the nearby lymph nodes, as well as the lungs,
the bones, the liver, and the brain. The carcinoma metastasis usually
spreads through the lymphatic system, whereas the sarcoma metastasis
most often spreads through the vascular system.

Unfortunately, there are no clear-cut warning signals of the various
types of cancer. The most frequent warning symptoms of cancer are unex-
plained bleeding, a sore that does not heal, a change in a wart or a mole,

frequent indigestion, difficulty in swallowing, persistent hoarseness or cough, and a lump or thickening in the breast or any other part of the body. However, cancers may start without any warning.

A few types of cancer will illustrate the diversity and similarity of the various cancers. (Summarized after Harrison, 1980; Silverberg, 1984; and other sources.)

Lung Cancer

Lung cancer accounts for 25% of all cancer deaths. In the early stages of lung cancer, the symptoms may include a persistent cough and shortness of breath. Symptoms associated with moderately advanced lung cancer include pneumonia and bloody sputum. In the advanced stages of the disease, weight loss, pain in the chest, severe shortness of breath, hoarseness, difficulty in swallowing, and fluid accumulation in the chest cavity may be present.

Annually, 120,000 people die of lung cancer. There is a definite relationship between cigarette smoking and lung cancer, and 85% of lung cancer deaths result from cigarette smoking. Two-pack-a-day smokers risk dying from this disease 30 times more than nonsmokers.

Other causes of lung cancer include arsenic, nickel, iron, isopropyl oil, asbestos, coal and tar fumes, petroleum mists, radioactive substances, and air pollution.

Individuals with lung cancer have a low survival rate; less than 10% survive 5 years after treatment. Moreover, the survival rate has *not* changed significantly since the early 1970s.

Breast Cancer

Breast cancer is measured to occur in 1 of every 11 women; there are about 90,000 new cases annually.

The symptoms associated with breast cancer frequently include a firm to hard lump (mass) that is not tender or a swelling in the breast. The skin may thicken and may be abnormally colored. Nipple retraction, nipple discharge, and dimpling of the breast may occur.

There is an 85% cure rate of breast cancer if it is detected and treated early in the course of the disease, though estimates reveal that 34,000 deaths annually are the result of breast cancer, with the highest incidence occurring in women 40 years old and older.

Multiple Myeloma

Multiple myeloma is one of the most deadly cancers. This disease is cancer of the bone marrow. Anemia may be the only symptom experienced by some victims, whereas others may experience severe bone pain and tenderness. Other symptoms may include quick loss of weight and spontaneous fractures, and occasionally, the skull may swell.

Bone cancers occur in those who have been frequently exposed to inordinate radiation or high doses of X rays. The survival rate after diagnosis is 1.5 to 2 years; however, in some instances, the cancer is so monstrous that death occurs only a few months after diagnosis.

Leukemia

Leukemia includes a group of intricate cancers. These cancers cause white-blood-cell production to occur abnormally and to push out the needed and healthy white blood cells, red blood cells, and platelets.

The symptoms associated with the leukemias are similar. They include a general sense of weakness and tiredness. The spleen, liver, and lymph nodes swell, and bruises and bleeding may occur easily. Other symptoms include weight loss and diminished appetite; and infections occur often. Frequently, individuals with leukemia are anemic and pale.

Among the children who survived the atomic bombings of Hiroshima and Nagasaki, there seems to be an increased incidence of leukemia, as well as among children who have been exposed to high doses of radiation. As a result of the high incidence of leukemia among these two groups, leukemia is thought to be caused, in some instances, by exposure to high doses of radiation. Pregnant women exposed to high doses of radiation also appear to be at a higher risk of having children with this disease. Furthermore, leukemia seems to occur more frequently among children with genetic abnormalities.

Leukemia can be divided into specific categories, which are determined by the type of white blood cell being affected. The leukemia that is most frequent among children and those under 20 years old is called *acute lymphocytic leukemia* (ALL), also known as *acute lymphoblastic leukemia*. More than 90% of these children experience a remission if the leukemia is treated aggressively. This remission can last, on the average, from 1 to 3 years, and there is a survival rate of 50% among individuals with ALL.

The most frequent leukemia among adults is called *acute myelocytic leukemia*, also known as *granulocytic leukemia*. In these cases, the rate of survival ranges from a few months to a various number of years.

There is a 3-year survival rate for 50% of those afflicted with chronic myelocytic leukemia, and a 5-year survival rate for 10% of this population.

Among individuals with chronic lymphocytic leukemia, 90% may experience temporary remission. A 5-year survival rate may be experienced by 40%–50% of those afflicted with this disease, and a 10-year survival rate can be achieved by 30%.

Liver Cancer

Liver cancer is most often fatal. The early symptoms of liver cancer are associated with gastrointestinal problems, including upset and sensitive stomach, a general sense of being weak, and nausea, vomiting, and constipation. As the cancer progresses, anemia may occur, as well as jaundice and rapid weight loss. Occasionally, individuals experience abdominal pain or the sensation of being full.

Cancer of the liver is nearly always deadly. Only 50% survive liver cancer for as few as 3 months after diagnosis. If the cancer has been confined to a tumor, surgical removal may be effective. Liver cancer may be treated with chemotherapy and radiation therapy.

Kidney Cancer

The symptoms associated with cancer of the kidney include the presence of blood in the urine, fever, and back or side pain. When the cancer is advanced, a lump may be discovered. Although the cause of kidney cancer is unknown, there appears to be a relationship between the cancer and kidney stones, as well as between kidney cancer and the drug phenacetin, which is used as a pain control.

A 50% survival rate may occur 10 years after treatment if the cancer has been detected and treated before it has the chance to spread farther than the kidney. If the cancer has spread beyond the renal vein, the lymph nodes, or the membrane surrounding the kidney, there is a marked decrease in survival rates.

Stomach Cancer

Stomach cancer afflicts more men than women and can occur in different forms. The symptoms associated with stomach cancer are imitative of digestive problems, and therefore, detection frequently occurs late in the course of the disease. Among the symptoms associated with cancer of the stomach are upper gastrointestinal ailments, including heartburn, indigestion, and feeling full although there has been little food consumption. With advanced stomach cancer, there may be a gradual weight loss, diminished appetite, anemia, and an aversion to meat. The most advanced symptoms include bloody bowel movements, acute pain in the stomach, and the presence of blood in vomit.

The incidence of stomach cancer increases among those with pernicious anemia, persistent gastritis, gastric ulcer, and achlorhydria.

There is a 5-year survival rate reaching 30% among those cases of stomach cancer that do not spread beyond the stomach and where surgery has proved successful. After a diagnosis of advanced stomach cancer, 50%

will live more than 6 months. The cure rate of those afflicted with stomach cancer is approximately 10%.

Cancer of the Uterus

Cancer of the uterus (and the endometrium) is seen most frequently among women ranging in age from 40 to 70 years old. There are different symptoms for menstruating and postmenopausal women.

Among women who menstruate, the symptoms include spotting between menstrual periods, abnormal menstrual flow, and vaginal bleeding following sexual intercourse.

The most frequent symptom among women who are postmenopausal is vaginal bleeding. In addition, abdominal cramps or discomfort may be experienced by some women.

An increase of endometrial and uterine cancers seems to occur among obese women, women with hypertension or diabetes, and those who have not had children. There is a greater prevalence of the disease among white women.

Of uterine cancer patients, 85% survive about 5 years if the cancer remains within the lining of the uterus (the endometrium). Once the disease spreads to the uterine muscles, the survival rate drops to 60%–70% living 5 years after treatment. Once the disease spreads to the lymph nodes surrounding the uterus, the cure rate falls dramatically.

Prostate Cancer

Prostate cancer is the second most common cancer among U.S. males (lung cancer is first).

Unfortunately, cancer of the prostate can exist without causing many symptoms. However, some men experience blood in the urine, pain or difficulty when beginning to urinate, and difficulty when stopping urination. There may also be the need to urinate frequently, although the urine flow may be weak. Back and pelvic pain, as well as impotence, can occur in the later stages of the disease.

Of patients under 60 years old, 50% have a survival rate of five years and beyond. Among those men who develop the disease after age 60, 50% die from causes other than prostate cancer.

ETIOLOGY

Only a small fraction of the people exposed to carcinogens develop cancer. Apparently, carcinogens are not the sole determinant of cancer, and it is possible that cancer is related to a *genetic deficiency of the immune system;* more specifically, the symptomatology of cancer and the phenomenon of metastasis point to an overfunction of B cells and T-helper cells and to the underfunction of the T-suppressor cells (Ader, 1981).

As described earlier, the immune system is comprised of a powerful and alert army of lymphocytes, plasma cells, and macrophages that defend the organism against the antigen invaders. The two main defensive forces are the B cells and the helper T cells. These cells are divided into several types, and they are located in various organs and parts of the body. The suppressor T cells control the actions of the B cells and the helper T cells; they perform the tasks of "military police," called in to restrain the overreacting B cells and helper T cells (Ader & Cohen, 1984).

The normal ratio of T helpers to T suppressors is 1.7 ± 5 (that is, there are about twice as many "soldiers" as "military police"). An overreaction of the suppressor T cells could paralyze the immune response, but in cancer, the suppressor T-cell "military police" fail to act. As a result, the unrestrained B cells and the helper T-cells fail to discriminate the healthy cells from the invading antigens and attack not only the antigens but the organs they are supposed to defend. In metastasis, the B cells and the helper T cells cross all bodily borders and spread destruction to several organs and parts of the organism, while the military-police suppressor T cells do nothing to prevent the catastrophe.

Several additional phenomena support the hypothesis that the hyperfunction of the immune defense system (i.e., the B cells and the helper T cells) is related to cancer. Old age brings a decline in the immune system, and therefore, elderly people are less capable of fighting diseases. Pneumonia and other infectious diseases kill elderly people, whereas younger people show more resilience and have a better chance in fighting against disease.

As mentioned above, cancer is related to a hyperactive immune system; accordingly, a decline in the immune system in old age should reduce the incidence of cancer. And this is precisely what takes place. The peak increase in cancer incidence and cancer mortality occurs between the ages of 45 and 65 and afterward goes down. At ages 65–69, cancer accounts for no more than 30% of deaths; cancer causes death in 12.5% of people over 80 years old.

The incidence of cancer compared to the incidence of acquired immunodeficiency syndrome (AIDS) supports the hypothesis that AIDS and the cancers are opposite diseases. According to estimates by the American Cancer Society (1986), there are about 870,000 new cancer cases a year in the United States and 450,000 cancer deaths. Cancer patients may develop all kinds of diseases, but so far, there is not a single case of a cancer patient's being afflicted by AIDS nor an AIDS patient suffering from cancer. Only *after* AIDS has played havoc with the organism may a cancerous disease finish the destructive job.

There is some evidence of T-cell abnormalities in *diabetes;* thus, one may hypothesize that diabetes is an autoimmune disease in which the immune system attacks the Langerhans islet cells. If the failure of the suppressor T cells is the main factor in autoimmune diseases, cancer belongs to the category of autoimmune diseases, and AIDS belongs to the opposite category: it is an antiautoimmune disease (Wolman, in press).

Genetic Factors: Male and Female Cancer Ratios

According to current statistical data, the life expectancy for men in the United States is 74 years; for women, 86 years. The difference of 12 years of life deserves special attention. During war periods, the longevity of women is quite understandable, but with the exception of the Vietnam war, the United States has not been at war for more than 35 years. In modern times, men and women are exposed to nearly the same risks; the question to be asked is: What is the reason for women's longevity in general and for their particular resilience to cancer and to AIDS?

The statistical data pertaining to the incidence of cancer and to cancer death cases are thought-provoking. In the United States, men and women are exposed to nearly the same carcinogens. Considering general population statistics, it is not surprising that of the 870,000 new cancer cases in 1984, 429,000 were male and 441,000 were female. The difference was less than 3%. However, the death cases represent a reverse picture: there were more male cancer deaths, that is, 244,000 male deaths compared to 205,000 female deaths. The differences was over 15%!

These differences have remained quite consistent. In the United States in 1977, 210,459 males and 176,277 females died of cancer. In 1979, 220,015 males died of cancer, compared to 183,380 females. Similar data have been reported the world over for deaths from leukemia and stomach and skin cancer; whereas there are no significant differences in the male–female incidence of cancer, the mortality rate is consistently higher for males.

One must conclude that there are biological and psychological differences between the male and the female immune systems. It is possible that these differences are related to the functions of the neuroendocrine system, and especially of gonadal secretions. The action of *estrogen* for or against cancer and AIDS requires careful scrutiny, and attention must be given to the difference between *male and female genetic factors.* There is some evidence that estrogen can exert a certain protection against cancer: about 90% of cases of endometrial cancer in women occur *after* menopause, when the levels of estrogen are reduced to a minimum. Furthermore, prostate cancer in men is often treated by estrogen. A combination of genetically determined biochemical and psychological factors is responsible for the somatopsychic and psychosomatic aspects of cancer.

Furthermore, the role of genetics in defects of the immune system can be exemplified as follows: a defect in adenosine deaminase (ADA), one of the riboside components of RNA, may adversely affect the functions of the immune system, and a lack of ADA may cause a severe deficiency of the immune system. Also, the Lesch–Nyham disease, an X-linked recessively transmitted disease of male children deserves to be mentioned.

A belief in genetic origins of cancer and specifically in alterations in the chromosomal complement was quite popular at one time, but a multiplicity of causes and the unmistaken role of physiological and psychological factors has militated against a simple biogenetic explanation of cancer's etiology (Lynch, 1982).

Obviously, biogenetic factors are *not* the sole cause of a disease. For instance, coronary heart disease is caused by a variety of factors, most of them environmental, and only 5% of individuals who suffer early myocardial infarctions are heterozygotes for the familial hypercholesterolemia related to atherosclerosis.

The Hammer-and-Anvil Interaction

Various types of cancer are associated with heavy smoking, heavy alcohol intake, age-related enlargement of the prostate, and so on. But how many heavy smokers, heavy drinkers, and men with enlarged prostates develop cancer, and how many do not? A similar question must be raised with regard to AIDS. Over 72% of all AIDS patients are male homosexuals. How many male homosexuals do not develop AIDS? Apparently, deficiency of the immune system and susceptibility to cancer are related to both genetic and psychological factors.

One need not dismiss the role of nutrition and chemicophysical factors in addition to psychological factors. One may, at this point, borrow some ideas from psychopathology. In most mental disorders, one can apply *hammer-and-anvil reasoning*. Some time ago, a mother and father brought to my office their 15½-year-old schizophrenic daughter. Her sister was a rather well-adjusted girl, and the parents maintained that they treated both girls exactly the same, which was, undoubtedly impossible. However, assuming a certain degree of similarity in parental behavior, one had to look to differences in the genetic predispositions of the two sisters. Whatever wrong the parents had done could be compared to blows of a hammer. The blows against the genetically sturdy background of one girl—that is, her anvil—caused insignificant scratches, but similar blows against a fragile genetic anvil could cause serious mental damage.

Most probably, this is the case in cancer. The various cancers are probably produced by carcinogenic bodies that affect genetically disposed organisms. The same antigens may not cause the disease if they are confronted with a genetically sturdy anvil. Genetically predisposed individuals do not develop the disease unless they are exposed to disease-producing bodies. The same reasoning, borrowed from psychopathology, may also apply to all other fields. Even the best seed would not grow if planted in an arid soil, and the most fertile soil will not produce anything without good seeds. In cancer, the disease-producing bodies are highly significant and indispensable causes of the disease, but they are only partial causes. The combination of the disease-carrying factors with a distinct genetic background, and with current personality traits and past psychological experiences, produces the total etiology of a disease. Thus, every organic disease has some psychological elements, and every mental disorder is related to a certain genetically transmitted weakness of the immune system.

In cancer, the hammer blows are not only the disease-carrying carcinogens but also the psychosocial influences that affect the functions of the immune system. The anvil presents a combination of genetic and acquired patterns of feeling, thinking, and acting.

Psychosocial Factors

As early as 1833, Tanchou, addressing the French Academy of Sciences, said:

> Cancer, like insanity, increases in a direct ratio to the civilization of the country and of the people. Flattering to the vanity of the French savant, that the average mortality rate from cancer at Paris during 11 years is about 0.80 per 1,000 living annually, while it is only 0.20 per 1,000 in London!!! Estimating the intensity of civilization by these data, it clearly follows that Paris is four times more civilized than London!!!!

Also, Bainbridge, in his book *The Cancer Problem* (1914), observed that, in their primeval condition, humans have been little subject to new growth, particularly to those of a malignant character. With a changed sociopsychological environment, there comes an increase in susceptibility to cancerous disease.

In an article entitled, "Cancer: A Disease of Either Election or Ignorance" (1925), Hay wrote:

> A study of the distribution of cancer among the races of the entire earth shows that cancer ratio is in about proportion to which civilized living predominates; so evidently something inherent in the habits of civilization is responsible for the difference of cancer incidence as compared with the uncivilized races and tribes. Climate has nothing to do with this difference, as witness the fact that tribes living naturally will show a complete absence of cancer until mixture with more civilized man corrupts the naturalness of habit; and just as these habits conform to those of civilization, even so does the incidence of cancer begin to show its head.

In 1957, Berglas noted that cancer may perhaps be just another intel-ligible natural process whose cause is to be found in our environment and *mode of life.* . . . Every one of us is threatened with death from cancer because of our inability to adapt to present living conditions.

In the preface to Berglas's book, Albert Schweitzer wrote:

> On my arrival in Gabon in 1913, I was astonished to encounter no cases of cancer. . . . I cannot, of course, say positively that there was no cancer at all; but like other frontier doctors, I can only say that if any cases existed, they must have been quite rare. In the course of the years, we have seen cases of cancer in growing numbers in our region. My observations incline me to attribute this to the fact that the natives are *living more and more after the manner of the whites.* (Quoted in Goldberg, 1981, p. 45)

Emotional Factors

The above-described role of genetic factors does not tell the entire story. Mason (1975) found that the mothers of leukemic children have a high level of the 17-hydroxy-corticosteroid hormone. He discovered a sim-ilar phenomenon in the urine of U.S. army recruits who had lost their mothers. Thus, he pointed to the link between psychological and endo-crinological phenomena.

Apparently, disappointment, frustration, and depression can adverse-ly affect the function of the adrenal glands and reduce their ability to produce the hormones that are used in the immunological defense of the organism. Cancer patients have weak immunological defenses and are unable to launch a successful fight against carcinogens and cancerous tissues (Lynch, 1976; Ormont, 1981). This is not a new discovery; as early as 1870, the oncologist James Paget noticed that disappointments, frustra-tions, and depression were frequently followed by an increase in cancerous tissues (Bammer & Newberry, 1982).

The relationship between smoking and lung cancer offers a useful insight into the physical-psychological interactions in cancer. In the United States, there are currently about 30 million heavy cigarette smokers and only a fraction of them dies of lung cancer, and not all victims of lung cancer smoke cigarettes. There is no question that tobacco is a carcinogen, but the fact that only a fraction of all heavy cigarette smokers die from lung cancer suggests the possibility that the lung cancer victims are somehow susceptible to cancer. Probably, their immune system is not capable of offering adequate protection against the carcinogen invasion.

Eysenck (1967) administered the Eysenck Personality Inventory to heavy cigarette smokers. He found that the lung cancer patients signifi-cantly differed from the other noncancerous heavy smokers. Probably, the susceptibility to lung cancer carries some biogenetic and psychosomatic elements. Specifically, individuals who tend to "bottle up" their emotional difficulties are prone to developing cancer. Similarly, Simonton and Simonton (1975) observed that individuals who repress their angry feelings tend to feel sorry for themselves and have a low self-image. Such individuals are also susceptible to cancer.

Ormont (1981) introduced a hormonal-immunological theory, following J. B. Cannon's idea of "wisdom of the body" (1981). Ormont maintained that every human body has some defects caused by its own constitutional genetic predisposition or by outside viruses and pollutants. However, the defense system of the organism (the immune system) usually finds the harmful elements and fights successfully against them. Stress disrupts the defensive process; it prevents the detection of the harmful elements, inhibits the fight against them, and allows the harmful cells unlimited multiplication and eventual destruction of the organism (Dotian, Keystone, Garfinkel, & Brown, 1982).

Several contemporary studies relate the predisposition of cancer to psychological factors, such as lack of closeness to one's parents, inability to express or difficulty in expressing negative emotions, and unconscious conflicts. Endocrine and immune processes and other pathophysiological mechanisms are the link between psychological problems and the etiology of cancer. According to Krantz and Glass (1984), depression and feelings of helplessness are associated with lower survival rates in cancer, whereas hostile feelings and anger are associated with a higher rate of survival.

Apparently, susceptibility to cancer is related to the above-described genetic and psychological developmental factors. Children need to be taken care of; they are born helpless, and they have no chance to survive unless taken care of. The fear of abandonment is the most frequent and most significant fear in childhood (Wolman, 1978). Adequate and affectionate parental care gives the child the feeling of security and reduces the fear of abandonment. Inadequate care and a fear of rejection give the child a feeling of insecurity and helplessness. These feelings often persist throughout one's lifetime. In many instances, feelings of loneliness and helplessness can reduce the biochemical resilience of the immune system and can render the organism unable to fight the cancer-carrying bodies, the carcinogens (LeShan & Worthington, 1956).

Soviet studies indicate that the subjecting of experimental animals to stressful conditioning procedures and especially to Pavlovian "experimental neurosis" facilitates the development of malignant tumors and even death (Schmale, Morrow, and Ader, 1977, p. 15). There is some evidence that environmentally induced psychological factors can increase susceptibility to cancer, and certainly, a frequent and ongoing exposure to stress reduces one's resilience.

Premorbid Background

The loss of someone dear, a feeling of loneliness and abandonment, a feeling of rejection, and the resulting pessimistic outlook on life are characteristic of individuals prone to developing cancer. Greene (1966) investigated 109 men, women, and children and found that leukemia or lymphoma had developed in individuals who had experienced separations or losses and who felt anxious and hopeless. LeShan (1977) conducted a 12-year study on over 400 cancer patients. Of these cancer-afflicted individuals, 72% had suffered a painful loss of someone they loved. The loss of the beloved person had taken place at various intervals, from a few months up to 8 years, before the onset of the disease.

THE COURSE OF THE DISEASE

The role of the immune system and its vulnerability to emotional stress offers at least a partial clue to prognosis. The emotional factors include the patient's own psychological makeup, as well as his or her environmental support system. Lonely individuals overconcerned with their health, hypochondriacs and anxiety-driven, lonely men and women, may succumb to the devastating growth of cancerous tissues. People who have lost their zest for life, whose life has no direction, who have no one to depend on or to care for, and who live from day to day have less chance of coping with the disease than socially involved and goal-directed individuals. Passivity and loneliness breed depression, and depression undermines the immune defenses. Active involvement with other people, an intensely active life, and devotion to a profession or an idea improve the ability of the immune system to combat cancer.

The emotional support of family members and friends plays a significant role in the cancer patient's morale and resilience. The negative attitudes of relatives and friends, their expressions of impatience and pessimism, and their lack of concern and care adversely affect the patient's ability to cope with cancer.

Bard (1972) reported a study of 100 seriously ill, hospitalized cancer patients. Cancer patients, Bard wrote, should be regarded as people under a special and severe form of stress. They expect prolonged and intense pain and live under a threat of disability and death, and they are therefore in a state of continuous, severe, and debilitating depression.

Prognosis

Additional evidence concerning the importance of psychological elements in cancer is derived from the widespread difficulty of making a precise prognostic evaluation. It is an undeniable fact that:

> Even the most experienced clinicians and pathologists have difficulty predicting the clinical course of many cancers. Tumors of the same type and stage at the time of diagnosis may go on to behave in different ways. At times, the cancer may completely disappear. The patient who was supposed to be dead in six

weeks is alive and well ten years later without a trace of cancer. Other patients . . . have cancers that neither grow nor shrink over the span of many
years. Still other patients, obviously, experience progression of the cancer causing the eventual death. (Kerr, 1981, pp. 3–6)

Greer, Morris, and Pettingale (1979) divided women afflicted with
breast cancer into four groups: (1) those who denied the illness; (2) those
who initially dismissed the severity of the problem but who showed a
willingness to fight the disease; (3) those who stoically accepted the illness;
and (4) those who felt helpless. A 5-year follow-up study indicated that the
first two groups, the denial and the fighting ones, had had a better clinical
outcome than the last two groups, the accepting and the helpless ones,
even though there were no medical differences between the groups in the
state and prognosis of the disease. Metastatic breast cancer patients who
expressed anger and hostile feelings lived longer than those who reacted
with feelings of helplessness.

Wittkower and Dudek (1973) reported a few studies that described
cancer-afflicted individuals as using defense mechanisms of repression and
denial. These patients were described "as leasing a double existence—with
a socially adequate but empty and meaningless facade and a tragic, tor-
mented and explosive unconscious self" (p. 26). Other studies have
stressed the fact that patients with breast cancer with metastases who
survived for long periods were characterized by self-confidence, in contrast
to the short-lived patients, who were incapable of expressing outwardly
aggressive and social impulses. Apparently, a self-assertive attitude increases the organism's resilience (Goldberg, 1981).

Resilience

The human organism is a somatopsychic and psychosomatic entity,
and the immune system is a biochemical and a psychological apparatus.
Undoubtedly, the functions of the immune system are affected by both
chemistry and emotions. Small wonder that the incidence of cancer is
higher in depressed and insecure individuals (Krantz & Glass, 1984; Simonton & Simonton, 1975).

Severe stress reduces the efficiency of the immune system, allowing
the growth and proliferation of cancerous cells, especially when the individual has little faith in his or her ability to fight and assert himself or
herself. Individuals having self-confidence, self-assertiveness, and determination increase the efficiency of the immune system and contribute to
the organism's resilience and survival.

A Case Description

Several years ago, a colleague of mine, an oncologist, referred to me a 50-year-
old business executive afflicted by cancer. The prognosis was grim, and the on-

cologist had advised the gravely depressed patient to undergo psychotherapy. The man was poorly dressed and unshaven. He started, "My doctor sent me to you. I am fatally ill and I will die in a few months. What can you do for me?"

I told him that no one was forcing him to stay in my office. He could leave and he would not be charged. He decided to stay and asked me, "What should I do?" My first suggestions to him was to go to a high-class men's store and buy himself three new suits. "Why do I need new suits?" he yelled. "Well," I replied, "so you will be buried in a dignified, high-class way."

He laughed. I ordered him to go back to work and not to sit at home. I told him to continue his usual way of life, to go to business lunches, and to take part in the social activities that he and his family used to take part in.

He continued to come to my office on a regular basis. I could not cure his cancer, nor could I promise longevity. The main aspect of our psychotherapeutic sessions was to strengthen his will to live, to point to his moral obligation to his wife and children, and to help him respect himself. Life is an obligation, and one's inner harmony depends on a reasonable balance between what one should and what one can do. He knew very well that he had a terminal disease, but he became determined not to give up. He fought his cancer, and despite the initial gloomy prognosis, he lived for 8 years.

In a chapter entitled "Exploring the Relationship between Personality and Cancer," Goldberg (1981) wrote:

> I know, for example, a chemotherapy patient who believes that she has avoided losing her hair through systematic imagery of her hair remaining full. I know of a woman who created the image of herself reacting with distaste towards sweets, and lost a good deal of weight as a result. (p. 118)

The aforementioned male and female differences in greater longevity and lower incidence of cancer-related mortality rates suggest that women have a higher level of resilience than men. However, highly motivated and self-confident cancer patients of both genders do better and live longer than poorly motivated, insecure, and depressed patients, although females do seem to be more capable of coping with hardships, frustrations, and pain. Pregnancy and labor present a challenge to every woman's psychological resilience, and only a fraction of women succumb to the stresses of their gender. By comparison, many men do not show a high level of resilience in breadwinning hardship, and much less in combat situations. Cancer is not a psychosomatic disease, but susceptibility to cancer and resilience are greatly influenced by one's psychological makeup, and the differences in male–female mortality rate is quite convincing. Moreover, at the present time, both males and females are exposed to nearly the same carcinogetic threats, and their resilience to cancer is a combination of biogenetic chemical predisposition and of biosocial, genetic, and acquired psychological traits.

As mentioned above, cancers are not psychosomatic disorders. There are no cancerous cells and tissues without carcinogens. Small wonder that the question "Do patients with cancer exhibit pathological behavior and

attitudes or are their responses to cancer adaptive and healthy?" is frequently asked (Fisher, 1981). In Feldman (1981), we read as follows:

> We have identified the most common patient concerns:
>
> 1) Requests for information about the results and side effects of chemother-
> apy or surgical procedures: the information often allays anxiety based on fears of
> the unknown.
>
> 2) Misperception, misinformation and confusion about how the treatment
> protocols can be managed, again serving to reduce anxiety.
>
> 3) The universal sense of isolation and alienation from the "healthy" world
> which seriously ill patients feel, and which is increased in a large institution.
>
> 4) The feeling of helplessness as experienced by a patient with a disease that
> is not understood and thus seems more mysterious and overwhelming.
>
> Furthermore, all three "Work and Cancer Histories" studies revealed how
> inculcated some cancer patients were with fear, shame, guilt fed by their own
> and others' perceptions of cancer as intractable, invidious, punishing—percep-
> tions surviving in literature and metaphor for centuries. One man and his wife
> whispered throughout the research interview, unconsciously acting out their
> stated apprehension that "someone" might learn of the husband's rectal cancer;
> they were so fearful that his employer might learn of it that they had not even
> shared the information with their adult son lest he inadvertently become the
> source of disseminating this shameful fact! A woman had delayed in returning
> to her beloved job until she had exhausted her financial resources. She had been
> certain that co-workers and customers would ostracise her because of her mas-
> tectomy. This had been her own mode of behavior toward other cancer victims;
> weren't they being punished for some "wickedness"? An older adolescent ex-
> plained his self-imposed isolation from peers on the basis that cancer was syn-
> onymous with death and being with him would place an unwarranted burden
> on them, creating anxiety in them about their own mortality, making them and
> him "additionally" uncomfortable. A doctor denied permission to include a
> patient in the "Work and Cancer Histories" research because he "never uses
> that word and I don't want anyone else to use it with my patients!"
>
> Such attitudinal assaults on the ability of the cancer patient to cope not just
> with the illness itself but with day-to-day life experiences require that special
> attention be directed in rehabilitation planning and implementation to the
> nature and effects of social attitudes and values that interact with the personality
> and cultural milieu of the patient, to the kinds of psychological defenses (hostili-
> ty, resistance, anger, etc.) the individual erects for protection against the assults,
> and to the evidence and patterns of stress points apt to affect the individual's
> involvement in the pursuit of a rehabilitation goal. (pp. 143–144)

Unfortunately, the role of one's personality traits, one's lifestyle, and
one's behavioral patterns, as well as the impact of psychosocial and cultural factors in the etiology of cancer, is still underestimated and inadequately
researched (Cullen, 1981).

REFERENCES

Ader, R. (Ed.). *Psychoneuroimmunology.* New York: Academic Press, 1981.
Ader, R., & Cohen, N. Behavior and the immune system. In W. D. Gentry (Ed.), *Handbook of
behavioral medicine.* New York: Guilford Press, 1984.

Bainbridge, W. *The cancer problem.* 1914.

Bammer, K., & Newberry, B. H. (Eds.). *Stress and cancer.* Toronto, Canada: Hogrefe, 1982.

Bard, M. The psychological impact of cancer and cancer surgery. *Proceedings of the American Cancer Society's National Conference on Human Values and Cancer,* Atlanta, 1972.

Cullen, J. W. Research issues in psychosocial and behavioral aspects of cancer. *Proceedings of the American Cancer Society, Third National Conference on Human Values and Cancer.* Washington, DC: American Cancer Society, 1981.

Dorian, B., Keystone, E., Garfinkel, P. E., & Brown, G. M. Aberration in lymphocyte subpopulations and functions during psychological stress. *Clinical Experimental Immunology,* 1982, *50,* 132–138.

Eysenck, H. J. *The biological basis of personality.* Springfield, IL: Thomas, 1967.

Feldman, L. F. The teaching of psychosocial and human issues: Rehabilitation and humanistic issues. *Proceedings of the American Cancer Society, Third National Conference on Human Values and Cancer.* Washington, DC: American Cancer Society, 1981.

Fisher, R. A patient's perspective on the human side of cancer. *Proceedings of the American Cancer Society, Third National Conference on Human Values and Cancer.* Washington, DC: American Cancer Society, 1981.

Gengerelli, J. A., & Kirkner, F. J. (Eds.). *Psychological variables in human cancer.* Berkeley: University of California Press, 1954.

Gladue, B. A., Green, R., & Hellman, R. E. Neuroendocrine response to estrogen and sexual orientation. *Science,* 1984, *225,* 1496–1499.

Goldberg, J. I. (Ed.). *Psychotherapeutic treatment of cancer patients.* New York: Free Press, 1981.

Greer, S., Morris, T., & Pettingale, K. W. Psychological response to breast cancer: Effects on outcome. *Lancet,* 1979, *13,* 785–787.

Harrison, T. R. (Ed.). *Principles of internal medicine* (9th ed.). New York: McGraw-Hill, 1980.

Kerr, M. E. Cancer and the family emotional system. In J. G. Goldberg (Ed.), *Psychotherapeutic treatment of cancer patients* (pp. 273–315). New York: Macmillan–Free Press, 1981.

LeShan, L. *You can fight for your life.* Philadelphia: Lippincott, 1977.

LeShan, L., and Worthington, R. E. Personality as a factor in the pathogenesis of cancer: A review of the literature. *British Journal of Medical Psychology,* 1956, *29,* 49–55.

Lynch, J. (Ed.). *Cancer genetics.* Springfield, IL: Thomas, 1976.

Lynch, H. T. (Ed.). *Genetics and breast cancer.* New York, Van Nostrand Reinhold, 1982.

Mason, J. W. Emotions as reflected in patterns of endocrine integration. In L. Levi (Ed.), *Emotions: Their parameters and measurements.* New York: Raven, 1975.

Ormont, L. R. Aggression and cancer in group treatment. In J. G. Goldberg (Ed.), *Psychotherapeutic treatment of cancer patients* (pp. 207–227). New York: Macmillan–Free Press, 1981.

Paget, J. *Surgical pathology.* London: Longmans, Green, 1870.

Schmale, A., Morrow, G., & Ader, R. Cancer, leukemia, and related diseases: Psychosomatic aspects. In B. B. Wolman (Ed.), *International encyclopedia of psychiatry, psychology, psychoanalysis and neurology* (Vol. 3, pp. 11–16). New York: Aesculapius Publishers, 1977.

Silverberg, E. *Cancer statistics,* New York: American Cancer Society, 1984.

Simonton, O. C., & Simonton, S. Belief systems and management of the emotional aspects of malignancy. *Journal of Transpersonal Psychology,* 1975, *7,* 29–47.

Soinetta, J. J. Problems of evaluation of psychosocial research. *Proceedings of the American Cancer Society, Third National Conference on Human Values and Cancer.* Washington, DC: American Cancer Society, 1981.

Wittkower, E. D., & Dudek, S. Z. Psychosomatic medicine: The mind-body-society interaction. In B. B. Wolman (Ed.), *Handbook of general psychology* (pp. 242–272). Englewood Cliffs, NJ: Prentice-Hall, 1973.

Wolman, B. B. *Children's fears.* New York: Grosset & Dunlop, 1978.

Wolman, B. B. *AIDS and cancer* (in press).

18

Pain

SURVIVAL AND POWER

Survival has always been and forever will be the main concern of all living creatures, including the human race. There is nothing more relevant, more significant, or more urgent in human life than survival. Survival depends on a supply of oxygen, water, and food, on appropriate temperature, and on opportunities for sleep and rest. Protection from hostile human beings, from natural disasters, from prey animals, from disease-carrying insects, from germs and viruses, and from other innumerable threatening situations are other prerequisites for survival.

Survival-supporting factors represent basic human needs. There are, however, scores of other fundamental needs, such as for good health, for dependable allies, for achievement, for social approval, for parental love, for adequate income, for comfortable garments, for convenient transportation, for knowledge, for sex, for entertainment, and so on.

Survival and satisfaction of one's needs depend primarily on one's own power. *Power can be defined as the ability to satisfy needs,* and survival is the arch need and the prerequisite of all other needs. Corpses have no needs, but living people have a great many needs.

Weakness means inadequate power; death is zero power. Human beings ascribe omnipotence to their gods, and no human being is omnipotent.

Omnipotence means unlimited power. All human beings crave maximal power, be it physical strength, health, wisdom, supply of food, money, or whatever else increases one's chances for survival and brings satisfaction of one's basic or derived or imaginary needs.

Usually, but not always, pleasure and pain are, respectively, the basic reactions to success and failure in life. Power is enjoyable; weakness is painful.

Obviously, pain and pleasure are the fundamental, although not always the appropriate, reactions to one's chances for survival. A necessary life-saving surgery can be very painful, and an enjoyable drug addiction can destroy the organism.

Elation and Depression

Elation and depression represent one's estimate of one's power. People "feel great" and are elated when they *believe* that they are strong, able to take care of their needs, and able to overcome hardships, threats, and dangers. Elation is a pleasant feeling, but it may or may not be commensurate with one's physical strength, health, achievements, and chances for survival.

Depression is basically a feeling of weakness. The feeling of weakness can be caused by physical weakness, illness, or handicap, as well as by sexual inadequacy, lack of support, defeat, frustration, loneliness, and any other hardship and stress. One may feel weak despite his or her strength.

We should draw a distinction between depression and other negative and unpleasant feelings, such as frustration, sadness, sorrow, and grief. *Depressed individuals feel helpless and tend to blame themselves for being helpless.* One can blame circumstances and other people for one's misfortunes, but in a state of depression, one is inclined to blame oneself. People afflicted by a physical disease may feel pain, unhappiness, loneliness, and weakness, but they may not blame themselves for their misery. People may feel weak, poor, rejected, or discriminated against and blame others, but in depression they view themselves as being the cause of their misery and thus the natural targets of blame. Depressed people feel guilty for being weak and resent themselves for being weak (Wolman, 1973).

In many instances, depression leads to *self-induced pain*. Depressed individuals are accident- and sickness-prone. They may invite pain in order to punish themselves for being helpless. In extreme cases, they may attempt suicide.

The Purpose of Pain

Pain should serve as an alarm signal of existing or impending threat to the organism. But psychosomatic pain can serve a variety of purposes. It can be, as has been mentioned, a self-induced punishment for committed or uncommitted sins. Quite often, pain becomes a method of avoiding unpleasant commitments and/or for soliciting compassion, help, and care. In some situations, a patient accompanied by an attentive family may become preoccupied with pain, and as Szasz (1982) described it, pain becomes "a career and a strategy." The patient pays continuous attention to the slightest pain and frequently goes for medical examinations. Pain-seeking patients reject the physician's opinions and look for more accommodating and more serious evaluations of a minor scar, an insignificant discomfort, or a displeasure. Quite often, the patients look for a second, third, or fourth opinion.

Students unprepared to take a test may develop a "splitting headache" that prevents them from taking the test. Apparently, people can simulate pain, and frequently, they can elicit pain. Children and adults can experience genuine pain with a conscious or unconscious wish to gain sympathy, forgiveness, and love.

The tendency to develop psychosomatic pain is a classic symptom of hysteria (Roy, 1982; Wolman, 1973). A patient of mine, a 38-year-old man, developed chest pains simulating angina pectoris whenever he suffered business setbacks and money losses. His pain was quite severe, and he felt incapacitated and unable to go to his office. A recently married 29-year-old woman complained of "excruciating pain" in her hand that made household chores and cooking almost impossible. Her frequent fights with her husband and his criticism of her cooking talents were the direct cause of her pain.

PAIN AND PLEASURE

There are many different types and incidences of pain experiences even though pain and pleasure are closely related to the vital functions of the organism and to its survival. Pain and pleasure should be the signals of danger and safety, respectively. A toothache or a stomachache usually indicates a decay, a wound, or a malfunction of the affected organ. Almost all diseases, trauma, and any other harm to an organism are accompanied by pain. Severe and life-endangering diseases usually produce unbearable pain. When the organism approaches fire or takes in poisonous substances that jeopardize life, pangs of pain are experienced.

However, a cavity in a tooth and a toothache are not the same. A cavity may cause the feeling of pain, but cavity and pain are two different things. A skin burn is accompanied by pain; even if the pain is removed or alleviated by medication, the burn still exists, indicating the place where the skin was damaged. Damage and pain do not always go together.

Pleasure feelings usually signal a smooth functioning of the organism. The intake of food, water, and fresh air elicits pleasurable feelings. Removal of pain, discomfort, and tension is experienced as pleasure.

Pain and pleasure are important factors in human motivation. Human beings seek pleasure-producing experiences and avoid painful ones. Scientists have frequently expressed the opinion that the pleasure–pain continuum is identical with the satisfaction–deprivation continuum. Some learning theorists (e.g., Skinner, 1959) have avoided using "mentalistic" terms for pain and pleasure. On the other hand, a psychoanalyst wrote that "The human being is organized on the prototype of a single cell which also functions on the pleasure-pain principle" (Deutsch, 1959, p. 132). Another wrote that pain may be:

> . . . decreased and even completely inhibited by psychological procedures, such as hypnosis, suggestion, and distraction. The most convincing cases are those in which major operations and obstetrical deliveries have been performed under hypnosis. Other patients have had amputations performed while praying to religious images, and have said they felt no pain. Simple suggestion by giving placebos frequently reduces ordinary pain to a remarkable degree. Distraction by arousing interest in things not connected with pain can be extraordinarily effective. (Cobb, 1958, p. 288)

Cobb quoted controlled experiments with graded stimulation to nerve endings: the extent of a wound bears only a slight relationship to the pain experienced, for the wound is not the only cause of the pain; the *significance* of the wound may be the paramount factor in determining the production of pain.

Bykov (1957, pp. 399 ff.) reported a series of experiments conducted by A. T. Pshonik. These experiments were devoted to the study of "the cortical dependence of pain reception and the interconnection existing between the pain and heat reception." Pain was caused by pricks of the needle and by the application of heat (63°C) to the skin. In preliminary experiments, the pain lasted for 10 seconds and resulted in vascular constriction and, consequently, a fall in the plethysmogram. The plethysmogram has been used by research workers as an objective yardstick of pain.

Some experiments threw light on what Bykov named "psychogenic pain." Pshonik applied 20 different combinations of the bell and a temperature below that of the pain stimulation and elicited in his subjects "the same vaso-constriction (a fall of the plethysmogram) and the same subjective pain sensations as the usual pain combinations of the bell and 63°" (Bykov, 1957, p. 341). The conditioned stimulus (the bell) transforms a subdolorific stimulation into a pain stimulation.

In some experiments described by Bykov, the unconditioned stimulus gave zero on the plethysmogram, but the conditioned stimulus (a combination of a tactile stimulus with the bell) changed the effect of the unconditioned stimulus and evoked a constriction of the vessels and, when applied with the light, evoked dilation.

Many functions of higher mammals are accompanied by pain or pleasure and the greater part of human functions are performed on the pain–pleasure level, but there are exceptions to this rule.

A crucial role in this issue has to be assigned to the experimentation in visceral conditioning conducted by Bykov and his associates (1957). Their studies proved beyond a doubt that some inner organs are responsive to stimuli but *do not respond* with the pain–pleasure reaction. At present, there is a large amount of evidence that pain and pleasure reactions are not universal, and that they probably start on an advanced evolutionary level. Lower biological species do not experience pain nor pleasure.

One may divide the pleasure process into three main levels: the *prehedonic*, the *hedonic*, and the *posthedonic*. The prehedonic level corresponds to Ukhtomski's prepotence or sheer-force conditioning (Ayrapetyants, 1959; Razran, 1965; Wenger, 1977). Conditioning on the hedonic level is related to reward and punishment. Certain functions of the human body are not accompanied by pleasure or pain, for instance, the division, growth, and decline of cells; the secretion of thyroxine; the growth of hair and nails; the growth of bones and muscles; and the growth of tumors in their initial stage. They are *prehedonic*. On the other hand, the secretion of semen, sucking, eating and drinking, rhythmical movements, the overcoming of obstacles, singing, hugging, and kissing are usually accompanied by pleasure. They are *hedonic*. Deprivation of food is painful; on the other hand, deprivation of certain nutritional values may become ultimately dangerous for the organism, yet it is not painful, at least in the beginning. Thus, pleasure applies to a certain part of human actions; some actions are guided by *prepleasure* or *postpleasure* factors that will be explained below.

The Posthedonic Level: The Antigone Principle

There are several instances in which men and women act in disregard of pain and pleasure. When a tired mother gets up in the middle of the night to take care of her infant, she certainly does not follow her wishes for comfort and pleasure. Restful sleep is definitely more enjoyable than sleepless nights spent at the crib of a sick child. When hungry parents give away the last piece of bread to their infants, they renounce pleasure and accept pangs of hunger willingly. Many people will risk their lives for their families and for their friends; some will do it for any human being in distress, as the history of the Danish resistance of the Nazis proved.

History is full of examples of men and women who have acted in an apparent renunciation of pleasure and a disregard of pain. Consider the early Christians who did not seek escape from the Roman persecutions and sang "Hallelujah" while being burned alive or thrown into cages of wild beasts. If avoidance of pain and pursuit of pleasure were the only motives of human actions, there would be no Christianity.

In medieval and contemporary times, Jewish people have been exposed to discrimination and persecution. The persecutors—whether the Crusaders, the flagellants, the Christian kings, or the Holy Inquisition—gave the Jews the choice of conversion, with all its privileges and joys, or terrible persecution and torture. Some Jews could not reject pleasure and withstand pain, but most of them refused to surrender. The heroic story of the Warsaw ghetto's fight against the Nazis in 1943 is symbolic of the history of humankind; the history of religious, national, and social movements knows many cases of self-sacrifice, courage, willing martyrdom, and heroism. Many men and women have chosen deprivation and pain and have refused to renounce or betray their friends, families, country, and ideals. An unconditional avoidance of pain and search for pleasure would have rendered loyalty, morality, and heroism absolutely impossible.

In some human actions, the pain–pleasure consideration seems to disappear. Bykov (1957) reported cases of wounded men who controlled their own pain. Undoubtedly, certain individuals are capable of suffering for the sake of others and of sacrificing themselves to make others happy. The prototype of this attitude is parenthood, or the willingness to give without taking.

Let us call this attitude the *Antigone principle,* after Antigone, the daughter of Oedipus. When Oedipus left Thebes, his two sons started a fight and one was killed. Creon, the new king, forbade the burial of the fratricidal brother. In the Greek religion, not being buried meant an eternal suffering of the soul. Antigone decided to save her brother's soul and to bury him, knowing very well that the king would have her executed. Thus, this willingness to sacrifice one's own life for a beloved person or ideal is called the *Antigone principle* (Wolman, 1965).

History is a huge and unsurpassed psychological laboratory. Not only does history bear witness to human actions guided by pleasure and pain, but it is full of actions of people who have made history by their relentless pursuit of truth, such as Galileo, or social justice, such as Johann Huss. Thousands of fighters for freedom of conscience, whether persecuted by religious or by secular authorities, whether tortured in dungeons or burned alive, have defended their convictions in total disregard of pain and pleasure.

Physiological Aspects of Pain

In 1973, scientists discovered opiate receptor sites in the brains of mammals and in other body tissues. This discovery followed earlier experimentation that had shown that the electrical stimulation of mammalian brains can substantially reduce acute and chronic pain. The analgesia was partially reversible by *naloxone,* an opiate antagonist.

Further research led to an assessment of the pharmacological role of enkephalins and eventually to the discovery of endogenous morphine compounds called *endorphins* (Boshes, 1983). The endorphins are opiate peptides, and they have been found in the limbic system, in the medial thalamus, and in the midbrain's periaqueductal gray matter, as well as in the sensory input areas of the spinal cord. Enkephalins have also been identified in the nerve terminals of the human and mammalian nervous system (Miller, 1981).

The first endogenous opiates, endorphins, were discovered in 1975 in the mammalian brain. According to Berger (1983, pp. 121 ff):

> There were two surprises. The first was that the compounds were peptides, unlike the plant and synthetic opiates. In fact, they were two pentapeptides— methionine-enkephalin and leucine-enkephalin—differing only in their terminal amino acid. The second surprise was that the sequence of methionine-enkephalin was identifical with the amino acid sequence 61-65 of the 91 amino acid pituitary peptide, β-lipotropin (β-LPH), that had been already discovered.
>
> Other endorphins were discovered in mammalian brain, pituitary gland, and gastrointestinal tract. Some of these endorphins were contained in the amino acid sequence of β-LPH: β-endorphin (β-LPH 61-69); α-endorphine (β-LPH 61–76), and γ-endorphin (β-LPH 61-77). Another endorphin, neoendorphin, is not contained in this sequence of β-LPH. All endorphins have opiatelike activity when tested on isolated tissue preparations, opiate-receptor-binding assays, or injected into the brains of living animals. However, the endorphins do differ from one another in potency and duration of activity. For example, α-neoendorphin is approximately 6.7 times as potent as methionine-enkephalin and 5 times as potent as β-endorphin in some tests of opiatelike activity. The enkephalins have opiatelike activity that is rapidly terminated by proteolytic enzymes in blood and tissues. In contrast, β-endorphin has potent and lasting opiatelike activity.

A more recently discovered endorphin, *dynorphin* (from the Greek word *dynis*, meaning "powerful"), contains the full structure of leucine-enkephalin as its first five residues, followed by 12 additional amino acids. This peptide is a quite potent opiatelike substance (Naranjo, 1986). Berger (1983) wrote:

> The adrenal medulla may contain as many as twelve endorphin peptides of various sizes. Enkephalin and other larger peptides that contain several copies of enkephalin occur within the adrenal medulla and are stored in epinephrine and norepinephrine-containing chromaffin granules. These endorphins from the adrenal medulla seem to be simultaneously released when the adrenal catecholamines are released. [Furthermore,] endorphin/opiate receptor sites have been found in high concentrations in the medial hypothalamus (which is involved in pain mediation), the substantia gelatinosa in the spinal cord (which is involved in pain mediation), the substantia gelatinosa in the spinal cord (which integrates sensory information), the area postrema (in which opiates produce nausea and vomiting), the solitary nuclei receiving visceral sensory fibers from the vagus and glossopharyngeal nerve, and the gastrointestinal tract. The area with the highest density of opiate receptors is the amygdala, a region in the brain involved in emotional behavior. The human pituitary gland, human brain, and human placenta have also been found to contain endorphins. (pp. 121–122)

β-Endorphin was believed to be the logical precursor of methionine-enkephalin, as the amino acid sequence of methionine-enkephalin is contained in that of β-endorphin. However, enkephalin and β-endorphin were later located in different neurons in the brain. The immu-nohistochemical research has demonstrated that β-endrophin and en-kephalin have different distributions in the mammalian brain. Enkephalin has been found in a large quantity of cell groups throughout the brain, from the spinal cord through the limbic system (Miller, 1981).

According to Berger (1983), further research suggests that the anterior lobe of the pituitary may tend to cleave the 31K precursor pro-opiomelanocortin to ACTH (1-39) and β-lipotropin (with some β-en-dorphin). The intermediate lobe, however, may tend to cleave pro-opiomelanocortin further to produce β-endorphin and ACTH and then may cleave ACTH into two fragments, a corticotropinlike intermediate-lobe peptide (CLIP, ACTH 18-39) and α-melanocyte-stimulating hormone (α-MSH, ACTH 1-13). Brain cells that contain pro-opiomelanocortin seem to produce β-endorphin and α-MSH in large proportions in a pattern sim-ilar to that of the intermediate lobe cells of the pituitary.

Because β-lipotropin and ACTH are found within the same secretory granules in the pituitary, it is presumed that β-lipotropin and perhaps some β-endorphin is released concomitantly with ACTH during times of stress (Berger, 1983).

NALOXONE

The interaction between chemical and psychological factors in control-ling pain and reversing the control is illustrated by research with naloxone, the opiate antagonist. Naloxone should theoretically reverse both the ef-fects of exogeneously administered opiates and the effects of the en-dorphins. A major strategy for investigating the possible roles of the en-dorphins has been to administer naloxone to humans and animals in various physiological states. Naloxone has been quite inactive in many normal human volunteers. However, naloxone has had some surprising effects in a number of specific human and animal studies that suggest a variety of possible roles for the endorphins. Naloxone has been reported to reverse the normal increase in pain threshold in pregnant rats, and it has decreased food-deprivation-induced analgesia in rats. Naloxone has been reported to reverse the analgesia produced by acupuncture in both hu-mans and animals. Naloxone has partially reversed the analgesia produced by electrical stimulation of the brain in both humans and animals. Nalox-one seems to reverse placebo analgesia, but it is unable to reverse or even modify the pain relief produced by alcohol intoxication and acetylsalicylic acid. Apparently, there is more to pain than chemistry. Naloxone has also been used to study the possible role of the endorphins in stress, shock, sleep, sexual behavior, and certain drug-intoxication states. Naloxone has reversed stress-induced and diazepam-induced eating behavior in rats (Levine, Gordon, & Fields, 1978).

Because opiates produce both euphoria during intoxication and dysphoria during withdrawal, naloxone has been used to investigate the possible role of the endorphins in the production of euphoric states. Naloxone was reported to be unable to modify the pleasure produced by a human male masturbating to orgasm, but it was able to decrease or block the pleasant tingling sensation that normal subjects felt when listening to their favorite musical selection (Berger, 1983).

Psychosomatic or Somatopsychic?

The discovery of the endorphins has pointed to the possibility of a somatopsychic etiology of pain. The term *endorphin* is an abbreviation of *endogenous morphine*.

Endogenous neutropeptides are neutrotransmitters produced by β-lipotropin and controlling pain—thus, acting in somatopsychic manner. Pain becomes neurochemical, similar to hunger, thirst, and other metabolic functions. In many instances, pain and comfortable feelings depend on the level of endorphins in appropriate parts of the brain (McKerns & Pantić, 1985). However, this rule has many exceptions, and according to Webb (1986), pain is provoked by a combination of neurochemical, neurophysiological, and psychological factors. Webb did not dismiss the role of neurotransmitters and peptides, but he maintained that the central pain experience is mediated by the ascending and descending spinal-cord nervous system. Obviously, experiences as perceived by an individual are communicated to the nervous system and produce psychosomatic reactions of pain or pleasure.

Attitude toward Pain

Pain is usually an alarm signal of the body; it points to an area attacked by antigens, or to an area that is infected, damaged, or unable to function. A toothache calls for help to teeth, and a knee pain draws the attention to a sick knee. But not all pain symptoms lead to the mobilization of one's resources in defense of the organism; as already mentioned, certain pains are self-defeating (Cooper & Croyle, 1984).

It is an open question whether a prior exposure to stress or pain leaves people more *vulnerable* or if it *immunizes* them. Some people, as it were, learn by experience and cope better when faced with a repeated stressful or painful experience. Some other people are already weakened and are less capable of facing stress or pain.

There are several types of pain: (1) acute; (2) recurrent; (3) chronic benign; (4) chronic periodic; and (5) chronic progressive. Acute pain is usually produced by an injury or a physical illness. Acute and recurrent pain can also be produced by anxiety and by recollection. Chronic benign pain is often caused by frustrations and depression. Chronic periodic pain and chronic progressive pain are often related to disease, sleep disturbances, and an exaggerated memory of past pain. Chronic pain may seriously affect one's self-esteem.

Some scientists maintain that pain is a poor protector against injury, for it comes too late in a sudden injury or in the slow progress of damage. In both instances, the pain fails to play a preventive or protective role. Thus, the attitude toward pain is a highly significant factor in human behavior.

Reaction to Pain

Some individuals are capable of perceiving pain as a teleological alarm signal of actual or potential damage to the organism that calls for an action in order to counteract the threat, to remedy the potential damage, or to prevent it. They believe that pain is a warning that, unless appropriate action takes place, the pain will increase and the damage will be more serious.

However, the intensity of pain is not always related to the degree of damage caused to the organism. Compare the intensity of a toothache to the mild or even unnoticed discomfort related to the initial phases of cancer or the acquired immunodeficiency syndrome (AIDS). Sometimes, pain may appear too late in a sudden injury or in a slow one, and it is often modified by the patient's reaction to it (Boshes, 1983, p. 23).

Some people tend to augment, to reduce, or to leave unchanged their perception of pain. Painful physiological corollaries of emotions perceived as painful call for perceptual reactance (Petrie, 1967). Hilgard (1973) and Hilgard and Hilgard (1975) explained the relationship of pain to hypnotic trance by a "neodissociative interpretation."

As discussed above, hysterics tend to be especially sensitive to pain. In contrast, schizoprenics may be very insensitive or totally insensitive to pain. Children are usually sensitive to pain, but many schizophrenic children are not (Wolman, 1970).

Many autistic children display aberrant reactions to physical pain and do not communicate feelings of distress by crying and whining. It appears that autistic children are insulated even against their own physiological reactions. They occasionally indulge in serious self-injury; they may bang their heads, bite their tongues, cut their hands, squeeze their fingers in the door, or sit on a hot radiator. All this occurs without a word of complaint.

Autistic children are usually toilet-trained at the same age as normal children. The relative ease of the training, like their lowered sensitivity to pain, stems from their low body cathexis and insufficient erotization of body surface and orifices.

THEORIES OF PAIN

In addition to the earlier theories (psychoanalytic and others), current research workers have suggested new interpretations. Two of them are briefly discussed here.

Melzack and Wall (1965) introduced the *gate control theory* of pain. According to this theory:

1. A spinal gate (SG) mechanism in the dorsal horn region of the spinal cord modulates the transmission of nerve impulses from afferent fibers to spinal cord transmission (T) cells. It is *assumed* that the substantia gelatinosa is the primary vehicle for gating.
2. The SG mechanism is controlled by the *relative* amount of activity in large-diameter (L) rapidly conducting and small-diameter (S) slowly conducting fibers. The large fibers tend to *inhibit* transmission; activity in the small fibers tends to *facilitate* transmission and to open the gate.
3. The SG mechanism is controlled by nerve impulses that descend from the brain.
4. A system of large-diameter, rapidly conducting fibers activates the cognitive processes that influence the modulating properties of the SG mechanism.
5. As soon as the output of the T cells exceeds the critical level, the *action system* is triggered. This system represents the neural areas that guide the sequential patterns of behavior typical of pain.

According to the *specificity theory* (Feuerstein, Labbé, & Kuczmierczyk, 1986), pain is communicated to the brain via an independent sensory system. The two basic components of pain are the physiological sensation of pain and the psychological awareness (perception) of pain. The primary element of pain is the specific, neurophysiological sensation. The awareness of a threat or of damage to the tissues is the perceptual aspect of pain that elicits the emotional reaction.

The American Psychiatric Association has introduced in the third edition of its *Diagnostic and Statistical Manual of Mental Disorders* (DSM-III; APA, 1980) several new concepts related to psychosomatic medicine, among them a new clinical category of Psychogenic Pain Disorder (307.80). According to the DSM-III, the predominant feature of psychogenic pain disorder is the complaint of pain in the absence of physical findings and with evidence of psychological, etiological factors.

The pain symptoms are not related to the anatomical distribution of the nervous system, and they cannot be accounted for by any organic pathology. There are no pathophysiological mechanisms that account for the pain.

Psychological factors are etiologically involved in the pain; usually, an environmental stimulus is related to a psychological conflict or need. The initiation or exacerbation of the pain permits the individual to avoid some activity that is noxious to him or her or enables him or her to get support from the environment. The psychogenic pain disorder can be accompanied by other localized sensory or motor function charges, such as paresthesias and muscle spasms. A description of a few particular pains follows.

HEADACHES

Headaches are the most frequently used means of eliciting compassion and forgiveness. "You're giving me a headache," people often say, seeking to be excused from an unpleasant task or commitment. Headaches are also a common symptom of emotional conflicts. There are many different types of headaches, defined by their etiology (e.g., reflex neuromuscular; migraine; migranoid; histamine, or allergic; focal infection; and hypertensive), or increased intracranial pressure by the type of pain (e.g., pulsating, bursting, bandlike, or continuous), or by the distribution of the pain (e.g., frontal, occipital, unilateral, or bilateral).

Some headaches could be conversion symptoms, which may result from repressed hostile or sexual impulses and may have a symbolic meaning to the patient.

Over 90% of all headaches are either *migraine headaches* or *tension headaches*, and about 50% of them are migraine headaches. According to Clark and Cumley (1973), the onset of migraine headaches often occurs among individuals ranging in age from 12 to 25. However, the onset may occur at any age. Typically, the person who is a victim of migraine headaches is very intelligent, driven, ambitious, and financially careful.

Three prominent features of migraine headaches are that: (1) the headache typically affects *one* side of the head, (2) there are periodic recurrences, and (3) migraine headaches are likely to be hereditary. The incidence of migraine headaches in most cases is once every 2 weeks. For women, the attack of these headaches may also be associated with their menstrual period. However, there are also individuals who do not show any regularity between attacks (Anderson & Franks, 1981; Lance, 1981).

The duration of a migraine headache may be from 1 hour to a week. Yet, individuals often experience similar pain and symptoms between attacks (Davis, Wetzel, & Kashiwaga, 1976).

The most outstanding symptom of a migraine headache is pain; typically, this pain is very intense and sharp, beginning in the temple, the eyeball, or the forehead. Victims of migraine headaches may also experience pain throughout the entire face and neck as well as in their arms. Some of the other symptoms, which precede a migraine headache, are disturbed vision, flashes of light that may be blinding, dizziness, and a sensitivity to noise. Blind spots may accompany the headache as the attack begins. While the person is experiencing a migraine attack, the skin may become sweaty, and although the person may have a fever, the arms and legs may feel cold to him or her. The face of a person with a migraine can appear pale and yellow, and finally, as the attack is nearing a climax, nausea and vomiting may occur.

There are several warnings of an oncoming migraine headache. These headaches seem to be related to periods of highs and lows in a person's life. Frequently, migraine headache sufferers may be in a rather good mood the evening before they experience an attack. These high spirits are sometimes accompanied by an increase in appetite. However, the following morning, they may awake feeling very depressed, restless, and confused. As the onset of the attack draws nearer, there may be a tendency to become absent-minded. Visual disturbance, as well as tingling sensations in the hands and arms or ringing in the ears, may be the warning signs that the migraine headache is upon the victim. (Clark & Cumley, 1973; Pearce, 1977).

The attacks are characterized by their periodic nature, prodromal disturbances (scotomata, occasional paresthesias, and speech difficulties), and pain. The pain may be unilateral and associated with photophobia. The actual pain is preceded by an initial phase of vasoconstriction, which produces the prodromata. The aberrations in central vasomotor functions are associated with excessive cranial vascular reactivity.

Migraine headaches may have a combination of psychosomatic and somatopsychic etiologies. According to Raskin (1985), migraine headaches are idiopathic and are possibly related to genetically transmitted dysfunctions of the brain stem, defective neurotransmitters, and an erratic pain-modulation system. Several hypotheses concerning the etiology of migraine headaches have been put forward, among them that the modulation or release of serotonin at the synaptic cleft is defective, or that the vasomotor regulation is defective. On the other hand, the onset of a migraine headache is quite often related to severe frustration, aggravation, depression, suppressed anger, and other emotional factors (Pearce, 1977). Small wonder that some research workers believe in the somatopsychic etiology of migraine headaches, whereas others believe in psychosomatic origins of migraine headaches. Most probably, migraine headaches are a classic case of the hammer-and-anvil scenerio: Psychological factors produce migraine headache whenever there is some degree of organic predisposition and weakness of the immune system.

Tension Headaches

As mentioned above, the vast majority of headaches are either migraine or tension headaches or a combination of the two. Tension headaches, often called *muscular-contraction headaches,* are another area where organicity (somatopsychic elements) and psychology (psychosomatic elements) converge. Tension headaches were believed to be a product of a sustained contraction of skeletal muscles of the neck, the shoulders, the scalp, and the face. However, this theory has been neither totally approved nor totally rejected. At the present time, there is no conclusive evidence that tension headaches are a product of emotional factors, although anxiety can produce muscular contraction and headaches (Martin, 1985).

In 1981, Fuijii *et al.* emphasized the importance of the perceived-pain threshold as a psychological variable. Furthermore, Martin (1985) reviewed 50 patients with muscle-contraction headaches and found that 41 of them (82%) manifested evidence of emotional conflicts that were being ineffectually dealt with. Anderson and Franks (1981) described a controlled comparison of patients with migraine and tension headaches. A personality distinction was made between the two groups of patients. The patients with migraine headaches were perfectionistic and success-oriented. The patients with tension headaches were more anxious and insecure. These authors studied several variables during periods of unstructured relaxation, mild stress, and recovery from stress. The variables included forearm and forehead muscle potentials, peripheral skin temperature, electrodermal response, heart rate, blood pressure, pain ratings, and scores on the Edwards Personality Inventory. Anderson and Franks concluded that the tension headaches were not associated with increased frontal muscular tension, and that the migraine group did not have increased vasomotor activity.

Martin and Mathew (1978) found no consistent difference between patients with tension headaches and control subjects in electromyographic (EMG) tracings of forehead or neck muscles or in pain thresholds for graded thermal stimuli. Among the headache group, the baseline levels of muscle tension in the forehead muscles were greater. In this group, 43% (10 of 23) had an increase in the severity of the headache following an inhalation of amyl nitrite, a finding suggesting that the pain of tension headache is associated with vasodilation rather than vasoconstriction.

Fuijii, Kachi, and Sobue (1981) reported that the EMG activity of temporal muscle, measured in 18 patients with muscle-contraction headaches, was significantly higher ($p < .01$) than in a control group of 30 patients. The level of muscle tension during headache-free time was greater in the headache group than in the control group.

It seems that the majority of muscle-contraction headaches are bilateral. The pain is usually nonthrobbing and more diffuse than other types of head pain, and the occipital and suboccipital areas are frequently painful and tender to palpitation. The onset is usually gradual, and there may be complaints of scalp tenderness during muscle-contraction headaches.

According to Davis *et al.* (1976), tension headache is a frequent symptom of depression. These researchers studied 74 patients with headaches: 40 were depressed (according to their scores on the California Psychological Inventory). Of the headaches studied, 39% were vascular, 31% were muscle-contraction, and 30% were a combination of the two. There was no association between the type of headache and personality types.

Cox and Thomas (1981) studied 74 patients with tension headaches. They applied the California Psychological Inventory and found that the majority of these patients were depressed.

OTHER PAINS

There can be no doubt that some pain is caused by organic factors and some by psychological factors. Consider, for instance, pectoral fibrositis, which is a muscular pain manifested on the left side of the body. Quite often, it is affected by the suffering individual's belief that he or she has a heart attack. It is possible that many other pains, including rheumatoid back pain, are caused—or at least are aggravated—by psychological factors (Seaman & Reder, 1963).

REFERENCES

American Psychiatric Association. *Diagnostic and Statistical Manual of Mental Disorders* (3rd ed.—DSM-III). Washington, DC: Author, 1980.

Anderson, C. D., & Franks, R. D. Migraine and tension headache: Is there a psychological difference? *Headache*, 1981, *21*, 63–81.

Ayrapetyants, E. S. *Higher nervous function and the receptors of internal organs.* Moscow: USSR Academy of Science, 1959.

Berger, P. A. Endorphins. In B. B. Wolman (Ed.), *International encyclopedia of psychiatry, psychology, psychoanalysis and neurology* (Progress Vol. 1, pp. 121–125). New York: Aesculpaius Publishers, 1983.

Boshes, B. Brain and behavior: Current research. In B. B. Wolman (Ed.), *International encyclopedia of psychiatry, psychology, psychoanalysis and neurology* (Progress Vol. 1, pp. 19–24). New York: Aesculapius Publishers, 1983.

Bykov, K. M. *The cerebral cortex and the inner organs.* New York: Chemical Publishing, 1957.

Clark, R. L., & Cumley, R. W. *The book of health.* New York: Van Nostrand Reinhold, 1973.

Cobb, S. *Foundations of neuropsychiatry.* Baltimore: Williams & Wilkins, 1958.

Cooper, J., & Croyle, R. T. Attitudes and attitude change. *Annual Review of Psychology* (Vol. 35, pp. 395–426). Palo Alto, CA: Annual Reviews, 1984.

Cox, D., & Thomas, D. Relationship between headaches and depression. *Headache*, 1981, *21*, 261–263.

Davis, R. A., Wetzel, R. D., & Kashiwaga, M. Personality, depression and headache type. *Headache*, 1976, *16*, 246–251.

Deutsch, F. (Ed.). *On the mysterious leap from the mind to the body*. New York: International Universities Press, 1959.

Feuerstein, M., Labbé, E. E., & Kuczmierczyk, A. R. *Health psychology: A psychological perspective*. New York: Plenum Press, 1986.

Fuijii, S., Kachi, T., & Sobue, I. Chronic headache: Its psychosomatic aspect. *Japanese Journal of Psychosomatic Medicine*, 1981, *21*, 411–419.

Hilgard, E. R. A neodissociative interpretation of pain reduction in hypnosis. *Psychological Review*, 1973, *80*, 396–416.

Hilgard, E. R., & Hilgard, J. R. *Hypnosis in the relief of pain*. Los Altos, CA: Kaufman, 1975.

Lance, J. W. Headache. *Annals of Neurology*, 1981, *10*, 1–10.

Levine, J. D., Gordon, N. C., & Fields, H. L. The mechanism of placebo analgesia. *Lancet*, 1978, *1*, 654–657.

Martin, M. J. Muscle contraction (tension) headache. In W. Dorfman & L. Cristofar (Eds.), *Psychosomatic illness review* (pp. 1–10). New York: Macmillan, 1985.

Martin, P. R., & Mathew, A. M. Tensions headaches: Psychophysiological investigation and treatment. *Journal of Psychosomatic Research*, 1978, *22*, 389–399.

McKerns, W., & Pantić, V. *Neuroendocrine correlates of stress*. New York: Plenum Press, 1985.

Melzack, R., & Wall, P. Pain mechanisms: A new theory. *Science*, 1965, *150*, 1971–1979.

Miller, R. J. Enkephalins and endorphins. In K. L. Melman (Ed.), *Drug therapeutics* (pp. 139–154). New York: Elsevier, 1981.

Naranjo, C. Drug-induced states. In B. B. Wolman & M. Ullman (Eds.), *Handbook of states of consciousness* (pp. 365–394). New York: Van Nostrand Reinhold, 1986.

Pearce, J. Migraine: A psychosomatic disorder. *Headache*, 1977, *17*, 125–128.

Petrie, A. *Individuality in pain and suffering*. Chicago: University of Chicago Press, 1967.

Raskin, N. H. Migraine. In W. Dorfman & L. Cristofar (Eds.), *Psychosomatic illness review* (pp. 11–22). New York: Macmillan, 1985.

Razran, G. Evolutionary psychology. In B. B. Wolman & E. Nagel (Eds.), *Scientific psychology* (pp. 207–252). New York: Basic Books, 1965.

Roy, A. (Ed.). *Hysteria*. New York: Wiley, 1982.

Seaman, G. J., & Reder, E. L. Psychogenic back disorders. *Psychosomatic Medicine*, 1963, *16*, 374–392.

Skinner, B. F. *Cumulative record*. New York: Appleton-Century-Crofts, 1959.

Szasz, T. S. Pain as a career and as strategy. In H. J. Wain & D. P. Devaris (Eds.), *The treatment of pain*. New York: Aronson, 1982.

Webb, W. L. Chronic pain. In W. Dorfman & L. Cristofar (Eds.), *Psychosomatic illness review* (pp. 196–209). New York: Macmillan, 1985.

Wenger, M. A. Emotions and autonomic physiology. In B. B. Wolman (Ed.), *International encyclopedia of psychiatry, psychology, psychoanalysis and neurology* (Vol. 4, pp. 307–311). New York: Aesculapius Publishers, 1977.

Wolman, B. B. Antigone principle. *American Image*, 1965, *22*, 186–201.

Wolman, B. B. *Children without childhood: A study of childhood schizophrenia*. New York: Grune & Stratton, 1970.

Wolman, B. B. *Call no man normal*. New York: International Universities Press, 1973.

19

Psychosomatic Issues in Sexuality and Gynecology

Sexual behavior represents a combination of physiological and psychological factors in males and females. Sexual behavior is regulated by the endocrine and nervous systems. Sexual arousal, penile tumescence in males, and vaginal lubrication in females belong to the realm of physiology. Sexual desires, courting, and sexual relations are psychological issues.

Chronic obstructive pulmonary disease, hypoxia, and decreased serum testosterone may cause erectile dysfunction. Sexual behavior can be seriously affected by renal failure, spinal cord lesions, hypophysectomy, adrenalectomy, and dysfunctions of the pituitary or adrenal glands and of the hypothalamus and the limbic system. Sexual behavior can be disturbed by alcohol, barbituates, and antihypertensive medication, as well as pelvic or genital pathology and a variety of other kinds of physical pathology.

A great many sexual dysfunctions can be caused by shortcomings, dysfunctions, deficiencies, and disorders of the nervous and endocrine systems. However, most sexual dysfunctions originate in *psychological factors,* such as depression, anxiety, feelings of shame, feelings of insecurity and inadequacy, unresolved oedipal involvements, masturbatory fantasies, guilt feelings, negative body image, ambivalent feelings about one's gender and inadequate or confused psychosexual identification, social maladjustment, and a host of other unconscious causes. In other words, human sexuality is a convincing proof that human behavior is a combination of psychosomatic and somatopsychic events. Whereas this volume is devoted to psychosomatic issues, one must keep in mind that nature crosses the mind and body bridge in both directions (Dropat & Holmes, 1963).

Psychoanalytic Interpretation

Freud (1905/1954) maintained that sexual disorders are caused by a fixation at or a regression to infantile sexuality. The so-called perversions that, according to Freud, include homosexuality, fetishism, sadomasochism, exhibitionism, transvestism, and voyeurism represent an infantile level of sexual development. For instance, fetishists cathect libidinally an inanimate object that symbolizes a part of the body of an ambivalently loved person. Fetishism is a mental state that leads the person to worship or love material objects. It is a fixation of neurotic investment on an object or a body part that is inappropriate to normal sexuality but that is needed by a person for the attainment of sexual gratification. Parts of the body, such as hair, hands, or feet, or any object of personal apparel can serve as a fetish. The fetish usually symbolizes the female phallus, and its use represents a denial of the fear of castration that might be suggested by the anatomical differences between the sexes. Fetishism is an unconscious defense against castration anxiety.

Transvestism represents, for the male, an identification with the phallic mother and, for the female, her wish to deny the lack of a penis. The compulsive exposure of the sex organs in exhibitionism is a defense against castration anxiety because of the shock or fright in the female object at the sight of a penis. Voyeurism serves similar defense needs. In his early thinking, Freud (1905/1954) regarded sadomasochism as a tendency to seek or inflict suffering as a way of achieving sexual arousal or gratification. In masochistic perversion, sexual gratification is felt as a result of pain inflicted by beatings, threats, humiliation, or subjugation at the hand of a sexual partner. Sadistic gratification is derived from inflicting such torment on the sexual partner. Perverts are capable of orgiastic release, but their orgasm is stimulated by the perverse act rather than by a normal heterosexual outlet. The capacity for genital orgasm is inhibited by an obstacle that is overcome or substituted for by the perverse act. Perverse behavior does not lack organization, as is often seen in the sexuality of "polymorphous perverts."

The factors that inhibit the normal development toward genital primacy are anxiety and guilt feelings related to the child's oedipal involvement with the parents. The oedipal complex refers to the complex emotional involvement with one's parents. In the preoedipal years, the child is involved with the mother and the father in different ways. By the third year, the child attains a more complex level of involvement with the parents. The child must relate to them as a member of a triad in which the child is the smallest and most dependent member.

The oedipal situation causes the upsurge of sexual feelings directed primarily toward the parent of the opposite sex. Little boys have sexual feelings toward their mothers, along with erections, desires to see their mother undressed, to sleep with her, and to get rid of the father. The little girl has sexual feelings for her father, wishes for a baby from him, and desires to get rid of the mother. The resolution of the positive oedipal complex leads to normal heterosexuality for both genders (Wolman, 1968; Wolman & Money, 1980).

The negative oedipal complex consists of sexual feelings directed toward the same-sex parent and feelings of rivalry toward the opposite-sex parent. The little boy wishes for approval and affection from his father and competes with his mother for his father's love. The little girl wishes for love and affection from her mother and competes with the father for her mother's affection. The negative oedipal complex exists in all children alongside the positive oedipal complex. When the balance of instinctual forces is shifted toward the negative oedipal complex, the likelihood of homosexuality is increased.

Castration anxiety is the key issue. Castration anxiety arises from the fear that the father will retaliate against the little boy for his sexual wishes to possess the mother. The balance of emotional patterns may shift as a result of this threat to the negative oedipal configuration, in which the son's loving attachment and submission to the father serve as a defense against castration fears. The little girl is more threatened by lack of love than by castration. If turning to the father does not satisfy her need for love and approval, she must cling to her mother, who is a safer love object.

In the perversions, infantile sexuality becomes predominant over adult sexuality (Meissner, 1980).

Sexual Inadequacy

With very few exceptions, sexual inadequacy is related to poor self-esteem, anxiety, low self-respect, and distorted body image. One of the most frequent disturbances in males is premature ejaculation. Premature ejaculation is the inability of a male to maintain penile erection long enough to complete penetration into the vagina. A sudden release of semen before the male reaches the peak of sexual arousal is a physiological process, but inferiority feelings and a lack of self-confidence are the frequent cause. According to Masters and Johnson (1970), the *fear* of sexual inadequacy is the greatest single cause of sexual inadequacy.

Premature ejaculation can be related to dysfunction or to prostate and urinary problems, but usually, it is caused by psychological factors. Quite often, it is related to feelings of insecurity and intense anxiety. In many instances, premature ejaculation is caused by the male's overconcern about pleasing the female partner. Some men worry about her hostile reaction. "She may dislike me," a patient of mine reported. "She may lose all respect for me and leave me," another patient complained.

Fensterheim and Kantor (1980) described the following case:

> A man complained of intermittent sexual impotency. Periodically he was able to attain and maintain an erection, but under those conditions he was usually disappointed in sex. At other times he was unable to either attain or maintain an erection. At these times he was aware of feelings of irritability and resentment, and often there were sharp words between the couple. Closer examination

revealed that the more actively the wife behaved in the sexual situation, the more apt the husband was to be impotent. Although such a pattern is usually associated with a fear of premature ejaculation, this did not seem to be true in this instance. Rather, the husband interpreted the wife's level of activity as demands being placed on him and he responded to these "demands" with resentment. Further examination showed a similar—although much lower response—to demands in nonsexual situations. (p. 317)

One of my young female patients complained of total frigidity. She did not experience any emotional reactions whatsoever during sexual relations, either vaginal or oral, although she had some lubrication. She believed she was unattractive, almost ugly, and she could not believe that any "worthwhile man" could be interested in her. A gynecological examination failed to show any physiological deficiency. Another allegedly frigid woman who disliked her husband had no sensual reaction to intercourse with her husband but could enjoy sex and even reach orgasm in occasional affairs with strangers. Apparently, sexual dysfunction can be caused by psychological attitudes and preferences.

SEXUAL DISORDERS IN ORGANIC DISEASES

Some organic diseases can cause sexual dysfunctions. Diseases of the central and autonomic nervous systems, diseases of the glands of inner secretion, chronic renal failure, insulin dependence in male diabetics, lumbosacral lesions, and so on adversely affect sexual functioning. However, in many instances, it is not the disease itself but the psychological reaction to the disease that causes sexual dysfunctions. Obviously, sexual disorders can be caused by both physical and psychological factors, or by a combination of both (Wise, 1985; Wolman & Money, 1980).

Take, for instance, the myocardial infarction. The psychological corollaries of myocardial infarction include fear of death, profound depression, and acute anxiety. The infarction itself hardly affects sexual functioning, but victims of cerebrovascular accidents tend to dramatically reduce their frequency of sexual intercourse and may suffer various sexual dysfunctions (Wise, 1985).

Carcinoma of the breast and mastectomy do not reduce sexual desire in females, nor do they prevent normal sexual functions. However, quite often, the psychological aftereffects of mastectomy seriously interfere with sexual behavior. In my clinical practice, I have worked with women who, after having a mastectomy, avoided sexual encounters. Mastectomy affected their body image and self-confidence: They felt ashamed and embarrassed and refused to have sexual relations (Frank, Dornbrush, Webster, et al., 1978).

GENDER IDENTITY AND ROLE

Gender identity is determined by the sex chromosomes. The male gender is determined by XY chromosomes, and the female gender by XX chromosomes. The loss of one X chromosome from the XX or XY pattern is not lethal. The addition of one or more X or Y chromosomes, called *mosaicism*, causes a variety of physiological and psychological disorders. Individuals with the XXY pattern (Klinefelter syndrome) are males, but their testes are small and sterile, their penises are small, and they are often mentally retarded.

XXX individuals are females. Some of them have behavioral problems, and many are not fertile. XXX individuals are phenotypically females who have gonadal streaks in place of ovaries.

Around the sixth week of gestation, the male fetus testes secrete two hormones: androgen and the Mullerian inhibiting substance (MIS). The female fetus does not secrete hormones in intrauterine life.

At birth, newborn infants are either males or females. This is their genotype, that is, the genetically determined gender. The parents can be healthy as phenotypes, but one of them or both may carry hidden recessive morbid genes. In this case, obviously, their genotype is not entirely healthy, and a single morbid gene can affect the future of their offspring.

The intrauterine environment and the antenatal environment exercise considerable influence on the not-yet-born organism. The influences become more and more diversified after birth and affect the development of the child in every possible way. Nutrition and the quality of physical care influence the chemistry of the body, and interaction with the parents and other people shapes the child's physical and psychological development. Both influences, the physical and the mental, act on the genotypical foundations and form the person's phenotype (Block, von Der Lippe, & Block, 1973; Mazut & Money, 1980).

Money (Money & Wiedekind, 1980) defined gender identity as the private experience of gender role, and he defined gender role as the public expression of gender identity. According to Money, gender role is everything that a person says or does to indicate to others or to himself or herself the degree that he or she is either male, female, or ambivalent. Gender role is the public expression of gender identity, and gender identity is the private experience of gender role. Thus, *gender identity–role* is the term used to express the unity of gender identity and gender role.

The differentiation of gender identity–role is a product of the interaction of prenatal and postnatal determinants or events, the latter outweighing the former in overall influence. In the differentiation of gender identity–role, identification signifies that an individual has established a mental schema in the brain by imitating and copying or modeling the behavior of members of his or her own assigned sex.

Gender identity–role disorders occur in individuals with normal external and internal reproductive anatomy. The sexual pathways of the central nervous system do not show morphological changes to which gender identity–role disorders might be attributed (Barnard, 1981).

According to Money (Money & Weidekind, 1980), some clinicians use the term *disorder* in connection with gender identity–role to refer only to male–female transpositions, sometimes known as *gender dysphorias*. These transpositions contain the syndromes of transexualism and transvestism and may include homosexuality and bisexuality, though neither of these are considered pathologies or disorders.

Some clinicians include in the category of disordered gender identity–role all the paraphilias. *Paraphilia* refers to a condition in which sexual arousal and performance depend on highly specific imagery, perceived or remembered, other than imagery of the erotic partner.

The paraphilias include masochism and sadism, rape and lust murder, voyeurism and exhibitionism, pedophilia and gerontophilia, amputeephilia (apotemnophilia), zoophilia, klismaphilia, coprophilia, urophilia, necrophilia, and fetishism. In all paraphilias, psychological factors affect the physical behavior. Transvestism, because of its associated fetishistic dependency on clothing, is a paraphilia. So is transexualism, for the transexual person can function erotically only by having, or imagining having, a body reassigned and transformed from that of the sex of birth.

A paraphilia becomes pathological when it becomes too severe, too insistent, and too noxious. The personal criteria of pathology are pain, suffering, and loss of the feeling of well-being. The social criterion may be too much harm to, or threat of endangering the health or well-being of, others.

The incidence of gender identity–role disorders is greater in males than in females. The embryology of the prenatal hormonal regulation of sex differentiation shows that nature's first choice is to differentiate the morphology of a female. The differentiation of male morphology requires that androgen be released by the fetal testes. Androgen also influences the brain pathways or thresholds that mediate erotic and mating behavior. It is likely that prenatal androgen has a masculinizing effect on the brain thresholds subserving the relationship of visual signals and images to erotic attraction and arousal. In males, the visual stimulus prompts the initiation of an erotic approach. Nature demonstrates the primacy of the visual image in male eroticism in the phenomenon of the pubertal orgasm dream (wet dream).

Transexualism represents the most extreme transposition in terms of time and completeness. In transvestism, the transposition is time-limited and alternates between male and female. Homosexuality, in its extreme forms of effeminate homosexuality in the male and virilistic homosexuality in the female, shows itself not only in erotic but also in neurotic behavior.

The transexual individual is genitally an anatomical male or female who expresses a strong conviction that he or she has the mind of the opposite sex and seeks to change his or her original sex legally and through hormonal and surgical sex reassignment. The age at which sex reassignment becomes urgent may be prepuberty or adolescence or young adulthood.

In the etiology of transexualism, there is no evidence of a hereditary factor. Transexualism has been recorded in some males with the 47, XXY chromosomal condition (Klinefelter syndrome), but most XXY individuals are not transexuals. Transexuality is probably a psychosomatic phenomenon, according to Money (Money & Wiedekind, 1980, p. 275). It is impossible to find a formula from which to predict transexualism on the basis of early childhood history, even among children who overtly wish to change sex. In some families, it is possible to recognize a covert collusion of the parents and the child with respect to the child's repudiation of his or her anatomic sex. Therefore, a diagnosis of transexualism is based initially on the individual's need for sex reassignment. Usually, physical examination yields nothing that contributes to the diagnosis. Very rarely, the EEG may show a temporal-lobe epileptic focus requiring neurosurgery, after which the sex problem may remit. Also, hormonal tests offer no evidence, and the issue seems to be totally psychogenic.

Homosexuality

Psychoanalysts relate homosexuality to the oedipal phase of development. The anxiety in relationship to the female genitals may be of at least two kinds: (1) the anxiety may arise from awareness that there are "penisless" beings and may encourage castration fears; or (2) castration anxiety could be rooted in early oral-aggressive impulses, and the female genitals may be seen as the castrating instrument capable of biting or tearing off the penis—the vagina dentata fantasy.

According to Freud, male homosexuality originates in identification with the mother. When the identification with the father, which would shape the young male child's emerging sense of himself as a man, is undercut, the child is drawn to his mother. The tendency of the mother to be oversolicitious and overprotective of and overinvolved with the male child contributes to the little boy's feminine identification. Such identification cannot be without considerable conflict, and the degree of anxiety depends largely on the extent to which the child has remained pathologically dependent on the mother and the degree to which he has been unable to establish some degree of separation from her without the threat of loss or abandonment. The identification with the mother underlies the homosexual impulse to view men as sexual objects.

A frequent component of this complex is a continually frustrated year-ning and longing for closeness, acceptance, and loving communication with the father. These wishes can be more-or-less consciously expressed directly in relation to the father, but more frequently, they remain rela-tively unconscious and are acted-out as wishes for approval and accep-tance from significant male figures in the patient's life. Homosexuals are often so intensely narcissistic that they are usually attracted to themselves. The narcissistic wish often expresses itself as the substitute for oedipal strivings; that is, once the homosexual male has identified himself with his mother, he begins to behave as he once wished his mother to behave toward him. This wish leads to a choice of libidinal objects, such as men or boys, who are quite similar to the individual himself (Meissner, 1980).

In the psychoanalytic view, some homosexuals show a need to give to others what they did not get themselves. They gain the satisfaction of "getting," through an identification with the one with/to whom they are giving. This is a form of "altruism" in which certain pleasures that the individuals cannot have themselves may be given to others and relished through an identification with these others. The wish to give and the affection for the other are usually ambivalent and mixed with envy, which may turn into resentment if the one given to is not as pleased as the giver expects him to be.

According to psychoanalytic theory, the boy's identification with the mother could be related to other pregenital components, including an anal fixation. This dynamic may lead to a masochistic striving to submit oneself to the father in the "passive" way that the mother does. The anal fixation, combined with maternal identification, may lead to a wish for anal inter-course. Feminine and passive men have not at all given up their uncon-scious striving to be masculine and to replace their father. By becoming the feminine part to a more masculine man, they can gain the strength and masculine power of the partner. Thus, the retreat from castration anxiety to a feminine identification does not replace the wish for identification with the father. The wish to be like the father, to gain power by being more like him, is ambivalent, as its ultimate aim is, in the oedipal context, to replace the father. Once the boy places the father in a position of power and omnipotence, he may try to regain some sense of strength by sharing in the father's power (Wolman, 1968, 1978).

Narcissistic and passive-anal fixations may occur in the same indi-vidual and may express themselves in various combinations in different forms of homosexuality. In situations in which the homosexual inclinations are excessively stimulated, such individuals may experience an over-whelming anxiety, which has been described in the psychoanalytic liter-ature as *homosexual panic*.

Fear of the penis is essential to female homosexuality, according to psychoanalytic theory. Often, the penis is seen by such women as a punishing, hurting, destructive, tearing, and biting organ. These fears and thoughts and feelings may impede the capacity for sexual enjoyment, to the extent that there is no sexual pleasure possible if it involves the penis.

For homosexual women, the male genital can be excluded by regression. The first love object of every human being is the mother, so that all women begin life with a primary homosexual attachment. When, in the course of later development, the emergence of normal heterosexuality is blocked, regression to the homosexual attachment may occur. Women regress from love of the father as a sexual object to a love of the mother as a sexual object. In female homosexuality, the rejection of heterosexuality is related to the castration complex, to penis fear, and to an early preoedipal fixation on attachment to the mother and loving attachment to the father. This is the psychoanalytic view.

However, if the mother is unable to positively reinforce the young girl's sense of growing femininity, this disappointment and disillusionment may draw her away from an increasing identification with the mother and toward an identification with the father. This paternal identification may lead her to seek woman as love objects. This resolution not only allows the woman to avoid oedipal competition with the mother but also has an element of continuing hostility toward the father, expressed in hostility toward men.

It is necessary to add at this point that there is a possibility of some degree of genetic predisposition to homosexuality.

PREGNANCY

Pregnancy represents a major step in the life of a woman. When a woman becomes pregnant, she experiences dramatic psychological changes as well as major physiological changes. Many pregnant women become introverted and passive. There is in the pregnant woman a growing preoccupation with her body, her physical and emotional needs, and her unborn child. Many women experience primitive modes of thinking and a preoccupation with fantasy. It is not uncommon for pregnant women to have fantasies about bearing a defective, damaged child (Belle, 1982).

The pregnant woman's view of her pregnancy and childbirth is closely related to her attitude toward and relationship with her mother (Shainess, 1977; Tolchin & Egan, 1978).

In women who have had a good relationship with their mothers, there is a resurgence of positive, warm, and longing feelings toward their mothers and a reawakening of many pleasant memories regarding their mothers. The strengthening of this bond between mother and daughter results in the pregnant woman's mother assisting her pregnant daughter. However, if there has been a poor mother–daughter relationship, the intensified recollection of that relationship may result in increased fighting and tension between the pregnant woman and her mother.

In order to have a psychologically healthy pregnancy, the woman must have satisfactorily resolved various stages of her relationship with her mother. If the woman is struggling with her own strong dependency needs, the fetus may be resented and feared as a parasite who drains her, sucks her dry, and eats her up like a cancer within. These fears can contribute to hypochondriasis during pregnancy. Becoming a mother involves a certain loss of autonomy. If this is an unresolved conflict, the pregnant woman may fear an intolerable loss of freedom in being tied down by the baby and burdened with responsibility (Shainess, 1977).

If a woman does not have a positive identification with her mother, she is quite likely to face a conflict in becoming a mother herself. The prospective mother who had an antagonistic relationship with her own mother may carry with her intense feelings of guilt because of her hostile and aggressive impulses toward her mother. Her guilt may prompt fears about her own pregnancy. She may believe that she cannot have a normal baby, that it will be retarded, that it will be a monster, or that she will die in childbirth.

The mother-to-be may have been very jealous of her mother as a rival for her father's affection and may also have been enraged by subsequent pregnancies that the mother had. So the pregnant woman may be concerned about awakening the animosity of others toward her; there may be an increase in superstitious fears. The pregnant woman may also fear that her baby will be a rival for her husband's love—a situation that she may have experienced with her own parents. So, too, a new baby may be perceived as the woman's sibling, toward whom she felt anger and jealousy (Doherty & Jacobson, 1982).

A woman's positive identification with her mother usually entails an acceptance of herself as a sexual being. If the woman has conflicts about being a sexual person, these concerns are likely to be intensified during pregnancy, increasing her guilt and anxiety. If a pregnant woman fears that masturbation could have injured her genitals, she may believe that the baby is damaged. Or she may believe that her body will be injured by the pregnancy and the delivery. Many women with uncomplicated pregnancies are afraid to have intercourse during pregnancy because they fear that coitus will result in damage to the fetus.

The study of psychosomatics in gynecology and obstetrics is not new. As early as 1930, Horney (reported in Kelman, 1967) related premenstrual tensions to psychological causes. Several psychoanalysts have related menstrual disturbances to psychosomatic issues and have believed that conflicts and ambivalence about motherhood are a psychosomatic cause of infertility (Nadelson, Notman, & Ellis, 1985).

About 50%–70% of pregnant women experience nausea, vomiting, and fatigue, often accompanied by a sense of disappointment because they believe they should be excited. Others respond positively in spite of the discomfort. In other words, reactions to pregnancy could be due to physiological or psychological causes or to a combination of the two. The fact is that women who view pregnancy as an illness tend to have longer labors than women who do not (Nadelson *et al.*, 1985).

POSTPARTUM DEPRESSION

Not all women experience depression after childbirth. It is not clear whether childbirth itself is the cause of postpartum depression. Clinical experience points to the fact that women who are inclined toward depressive moods tend to react emotionally to childbirth. The postpartum depression is rarely a purely somatopsychic phenomenon (Weissman & Paykel, 1947).

MENOPAUSE

Similar reasoning could be applied to menopause. Menopause is a physiological occurrence common to all females, but not all of them experience the same symptoms, such as headaches, sleep disturbances, irritability, palpitations, and depression. However, women who depend on their childbearing roles as a source of self-esteem and feminine identification are apt to develop more symptoms (Nadelson *et al.*, 1985).

REFERENCES

Barnard, J. *The female world.* New York: Macmillan–Free Press, 1981.

Belle, D. (Ed.). *Lives in stress: Women and depression.* Beverly Hills, CA: Sage, 1982.

Block, J., Von Der Lippe, A., & Block J. H. Sex role and socialization. *Journal of Consulting and Clinical Psychology,* 1973, *41,* 321–341.

Doherty, W. J., & Jacobson, N. S. Marriage and the family. In B. B. Wolman (Ed.), *Handbook of developmental psychology.* Englewood Cliffs, NJ: Prentice-Hall, 1982.

Dorpat, T. L., & Holmes, T. H. *Psychosomatic obstetrics, gynecology and endocrinology.* Springld, IL: Thomas, 1963.

Fensterheim, H., & Kantor, J. S. The behavioral approach to sexual disorders. In B. B. Wolman & J. Money (Eds.), *Handbook of human sexuality* (pp. 313–324). Englewood Cliffs, NJ: Prentice-Hall, 1980.

Frank, D., Dornbrush, R. L., Webster, S. K., *et al.* Masectomy and sexual behavior. *Sexuality and Disability,* 1978, *1,* 16–26.

Freud, S. Three essays on the theory of sexuality. *Standard Edition* (Vol. 3). London: Hogarth Press, 1954. (Originally published, 1905.)

Kelman, H. (Ed.), *Feminine psychology.* New York: Norton, 1967.

Masters, W. H., & Johnson, V. E. *Human sexual inadequacy.* Boston: Little, Brown, 1970.

Mazur, T., and Money, J. Prenatal influences and subsequent sexuality. In B. B. Wolman & J. Money (Eds.), *Handbook of human sexuality* (pp. 3–14). Englewood Cliffs, NJ: Prentice-Hall, 1980.

Meissner, W. W. Psychoanalysis and sexual disorders. In B. B. Wolman & J. Money (Eds.), *Handbook of human sexuality* (pp. 285–311). Englewood Cliffs, NJ: Prentice-Hall, 1980.

Money, J., & Wiedekind, S. Gender identity/role: Normal differentiations and its transpositions. In B. B. Wolman & J. Money (Eds.), *Handbook of human sexuality* (pp. 269–284). Englewood Cliffs, NJ: Prentice-Hall, 1980.

Nadelson, C., Notman, M., & Ellis, E. Psychosomatic aspects of obstetrics and gynecology. In W. Dorfman & L. Cristofar (Eds.), *Psychosomatic illness review* (pp. 162–179). New York: Macmillan, 1985.

Shainess, N. Pregnancy: Psychiatric aspects. In B. B. Wolman (Ed.), *International encyclopedia of psychiatry, psychology, psychoanalysis and neurology*. New York: Aesculapius Publishers, 1977.

Thorne, F. C., & Pishkin, V. Diagnosing personality states. In B. B. Wolman (Ed.), *Clinical diagnosis of mental disorders: A handbook* (pp. 807–857). New York: Plenum Press, 1978.

Tolchin, J., & Egan, J. Fears in childhood and pregnancy. In B. B. Wolman (Ed.), *Psychological aspects of gynecology and obstetrics* (pp. 169–176). Oradell, NJ: Medical Economics, 1978.

Weisman, M., & Paykel, E. *The depressed woman*. Chicago: University of Chicago Press, 1974.

Wise, T. N. Sexual dysfunction in the medically ill. In W. Dorfman & L. Cristofar (Eds.), *Psychosomatic illness review* (pp. 180–195). New York: Macmillan, 1985.

Wolman, B. B. *The unconscious mind*. Englewood Cliffs, NJ: Prentice-Hall, 1968.

Wolman, B. B. (Ed.). *Clinical diagnosis of mental disorders: A handbook*. New York: Plenum Press, 1978.

Wolman, B. B., & Money, J. (Eds.), *Handbook of human sexuality*. Englewood Cliffs, NJ: Prentice-Hall, 1980.

20

Psychosomatic Issues in Diabetes, Arthritis, Thyroid Diseases, Muscular Tensions, and Infectious Diseases

THE IMMUNE SYSTEM

The diseases described in the following pages are not purely psychosomatic, but psychological factors play a significant role in their etiology, their degree of severity and their potential prognosis. A survey of the physiological dysfunctions of the human organism can hardly find a case totally free of psychological influences. Whenever a human body is exposed to disease-carrying viruses, bacterias, or any other harmful element, the host's immune system and its defensive army of lymphocytes, B cells, and T cells fight the invaders (Stein, Keller, & Schleifer, 1981).

There is no question that the biochemical structure and the physiological functions of the immune system are genetically determined (Möller & Möller, 1983). Moreover, the biological rhythms of the organism depend on genetic factors (Luce, 1970). However, the human organism and its behavior are not 100% stable, unyielding, and unchangeable. Human life represents a process of changes induced by a variety of factors, and socio-psychological events play a highly significant role in these changes. The immune system is not an isolated system: Its functions are greatly influenced by one's attitudes, emotions, and other personality traits, as well as by interactions between the organism and its environment (Gentry, 1984; Goldberger & Breznitz, 1982; Wall, 1979).

Ader and Cohen (1984) described these interactions as follows:

> As a result of research in psychosomatic and behavioral medicine, it has become clear that there is probably no major organ system or homeostatic defense mechanism that is not subject to the influence of interactions between psychological

and physiological events. The complex mechanisms underlying these interactions and their relationship to organic disease, however, are imperfectly understood. Perhaps least understood of all are the interrelations between behavioral and immune processes. . . . We cannot yet clarify the mechanisms involved, but we can provide some documentation of the potential impact of psychosocial factors on immune processes and on pathophysiological processes that involve immune responses. . . . We would contend, however, that like all other physiological systems operating in the interests of homeostasis, immune processes are sensitive to the influence of the central nervous system. As such, the immune system would stand as the mediator of the effects of psychosocial factors on the predisposition to and the precipitation and perpetuation of a variety of diseases. (p. 117)

Psychosomatic research is not limited to diseases that are produced by psychological factors; it also deals with a great many diseases of which psychological issues are not the sole cause but contribute to the etiology, severity, and course of the disease (Wittkower, 1969). Psychosomatic research studies anxiety, depression, and other emotional states and analyzes their role in neurochemical changes. For instance, research discovered that individuals in a state of bereavement experience a depressed function of T cells in the immune system (Barthrop *et al.*, 1977). A study by Rogers, Dubey, and Reich (1979) discovered significant changes in the functions of the T cells in individuals under stress. In other words, mourning and stress, as well as other emotions, can influence the functions of the immune system and its ability to fight disease.

DIABETES MELLITUS

Diabetes mellitus is not a psychosomatic disease. It is a metabolic disease related to abnormal carbohydrate oxidation that causes excessive amounts of sugar in the blood and the urine. Diabetes mellitus is a disease associated with a serious deficiency of insulin production that adversely affects the metabolism of glucose. Diabetes can have a great many physical and mental complications: diabetic patients may suffer vascular disorders, weakness, chronic renal failure, myocardial infarction, loss of weight, cataracts, blindness, strokes, autonomic and peripheral neuropathy, loss of appetite, muscle tenderness, excessive fatigue, depression, and impairment of cognitive functions, with occasional delusions and hallucinations. The initial symptoms of diabetes mellitus are a high level of blood sugar and the presence of sugar in the urine (Tager *et al.*, 1979).

Etiological research on diabetes mellitus points to genetic and immunological predisposition (Ellenberg & Rifkin, 1983). Genetically and immunologically predisposed individuals may develop islet-cell antibodies, and their B cells are unable to produce adequate amounts of insulin. Any type of physical stress, and especially infections or traumas, can trigger or aggravate diabetes mellitus. The disease is more prevalent in old age. But all this is one side of the coin; psychological factors are the other side.

Emotional upheavals, adverse life situations, severe frustrations, or family losses can contribute to the etiology. They may trigger the onset of diabetes mellitus and/or aggravate the course of the disease. Undoubtedly, many individuals who develop diabetes may have islet-cell antibodies for years before clinically identifiable diabetes mellitus appears. Psychologically stressful events may have little impact on one's initial susceptibility to this apparently genetically and immunologically determined disease, but like physical stresses, they may trigger the clinical manifestations of diabetes by increasing the demands for insulin production by the B cells, which are already depleted. On the other hand, it is quite possible that early losses could adversely affect immunological competence (Jacobson & Leibovich, 1985, p. 125). Moreover, emotional arousals can offset the hormonal secretion that influences the metabolism of glucose.

Diabetes could be a product of a single emotional crisis, but more often, it results from a chain of severe crises (Holmes & Masuda, 1974). The treatment of diabetes requires self-discipline, and the success of the treatment depends on intense and unswerving patient–doctor cooperation. However, diabetes, as well as the stress it creates, can make the patient unable to cooperate. It is not easy to acquire the complex skills needed for handling the disease, and many diabetic patients get easily discouraged. Their moods change rapidly, and in depressed or angry moods, they blame family members and create unbearable tension that pushes away all who try to help them.

Because diabetes requires rigorous dieting and continuous efforts to regulate daily functions, any negligence may cause the dangerous symptoms of hypoglycemia and acidosis, or even more severe and life-jeopardizing complications. In many instances, diabetes adversely affects the functions of the central and the peripheral nervous systems (Bale, 1973).

Diabetic patients are exceedingly sensitive and tend to overreact to stress. Emotional reactions to stress may produce health-damaging hormones and may adversely affect the fat and glucose metabolism (Schade & Eaton, 1980). Moreover, stressful events may trigger more severe diabetic symptoms and may aggravate the course of the disease by increasing the demand for insulin production by the B cells, which have little left to give (Jacobson & Leibovich, 1985).

It is rare and almost impossible to develop psychosomatic disorders that do not serve a purpose. On several occasions, patients of mine have maintained that their ailments were physical when they were psychosomatic; occasionally, the opposite was true. Only by a thorough examination were their hypotheses dismissed.

A Case Report

Many years ago, I had in psychotherapy a highly active elderly woman who was a gifted writer and who worked as an editor in a publishing house. Once in a while, she complained about a variety of physical symptoms that could have indicated peptic ulcer or any other gastrointestinal and, possibly, even cardiovascular dysfunction. She went to her family doctor, who could not find anything wrong with her. She went to another doctor and underwent several tests: all of them were negative.

In her case, I did not suspect any psychosomatic disorder. The woman was in the last phase of psychotherapy and was functioning reasonably well. I firmly believe that every psychosomatic disorder serves a distinct purpose, and in her case, I could not see any reason for psychosomatics. I sent her to a competent endocrinologist, who correctly diagnosed diabetes mellitus.

OSTEOARTHRITIS

There are several types of arthritis, the most common types being degenerative and rheumatoid arthritis. The degenerative form, osteoarthritis, is typically a disease related to the aging process. The degenerative process of aging starts as early as the third decade of life and, over the years, affects the cartilage fibers. Usually, osteoarthritis causes stiffening of the joints, increasing levels of pain, and progressive limitation of mobility.

In most cases, osteoarthritic changes start in the joint cartilage. In some instances, arthritic diseases are caused by torn ligaments, fractures, and other injuries, but in the majority of cases, arthritis is not a traumatic but a developmental condition typical of aging. In some instances, elderly osteoarthritic patients become disabled and cannot use their arms and/or legs.

Distinct personality traits predispose one to arthritic diseases. Alexander (Alexander & Flagg, 1965) described the mental traits of arthritic women as follows:

> In adolescence, these women show tomboyish behavior. As adults, they control their emotional expressions and attempt to control their husbands and children. They are demanding toward their children and at the same time they over-protect and indulge them. This domineering attitude is a combination of a tendency to dominate and a masochistic need to serve other people. Most arthritic women reject the feminine role. They compete with men and view the female role as submissive and humiliating. They are inclined to choose passive men as mates.
>
> The precipitating emotional factor in the onset or exacerbation of the illness can be related to a few significant factors: (1) the disease begins when the unconscious hostility toward and rebellion against men has been increased because of certain situations and threatens to erupt, e.g., when a patient is abandoned by a man with whom she had felt safe or if he begins to assert himself

instead of being compliant. (2) Any event which tends to increase hostility and guilt feelings previously can also precipitate the illness. Guilt feelings over aggressive attitudes may be mobilized when the patient cannot masochistically expiate it by serving others. (3) If a woman is forced to accept the feminine role, against which she reacts with an increased masculine protest, she is liable to develop arthritis. (p. 908)

Although the masculine protest reaction is the most conspicuous rebellion against being dominated, the chronic, inhibited, hostile state can usually be traced back to the early family constellation, consisting of a domineering and demanding mother and a dependent, compliant father. In such an atmosphere, the girl develops a dependence on, and a fear of, the aggressive mother but at the same time harbors strong rebelliousness, which she does not dare to express because of a fear of rejection. Such inhibited rebellion against the mother forms the nucleus of the hostile impulses of such women and is later transferred to men and everyone within the family. When they become mothers, these women reverse the situation and control their children as they had been controlled in the past.

The predisposing personality factor results from restrictive parental influences, which prohibit the free expression of frustration of the child. When, because of punitive measures, this discharge becomes associated with fear and guilt, a "psychological straitjacket" results that persists into adult life. Arthritic patients attempt to discharge aggression through muscular activity (exercise, sports, etc.) and to relieve the restrictive influences of strict conscience by serving others. If this equilibrium is disturbed by anything that blocks the discharge of hostility and the simultaneous guilt-relieving behavior patterns (helping and controlling others at the same time), chronic inhibited aggression leading to increased muscle tonus may aggravate or precipitate the arthritic process.

In the patient with far-advanced arthritis who is physically crippled, a stoical and optimistic attitude is seen.

Alexander and his Chicago collaborators found the same chronic inhibited, rebellious state in males but saw it to be more a reaction against unconscious passive-dependent or feminine traits, for which such patients overcompensate with aggressive impulses. The inhibition of these aggressive impulses creates a psychodynamic picture similar to that seen in female patients.

RHEUMATOID ARTHRITIS

Rheumatoid arthritis is an *autoimmune disease* that belongs to the same category as ulcerative colitis, systemic lupus erythematosus, hemolytic anemia, cancer, and Hashimoto thyroiditis. Rheumatoid arthritis is associated with a serious inflammation of the membranes that line the joints. It is a progressive disease, but the speed and course of the disease are rather unpredictable.

Apparently, susceptibility to rheumatoid arthritis is a product of both genetic predisposition and psychosocial interaction. Even the best seed will not be fertile if it is planted in arid soil, but in some instances, a bad seed may develop reasonably well if properly taken care of. There are no simple answers to the nature–nurture issues, and not all organisms react in the same way to the same stressful situations. The immune system mediates between the pathophysiological, biochemical, and endocrinological determinants and the psychosocial events processed by the central nervous system (Ader & Cohen, 1984).

According to Moos and Solomon (1964, 1966), rheumatoid arthritis patients are exceedingly conscientious and rigid. Most of them felt rejected by their parents and have developed a self-sacrificing, almost masochistic attitude. All of them view their life as a continuous chain of stressful situations. Patients with rapidly progressing diseases experience acute anxiety and severe depression.

Rheumatoid arthritis patients tend to see their bodies as filled with fluid and angry impulses. The arthritic dramatizes in his or her body scheme a conflict about expressing anger. This body image results from inconsistent parents; the fathers were ordinarily calm but occasionally burst forth in anger, and the mothers were self-sacrificing, prohibitive, and seductive figures. Arthritis patients attach unusual significance to their bodies and unconsciously desire to exhibit them, but they overtly deny this desire and complain of shyness and inadequacy.

In one study, 28 children (23 girls and 5 boys) with rheumatoid arthritis who ranged in age from 2 to 6 were observed. They had a close and intense mother–child relationship, which predated the illness but which was also reinforced by it. The mothers had the following characteristics in common: (1) deep deprivation in childhood; (2) a marked tendency toward depression; (3) a slavish devotion to the arthritic child, as well as in other areas of their lives; and (4) a marked difficulty in expressing their feelings, either positive or negative.

According to research data reported by Ader and Cohen (1984), Weiner (1977), and others, in almost all cases of rheumatoid arthritis, there is a high incidence of parental separation or divorce or of death of one of the parents or a close relative. Depression is the common personality feature of all rheumatoid arthritis patients. It is possible that a prolonged state of depression affects the hypothalamic-pituitary-adrenal axis, suppresses the resilience of the immune system, and is conducive to the pathological changes of rheumatoid arthritis.

BACKACHE

Low-back pain can come from a great many different causes. It can be congenital; some people are born with defective spinal columns and therefore suffer backache. Some backaches are caused by disease, such as rickets, osteomyelitis, rheumatoid arthritis, tuberculosis, syphilis, lumbago, or gout. Low backache can be a product of a sprain or injury to the vertebrae or the spine and its nerves, muscles, or ligaments.

Many backaches are caused by a combination of physical and psychological factors, for example, obesity or poor posture. With some exceptions obesity has psychological causes (see Wolman's *Psychological Aspects of Obesity*, 1982). People gain weight by overeating, and they overeat for various psychological reasons.

Seaman and Reder (1963) described three major types of psychosomatic back disabilities and two lesser types. The first of the lesser types is the backache in overworked women and asthenic men. The symptoms resemble those of low-back pain due to disk damage and are relieved by a decrease in the work load and exercises that increase abdominal strength. Another lesser type of backache is found in hypochondriacs with multiple complaints who frequent outpatient clinics and who go from one physician to another.

The most common cases of psychosomatic backache are related to a direct blow to the back. The patient usually has a poor work record, for which she or he blames others. Seaman and Reder (1954) listed as the second major type of psychosomatic back pain the kind that occurs in intelligent young women following exposure to cold air, stress to the back, and/or an emotional upset. The pain may be quite severe, associated with muscle spasm, and a partial relief of pain in extension and hyperextension and increase in pain in flexion of the back.

The third type of psychosomatic back disability follows surgery for herniated disk. The diagnosis of psychogenic back disability or proneness to it should be made before the operation because such a patient may use the organic disability for emotional gratification.

Dorpat and Holmes (1963) studied the pain and muscle activity patterns in 65 subjects ranging in age from 14 to 56. They found that backache symptoms or increased muscle tension appeared in situations in which the individuals were *unable to take positive measures* to resolve their difficulties for fear their action might add to their insecurity and frustration. Fear of retaliation for angry feelings inhibited their action. The rigid posture and increased pain reflected their conflicting emotion.

Low-back pain is often caused by depression and consequently by poor posture; however, poor posture can have a variety of other causes. The upright posture of human beings goes against the usual posture of other species. Thus, human beings must be aware of the need to control their posture consistently, whenever they walk, stand, or sit. Small wonder that the frequent day-to-day bent-over position in clerical work, in reading and writing, and in many other situations may cause low back pain.

There are, however, frequent psychological reasons for poor and pain-producing posture. Every human being may, occasionally, walk in an inappropriate, not-straight posture, but depressed individuals do it frequently and consistently. In my clinical practice, I pay attention to *body language* for emotions; one's attitude toward oneself speaks louder in this nonverbal communication. Whenever patients enter my office, my initial impression is based on how they come in, how they stand up and sit down. In a great many instances, their bent or rigid posture reflects their lack of self-esteem and their depressed attitude.

Most often, low-back pain is a psychosomatic symptom that may have serious physical consequences. Let us compare it to ulcers. Ulcers are usually psychosomatic phenomena, but once they have started, they become a physical illness. Moreover, when the duodenal wall or the stomach has been perforated, surgery may be unavoidable.

Similar reasoning could be applied to low-back pain. Even when purely psychological causes produce the psychosomatic symptoms, the necessary treatment may be surgical. Although the cause of the low-back pain could be poor posture that conveys an unconscious plea for sympathy and help, the outcome may go far beyond the wished for and hoped-for results. Nearly all psychosomatic disorders serve a distinct purpose, such as avoiding responsibility, escaping from a difficult situation, reducing guilt feelings, or soliciting compassion, but the escape is from the frying pan into the fire.

Diseases of the Thyroid Gland

The thyroid gland is a gland of inner secretion. It is located in the neck and is one of the major glands of the endocrine system. It is comprised of a great many *acinar cells*, which are combined into ball-like units called *follicles*. The hormones produced by the thyroid gland are *thyroxine, triiodothyronine*, and *thyrocalcitonin*, and they are carried by the cardiovascular system through the veins of the thyroid gland. The main function of the thyroid gland and the thyroxine and triiodothyronine is the metabolism of *iodine*. The thyrocalcitonin participates, together with the parathyroid, in controlling the level of calcium in the blood. Thyroxine and triiodothyronine influence the metabolic processes in the entire human body (Hall, 1985).

Many possible physical disorders are related to the thyroid gland. A

severe and innate *hypothyroidism* leads to *cretinism*. The lack of or inadequate function of the thyroid gland prevents physical and mental growth.
Cretins are usually exceedingly short and mentally retarded. However, in
many instances, early treatment with radioactive iodine has reversed the
process of cretinism.

Thyrotoxicosis

Like many other diseases of the thyroid gland, *thyrotoxicosis* can be
produced by either physical or emotional factors, or both.

The onset of thyrotoxicosis, following an acute emotional trauma (e.g.,
a war experience or the witnessing of the accidental death of a loved one),
is called *Basedow shock*.

Kracht and Kracht (1952) demonstrated a "fright thyrotoxicosis" in
wild rabbits that occurred when they were exposed to a barking dog. The
hyperthyroid response of all the rabbits was so marked that the animals
died in a "thyroid crisis" (extreme hyperthyroidism) if they were left in the
presence of the dogs, unless they received thyroid treatment. Kracht and
Kracht viewed the phenomenon as a specific thyroidal reaction to stress
based on their histological findings of marked hyperactivity in the thyroid
glands and normal cytology in all other endocrine glands in the animals at
autopsy.

Hetzel, De La Nabe, and Hinkle (1952) artificially produced changes in
protein-bound iodine (PBI) blood levels in euthyroid and hyperthyroid
subjects. The hyperthyroid subjects showed little PBI-level change when
they were relaxed, and the authors observed a drop in the PBI value in two
patients after the patients had verbally expressed their emotional conflicts,
especially resentment.

Bursten (1961) drew a distinction between psychosis and thyrotoxicosis. His research included 8,000 psychotic patients, and only 10 of them
were afflicted by thyrotoxicosis. It is highly probable, however, that thyrotoxicosis can cause psychological disorders, although it may also be
caused by them: it may be somatopsychic as well as psychosomatic.

According to the psychoanalytic "specificity conflict theory," thy-
rotoxic patients struggle against the fear of death. They use the defense
mechanisms of denial and counterphobic escape (Taylor, 1987). This theory supports the psychosomatic notion of thyrotoxicosis.

Hyperthyroidism

The physical symptoms of hyperthyroidism are: (1) tachycardia, (2)
goiter, (3) soft moist skin, (4) hyperhydrosis, (5) heat sensitivity, (6) ex-
ophthalmos, (7) dyspnea, (8) weight loss, (9) palpitations, (10) muscular
weakness, and (11) loose stools. The highest incidence of hyperthyroidism

is in 20- to 40-year-old men. The most common mental symptoms of hyperthyroidism are nervous tension, restlessness, inability to concentrate, emotional lability, and hyperkineses. In extreme cases of hyperthyroidism, the
patients develop symptoms resembling manic-depressive psychosis
(Whybrow & Prange, 1981).

Hypothyroidism (Myxedema)

The most common symptoms of myxedema are weight gain, vague
aching pains in the legs, memory impairment, constipation, deafness, loss
of hair, dry skin, cold intolerance, excessive fatigue, lability of mood, and
anxiety. In some instances, the patients develop manic-depressive and
paranoid-schizophrenia-type symptoms (Hall, 1985).

MUSCULAR TENSIONS

Muscles are the basic tools for all bodily motion. The *striated muscles*
control the skeletal movements; the *smooth muscles* control the movements
of the inner organs. Voluntary decisions are in charge of the striated muscles, but there is no conscious control over the smooth muscles.

Muscle tensions can be caused by purely physical factors, such as
brain damage, cerebral palsy, or a stroke. They may, however, be caused
as well by psychological factors, such as tension headaches, severe anxiety,
and depression.

Nocturnal *bruxism* is one of the potential psychosomatic muscular-
tension syndromes. The main symptom is a forceful grinding of the teeth
in sleep. Bruxism can be related to muscular pain or soreness of the den-
ture. Most often, it is a psychogenic reaction to emotional stress during the
preceding day or to anticipated stressful events on the following day
(Funch & Gale, 1980).

Lower back pain, described elsewhere in this chapter, is also a case of
muscular tension.

INFECTIOUS DISEASES

Ader and Cohen (1984) reported several instances of psychological
predisposition to infectious diseases. According to the research data described by these authors, susceptibility to streptococcal disease is related to
chronic stress. Resilience to respiratory diseases is related to "ego
strength" as measured by the Minnesota Multiphasic Personality Inventory. Emotional states influence physical health, and certain personality
types are more susceptible to viral respiratory infections. A study of 1,000

cadets at the West Point Military Academy, as reported by Kasl, Evans, and Neiderman (1979), found that cadets with a high risk of EBV (Epstein–Barr virus) leading to a clinical disease had highly ambitious, overachieving fathers.

The fact is that despite exposure to pathogenic factors, only a small number of infected individuals actually succumb to and develop disease. The interpretation can go two ways: the cause may be either genetically transmitted resilience or the impact of psychosocial factors, or both. Most probably, it is both (Farber, 1982). Gunderson and Rahe (1974) described the role of life stress in resilience or lack of resilience in the face of invading diseases.

REFERENCES

Ader, R., & Cohen, N. Behavior and the immune system. In W. D. Gentry (Ed.), *Handbook of behavioral medicine* (pp. 117–173). New York: Guilford Press, 1984.

Alexander, F., & Flagg, G. W. The psychosomatic approach. In B. B. Wolman (Ed.), *Handbook of clinical psychology* (pp. 895–947). New York: McGraw-Hill, 1965.

Bale, R. Brain damage in diabetes mellitus. *British Journal of Psychiatry,* 1973, *122,* 337–341.

Bartrop, R. W., *et al.* Depressed lymphocyte function after bereavement. *Lancet,* 1977, *1,* 834–836.

Bursten, B. Psychoses associated with thyrotoxicosis. *Archives of General Psychiatry,* 1961, *4.*

Dorpat, T. L., & Holmes, T. H. *Psychosomatic obstetrics, gynecology and endocrinology.* Springfield, IL: Thomas, 1968.

Ellenberg, M., & Rifkin, H. (Eds.). *Diabetes: Theory and practice.* New York: Medical Examination Publishing, 1983.

Farber, S. L. Genetic diversity and different reactions to stress. In L. Goldberger & S. Breznitz (Eds.), *Handbook of stress* (pp. 123–133). New York: Macmillan–Free Press, 1982.

Funch, D. P., & Gale, E. N. Factors associated with nocturnal bruxism and its treatment. *Journal of Behavioral Medicine,* 1980, *3,* 385–397.

Gentry, W. D. (Ed.). *Handbook of behavioral medicine.* New York: Guilford, 1984.

Gunderson, E. K., & Rahe, R. H. (Eds.). *Life stress and illness.* Springfield, IL: Thomas, 1974.

Hall, R. C. Psychiatric effects of thyroid hormone disturbance. In W. Dorfman & L. Cristofar (Eds.), *Psychosomatic illness review* (pp. 107–123). New York: Macmillan, 1985.

Hetzel, B. S., De La Nabe, D. S., & Hinkle, L. Rapid changes in plasma PBI in euthyroid and hyperthyroid subjects. Washington, DC: *Transactions of the American Goiter Association,* 1952.

Holmes, T. H., & Masuda, M. Life change and illness susceptibility. In B. S. Dohrenwend & B. P. Dohrenwend (Eds.), *Stressful life situations: Their nature and effect.* New York: Wiley, 1974.

Jacobson, A. M., & Leibovich, J. B. Psychological issues in diabetes mellitus. In W. Dorfman & L. Cristofar (Eds.), *Psychosomatic illness review* (pp. 124–133). New York: Macmillan, 1985.

Kasl, S. V., Evans, A. S., & Neiderman, J. C. Psychosocial risk factors in the development of infectious mononucleosis. *Psychosomatic Medicine,* 1979, *41,* 445–466.

Kracht, J., & Kracht, V. Histopathology and therapy of the shock thyrotoxicosis in wild rabbits. *Archives of Pathological Anatomy,* 1952, *321,* 238–274.

Luce, G. G. *Biological rhythms in psychiatry and medicine.* Washington, DC: National Institute for Mental Health, 1970.

Marx, J. L. Diabetes: A possible autoimmune disease. *Science,* 1984, *225,* 1381–1383.

Möller, E., & Möller, G. (Eds.). *Genetics of the immune response.* New York: Plenum Press, 1983.

Moos, R. H., & Solomon, G. F. Personality correlates of the rapidity of progression of rheumatoid arthritis. *Annals of Rheumatic Diseases,* 1964, *23,* 145–151.

Moos, R. H., & Solomon, G. F. Social and personal factors in rheumatoid arthritis: Pathogenic considerations. *Clinical Medicine,* 1966, *73,* 19–26.

Rogers, M. P., Dubey, D., & Reich, P. The influence of the psyche and the brain on immunity and disease susceptibility: A critical review. *Psychosomatic Medicine,* 1979, *41,* 147–164.

Schade, D., & Eaton, R. The temporal relationship between endogenously secreted stress hormones and diabetic decompensation in diabetic men. *Journal of Clinical Endocrinological Metabolisms,* 1980, *50,* 131–136.

Seaman, G. J., & Reder, E. L. Psychogenic back disorders. *Psychosomatic Medicine,* 1954, *19,* 374–392.

Stein, M., Keller, S., & Schleifer, S. The hypothalamus and the immune response. In H. Weiner, M. Hofer, & A. Stunkard (Eds.), *Brain, behavior and bodily disease.* New York: Raven, 1981.

Tager, H., *et al.* A structurally abnormal insulin causing human diabetes. *Nature,* 1979, *281,* 122–125.

Taylor, G. J. *Psychosomatic medicine and contemporary psychoanalysis.* New York: International Universities Press, 1985.

Wall, P. D. Brain and mind. *Excerpta Medica,* 1979, *New Series,* 293–304.

Weiner, H. *Psychobiology and human disease.* New York: Elsevier, 1977.

Whybrow, P. C., & Prange, A. J. A hypothesis of thyroid-catecholamine-receptor interaction: Its relevance to affective illness. *Archives of General Psychiatry,* 1981, *38,* 106–113.

Wittkower, E. D. A global survey of psychosomatic medicine. *International Journal of Psychiatry,* 1969, *7,* 499–516.

Wolman, B. B. *Psychological aspects of obesity.* New York: Grosset & Dunlap, 1982.

21

Psychosomatic Issues in Mental Disorders

Every mental disorder can lead to the development of psychosomatic symptoms. The mind–body relationship is either somatopsychic or psychosomatic, and every deviation from well-adjusted and balanced behavior can easily lead to the formation of mental or physical symptoms.

The words *fear* and *anxiety* are often used interchangeably. The psychosomatic reactions to fear and anxiety are very much the same: both involve the autonomic nervous system, specifically its sympathetic part, which affects the activity of the gastrointestinal system, increases the secretion of adrenalin, speeds up the heart rate, and so on. However, *fear is a reaction to a specific real or unreal danger*, such as, for instance, vicious dogs or goblins, whereas *anxiety denotes a general gloomy feeling of impending doom*.

Fear is an instant reaction to danger. It is related to a low estimate of one's own power as compared to the power of the threatening factor. *Fear disappears with a change in the balance of power*. In the presence of an adult who is perceived by the child as offering protection, the child's fear will be allayed. The disappearance of the threatening person, animal, or object puts an end to a child's fear. The child's changing estimate of his or her own power in comparison to the danger removes his or her fear.

Anxiety is not a reaction to a particular threat. *It is a general and lasting state of mind*. Anxiety deals with no specific object; it reflects an overall weakness, ineptitude, and helplessness. Anxiety is tantamount to a loss of self-esteem. Expecting impending doom, one may withdraw from her or his usual activities and may become tense, irritable, and seclusive, as if mentally paralyzed. Anxiety may adversely affect one's intellectual functioning. The state of anxiety may make a person momentarily forget things that he or she knows, to stutter or stammer, and to be unable to communicate his or her thoughts as if his or her mind has gone blank.

It is important to distinguish between these two emotions. Fear is an emotional reaction to a certain threat. The individual who fears perceives the threatening person, animal, object, or situation as being *stronger than himself or herself,* and thus as being capable of *harming him or her.* Fear is related to perceiving oneself as weak in comparison to the threatening force, but fear can be allayed by the presence of a strong and friendly person. It can also be overcome by familiarizing oneself with the source of the threat and recognizing one's ability to cope with the threatening person or situation.

Anxiety results from an overall feeling of weakness and inability to cope with dangers. A frightened person feels that he or she cannot stand up to a *particular danger.* An anxious individual continually underestimates her or his ability to cope with life in general. The presence of powerful allies and familiarity with the threat does not solve the problem. Anxiety does not come from outside the person; it comes from within, from the unconscious (Wolman, 1984).

This distinction is especially significant in child psychology. A child who fears dogs may be otherwise a happy child, active and outgoing. The problem is limited, and whoever tries to help her or him can depend on the child's resources. Moreover, the process of growth and development will increase the child's powers and faith in himself or herself, and self-confidence may help the child to overcome his or her fears (Ackerman, 1961; Schaffer, 1977).

An anxious child is not anxious because of an external threat; the threat is in himself or herself. Anxiety states can originate in biochemical elements of the human body, in deeply rooted personality traits, in sociopsychological environments, or in a combination of mental and physical factors (Wolman, 1978a,b).

The most common psychogenic sign of anxiety is arousal of the peripheral nervous system. The symptoms of anxiety are sweating, rapid heart rate, and tension in the skeletal muscles. Sometimes, anxiety states lead to trembling, loss of control over the bladder and the bowels, a loss of appetite, and an increase in blood pressure. Anxiety symptoms are not universal: some individuals develop diarrhea, whereas others may have constipation, and still others may develop tachycardia. The nature of the symptoms may depend on one's genetic predisposition or personality type or on the type of stressful situation.

SCHOOL PHOBIA

School-phobic children refuse to go to school for a variety of reasons. In some instances, their avoidance of school is caused by harsh and unfair teachers, by the fear of being hurt and/or of being ridiculed by their school-mates, or by the fear of scholastic failure and the resulting parental punishment.

In a way, school phobia is a misnomer. Most, if not all, the so-called school-phobic children are not phobic at all; they do not avoid school, but they feel compelled to stay at home.

The majority of children with school phobia do well in school. Apparently, they do not fear scholastic failure, but *they dread separation and abandonment at home.* Children who have witnessed a death in the family are prone to having school phobia; they imagine that their presence at home can prevent bad things from happening. A death in the family or a parental illness rarely causes school phobia in a child who is otherwise well adjusted; but traumatic events precipitate school phobia in children who are susceptible to anxiety.

School phobia also has other causes. Sometimes, it develops gradually as a by-product of a child's deep-rooted anxiety, which makes him or her cling to the protective home environment. Sometimes, it is produced by a faulty parent–child relationship.

Some anxious mothers fear being home alone; as their husbands must leave the house to go to work, the wives resort to their children for company. They may not admit this to themselves; as a rule, they are not fully aware of this wish, but they never miss the opportunity to "allow" the child to skip school on rainy days. In many instances, the child empathizes with the mother's wish and makes his or her own excuses for not going to school.

Quite often, school phobia is caused by the child's worry that something horrible may happen to the mother and/or the father in the child's absence. Normally, parents are perceived by their children as being strong, friendly, and dependable. But when one or both of the parents display true or imaginary illnesses, confide in and complain to the child, or present themselves as weak and despondent creatures, the child may worry about the parents instead of their worrying about him or her.

There is a fundamental difference between truancy and school phobia. Some children avoid school; they are truants, and they run away from school. However, there are some children who do not run *away* from school but run *toward* something that alleviates their anxiety. They are not truants.

It is important to repeat that phobic children do not run away from the objects of their phobias; phobic children "run home" to their mothers. They are afraid to be away from home because they worry that something may happen when they are gone. They may develop headaches, belly-aches, nausea, dizziness, and other psychosomatic symptoms to justify their insistence on staying home. Phobic children are not malingerers or liars; their headaches are real and they actually do throw up. Their symptoms develop unconsciously, and they sincerely believe that they must stay home because of their physical illnesses (Wolman, 1978a).

CONVERSION HYSTERIA

Originally Freud believed that hysteria represented a series of symbolic representations of unconscious memories of past traumas. Originally, Freud believed that hysterics suffer mainly from reminiscences. With the development of the structural theory in later works, Freud (1905/1962) related conversion hysteria to mechanisms of defense, mainly to identification, displacement, repression, and regression.

Mental life originates in the organism, and physical energy is the arch-source of all mental energies. When the outlets for mental energies are blocked, some amounts of these energies are discharged along physical paths, such as crying spells, temper tantrums, hysterical laughing and screaming, fainting, diarrhea, and throwing up (Breuer & Freud, 1895/1962).

Conversion hysteria can imitate almost any physical disease or handicap. Many a hysteric develops a complete loss of desire to eat, to have sexual relations, or to do anything at all. Conversion symptoms include hysterical blindness, hysterical heart attacks, and even simulated pregnancy. Hysterics may experience the most severe pain in almost every part of the organism; disturbance of talking and walking, partial or complete motor paralysis, sleeptaking and sleepwalking, and tonic and clonic spasms belong to the galaxy of conversion symptoms (Nemiah, 1985).

The mental symptoms of hysteria are no less spectacular. Conversion hysterics are apt to exaggerate; they are carried away by true or imaginary victories and defeats. Hysterics occasionally experience hallucinations and delusions; discontinuity of awareness of oneself, the so-called split personality, is one of the classic symptoms of conversion hysteria.

Such a split in the ego may take place when the ego is exposed to powerful and mutually exclusive demands made by external reality and the id. The ego can serve these two lords when it is itself strong enough to control the excessive demands of the id and to manipulate the external world. Weak egos, however, may not be able to do so. Sometimes, two mental attitudes may develop and exist alongside each other: one attitude is related to reality, and the other one (a psychosis) is influenced by instincts and detaches the ego from reality. Yet, the personality split in hysteria never goes as deep as it does in psychosis, nor is it as lasting. In all neuroses, two attitudes develop that are contrary to each other and independent of each other. One of them represents the reality-oriented ego and the other the repressed material of the id.

The third edition of *The Diagnostic and Statistical Manual* of the American Psychiatric Association (DSM-III; APA, 1980) describes conversion hysteria, and its description is summarized as follows:

> *Conversion Disorder (or Hysterical Neurosis, Conversion Type).* The predominant disturbance is a loss of or alteration in physical functioning that suggests physical disorder but which is an expression of a psychological conflict or need. This disturbance is not under voluntary control.
>
> Conversion symptoms resemble the symptoms of neurological diseases such as paralysis, aphonia, seizures, coordination disturbance, akinesia, dyskinesia, blindness, tunnel vision, anosmia, anesthesia, and paresthesia. Sometimes, conversion symptoms involve the autonomic or endocrine system. Vomiting as a conversion symptom can represent revulsion and disgust, pseudocyesis (false pregnancy) often represents a wish for and a fear of pregnancy.
>
> The inner conflict about the expression of rage may be expressed as "aphonia" or as a "paralysis" of the arm. When the individual views a traumatic event, a conflict about acknowledging that event may be expressed as "blindness." The conversion symptom has a symbolic value that represents the underlying psychological conflict.
>
> Often conversion symptoms enable one to avoid a noxious activity or to get support from the environment that otherwise might not be forthcoming. For example, a person with marked dependency needs may develop "blindness" or inability to walk or stand to prevent desertion by a spouse. (p. 247)

The sensory conversion symptoms include *anesthesias,* or losses of sensitivity; *hypoesthesias,* or partial losses of sensitivity; *hyperesthesias,* or excessive sensitivity; and *paresthesias,* or exceptional sensations such as tingling. Blindness, deafness, loss of touch, and pain sensitivity in various parts of the body, as well as occasional loss of the sense of smell, are some of the anesthesias. Loss of pain sensitivity is referred to as an *analgesia.*

The motor symptoms of conversion hysteria are varied and numerous. Loss of or disturbances in the motor ability of various muscles may occur. Actual paralyses usually involve a single limb (a leg or an arm). Occasionally, a *hemiplegia* is seen in which the entire left or right side of the body is affected. The loss of function may be selective and may be related to the patient's occupation, as in *aphonia* in a singer. The most numerous motor symptoms are tremors (shaking and trembling of the muscles) and *tics* (unconscious muscular twitches). *Contractures* may also occur, involving the flexion and extension of the fingers and/or the toes or rigidity of the knee and/or elbow joints. The contractures and paralyses may result in walking disturbances. An example is *astasia-abasia,* a disorganized walk with the legs wobbling about in every direction.

Many patients experience disturbances in expressive speech, such as *aphonia* (the diminution of speech to a whisper) and *mutism* (complete inability to speak). Hysterical *convulsions* or *fits* resembling epileptic seizures are among the symptoms of conversion hysteria. It is highly typical of hysterics that their convulsions usually occur in the presence of other people.

Visceral symptoms include headaches, sensations of choking, breathing difficulties, cold and clammy extremities, nausea, vomiting, belching, and many vague pains and aches. Persistent hiccoughing and sneezing occur in some patients. In *anorexia nervosa*, the patient loses his or her appetite for food, cannot keep food down, may not be able to swallow food, and becomes emaciated through the limitation of nourishment.

Hysterics often simulate a large variety of illnesses, such as tuberculosis, appendicitis, and surgical illnesses. It is important to distinguish between hysterical and organic disturbances. Some of the criteria to be used are the *belle indifférence* of the hysteric to the symptom; the frequent failure of the dysfunction to follow a correct anatomical or nerve-distribution pattern; contradictions, as when the person who is hysterically blind avoids bumping into persons or objects; and the susceptibility of the symptoms to removal by hypnosis or suggestion.

There is usually a secondary gain in the conversion reaction, so that the patient's illness enables him or her to avoid or solve some problem or conflict. The symptoms prevent the individual from having to face the traumatic situation, bring him or her sympathy, and enable him or her to control others. More specifically, the symptoms may serve any or all of the following purposes: (1) removal of the patient from an unpleasant or traumatic situation; (2) a regaining of attention, concern, status, or the patient's lost position as the center of attention and affection; (3) self-punishment to alleviate guilt; (4) punishment of others, making them feel that their inconsiderate treatment has made the patient sick; (5) a perpetuation of actual physical or organic illness hysterically after the organic condition has cleared up, which allows the patient to exploit the illness for unconscious gains; (6) receipt of monetary compensation when covered by insurance; and (7) iatrogenically induced symptomatology discussed by the physician, which is absorbed because of the suggestibility of the hysteric. (Alexander & Flagg, 1965, p. 964).

Quite often, the psychosomatic symptoms clearly indicate the patient's conscious or unconscious wishes. I had a patient who developed a host of psychosomatic symptoms when his careless behavior caused severe financial losses in his business. His symptoms were supposed to relieve his guilt feelings. Another patient, a young woman who was being pressured by her parents to marry an old and wealthy relative, developed nausea and vomiting. When she spoke about this parental pressure, she used the following words: "I can't *stomach* it." A man whose failing business necessitated a bold and somewhat risky action developed chest pain. He said, "I don't have the *heart* to do what my accountant and other people have suggested."

Depression

Hysteria was one of the most frequent occurrences in Victorian Vienna, and sexual dysfunction was the most frequent complaint of Freud's patients. Today, feelings of futility and a lack of purpose in life are probably the most frequent symptoms. Sex was the main worry of Freud's middle- and upper-class patients, especially in the peaceful period between 1880 and 1914, before World War I. In the turbulent era after World War II, facing the threat of World War III, people have been more concerned with *survival*. Survival is the universal arch-need, the basis of all other needs, and in times of insecurity, the main concern is how to overcome the feeling of pervading helplessness.

Survival and the satisfaction of the basic needs depend on *one's own power and the power of one's allies*. The failure of one's own power and an inability to secure the cooperation of others are the main contemporary issues.

One may thus suggest a definition for depression that differentiates it from any other unpleasant feeling, such as sadness, unhappiness, frustration, sorrow, or grief. Depression should be defined as a *feeling of helplessness and blaming oneself for being helpless*. Depression is self-directed hatred.

Depression can occur in a variety of situations, and it is not limited to the classic syndrome of unipolar depressive or bipolar manic-depressive psychosis. People afflicted by a physical disease can feel pain, loneliness, and unhappiness without blaming themselves. However, if they blame themselves, they are depressed. Depression can be associated with several mental disorders; sociopaths, for instance, may blame themselves for being weak and may try to compensate by overt aggression, which gives them the feeling of power. Schizophrenics are often more depressed than manic-depressive psychotics, and their depression carries profound feelings of self-hatred. Depressed people tend to love and hate themselves (Brown, 1978).

Love is here defined as a willingness to give, to care, and to protect. Eros, the god of love, is also the god of life, for whoever loves defends and protects the life of the loved ones. When love is sexual, it may lead to the creation of new life. Hatred is here defined as the desire to hurt, destroy, and kill. The god of war, Ares, is the god of destruction and death. Whoever hates attacks and hurts.

Love and hate are often ambivalent. A neonate's love and hate are primitive, self-centered, and narcissistic. All human beings are born lovers and haters, and their interactions in early childhood determine the balance of the intraindividual and interindividual cathexes of libido and destrudo.

One may relate Freudian concepts of cathexis to overt behavior and may distinguish four categories of human relations: hostile (H), instrumental (I), mutual (M), and vectorial (V). A *hostile* attitude is destructive. An *instrumental* attitude aims at using others for one's own benefit: infants are takers, and their attitude is *instrumental*. Through growth and learning, they acquire the *mutual* attitude of giving and taking: in mature sex and marriage, one gives and takes. One may become capable of giving without taking: mature parents display a *vectorial* attitude toward their children.

In observing mental patients one can't help noticing three distinct patterns of behavior. Some patients are *hyperinstrumental*, loving only themselves and exploiting others. At the other extreme are the *hypervectorials*, who love others too much at their own expense. In the third category are the *dysmutuals*, who swing from one extreme to the other. Hyperinstrumental sociopaths are extremely selfish, hypervectorial schizophrenics too unselfish, and dysmutual manic-depressives go from one extreme to the other. Hypervectorial schizophrenics love others too much; thus, no love is left for themselves, and they often hate themselves for not loving enough. When their defense mechanisms fail, they may break loose in catatonic fury. Dysmutual depressives swing from being very friendly to being very hostile. Sociopaths are too selfish, schizophrenics too unselfish, and manic-depressives exaggerate in both directions (Wolman, 1973, 1987).

Studies of manic-depressive and related disorders point to rejection in early childhood. This rejection, if started in the earliest years, gives rise to "anaclitic depression." Parental rejection need not be associated with pathological hostility, an infant may feel rejected when the mother is sick and unable to take care of him or her, when she is pregnant with another child, or when she is too busy working or is overburdened with a large family. The child who becomes a manic-depressive is usually the "Cinderella" in a family, usually composed of a hostile mother, an uninterested or hostile father, and favored siblings. Manic-depressive patients are "love addicts" always in search of someone to love them. When they feel loved, they experience a blissful manic feeling, but they are *insatiable* in their need to be loved. They are in constant search of new loves. Thus, although they believe themselves to be very friendly, others perceive them as being weak and overdemanding individuals. Manic-depressive patients are usually permanently depressed; a happy mood sometimes breaks through the clouds, but it cannot disperse them. They are usually kind and friendly to strangers, whom they expect to win over, but they may be hostile to the members of their family. Quite often, they try to win love by being weak. Sometimes, they work hard toward a goal, but when they come close to victory, they act out their "Sisyphus complex" and defeat themselves.

Etiological Factors

My studies have led me to establish a link among the various degrees of depression, viewed as a nosological entity, on a continuum of neurotic symptoms through hysteroid character neurosis, latent psychosis, and full-blown psychotic depression. Moods of elation and depression are reflections of shifts in the balance of libidinal cathexes from self-love to object love, from self-hate to object hate, from love to hate, and vice versa. I have called this group of disorders *dysmutual depression*, because mutual relationships are disturbed and the underlying dynamic is that of self-depreciation, self-accusation, and self-defeating behavior (Wolman, 1973, 1984).

There has been a good deal of evidence that lack of maternal love causes severe depression and "affect hunger." The rejected child may try to win love by intentional suffering and may escape into illness. "The discouraged child who finds that he can tyrannize best by tears will be a cry-baby, and a direct line of development leads from the cry-baby to the adult depressed patient," wrote Kurt Adler (1967, p. 332).

Many manic-depressive patients come from large families where no one was genuinely interested in the child's welfare. As a result of the lack of a true and meaningful relationship in childhood, the manic-depressive suffers from feelings of insecurity and rejection (Cartwell & Carlson, 1983).

My clinical observations have led me to believe that manic-depressive patients have been exposed in childhood to a sort of *emotional seesaw* of acceptance and rejection, care and abandonment. The mothers of my severely depressed patients did not like their children; however, when the children were in serious trouble or gravely ill, the mothers turned around and showered them with affection. These emotional swings were conducive to a self-defeating attitude in the offspring, for sickness was the only way to win love.

Mothers of manic-depressive patients are neither considerate nor warm persons. Some are sociopathic, concerned about no one but themselves, resenting the burdens of motherhood, and often displaying violent tempers and brutality. The child who will become a depressive psychotic is treated by the mother with rejection and sometimes with hate; in many cases, the child is forced to compete unsuccessfully with a more privileged sibling (Kashami *et al.*, 1983; Schaffer, 1977).

Future manic-depressives are treated with outright dislike, except when they are seriously ill. They are unwanted and unloved members of the family and are treated as a burden and a handicap, except on those rare occasions when their sad condition forces the parents into a position of caring. In most cases, adequate maternal care is given to the infant in the first few months of life; the rejection comes somewhat later. Thus, manic-depressives have a tendency to regress to infancy and even to a passive, prenatal intrauterine life. Regression goes back not to the point of frustration or rejection, but below that point, to the true or imaginary era of the "lost paradise" of safety and love. In milder, neurotic cases of hysteria and depressive neurosis, the regression is usually to the oral stage, the main objective of which is to *win love*. Whatever psychosomatic symptoms develop, all are geared to this goal of gaining love (Wolman, 1973).

Making oneself clumsy and sick serves this purpose. The goal is to win love by self-defeat. Usually, infants receive love from the parents. However, when love is withheld from a child, or when it is given in an unfriendly manner, the infant is unable to develop a proper emotional balance. Uncertain that his or her emotional needs will be satisfied, the infant feels permanently hungry. Thus, *manic-depressive patients consume gross quantities of food*, a behavior indicative of their oral-cannibalistic fixations. Unable to get love, they grab food; many depressed patients are overweight. They tend to overeat constantly, as if trying to fill the emotional void (Wolman, 1982). They overeat to make themselves less attractive, less capable of an active life, less successful, and less healthy. They overeat in order to deepen the self-defeat, and to prove to themselves that they are weak and unable to control their being overweight; in the back of their minds looms the unconscious hope of gaining love by self-destructive behavior.

Depression can be exogenous or endogenous. In exogenous depression, outside and recent events cause the depressed feeling. Exogenous depression can start as a reaction to real misfortunes, such as the loss of someone dear, a serious defeat in one's career, or a loss of money or of a job. No one is happy when one of these things happens, but only some people react with quiet and helpless self-directed anger. Life events play a significant role in the etiology of depressive disorders (Goldberger & Bresnitz, 1982, p. 578).

Endogenous depression is not related to any particular misfortune nor to any other recent event. Sometimes, my patients say, "Everything is all right; my wife is sweet and loving, my children do well in school, my job or business is doing well—why am I so depressed?" Usually, this question indicates endogenous depression, related to early childhood experience (Kashami & Carlson, 1985).

The possible role of genetic factors in the etiology of depression is highly controversial. However, according to Farber (1982), offspring of bipolar parents exhibit symptoms such as hyperactivity, short attention span, poor frustration tolerance, explosiveness, and inadequate school performance.

A host of psychosomatic symptoms is associated with various types and levels of depressive disorders (Howells, 1980). According to Katon, Kleinman, and Rosen (1982), at least 26% of patients who come to physicians complaining about physical disease are depressed, and their depression has led to the development of psychosomatic symptoms. Apparently, a great many psychosomatic conversion symptoms are related to underlying depressive disorders (Beckham & Leber, 1985, p. 684). Exposure to stressors alone is almost never a sufficient explanation for illness in ordinary human experience, just as genetic studies have shown that biological vulnerability alone does not produce psychiatric disorders. Other factors that require consideration include the characteristics of the stressful situation, individual biological and psychological attributes, and the social supports available to the individual at risk.

The characteristics of a stressor that are presumed to mediate its impact include such dimensions as its magnitude, its duration, its novelty, and its predictability. The relevant personality variables include coping skills, personality style, age at exposure, biological vulnerabilities, and response thresholds. The social factors include the availability of benevolent and supportive relatives and friends, access to helping resources, social influence and social class, community attitudes, and the prevailing group morale.

Moreover, it is becoming increasingly apparent that a simple count of the reported stressful precipitants is not fruitful. Improved strategies include the adoption of a multifactorial model that takes into account the effects of historical and concurrent burdens and buffers. Another interesting approach is to test hypotheses regarding the role of particular combinations of events within specified periods of time. This strategy is exemplified by Dohrenwend and Dohrenwend's *pathogenic triad* (1981). They postulated that depression is more likely to occur following the advent within a short period of time of fateful loss events (e.g., the death of one's spouse), events that exhaust the individual physically (e.g., a major medical illness), and the disruption of social supports (e.g., a geographical move). The combined impact of such events would be associated with a greater incidence of psychopathology in previously healthy people than would be observed either in the absence of such events or in their separate occurrence or in their association with other categories. While the utility of this approach remains to be tested, it is innovative and promising (Rabkin, 1982, pp. 580–581).

REFERENCES

Ackerman, N. W. *The psychodynamics of family life.* New York: Basic Books, 1961.
Adler, K. Adler's individual psychology. In B. B. Wolman (Ed.), *Psychoanalytic techniques.* New York: Basic Books, 1967.
Alexander, F., & Flagg, W. N. The psychosomatic approach. In B. B. Wolman (Ed.), *Handbook of clinical psychology* (pp. 855–947). New York: McGraw-Hill, 1965.
American Psychiatric Association. *Diagnostic and statistical manual of mental disorders* (3rd ed.— DSM-III). Washington, DC: 1980.
Beckham, E. E., & Leber, W. R. *Handbook of depression: Treatment, assessment and research.* Homewood, IL: Dorsey Press, 1985.
Breuer, J., & Freud, S. (1895) Studies in hysteria. *Standard Edition* (Vol. 1). London: Hogarth Press, 1962.
Brown, G. W. *Social origins of depression: A study of psychiatric disorders in women.* New York: Macmillan–Free Press, 1978.

Cartwell, D. P., & Carlson, G. A. (Eds.). *Affective disorders in childhood and adolescence*. New York: Medical Scientific Books, 1983.

Dohrenwend, B. P., & Dohrenwend, B. S. (Eds.). *Stressful life events: Their nature and effects*. New York: Wiley, 1974.

Farber, S. L. Genetic diversity and differing reactions to stress. In L. Goldberger & S. Breznitz (Eds.), *Handbook of stress* (pp. 123–133). New York: Macmillan–Free Press, 1982.

Freud, S. Fragment of an analysis of a case of hysteria. *Standard Edition*, (Originally published, 1905.) London: Hogarth Press, 1962.

Goldberger, L., & Bresnitz, S. (Eds.) *Handbook of stress: Theoretical and clinical aspects*. New York: Macmillan–Free Press, 1982.

Howells, J. G. (Ed.). *Advances in family psychiatry*. New York: International Universities Press, 1980.

Kashami, J. H., & Carlson, G. A. Major depressive disorders in a preschooler. *Journal of the American Academy of Child Psychiatry*, 1985, 24, 490–494.

Kashami, J. H., *et al.* Depression in a sample of 9-year old children: Prevalence and associated characteristics. *Archives of General Psychiatry*, 1983, 40, 1217–1223.

Katon, W., Kleinman, A., & Rosen, G. Depression and somatization: A review. *American Journal of Medicine*, 1982, 72, 127–135.

Nemiah, J. C. Somatoform disorders. In H. I. Kaplan & B. J. Sadock (Eds.), *Comprehensive textbook of psychiatry* (4th ed., pp. 924–942). Baltimore: Williams & Wilkins, 1985.

Rabkin, J. G. Stress and physical disorders. In L. Goldberger & S. Breznitz (Eds.), *Handbook of stress* (pp. 566–584). New York: Macmillan–Free Press, 1982.

Schaffer, H. R. (Ed.). *Studies in mother-infant interactions*. New York: Academic Press, 1977.

Solomon, S. Application of neurology to psychiatry. In H. I. Kaplan & B. J. Sadock (Eds.), *Comprehensive textbook of psychiatry* (4th ed.). Baltimore: Williams & Wilkins, 1985.

Wolman, B. B. *Call no man normal*. New York: International Universities Press, 1973.

Wolman, B. B. *Children's fears*. New York: Grosset & Dunlap, 1978a.

Wolman, B. B. *Treatment of mental disorders in childhood and adolescence*. Englewood Cliffs, NJ: Prentice-Hall, 1978b.

Wolman, B. B. Depression and obesity. In B. B. Wolman (Ed.), *Psychological aspects of obesity: A handbook* (pp. 88–103). New York: Van Nostrand Reinhold, 1982.

Wolman, B. B. *Interactional psychotherapy*. New York: Van Nostrand Reinhold, 1984.

Wolman, B. B. *The sociopathic personality*. New York: Brunner/Mazel, 1987.

22

Mental Disorders: Schizophrenia

Schizophrenia is one of the most popular misnomers in the history of psychiatry. This complex and severe psychosis was, for a while, called *dementia praecox*, a term implying that the patients afflicted by this disorder were demented. In 1911, E. Bleuler changed the name to schizophrenia, implying a splitting of one's mind.

At the present time no one views schizophrenia as a dementive state or as split personality. The third edition of *the Diagnostic and Statistical Manual of Mental Disorders* of the American Psychiatric Association (DSM-III; APA, 1980) suggests these diagnostic criteria: (1) delusions; (2) auditory hallucinations; (3) illogical thinking; and (4) grossly disorganized behavior.

The etiology of schizophrenia is highly controversial. Some researchers point to the possibility of genetic factors; others believe in biochemical origins; and still others emphasize the role of psychosocial causes.

There is no evidence that schizophrenia is inherited, but one can't deny the probable genetic predisposition to schizophrenia (Mirsky & Duncan, 1986; Walker & Shaye, 1982).

GENETICS

According to Kallmann (1953), schizophrenia depends on a recessive mutant gene that produces enzyme deficiency. The incidence of schizophrenia (which is 0.85% in the general population, 1.8% in step siblings, and 2.1% in husbands and wives) served as a basis for Kallmann's hypothesis.

Among blood relatives, the incidence is much higher. Among first cousins, it is 2.6%; among grandchildren, 4.3%; among children, one of whom is schizophrenic, 16.4%; among same-sex dizygotic twins, 17.6%; among children of two schizophrenic parents, 68.1%; among monozygotic twins separated for 5 or more years 77.6; and finally, among monozygotic twins who have not been separated, 91.5%. The total expectancy of the various types of schizophrenia varies from 7.1% for half-siblings to 14% for full siblings and two-egg twins, and up to 86.2% for one-egg twins (Kallmann, 1953, p. 145).

Kallmann (1953) observed a close relationship between a low resistance to schizophrenia and a low resistance to pulmonary tuberculosis. He noticed that the severe deterioration in schizophrenia is related to a highly asthenic physique and to low athletic elements in the body structure. The athletic body type was found most frequently in paranoid schizophrenics. The pyknic physique gives the worst prognosis. The predisposition to tuberculosis and to schizophrenia was related by Kallmann to a hereditary weakness of the reticuloendothelial system.

Kallmann (1953) proved that the probability of schizophrenia is higher among blood relatives than among nonrelated individuals. However, his work did not prove that schizophrenia is an inherited disorder, and a dominant heredity is highly improbable; most researchers have rejected the possibility of recessive heredity and have emphasized the importance of environmental factors (Berger, 1981; Fish, 1981; Goldstein, 1985; Jackson, 1960; Kety, 1960; Rosenthal, 1970; Walker & Shaye, 1982; Wender, Rosenthal, Kety, Schulsinger, & Weiner, 1974; Zubin & Steinhauser, 1981).

In a review of the literature on the genetics of schizophrenia, Jackson (1960) wrote, "Regarding twins who are alleged to have been reared apart and who both developed schizophrenia . . . an exhaustive search of American and European literature of the past forty years has uncovered only two such cases" (p. 40). Furthermore, according to the laws of recessive inheritance, the rate of expectancy for monozygotic twins should be 100%, whereas in Kallmann's findings (1948; 1953), it was 85%. Kallmann found a 68% expectancy rate for the children of two schizophrenic parents, but it should have been 100%. Furthermore, Gregory's studies (1960) show that the incidence of schizophrenia in relatives does not follow either simple dominant or simple recessive patterns.

In my own research (Wolman, 1966), I found that only 6% of offspring of schizophrenic parents were schizophrenic, and that 60% of them did not show any significant pathology at all.

However, the controversy about genetics is still very much alive, and according to Roizin and Willson (1983) a large body of evidence suggests that schizophrenia is a genetically determined illness affecting the central nervous system.

Since Kallmann's initial exploration (1948;1953) of genetic factors in the transmission of schizophrenia, there have been some indications of a possible gene–environment interaction. Also, the results of research on the toxicity of serum, urine, and spinal fluid in schizophrenics have been controversial.

NEUROCHEMISTRY

Studies of the amino acid metabolism of schizophrenics have led to the hypothesis that schizophrenia may be related to disturbances in this metabolism. According to Kety (1960):

> That disordered amino acid metabolism is a fundamental component of some forms of schizophrenia remains an attractive though fairly general hypothesis. The chromatographic search for supportive evidence is interesting and valuable, and the preliminary indications of differences that are characteristic of even a segment of the disease rather than artifactual or incidental has not yet been obtained. (p. 127)

The possible role of biochemical elements in schizophrenia is still a controversial issue (Berger, 1981; Roizin & Willson, 1983). According to Berger (1981), a synthetic analogue of enkephalin (FK 33-824, D-Ala^2, methyl-Phe^4, methionine^5 sulfoxide carbinol enkephalin) has been reported to decrease psychotic symptoms in schizophrenic patients. In one uncontrolled pilot study, nine patients received .5 mg and 1 mg FK 33-824 for 2 days. A significant improvement in symptoms, which lasted from 1 to 7 days, was reported. In another single-blind study, researchers reported that FK 33-824 had a strikingly positive effect on the hallucinations of nine chronic psychotic patients.

Also, a decrease in schizophrenic symptoms was reported in a single-blind study of 6 patients, in a double-blind study of 6 patients, and in a double-blind study of 8 patients, following the administration of DTγE. However, in another study, placebo produced the same reduction in the schizophrenic symptomatology of 13 patients. Hence, the possible antipsychotic activity of DTγE will require further investigation.

Endorphin

The stiffness caused by intraventricular β-endorphin injections in rats has been compared to the catalepsy produced in these animals by neuroleptics. Though not all investigators agree that β-endorphin is an endogenous neuroleptic and that schizophrenic symptoms may reflect an endorphin deficiency. Furthermore, in a single-blind study, 3 of 4 schizophrenic patients were reported to benefit from 15 intravenous doses of 1.5–9 mg of β-endorphin. However, improvement was not obvious in a careful double-blind study of 10 schizophrenic patients given 20 mg of β-endorphin.

In contrast to those studies suggesting an endorphin deficiency in schizophrenia, there are currently several studies that suggest an increase in endorphin activity in schizophrenia. In a double-blind crossover study, the condition of six of eight schizophrenic subjects briefly worsened after β-endorphin treatment when compared with placebo trials. The symptoms of only one schizophrenic patient worsened after placebo injection.

Endorphin fractions other than β-endorphin and enkephalin have been found in elevated levels in the cerebrospinal fluid (CSF) of unmedicated schizophrenic patients. When these patients were medicated, the increased concentrations returned toward normal. There have also been reports of elevated CSF concentrations of β-endorphin in some schizophrenic patients. Chronic schizophrenic patients had values of 35 fm/ml in contrast to the values of 760 fm/ml in the acute schizophrenic patients. Another group of investigators studied over 60 CSF samples from chronic schizophrenic patients and normal controls and found that the β-endorphin concentrations in both groups, measured by radioimmunoassay, were between 3 and 12 fm/ml. One other study that compared β-endorphin levels in schizophrenic patients, normal controls, and neurological controls found similar levels (approximately 10–15 fm/ml) in all three groups. These results show great disparity in the CSF β-endorphin levels of both schizophrenic patients and normal controls. Thus, the possible question of altered CSF β-endorphin concentrations in schizophrenic patients remains unanswered (Fish, 1981; Roizin & Willson, 1983).

The reported improvement in schizophrenic symptoms following hemodialysis is further evidence of an endorphin excess in schizophrenia (Berger, 1983). Unfortunately, the hemodialysis trial was not double-blind, and preliminary results from double-blind studies on the use of hemodialysis in schizophrenia are somewhat disappointing. In addition, there has been no confirmation of elevated leu-5-β-endorphin concentrations in either the dialysate of 10 patients or in the plasma of 98 schizophrenics compared to 42 normal controls (Berger, 1983, pp. 123–124).

Roizin and Willson (1983) reported the possibility that schizophrenia is associated with the presence of circulating immunoglobulins capable of binding to neuronal nuclei or cytoplasm in specific areas of the human brain. Moreover, extraneural involvement of immunological mechanisms in schizophrenic subjects has been demonstrated by the use of hemoglobins and a study of serum specimens of schizophrenics.

The finding of a dopamine-β-hydroxylase deficit in postmortem schizophrenic brains has raised the possibility that some of the catecholamine terminals in cortical areas of schizophrenic brains store small amounts of dopamine instead of noradrenaline. Also, some researchers have reported increases in the number of dopamine receptors in the CNS of schizophrenics as measured by neuroleptic binding (Roizin & Willson, 1983, pp. 32–33).

NEUROPHYSIOLOGY

According to Roizin and Willson (1983), investigators have devoted considerable time to the study of potential neurophysiological abnormalities in schizophrenics—in particular, to study of the possibility that the disease is related to the dysfunction of a specific portion of the nervous system. Scientists using visual techniques, evoked potentials, electroencephalography, and handedness, footedness, and eye-dominance studies have concluded that many schizophrenics show abnormalities in left-hemisphere function. Still other reports, based primarily on measurements of callosal function, suggest that the corpus callosum may be impaired. However, no definite correlation has been established between these functional abnormalities and structured pathology.

Some researchers are concerned with a variety of pathobiological and pathochemical processes that may, directly or indirectly, affect the CNS and that may be manifested clinically in schizophrenic behavior or schizophrenialike psychosis. Some of the most outstanding examples are: (1) visceral involvement, such as degeneration of the liver; fibrosis of the intestine, kidney, and spleen; and metaplasia of the bone marrow; (2) endocrine disorders caused by degeneration and/or atrophy of the adrenal cortex, the ovaries or testes, the pituitary thyroid, and the parathyroid; and (3) cardiovascular hypoplasia (including that of cerebral blood vessels and capillaries), which, at times, is associated with status lymphaticus or constitutional infantilism.

Another possible biochemical pathogenic mechanism in schizophrenia was suggested by detection in the serum of schizophrenic subjects of an abnormally high content of creatinine phosphokinase, an enzyme derived from striated muscle. This enzyme is present in abnormal quantities when muscle destruction has occurred as a result of trauma or neuromuscular disease. Biopsies of striated muscles from schizophrenics have revealed evidence of muscle cell degeneration; its relationship to CNS functions is unknown (Roizin & Willson, 1983, p. 34).

STRESS AND SCHIZOPHRENIA

Several authors have related the etiology of schizophrenia to stressful events. An examination of the studies in this area provides the following information about the relationship between stressful life events and psychiatric syndromes. First, there is no evidence that the stressful events reported by schizophrenics are more frequent than those reported by other diagnostic groups preceding illness onset. Moreover, the one study that evaluated the magnitude of stress associated with these events found that the events reported by schizophrenic patients were less objectively hazardous or "troublesome" than those reported by depressives. Finally, no investigator has gathered evidence to indicate that the events reported by schizophrenic patients either are of a singular nature or fall into categories different from those associated with other psychiatric patients (Lidz, Fleck, & Cornelison, 1979; Heston, 1970).

Given the discrepancies in design and the unevenness of the methodological rigor of these studies, one cannot justifiably conclude that they have disproved the possibility of an association between stressful life events and schizophrenia onset; rather, they have failed to provide positive evidence of such a link. In order to clarify findings and to permit a comparison of findings, researchers must give least three variables further attention: the magnitude of the objective hazard associated with the reported events; their fatefulness (i.e., the independence of the patient's behavior); and the unit of time in which they occurred (Rabkin, 1980, p. 576).

SOCIOPSYCHOSOMATIC THEORY

One need not exclude the possibility of the hammer-and-anvil effect, but apparently, the sociopsychological issues are the hammer and the physical symptoms of schizophrenia are of psychosomatic origin. Thus, Kety (1960) wrote:

> The disturbances in behavior and activity which make the schizophrenic process would also be expected to cause deviations from the normal in many biochemical and metabolic measures: in urine volume and concentration, in energy and nitrogen metabolism, and in the size and function of numerous organic systems. The physiological and biochemical states of the patient are of interest as part of a total understanding of the schizophrenic process; it is important, however, not to attribute to them a primary or etiological role. (p. 123)

Psychoanalytic theory has related somatic symptoms to hypochondriasis and self-hypercathexis. Fenichel (1945) wrote, "It may be assumed that certain psychogenic factors, namely a dammed up state of being and a narcissistic withdrawal, . . . create organic changes which then in turn give rise to hypochondriacal sensations" (p. 261). And further on:

> Many schizophrenics begin with characteristic hypochondriacal sensations. The theory of hypochondriasis, which maintains that organ cathexis grew at the expense of object cathexes, makes this early symptomatology intelligible. The beginning of the schizophrenic process is a regression to narcissism. This brings with it an increase in the 'libido tonus' of the body (either of the whole body or, depending on the individual history, of certain organs), and this increase makes itself felt in the form of the hypochondriacal sensations (Federn, 1952; Fenichel, 1945, p. 418; Schur, 1955).

This theory does not, however, sound very convincing; narcissistic individuals usually take good care of themselves. But when one cares so much for others as to neglect oneself, the *hypocathected* body may react with symptom formation. Schizophrenics suffer from low vitality and lack of energy. A great many of them suffer a variety of respiratory diseases and skin diseases, usually developed in their least cathected organs. A patient of mine who doubted her manual dexterity had a severe skin rash on her hands; another, who believed she was ugly, had a facial rash; still another, who doubted her femininity, had a skin rash on her pubic area. The theory of self-hypocathexis is schizophrenia, first introduced by Federn (1952), explains the decline in sensitivity to pain, the generally lowered tonus, and the passivity in schizophrenia. The schizophrenic tendency toward self-mutilation is explained by the theory of a *decline* in self-cathexis.

The hypothesis that somatic symptoms result from a hypocathexis of bodily organs supports the *sociopsychosomatic* theory as follows: Noxious *environmental* (social) factors cause an imbalance in *interindividual cathexes.* This imbalance produces a severe dysbalance in the *intraindividual cathexes,* which, in turn, introduces a disorder in the personality structure (psychological factors). The personality disorder causes somatic changes, either through a transformation of deficiency in mental energy into organic deficiencies or through the process of conditioning (Wolman, 1966).

DOWNWARD ADJUSTMENT

Let us review a few somatic symptoms in schizophrenia. It is believed that the following four changes usually take place in the cardiovascular system of schizophrenics: (1) a decrease in the size of the heart; (2) a decrease in the volume of the blood flow; (3) a decrease in the systematic blood pressure; and (4) an exaggerated tendency toward vasoconstriction and hence a diminished blood supply. Trying to escape from anxiety, schizophrenics avoid certain psychological functions. Quite often, certain cerebral centers that supercede the visceral functions are in a state of hypo-functionality in schizophrenics.

Because the vascular mechanisms play an important role in the control of the body temperature, several authors have implied that the schizophrenic suffers from a defect in the vasomotor systems or in the nerve control apparatus of this system located in the hypothalamus. Defects in the circulatory system may be caused by an inadequate supply of oxygen. Kety (1960) showed no differences between the oxygen consumption and the flow of blood in the brains of schizophrenics and normals.

It is an undeniable fact that cyanosis, or a blueing of the hands and feet caused by venous stasis, is frequently observed in schizophrenics. This symptom was interpreted by Shattock (1950) to be a constriction of the small arterioles of the skin. Arieti (1955, p. 365) remarked that, in the passive behavior of schizophrenics, vasoconstriction is a compensatory mechanism that prevents loss of heat. Furthermore, the bizarre postures of catatonics activate antigravity vasoconstrictor mechanisms. Without these mechanisms, edema due to blood stasis would be very frequent.

Schizophrenia is an effort to survive on a lower level of living, and the psychosomatic changes are a continuation of the downward adjustment process. One cannot help speculating about the neurological and biochemical counterparts of this process, but all observed phenomena point to a process of reducing the way of living in order to preserve life itself. One may hypothesize that a regression from the conscious to the unconscious and from an active organic life to the schizophrenic inactive pattern is an energy-saving way of living when a full life seems to be inaccessible. The increased reliance of schizophrenics on olfactory sensations brings additional proof of this downward adjustment (Wolman, 1966).

MENTAL PROCESSES

Assuming that the higher mental processes, such as perception and thinking, are related to the central nervous system, and that the visceral functions are related to the autonomic nervous system, Russian neurophysiologists have tried to discover whether and how the higher mental processes can influence the visceral functions. They have applied conditioning methods: Soviet research workers have conducted hundreds of experiments on visceral conditioning; the experimental work has included the kidneys, the liver, the cardiovascular system, the respiratory apparatus, the gastrointestinal system, the glandular system, the metabolic processes, and exchange of heat (Wolman, 1966). These studies have shown that the cerebrum regulates the activities of the entire body, including the functions of the inner organs. Summarizing the studies conducted by himself and other workers, Bykov (1957) wrote about the "corrective influence of the cerebral cortex" and stated that positive impulses coming from the cortex to an active organ inhibit its activity, but inhibitory impulses increase the cortex's activity. Furthermore, Bykov (1957) assumed that:

> The complex functions of the viscera are formed at different cerebral levels. The impulses arising in the cerebral cortex as a result of conditional temporary connections affect the adjacent subcortical centers, where the forms and intensity of the stimulations conveyed to the working effector apparatus take a definite shape. (p. 145)

One is inclined to believe that the overworked cortical centers interfere with the work of other organs. One may say that new connections are formed, and that the inner organs become conditioned to react in an unusual way that is detrimental to the survival of the organism. This influence is, most probably, *inhibitory;* hence the reduced vitality of schizophrenics and action in the direction of a "downward adjustment" (Lynn, 1960).

At this point, it is worthwhile to invoke Pavlov's research and post-Pavlovian research on schizophrenia and to utilize their findings in support of the sociopsychosomatic theory of schizophrenia. According to this theory, schizophrenia starts as a psychological reaction to noxious social factors. The social factors cause a reversal in the system of interindividual cathexes, which, in turn causes a dysbalance in intraindividual cathexes and other pathological changes in personality structure. These psychological changes produce disturbances in the functioning of the central and autonomic nervous systems and affect the glandular system and the metabolism (Wolman, 1966).

CONDITIONING

Pavlov (1927) wrote that schizophrenia is the result of a general protective inhibition of the cortex that prevents further overstimulation of the overworked nerve cells. It is possible that several schizophrenic symptoms are produced by the cortical protective inhibition, but the cortical and subcortical protective inhibition is produced by psychological disorder and psychological disorder is caused by noxious social factors.

One may interpret the low sympathetic time of schizophrenics as a defensive conditioning in reaction to overstimulation; one may, however, also view the overstimulation in the framework of environmental, interactional components. Conditioning is an interactional process and social stimuli lead to a conditioned defensive reaction that could be "psychosomatic." According to Bykov (1957):

> It may be assumed that in acting on the functioning cells of the salivary glands, the nervous impulses from the cortex along the efferent nerves reduce the excitation of the salivary glands to a minimum. . . . A weak excitation on reaching a slightly functioning gland increased its activity, whereas a strong excitation inhibited it. However, our knowledge so far of the essence of the phenomenon is too limited to enable us to be dogmatic in the assertion of the hypothesis. A further study . . . may possibly suggest another interpretation of the described factors. (p. 140)

Furthermore, "The constancy of metabolism computed to a unit of body surface . . . is found to be eliminated as a result of chloralhydrate poisoning; for example, after, we may assume, the activity of the cerebrum has been excluded" (Bykov, 1957, p. 156). The general metabolism can be changed through work signals; the sound of a metronome and the command "Get ready for the experiment" caused a marked increase in oxygen consumption and pulmonary ventilation. In Shatenshtein's experiment, "a man who remained quietly lying on a couch showed an increase in metabolism when [it was] suggested that he had just completed some very hard muscular work" (Bykov, 1957, p. 179). In Yefimov's experiment, the rate of metabolism went up when the subject imagined that he was doing some work. In other words, high-level psychologically conditioned stimuli can affect the functions of the autonomic nervous system and can produce somatic changes.

These facts should be related to the observed somatic changes in schizophrenia. Schizophrenia seems to be a peculiar state of an "over-mobilized ego."

ANALGESIA

Analgesia offers a good opportunity for further clarification of the nature of schizophrenia. Bleuler (1911/1950) wrote:

> Even in well-oriented patients one may often observe the presence of a complete *analgesia*, which includes the deeper parts of the body as well as the skin. The patients intentionally or unintentionally incur quite serious injuries, pluck out an eye, sit down on a hot stove and receive severe gluteal burns. (p. 57)

Bleuler believed that the "catatonic anaesthesias of which many authors speak are merely analgesias" (p. 214).

Two mechanisms are probably at work here. One is conditioning. In experiments conducted by Bykov and his associates, pain was increased and decreased by verbal stimuli (Bykov, 1957, pp. 342 ff.). The other mechanism is the decline of self-cathexis and thus the inevitable impoverishment of vitality. This makes schizophrenics less able and less eager to protect themselves. However, in the face of a great danger, the schizophrenic who is not too deteriorated often displays a self-defensive reaction. The severely deteriorated may have lost this ability, and with their lowered sensitivity to pain, they may fall prey to any danger.

Arieti (1955) described severely deteriorated schizophrenics as follows:

> It seems as though the patients who have reached this stage are insensitive to pain. They appear analgesic not only to pin pricks, but to much more painful stimuli. When they are in need of surgical intervention and require sutures in such sensitive regions as the lips, face, skull or hands, they act as though they cannot feel anything, even in the absence of any anesthetic procedure. I have many times sutured wounds caused by their violent and assaultive behavior, without eliciting any sign of pain, or resistance. Other patients seem to feel some pain, but far less than normal persons would. [They] also appear insensitive when the flame of a candle is passed rapidly over the skin. They may sit near the radiator, and if they are not moved, they may continue to stay there even, when, as a result of close contact, they are burned. (p. 373)

The same patients "seem to have lost the sensation of taste. When they are given bitter radishes or teaspoons of sugar, salt, pepper or quinine, they do not show any pleasant or unpleasant reaction" (p. 374).

The Schizophrenic Paradox

And this is the schizophrenic paradox: *real life is sacrificed for a pseudoprotection of life* (Wolman, 1966). Schizophrenics feel that they have to give away their lives to protect those on whom their survival depends. The lavish hypercathexis of the "protectors" leads to impoverishment and death. A classic case of psychosomatic analgesia was described by Shattock (1950):

> A schizophrenic woman set fire to the blanket in which she was wrapped. She was found two hours later "sitting contently on the floor, her legs badly burned, her charred tibiae exposed. Third degree burns also covered her chest, abdominal wall, back and hands. She spoke pleasantly, begging to be left where she was, exculpated everybody, and discussed philosophically whether the absence of religious beliefs was a matter of importance in her present condition. The patient denied repeatedly that she was in any pain and remained cheerful and argumentative for half an hour, while her body was lifted with difficulty from the burning floor boards. She then complained of pain in her shoulders, the only part of her body which was not burned, and a few minutes later collapsed and died.

References

American Psychiatric Association *Diagnostic and statistical manual of mental disorders* (3rd ed.— DSM-III). Washington, DC: Author, 1980.

Arieti, S. *Interpretation of schizophrenia*. New York: Bruner, 1955.

Berger, P. A. Biochemistry and the schizophrenias: Old concepts and new hypotheses. *Journal of Nervous and Mental Diseases*, 1983, *171*, 123–124.

Bleuler, E. *Dementia Praecox or the group of schizophrenias*. New York: 1950. (Originally published, 1911.) 1950.

Bykov, K. *The cerebral cortex and the inner organs*. New York: Chemical Publishing, 1957.

Federn, P. *Ego psychology and the psychoses*. New York: Basic Books, 1952.

Fenichel, O. *Psychoanalytic theory of neuroses*. New York: Norton, 1945.

Fish, B. Neurobiological antecedents of schizophrenia in children: Evidence for an inherited, congenital neurointegrative defect. *Archives of General Psychiatry*, 1981, *34*, 1297–1313.

Goldstein, M. J. *The UCLA family project*. Presented at NIMH High Risk Consortium, San Francisco. Washington, DC: NIMH, 1985.

Gregory, L. Genetic factors in schizophrenia. *American Journal of Psychiatry*, 1960, *116*, 961–972.

Heston, L. B. Effects of child rearing by schizophrenic mothers. *Journal of Psychiatric Research*, 1970, *4*, 153–267.

Jackson, D. D. (Ed.). *The etiology of schizophrenia*. New York: Basic Books, 1960.

Kallman, F. J. Genetic theory of schizophrenia: Analysis of 691 twin index families. *American Journal of Psychiatry*, 1948, *103*, 309–322.

Kallman, F. J. *Genetics in relation to mental disorders*. New York: Norton, 1953.

Kety, S. S. Recent biochemical theories of schizophrenia. In D. D. Jackson (Ed.), *The etiology of schizophrenia*. New York: Basic Books, 1960.

Lidz, T., Fleck, S., & Cornelison, A. R. *Schizophrenia and the family*. New York: International Universities Press, 1979.

Lynn, R. Russian theory and research in schizophrenia. *Psychological Bulletin*, 1960, *60*, 486–498.

Mirsky, A. F., & Duncan, C. C. Etiology and expression of schizophrenia: Neurobiological and psychological factors. *Annual Review of Psychology*, 1986, *37*, 291–319.

Pavlov, I. P. *Lectures on conditioned reflexes*. New York: Liveright, 1927.

Rabkin, J. G. Stressful life events and schizophrenia: A review of the research literature. *Psychological Bulletin*, 1980. *87*, 408–425.

Roizin, L., & Willson, N. Central nervous system in schizophrenia. In B. B. Wolman (Ed.), *International encyclopedia of psychiatry, psychology, psychoanalysis and neurology* (Progress Vol. 1, pp. 31–35). New York: Aesculapius Publishers, 1983.

Rosenthal, D. *Genetic theory and abnormal behavior*. New York: McGraw-Hill, 1970.

Schur, M. Comments on the metapsychology of somatization. *Psychoanalytic Study of the Child*, 1955, *10*, 119–164.

Shattock, M. F. The somatic manifestations of schizophrenia: A clinical study of their significance. *Journal of Mental Science*, 1950, *96*, 32–39.

Stockings, G. T. Schizophreni in military practice. *Journal of Mental Science*, 1945, *91*, 110–112.

Walker, E., & Shaye, J. Familial schizophrenia: A predictor of neuromotor and attentional abnormalities in schizophrenia. *Archives of General Psychiatry*, 1982, *39*, 1153–1160.

Wender, P. H., Rosenthal, D. Kety, S. S., Schulsinger, F., & Weiner, J. Crossfostering: A research strategy for classifying the role of genetic and environmental factors in the etiology of schizophrenia. *Archives of General Psychiatry*, 1974, *30*, 121–128.

Wolman, B. B. *Vectoriasis praecox or the group of schizophrenias*. Springfield, IL: Thomas, 1966.

Zubin, J., & Steinhauser, S. R. How to break the logjams in schizophrenia: A look beyond genetics. *Journal of Nervous and Mental Diseases*, 1981, *169*, 477–492.

IV

Treatment Methods

23

Basic Premises

ETIOLOGICAL CONSIDERATIONS

The treatment of psychosomatic disorders necessitates the cooperation of several professions. The prevention of psychosomatic disorders requires the help and guidance of pediatricians, child psychologists, child psychiatrists, social workers, guidance workers, and educators, for many psychosomatic problems are related to parent–child interaction and other types of social relations. Moreover, although psychosomatic problems are not innate, a search for a genetic predisposition is usually advisable. The treatment process itself depends on the skills of psychiatrists, psychologists, and psychoanalysts, with the close cooperation of psychiatric social workers and quite often medical practitioners in a variety of fields, including, sometimes, the entire hospital staff.

At present, there are several approaches to the treatment of psychosomatic disorders, such as the pharmacophysiological, the psychoanalytic, and the behavioral approaches. It is not easy to decide which approach is the most productive, for psychosomatic disorders are related to a host of genetic, biochemical, and psychological factors. For instance, the serum pepsinogen level is genetically determined, but it can be used as an indicator of susceptibility to the psychosomatic disease of peptic ulcer. There are genetically predisposing factors in other disorders, such as cardiovascular diseases. There are hundreds of books and articles dealing with treatment methods for particular psychosomatic problems, and the search for better methods goes on unabated.

At present, there is a tendency in psychosomatic medicine to apply general rules rather than to view it as a treatment method for specific psychosomatic disorders. Psychosomatic medicine utilizes a broad-minded approach to all patients and all disorders, with a distinct emphasis on the interaction between the organic and the psychosocial determinants (Leigh, Feinstein, & Reiser, 1982; Lipowski, 1985). Certainly, every type of psychosomatic disorder requires a specific approach and a specific treatment tech-

239

nique, but this volume is devoted to the general foundations and to the basic treatment methods.

Present-day therapeutic strategy is directed at multiple etiological factors. Several researchers have promoted this approach. They have pointed to significant correlations between illness onset and the proximal occurrence of significant life stresses, ranging from the death of a spouse to a minor violation of the law. However, stresses of larger magnitude or cumulative stresses correlate better with the subsequent onset of serious illness (Goldberger & Breznitz, 1982; Pichot, 1985).

The noxious factors seem to operate from moments to years following the significant life event(s). These factors may be clustered into four groups: genetic-biological, environmental-social, psychological-behavioral, and autonomous habits. For example, some patients experience personal stresses, such as getting married and moving, that increase their cigarette smoking; the result is a bronchitic infection and an asthmatic condition. Another patient's stresses may lead to depression and personal negligence, which lead to contracting a cold and to an asthmatic condition. In these examples, it is equally possible that cigarette smoking or personal negligence is present but not important in the actual pathophysiological induction of wheezing (bronchospasm). Cigarette smoking, like asthma, may be the result of the patient's individual reaction to the stressors. Thus, identifying the risk factors correlated with illness allows for an analysis of the discrete variables related to the onset of disease (Lehrer & Woolfolk, 1984).

The admixture of biological, psychological, and social predisposing factors is consistent with Alexander's notions of these illnesses as spectrum diseases. Individuals with similar disease may vary in the degree of vulnerability contributed by each of these factors. For example, genetic factors may have placed some ulcer patients at risk for the development of peptic ulcer disease regardless of stresses, whereas others without such loading may develop ulcers as a result of their living style or their coping strategies (Garrick & Kimball, 1983).

GENERAL RULES

A few general psychotherapeutic rules should be followed in the treatment of almost all stress cases:

1. The patient should be encouraged to retain a sense of his or her competence and self-respect. This necessitates his or her accepting whatever unalterable limitations are placed on his or her life plans by loss or injury.
2. The person should continue realistic and adaptive action including maintenance of social relationships and development of new, adaptively useful ones. (Horowitz, 1982, p. 728)

As in all other maladjustments and disorders dealt with by the healing profession, psychosomatic treatment aims at the removal of psychosomatic symptoms and the prevention of their recurrence. One must emphasize the importance of dealing with the underlying psychological causes without taking lightly the resulting physical symptoms. In the initial phase of a psychosomatic disorder, the treatment must emphasize the etiology, in hopes that the removal of the causes will forever remove the possibility of relapses and the recurrence of the symptoms. However, at no time should one overlook the present physical symptoms and their current or potential damage to the organism. For instance, in the advanced phases of peptic ulcers, the removal of psychological stressors will not cure the ulcers, and ignoring the psychological etiological factors could cause serious aggravation of the disease. The treatment must deal with all aspects of the disease, including the psychological etiology and the resulting physical symptoms and their combination.

A general textbook of health describes the necessity of combining physical and psychological approaches: "When a patient is proved to have peptic ulcer, the physician will place him or her on a regimen of diet, rest and avoidance of fear and worry. . . . Rest and avoidance of emotional upset are quite important in the care of the ulcer patient" (Clark & Cumley, 1973, p. 454). This psychological care must be combined with the necessary medical treatment methods.

According to Goldberg (1981), research designed to study the immune system suggests that the organism normally has the capacity to fight cancer successfully. The immune system's mechanisms of resistance to disease have been formulated on both the psychological and the physiological levels: (1) the neuropsychological defense mechanisms protect the organism against intruding agents on the mental level, and (2) the biochemical elements of the immune system protect the organism from intruding agents on the physical level.

There is no evidence concerning a psychosomatic etiology for the various cancer diseases. There is, however, accumulating evidence attesting to the importance of psychological factors in the background and the predisposition of cancer patients. Thus, one may hypothesize that environmental factors contribute to etiology in those individuals whose state of mind increases their predisposition to cancer (Lockhart, 1981). Thus, the therapeutic intervention should take into consideration all of the available physicochemical and psychological methods (Kimball, 1981).

Furthermore, even the purely physicochemical treatment of cancer need not overlook elements in the patient's psychological makeup, such as:

1. The patient's attitudes and beliefs
2. Stress and its relationship to the immune system
3. Early childhood experiences

4. Visual imagery as a bio-feedback system
5. Secondary gains of illness
6. Family support systems
7. Life goals
8. Possibility of recurrence and the threat of death (Bilick & Nuland, 1981, p. 60)

Obviously, a person afflicted by a physical disease is also suffering emotionally. In many instances, a person's emotional suffering leads to physical symptoms, that is, to psychosomatic disorders. Certain general diagnostic clues and psychological treatment methods are described in the following chapters. There are no general physicochemical treatment methods, and every psychosomatic disorder requires highly specialized treatment techniques that cannot be dealt with in this volume (Ramsay, Wittkower, & Warnes, 1976).

REFERENCES

Bilick, H. A., & Nuland, W. A psychological model in the treatment of cancer patients. In J. Goldberg (Ed.), *Psychotherapeutic treatment of cancer patients*. New York: Macmillan–Free Press, 1981.

Clark, R. L., & Cumley, R. W. *The book of health* (3rd ed.). New York: Van Nostrand Reinhold, 1973.

Garrick, T. R., & Kimball, C. P. Recent developments in psychosomatic disorders. In B. B. Wolman (Ed.), *The therapist's handbook* (2nd ed., pp. 514–528). New York: Van Nostrand Reinhold, 1983.

Goldberg, J. (Ed.). *Psychotherapeutic treatment of cancer patients*. New York: Macmillan–Free Press, 1981.

Goldberger, L., & Breznitz, S. *Handbook of stress: Theoretical and clinical aspects*. New York: Macmillan–Free Press, 1982.

Horowitz, M. J. Stress response syndromes and their treatment. In L. Goldberger & S. Breznitz (Eds.), *Handbook of stress*. New York: Macmillan–Free Press, 1982.

Kimball, C. P. *The biopsychosocial approach to the patient*. Baltimore: Williams & Wilkins, 1981.

Lehrer, C., & Woolfolk, R. L. (Eds.) *Clinical guide to stress management*. New York: Guilford Press, 1984.

Leigh, H., Feinstein. A. R., & Reiser, M. F. The patient evaluation grid. *General Hospital Psychiatry*, 1980, 2, 3–9.

Lipowski, Z. J. *Psychosomatic medicine and liason psychiatry*. New York: Plenum Press, 1985.

Lockhart, R. A. Cancer in myth and dream. In J. Goldberg (Ed.), *Psychotherapeutic treatment of cancer patients*. New York: Macmillan–Free Press, 1981.

Pichot, P. *Psychiatry: The state of the art*. New York: Plenum Press, 1985.

Ramsay, R. A., Wittkower, E. D., & Warnes. H. Treatment of psychosomatic disorders. In B. B. Wolman (Ed.), *The therapist's handbook* (pp. 451–519). New York: Van Nostrand Reinhold, 1976.

24

Differential Diagnosis

Nosology: Classification of Diseases

Every treatment process must start with diagnostic procedures. One cannot successfully treat a nonexisting or a misunderstood or a misdiagnosed condition. A correct determination of the nature, degree, and severity of a particular disorder is an absolutely necessary prerequisite for choosing an appropriate treatment method.

The choice of a treatment method and the planning of treatment strategy require a thorough evaluation of the patient in need of treatment. It is of the utmost importance to take into consideration the biochemical and psychological ingredients, the potential genetic predisposition, the relevance of childhood experiences, and whatever else could improve or reduce the chances of therapeutic success.

To diagnose means to discern and to find out in what way and to what extent a particular disease differs from other morbid conditions, as well as what it has in common with some of them, and whether it does belong to a certain category or class of physical or mental disorders. Classification serves the above-mentioned purposes, and the success of diagnostic procedures hinges on the process of classification (Wolman, 1978).

As mentioned above, the purpose of classification is to facilitate diagnosis; to diagnose means to discern, that is, to find out to what extent a particular disease, disorder, or dysfunction differs from other diseases, disorders, or dysfunctions, and what it has in common with similar ones. Every case is unique—that is, it is an *idiophenomenon*—because it is a disease or a disorder of a *particular person* in a particular period. However, if it shares certain characteristics with other cases, these common characteristics permit putting them together into categories or classes and forming general *nomothetic* conclusions, which help in forming a strategy of treatment (Wolman, 1981).

Classification is the name of the process of grouping together objects or events or concepts on the basis of at least one common trait or characteristic. One can choose any criterion or any common element. Thus, one could divide all cases of physical and mental disorders into male and female, childhood and adult, hospitalized and ambulatory, rich and poor, urban and rural, and so on, depending on the vantage point of the person who is doing the classifying. A hospital administrator who assigns rooms to patients may use as criteria their age and sex or their level of income and the kind of insurance they have. A sociologist or an anthropologist who studies mental disorders is interested in ecological factors, class, race, religion, ethnic background, family dynamics, and so on. There are innumerable means of classification: one could divide patients into those who are married or single; those on medication or in psychotherapy, or those receiving both; those who are correctly diagnosed or misdiagnosed; those receiving or not receiving treatment; and so on.

What are the objective criteria for the choice of a classification system? Classification is a procedure of formal logic. It means grouping together objects, bodies, or concepts. It is a selective procedure; it is perfectly logical to classify one's students according to age, sex, religion, race, ethnic origin, and so on. One can divide them into those who wear glasses and those who don't, into those whose marks are above or below the average, or into those who play tennis and those who don't. Each of these classifications may serve a *purpose*.

No classificatory system, as such, is better or more essential than another. Real-estate brokers may classify their acquaintances into those who buy and those who take up time without buying; a neighbor who is a bridge player classifies the same people as nonplayers, beginners, good players, and masters.

Scientific classification enables the formation of general concepts, for when objects or events are put together into a class or category on the basis of at least one common denominator, it becomes possible to make generalizations. These generalizations, often called *empirical laws*, enable science to move away from idiophenomena and to generalize communication (Nagel, 1961).

There are two rules for scientific classification: *economy* and *usefulness*. A classification is economical when: (1) no object within a given system of classification belongs to more than one class, and (2) every object belongs to a certain class. For example, if we divide tables in a storage room according to height and classify those below 3 feet as low and those above 4 feet as tall, we have left out some tables. If we classify as low those that are below 4 feet and as tall those that are above 3 feet, those between 3 and 4 feet belong to both classes, and our classification is uneconomical.

The classification of mental disorders based merely on symptomatology is usually uneconomical. Consider autistic patterns of behavior, typical not only of schizophrenic children but also of children who have had encephalitis or anoxia (Wolman, 1970). Hallucinations may accompany a great many disorders. So may depression, anxiety, phobias, homosexual impulses, psychosomatic disorders, addictions, antisocial behavior, and so on. Most of these symptoms accompany more than one type of mental disorder.

All clinicians would agree that diagnosis is the ultimate purpose of the classification of behavioral disorders. However, this agreement borders on tautology: Nosology is the science of the classification of diseases; classification is a systematic arranging of objects or ideas in classes; and diagnosis means discerning, or distinguishing, that is, finding out the specific traits or characteristics that enable the clinician to put a particular disease or disorder into a class of similar cases.

In other words, when a clinician studies a case of a disease and arrives at a conclusion concerning the particular nature of the case, further decisions about what action to take are greatly facilitated if it is possible to relate the particular case to a class or category of similar cases. An adequate classificatory system enables the clinician to reason, for example, as follows: "Mr. A cannot go to sleep unless he touches the alarm clock innumerable times. He always brushes his teeth in the same manner, four times up and four times down. He feels miserable when he is unable to have his lunch at 12:15," and so on. His sex, age, and occupation are coincidental to a diagnosis, but the above overt symptoms permit a diagnosis of his case as an obsessive neurotic, provided that all other cases with similar symptoms have been put together in the same class. Thus, an adequate classificatory system is a necessary prerequisite for a clinical diagnosis and for the resulting treatment strategy.

Imagine a therapist who does not have any classificatory system. Suppose the therapist noticed certain symptoms but was unable to relate them to any of the nosological categories. What kind of treatment should be applied? In medieval times, headaches were often treated by bloodletting, which must have been fatal for some patients. Some mentally disturbed individuals were treated by exorcism, cold packs, and flogging.

Wolman's *Dictionary of Behavioral Science* (1973) defines *diagnosis* as "Identification of diseases, handicaps, and disorders on the basis of observed symptoms; diagnosis is classification on the basis of observed characteristics" (p. 99).

A correct assessment of the distinct features (symptoms) common to a certain class or group of disorders is the mainstay of clinical diagnosis, and an adequate classificatory system facilitates diagnostic procedures (Zubin, 1978).

There are four clinically significant criteria for the classification of disorders: symptomatology, etiology, prognosis, and treatment. These are not identical and are not even similar terms. In many instances, symptomatological considerations are essential. Consider hypertension: Patients with abnormal Q–T intervals on an electrocardiogram or with a previous history of myocardial infarction are at high risk for a sudden cardiac death. Individuals with high resting levels of blood pressure and a high sensitivity to the dietary intake of sodium chloride are potential hypertension cases. People who have high serum levels of cholesterol, who have high levels of arterial blood pressure, and who are heavy smokers are at risk for an acute myocardial infarction. Obviously, symptoms are relevant diagnostic clues (Herd, 1984).

It must be emphasized that every diagnostic investigation should pay special attention to *etiology*, for some symptoms can be misleading, and a rational nosology greatly depends on a study of the precursors of the illness. The precursors of any disease can be somatic, that is, either genetic or physical, chemical, or environmental factors. In the first case, the disorder is *genosomatic;* in the second case, it is *ecosomatic*. Some disorders are related to patients' interactions with their social environment; thus, these disorders are *sociopsychogenic* (Krauss & Krauss, 1977).

THERAPEUTIC CONSIDERATIONS

Empirical science serves as a basis of the applied sciences, which deal with treatment methods. The applied sciences prescribe actions directed toward a certain goal. For example, education, which is an applied science, sets goals and develops means leading toward the attainment of educational goals. Medicine attempts to cure disorders and develops physical, chemical, and psychological methods that should enable practitioners to attain the therapeutic goal (Wolman, 1978).

The empirical science of pathology is the very foundation of the applied science of treatment. An adequate therapy is based on empirical knowledge, and the empirical study must not overlook its main application. In short, a therapy that is not based on scientific pathology is quackery, but empirical research in pathology that is not related to therapy goes nowhere and could be useless, for it may deal with insignificant and irrelevant issues.

It seems that therapeutic planning should be considered when developing a classificatory system. This consideration raises several relevant questions concerning the aims, the methods, and the overall philosophy of therapy. What is actually the goal of treatment?

Other applied sciences have a much easier road. Consider education. Educational science has a built-in *goal*, which is determined by the biological process of growth and maturation. The inherent goal of all educational systems, whether John Dewey's or J. F. Herbart's, whether American or Soviet, is to help and guide children in the natural process of becoming mature adults. However, because conceptions of maturing and adulthood greatly depend on cultural settings and social philosophies, educational science must determine the *transcendent* goals appropriate for each society and culture.

It seems that health should serve as the inherent goal of all treatment methods, but this is one of the highly controversial issues in current research.

During World War II, Stockings (1945) suggested that military psychiatrists diagnose schizophrenic patients on the basis of their reaction to the methods of treatment used. Those schizophrenics who reacted favorably to IST (insulin shock treatment) were labeled *dysglycotics,* and those who responded to ECT (electric shock treatment) were called *dysoxics.* However, this system is open to severe criticism for lack of evidence concerning the efficacy of the treatment methods.

In diagnostic procedures, one could apply the formula of independent variables, intervening variables, and dependent variables. Assuming that etiological factors, whatever they are, are the independent variable, the clinician, armed with a knowledge of the intervening variables, should be able to predict the symptoms, that is, the dependent variable. Or with a knowledge of symptoms (the dependent variable) and the intervening variables, he or she should be able to explain (i.e., to "predict" in reverse time order) what caused the symptoms. For instance, if a patient has a fear of open spaces (agoraphobia), the clinician applies his or her knowledge of the appropriate conceptual system, which may serve as the intervening variable (Wolman, 1981). By the same token, when the clinician finds the underlying etiology, she or he should be able to predict that the patient will fear open spaces.

I use this method in my psychotherapeutic practice, which I call *interactional psychotherapy* (Wolman, 1984). Accepting a modified psychoanalytic model (to be explained later) as the intervening variable, I have pursued diagnostic interviews either starting from the etiological data, which lead to an anticipatory hypothesis about the symptoms or starting from symptoms and hypothetically deducing their causes.

An adequate classificatory system must relate the therapeutic goal to the relevant etiological and prognostic factors. This suggestion hinges on accepting the causal principle and its application both to past events (i.e., the etiology, or the study of causes) and to the possible outcomes, which are anticipated by prognostic studies (Zubin, 1978).

Diagnosis and Behavioral Methods

In behavior modification, the diagnostic process endeavors to describe the patient's complaints in objective terms, and at the same time to search for the antecedent and maintaining factors and the probable means by which each problem can be resolved. Presenting complaints are usually divided into *behavioral excesses* (e.g., exhibitionism, compulsive checking, frequent rage reactions, and overeating) and/or *behavioral deficits* (e.g., impotence, social withdrawal, and timid and unassertive reaction patterns). In essence, the behavior modifier endeavors to increase or decrease the frequency of specific behaviors, depending on their social context. A thorough search is conducted to uncover and clarify the variables in the patient's biological, psychological, and sociological systems that maintain the current problem behaviors. This behavioral analysis is continually modified and refined as more information is gained about the patient. Frequency distributions are compiled: How many aggressive outbursts, how many avoidance responses, how many negative self-statements, or how many delusional remarks has the patient emitted? Self-monitoring is also highly recommended, especially for well-motivated patients who can count their own positive and negative responses to a wide variety of stimuli (Agras, 1984).

In his or her day-to-day work, the behavioral clinician, like any other therapist, attempts to understand his or her patients' personal constructs, their presenting complaints, and the factors that have given rise to their difficulties, conflicts, perceptual distortions, and idiosyncrasies. Thus, history taking, assessment, and evaluation combine to yield an accurate portrait of the patient in a unique network of social interactions. But unlike in general psychiatric anamnesis, no less attention is paid to overt behavior than to verbal reports of feelings, thoughts, and fantasies. Behavior modifiers do not regard the task of diagnosis as that of assigning the patient to a category and then applying the treatments that are considered best for the members of that category. Questions starting with *how, when, where, what,* and *who* are found to be more productive in eliciting the significant personal and situational variables that are causing and maintaining the emotional disturbances. The upshot of a functional analysis is a detailed and specific range of hypersensitivities, shortcomings, avoidance behaviors, and social inadequacies (Cautela, 1968; Godfried & Kent, 1970; McReynolds, 1975).

Specificity is the hallmark of behavior therapy. Where a traditional therapist may speak of a patient as "an obsessive-compulsive personality with passive-aggressive tendencies," behavior therapists would say, "Mr. Smith washes his hands on an average of 96 times a day; he is inhibited with most authority figures, although he is inclined to overassert his authority with subordinates; he avoids intimate contacts with women, a behavior that he attributes to his premature ejaculation; he is hypersensitive to criticism, rejection, and disapproval." Each of the foregoing problem areas would then be even more clearly articulated, with special emphasis being devoted to particular eliciting and maintaining conditions.

Lazarus (1981) proposed a detailed and systematic assessment process. During diagnostic interviews and throughout the course of therapy, his *multimodal orientation* examines seven interactive modalities: overt behavior, affective responses, sensory reactions, emotive imagery, cognitive processes, interpersonal relationships, and a "biological modality" especially characterized by indications and contraindications for the use of medication. The acronym BASIC ID (derived from *behavior, affect, sensation, imagery, cognition, interpersonal,* and *drugs*) provides a useful mnemonic for remembering these separate yet interrelated modalities. Although *overt behavior* and *interpersonal responses* are amenable to direct observation, the other modalities depend on verbal reports. Affect, imagery, sensation, and cognitive processes are hypothetical constructs—"off limits" to radical behaviorists, but clinically crucial to behaviorally oriented therapists. The application of various sensory exercises is clearly behavioral; however, the statement, "I have an image of my late mother's funeral" is, strictly speaking, verbal behavior. Yet, within the multimodal framework, it is assumed that associated "verbal operants," involving interrelated "affective responses," "cognitions," and "subjective sensations." can be elicited: "The image makes me feel sad and sorry for myself, as I keep thinking that I am to blame for her premature death, which in turn, makes me feel tense all over" (Wilson & Lazarus, 1983, p. 124).

PROGNOSTIC CONSIDERATIONS

All practitioners in the healing professions are concerned with prognosis. One classificatory system went so far as to link it to the anticipated outcome. According to Zilboorg and Henry (1941):

> The most distinguishing point of the Kraepelinian system was the prognostic attitude, closely connected with diagnosis. The Hippocratic principles of prognosis thus entered into psychiatry under a very singular guise. One diagnosed by prognosis, as it were, and if the prognosis proved ultimately correct, the diagnosis was considered correct. This was a departure from a vital and sound principle of general medicine. One cannot say that because a disease ends in a certain definite way it is a certain definite disease. Kraepelin himself was apparently unaware of this singular deviation from medical principles and did not foresee that the fatalism with which it was imbued weakened even further the rather unstable and never too strong rational therapeutic interest with regard to mental diseases. There is no doubt that it was not Kraepelin's intention to diminish the therapeutic efforts or to keep them only within the limits of the aging tradition of hospital management and humanitarian tolerance. But the therapeutic efforts were to become based on the complacent, expectant attitude that if the disease is a manic-depressive-psychosis the patient will get well, and if it is a dementia praecox the patient will deteriorate—or, in the most turgid language of psychiatric formalism, if it is a manic-depressive-psychosis "the prognosis is good for the attack," and if it is a dementia praecox the prognosis is unfavorable. (p. 456)

PSYCHOSOCIAL FIELD

The very nature of human behavior renders clinical predictions exceedingly difficult if not totally impossible. Human beings do not act in a vacuum, and their behavior almost always represents a psychosocial field. Every observer, no matter how objective, influences the observed. In physics, under Einstein's influence, there has been a growing awareness of the fact that any observer–observed situation represents a field. According to Jeans (1958):

> Every observation involves a passage of a complete quantum from the observed object to the observing subject, and a complete quantum constitutes a not negligible coupling between the observer and the observed. We can no longer make a sharp division between the two. . . . Complete objectivity can only be regained by treating observer and observed as parts of a single system. (p. 143)

The difference in the choice of vantage point can lead to far-reaching differences in the results of observation. Compare, for instance, Sigmund Freud's and Harry Stack Sullivan's ideas concerning schizophrenia: The reclining position of the patient and the sparse communication from the mostly silent psychoanalyst facilitated transference phenomena. Freud, the keen observer, noticed them and made them the cornerstone of his therapeutic method. However, when a psychotic patient was asked to recline with a psychoanalyst sitting behind the couch, a different reaction took place. Silence was probably perceived as rejection, and the invisible analyst became a threatening figure. The patient withdrew even more and would not dare to communicate his or her true feelings. Such behavior gave the impression of narcissistic withdrawal and lack of transference feelings toward the psychoanalyst.

Sullivan worked in a hospital where patients were moving back and forth and were acting out their feelings. He saw patients in interpersonal relations, and being a keen observer, he did not fail to notice the socially induced changes in their behavior. The here-and-now interaction became the clue to understanding the psychotic patient. Most probably, what has been observed in *participant observation* was not the patient as an isolated entity but the patient in interaction with the therapist, that is, a *psychosocial field*.

One must therefore conclude that the present status of mental patients is only one of the many determinants of their future behavior. How they will act in the future will be greatly influenced by their interactions with several other people (among them, the therapist), and it is therefore rather unpredictable (Wolman, 1988).

KIMBALL'S DIAGNOSTIC METHOD

Psychosomatic illnesses are best treated by a comprehensive, holistic, or psychosomatic method. Medicine, in general, tends to respond only to the symptoms of disease, while ignoring the precursors of illness, early developmental factors, and their relationship to the illness. Even in psy-

chosomatic disorders, clinical medicine pays little attention to the physiological or psychological factors that led up to these disorders.

Partly to blame for this is the fact that there is really no such thing as a
"psychological disorder." Also, the psychosomatic approach is an imper-
fect science. Kimball (1978) compared it to detective work—to finding the
pieces of the puzzle and fitting them together. But there is no psychosomatic formula that applies to every case; each patient requires a unique
study. Along with its analytic functions, this approach is also a synthetic
process, bringing together many analyses for a total picture of the person
and the disorder.

In the psychosomatic approach, when one meets with a patient one
tries to find out as much as possible about the patient's early environment,
preillness, the illness-onset situation, the early illness experience, the
phases of illness, and the aspects of coping behavior. With this information, we will ultimately construct a "life chart" for that individual that will
help us to understand her or his particular psychosomatic disorder.

We begin this life chart with any information we can secure about
pertinent genetic factors, such as a family history of depressive illness or
cardiovascular reactions. We also look for family situations that may be, or
that have been, stressful to the patient. For example, families who are new
to a culture manifest illnesses different from those manifested by long-
acculturated families. Children of Puerto Rican immigrants in the 1950s
showed a high incidence of psychosomatic disorders, especially asthma
and ulcerative colitis. The family's socioeconomic class, the age and health
of the mother, and the specific patterns of response already present at birth
are just some of the factors that affect the potential for illness in a patient.

We next observe the patient's early illness patterns and what brought
them on. The emergence of these patterns may hint at fixations and behavior patterns that may still be present. The illness state is partially a learned
one, involving such things as the "permission to be ill" given by the family
and the culture. The "ill family" is spoken of almost as often as the "ill
individual." The reactions of the family and the culture to the illness state
in childhood may affect the patient's reactions to the illness state as an
adult.

Stress affects the onset and the severity of a disorder. The stress of
loss, particularly the death or divorce of the parents, seems to have a
profound influence on psychosomatic disorders. This stressful separation,
and the developmental stage during which it occurred in the patient's life,
affects how the patient ultimately deals with the events and emotions that
accompany illness. Illness itself is a stressor, and the patient deals, to a
great degree, with disease in the same way that he or she deals with stress.

Another important area of the patient's life to investigate is the onset
of the illness. It may be impossible to treat the patient's illness without first
identifying and/or attending to the business problems or marital tensions

that the patient is undergoing, and that may have prompted the acute phase of the illness.

As the patient receives treatment for the disorder, it is still helpful to monitor his or her emotional and adaptive reactions. At this point, the life chart makes it easier to identify changes in the patient's states of consciousness and to take immediate steps toward calming delusions and agitation or toward attending to the patient's anxiety or sadness states.

Kimball (1978) maintained that it can be very helpful in the treatment of psychosomatic illnesses to create a life chart, or history, of the patient. This life chart should focus on early developmental factors, major events or stressors in the preillness phase, the events surrounding the onset of the illness and the experiences of the early illness and the acute illness, as well as the progress of adaptive coping behavior in the convalescent and rehabilitative phases of illness. The more complete the life chart, the more hints and clues will be provided about the most effective methods of treatment.

DIAGNOSTIC DIFFICULTIES

There are no clear-cut devices in diagnosing psychosomatic disorders. In my own clinical practice, I abide by a simple rule: "Body comes first." I try to make sure that the problem is not biochemical *before* I turn to psychology. Once, I had a patient who maintained that he had a bad cardiac case. If this had been true, it would have been rather inappropriate to apply psychotherapy. I referred him to a competent cardiologist, who kept him in the hospital for a few days. My patient underwent a series of thorough cardiovascular examinations, which all turned out to be negative. These negative results allowed me to apply psychotherapy that cured this patient of all psychosomatic symptoms.

Sometimes, people come to my office with misdiagnosed physical diseases. They are made to believe that "it was all in the mind." One case, already mentioned in this book, was a woman who suffered from allegedly psychosomatic fainting spells. Psychosomatic symptoms always serve a purpose; this is called *primary* or *secondary gain* in psychoanalysis. In this woman's case, the symptoms could not have served any conscious or unconscious purpose; thus, I excluded the possibility of psychosomatics. I referred her to an expert endocrinologist, who properly diagnosed her condition.

A description of my own patients follows:

The patient, Dr. J., was a biologist with a doctor-of-science degree. His knowledge of biochemistry, pharmacology, and physiology was astounding. Originally, he had planned to become a physician, but he was more interested in research than in practice. He spoke with authority on issues in his competence, and psychosomatic medicine was one of his favorite topics. He was a borderline manic-depressive with a strong self-destructive tendency. His professional career had been inconsistent and spotty; after long periods of hard work, he would abandon his projects, run away, and turn to something else. Apparently, he avoided people and shied away from success and then rationalized his defeats.

Once, he began complaining about nausea and loss of appetite; he proudly declared that he had developed anorexia nervosa and was pleased with his new symptoms.

I disagreed with his self-diagnostic statements. I believe that physical diseases can strike anyone, and neurotics are not immune to TB, pneumonia, and typhoid fever. I have always been opposed to the throwing of all physical symptoms into the waste basket of psychosomatics. In all the years of my practice, whenever a patient has complained of a pain or an ailment, I have demanded a thorough medical examination. Accordingly, I asked Dr. J. to consult his physician. He chided me. "I knew," he said sarcastically, "that you would send me for a physical. That's your old-fashioned philosophy; body comes first."

However, on my insistence, he went to see his family physician. The next day, he reported triumphantly, "My doctor could not find anything wrong with me. It's all in my mind. It's psychosomatic, positive."

As time went on, his complaints became more frequent, and he began to lose weight. I worried about him, for his symptoms did not look psychosomatic to me. I sent him for a physical checkup, this time to an internist with whom I closely cooperated. The report was optimistic, diagnosing mild gastrointestinal trouble, and a medicine was prescribed. Although I kept on insisting on a *thorough* checkup, I tried to convince myself that my worries were irrational. The patient, however, adamantly refused to go for further examinations, and I was torn by an inner conflict; my conscious sided with the internist, but my unconscious was full of worries.

A week passed, and Dr. J. reported a strange dream. In his dream, his brother, with whom he had strongly identified, had been hit in the kidneys by a bomb and was dying. At this point, I became absolutely convinced that Dr. J. had cancer of the kidneys or some other serious kidney disease.

I decided to act immediately. I did not communicate my suspicions to Dr. J., but I put an ultimatum to him: Either he would immediately go for a GI series or I would refuse to see him any longer. I sent him to a top internist. The examination revealed cancer of the kidneys. Dr. J. was hospitalized immediately and, unfortunately, never came back.

It was a terrible shock. One gets attached to a patient, and I felt horribly about Dr. J. I should have been more inclined to listen to the voice of my unconscious. Had I been more determined and less influenced by the two physicians, I would have said, "Go to a top specialist, or I will refuse ever to see you again." I did say that the last time he came to my office, immediately after he told me his dream. I doubt whether an early intervention on my part could have helped, but even today I feel sad when I think of poor Dr. J.

Brill (1972) described some cases of misdiagnosis. The following case involved psychosomatics in a spectacular fashion:

A male employee of about 40 was in sick bay with lobar pneumonia. It was in the days before serum was in general clinical use, and antibiotics were only a Utopian dream. The medical treatment was limited to nursing care, supportive medication, and oxygen, and a form of supportive psychotherapy was recognized as a key issue in treatment; the usual experience was that, once the patient had lost hope and confidence, a fatal outcome was virtually assured.

The patient was on the mend, with a falling temperature and a sense of well-being that augured well. Then came a visit from an authoritative figure who harangued him without mercy on an ethical issue. An emergency call from the ward was too late. I failed to relieve his emotional state; his temperature shot up within an hour, and a spectacular deterioration of his physical condition followed. Within 36 hours, he was dead. I have always wondered if he would have lived if I had maintained protection of his psychic state.

Another case appears to be a clearcut somatopsychic reaction. On one of our wards in the early 1930s was a woman with a cerebellar tumor that was considered inoperable. She was querulous, complaining, demanding, difficult, and given to bouts of screaming and paranoid projections. Early one day, she demanded to see the priest to get the last rites. I examined her and found no change and no indication for calling the priest, who at the time was miles away. Firmly and gently, I explained that the priest would be by to see her as soon as feasible. Her response was hostile and vigorous, not that of a dying woman. My reassurance was firm, protracted, and full of confidence, and finally, she listened. At dusk, the Catholic chaplain arrived. We asked him to see her, and she requested him to administer the last rites. He had hardly finished, when her condition changed, and I watched her die during the next 2 hours. I was so incredulous that I checked my findings by ophthalmoscope and actually saw the blood in the retinal vessels break into segments in typical fashion. This was perhaps a failure of evaluation in the first instance, but it also involved a failure in alleviating tension and anxiety.

Some Recent Developments

Leigh and Reiser (1980) introduced the Patient Evaluation Grid (PEG) as a comprehensive diagnostic tool. The Patient Evaluation Grid has three dimensions and three time contexts. The dimensions are biological, personal, and environmental, and the time contexts distinguish between current, recent, and background.

The *biological dimension* contains information on the patient as tissues, organs, and disease. The *personal dimension* refers to the psychological and behavioral aspects of the patient. The *environmental dimension* contains information related to the physical and social environment of the patient.

The *current context* refers to the present state of the patient in each of the dimensions: physical state, mental status, and family relationships.

The *recent context* pertains to recent changes and events: recent surgery, the development of symptoms and signs, changes in sleep pattern, recent onset of depression, and life changes. The *background context* refers to genetic factors, personality type, habitual coping mechanisms, and cultural factors, such as sick-role expectations and religious convictions (Leigh & Reiser, p. 235).

Another approach to diagnostic issues was introduced as *consultation-liaison psychiatry*. According to Leigh and Reiser (1980) and Lipowski (1985) consultation-liaison psychiatry applies the psychosomatic approach to the evaluation and management of patients in the general medical setting. The consultation-liaison psychiatrist works collaboratively with the internist or the surgeon in a comprehensive evaluation process, including an assessment of stressors in the patient's environment, any changes in behavior (e.g., in sleep or drinking habits) or moods (e.g., depression or anxiety) that may have contributed to the disease, and aspects of the patient's personality that may prove to be important in the planning of treatment. The consultation-liaison psychiatrist helps the nonpsychiatric physician and other health-care workers in a comprehensive psychosomatic approach to the patient, offering to them a comprehensive diagnostic evaluation (Lipowski, 1985).

References

Agras, W. S. The behavioral treatment of somatic disorders. In W. D. Gentry (Ed.), *Behavioral medicine: A new paradigm* (pp. 479–530). New York: Guilford Press, 1984.

Brill, H. Somato-psychic interaction as seen in treatment failures in a mental hospital. In B. B. Wolman (Ed.), *Success and failure in psychoanalysis and psychotherapy* (pp. 153–159). New York: Macmillan, 1972.

Cautela, J. R. Behavioral type and the need for behavior assessment. *Psychotherapy: Theory, Research and Practice*, 1968, 5, 175–179.

Godfried, M. R., & Kent, R. W. Traditional versus behavioral personality assessment: A comparison of methodological and theoretical assumptions. *Psychological Bulletin*, 1972, 77, 409–420.

Herd, J. A. Cardiovascular disease and hypertension. In W. D. Gentry (Ed.), *Handbook of behavioral medicine* (pp. 222–281). New York: Guilford Press, 1984.

Jeans, J. *Physics and philosophy*. Ann Arbor: University of Michigan Press, 1958.

Kimball, C. P. Diagnosing psychosomatic situations. In B. B. Wolman (Ed.), *Clinical diagnosis of mental disorders: A handbook* (pp. 677–708). New York: Plenum Press, 1978.

Krauss, H. H., & Krauss, B. J. Nosology: Wolman's system. In B. B. Wolman (Ed.), *International Encyclopedia of Psychiatry, Psychology, Psychoanalysis and Neurology* (Vol. 8, pp. 86–88). New York: Aesculapius Publishers, 1977.

Lazarus, A. A. *The practice of multimodal therapy*. New York: McGraw-Hill, 1981.

Leigh, H., & Reiser, M. F. *The patient: Biological, psychological and social dimensions of medical practice*. New York: Plenum Press, 1980.

Leigh, H., Feinstein, A. R., & Reiser, M. F. The patient evaluation grid: A systematic approach to comprehensive care. *General Hospital Psychiatry*, 1980, 2, 3–9.

Lipowski, Z. J. *Psychosomatic medicine and liason psychiatry.* New York: Plenum Press, 1985.

McReynolds, P. (Ed.). *Advances in psychological assessment.* San Francisco: Jossey-Bass, 1975.

Nagel, E. *The structure of science.* New York: Harcourt Brace, 1961.

Stockings, G. T. Schizophrenia in military psychiatric practice. *Journal of Medical Science,* 1945, *91,* 110–112.

Wilson, G. T., & Lazarus, A. A. Behavior modification and therapy. In B. B. Wolman (Ed.), *The therapist's handbook* (2nd ed., pp. 121–154). New York: Van Nostrand Reinhold, 1983.

Wolman, B. B. *Children without childhood: A study in childhood schizophrenia.* New York: Grune & Stratton, 1970.

Wolman, B. B. *Dictionary of behavioral sciences.* New York: Van Nostrand Reinhold, 1973.

Wolman, B. B. (Ed.). *Clinical diagnosis of mental disorders: A handbook.* New York: Plenum Press, 1978.

Wolman, B. B. *Contemporary theories and systems in psychology* (2nd ed.). New York: Plenum Press, 1981.

Wolman, B. B. (Ed.). *The therapist's handbook* (2nd ed.). New York: Van Nostrand Reinhold, 1983.

Wolman, B. B. *Interactional psychotherapy.* New York: Van Nostrand Reinhold, 1984.

Zilboorg, G., & Henry, G. W. *A history of medical psychology.* New York: Norton, 1941.

Zubin, J. Research in clinical diagnosis. In B. B. Wolman (Ed.), *Clinical diagnosis of mental disorders: A handbook* (pp. 3–14). New York: Plenum Press, 1978.

25

Psychoanalytic Methods

As described in Chapter 3, psychoanalysis has had a long tradition in dealing with psychosomatic disorders. According to Freud, physical energy is the arch source of mental energy. When the outlets for mental energies are blocked, some amount of these energies is discharged along physical paths in hysterical laughing and screaming, fainting, diarrhea, throwing up, and so on (Breuer & Freud, 1895/1955).

Conversion hysteria can imitate almost any physical disease or handicap. Conversion symptoms include hysterical blindness, hysterical heart attacks, and even simulated pregnancy. Hysterics may experience the most severe pain in almost any part of the organism; disturbances in talking and walking; partial or complete motor paralysis; sleep talking and sleepwalking, and tonic and clonic spasms.

Hysterics occasionally experience a discontinuity in self-awareness. The so-called split personality is one of the classic symptoms of conversion. Such a split in the ego may take place when the ego is exposed to powerful and mutually exclusive demands made by external reality and the id. The ego can serve these two lords when it is itself strong enough to control the excessive demands of the id and to manipulate the external world. Weak egos, however, may not be able to do so. The personality split in hysteria never goes as deep as it does in psychosis, nor is it as lasting. In all neuroses, two attitudes develop that are contrary to each other and independent of each other.

The Oedipus complex is at the core of conversion hysteria. The unresolved oedipal conflict leads most often to urethral eroticism and a prevalence of masturbatory practices and bed-wetting. Bed-wetting in boys serves sexual gratification in a passive way; it symbolizes ejaculation (Sulloway, 1983).

FREE ASSOCIATION

Just before he published his structural theory in *The Ego and the Id* (1923/1962), Freud described his method and explained that his deterministic point of view had led him to substitute free association for hypnosis. In free association, the repressed memory of traumatic experiences comes to the surface. According to Freud, unraveling the unconscious and making it conscious remove the causes of the symptoms. The symptoms are the effects of repressed traumas; the removal of the causes leads to the disappearance of the effects. Thus, adhering to free associations, the fundamental rule of psychoanalysis does not contradict the cathartic method; it merely modifies it.

The method of free association was a turning point in the psychoanalytic treatment of mental disorders. All previous healing methods had been based on a clear-cut division of roles between the therapist and the patient. The therapist, be it a physician, a dentist, or a nurse, "treated" the patient, and the patient received treatment. The therapist was active; the patient, passive. Freud's method revolutionized the doctor–patient relationship. The psychoanalyst took on the role of a reserved listener whose undivided attention was given to the patient's free association. The patient's communication deviated from "reporting" to the doctor. In free associations, the patient's mind jumped from one topic to another and often included irrational thoughts and fantasies.

Free association facilitated regression in the patient and the uncovering of unconscious processes. The analyst was supposed to restrain himself or herself, and to avoid giving any stimuli or any reality cues. The stimulus deprivation, the reclining position, and the dependent attitude of the analyst produced topographical and structural regression in the patient. In the artificial setting of the analyst's office, repressed unconscious thoughts came to the surface and lay bare the primary process.

Freud did not fight against symptoms; he began to unravel the causes of mental disorders. The causes are buried in the unconscious, and they must be brought up to the surface and resolved. The lowering of ego defenses permits access to the repressed material and a reexperiencing of past traumas. One cannot fight an invisible enemy; obtaining insight into and a resolution of unconscious conflicts became a guiding principle of psychoanalytic technique, and it has been incorporated by disciples and dissidents alike.

RESISTANCE

People under stress are usually aware of the fact that they need psychological help; yet, they tend to procrastinate in seeking it. It is apparently much easier to ask for help for a physical ailment than for a mental or psychosomatic disorder.

Even when a person decides to seek help, he or she may soon find out that it is not easy to cooperate with the psychoanalyst. It is easier to sit in a dental chair and let the dentist do the job, or to lie on the physician's examination table and let him or her do the work. The psychoanalytic couch presents new and unpredicted difficulties. The analyst pronounces the fundamental rule of free associations: "Please tell me everything that comes to your mind, pleasant or unpleasant, relevant or irrelevant, important or unimportant. Tell me everything that crosses your mind, and do not withhold anything at all."

Nothing seems easier than compliance with this simple rule; yet, patients resist it. Freud (1933/1962) compared resistance to a "demon" who refuses to come to light because to do so might mean his or her end; patients act as if they are afraid of letting their thoughts flow freely. In most cases of psychosomatic disorders the patients offer stiff resistance as if afraid to give up their chosen protection against embarrassment, anxiety, or guilt (Fenichel, 1945; Freud, 1933/1962).

Apparently, the same forces that have repressed unacceptable wishes resist the reopening of buried conflicts. These forces keep on repressing these conflicts and resisting the unraveling of what has been repressed. Fear of the repressed material prevents its being unrepressed.

Resistance can take almost any form and shape. Failure to verbalize in free association, periods of prolonged silence, breaking appointments or coming late to them, blocking memories, and reacting antagonistically to treatment are frequent signs of resistance. Patients resist by producing hosts of long, foggy, and involved dreams that belabor the same theme; by being drowsy and falling asleep on the couch; by discussing their problems with outsiders; by producing nonsensical associations; by being irritable and hostile to the analyst; and so on (Freud, 1933/1962; Wolman, 1968).

Originally, the concepts of repression and resistance were interpreted in terms of the topographical theory: the conscious was the repressing and resisting censor, and the unconscious pressed for discharge of the repressed material.

With the introduction of the structural theory (Freud, 1923/1962), the ego itself became the repressing and resisting censor. Topographically, the ego belongs to all three strata: the conscious, the preconscious, and the unconscious. The unconscious part of the ego is the repressing agency, and repression itself is an unconscious process. The battle between the id forces that press for repetition compulsion and the ego forces that block the immediate discharge of energy is fought in the murky waters of the unconscious.

In resistance, the patient may forget most recent events and may be unable to free-associate; the associations may go in every possible direction, preventing a continuous flow. The patient may accept the analyst's interpretation and apply it to everyone except herself or himself. Some patients use the "fundamental rule" in a resistive way, repeating the same material again and again.

Resistance often utilizes defense mechanisms, especially projection, reaction formation, and displacement:

> They can be observed in operation alike in dreams, symptom formations, and everyday life and, to the extent that they contribute under ordinary circumstances to harmonious adaptation, are difficult to reduce in analysis: although of course from the analyst's point of view they are easy enough to detect. Projection having originally functioned actively at a period before reality-proving is advanced is extremely hard to bring home to the patient, as in the obvious case of the paranoidal system. Reaction formation, being essentially a fixed form of anticathexis dealing with specific forms of repressed instinct, is easier to establish intellectually than emotionally; and displacement, though relatively easy for the patient to recognize and appreciate, is so continuously in operation in everyday life that its pathological and defensive forms can well be screened. (Glover, 1958, p. 62)

Unresolved resistance may bring a stalemate in analysis. Each clinical type—indeed, each individual—displays a variety of resistive patterns related to the level of fixation, the type of disorder, and the patient's life history. Patients afflicted by psychosomatic symptoms are exceedingly resistive and tend to hold onto their symptoms.

TRANSFERENCE

Transference is at the same time the greatest aid in and the greatest obstacle to psychoanalytic treatment. In negative transference, the patient views the analyst as an unfair, rejecting parental figure. The patient becomes irritable and hostile, looking for errors and unfairness in the psychoanalyst's behavior.

Positive transference can also erect stumbling blocks in the road to cure. The enamored patient requests special attention and "tender loving care" from the analyst. At the peak of positive transference, the patient is interested not in the treatment but in obtaining the psychoanalyst's affection.

INSIGHT

Usually, insight is the prerequisite of cure, but not necessarily in psychosomatics. Insight cannot be gained by mere interpretation of conscious behavior (often called *confrontation*) and interpretation of the unconscious. Psychoanalysis may become interminable unless resistances are overcome.

Thus, a prolonged process of working through must follow the therapeutic process. The patient must expose deeper and deeper layers of infantile conflicts and gradually, step by step, resolve them.

The withdrawal of cathexes from infantile fixations enriches the patient's personality and puts new emotional resources at the disposal of her or his ego. The need for energy-absorbing psychosomatic symptoms subsides, and each step forward frees the mental energies. In the terminal phase, patients may tend to invest their energy in new adventures.

One could compare the patient in the final phase of analysis to a car whose power has been increased. An increase in the power of an automobile engine requires a proportional increase in the power of the brakes and the steering mechanism. Similarly, a gradual resolution of mental conflicts frees the mental energies; these energies must be put to rational use.

Freud and almost all Freudians have observed that a purely intellectual approach to emotional problems can hardly result in their resolution. The emotional experience of transference emerges as the main vehicle of cure (Blanck, 1983; Greenson, 1967; Menninger, 1958; Wolman, 1967).

ALEXANDER'S TECHNIQUE

Alexander and French (1946) deviated from Freud in the handling of transferences. The very idea that transference must be handled and not just allowed to develop was a new one.

Alexander and French believed that treatment is an "emotional experience," and that what occurs during its course is more than transference and therefore must not be left to coincidental developments. Though the patient relives in transference emotional involvements of his or her childhood, the mere reliving cannot be healing. Past emotions must be reexperienced in a setting that enables correction. Thus, "corrective emotional experience" must be offered to the patient.

This experience must be geared to the patient's needs: a rigid everyday schedule may not be appropriate for some patients. Alexander maintained that, in many cases, less frequent interviews are just as productive as the classic procedure with daily sessions.

Alexander, French, Selesnick, and others experimented with less frequent interviews and also with interruptions in treatment (Seleznick, 1967):

> At propitious moments the analyst may manipulate the frequency of analytic
> interviews or recommend a temporary interruption of treatment. In some cases,

as for example, with acting-out patients, it may be necessary to increase the frequency of the interviews in order to develop a more intense transference relationship. This encourages a tendency toward identification with the analyst, who then has an opportunity to exert a restraining influence on the patient's impulses. Frequently, however, especially with those patients who use analysis as a substitute for life experiences, it is better to reduce the frequency of the interviews or to set a tentative termination date for the analysis. Owing to these experimental manipulations, dependency on the analytic situation becomes a focal issue. The patient may discover that he can manage quite well without the analyst, and soon a more permanent separation may be recommended. Preparatory interruptions were found to be an excellent means of gauging the proper time for terminating the treatment. Alexander, French, and some of their colleagues at the Chicago Psychoanalytic Institute learned that the emotional reaction to previous interruptions is a more important clue than such criteria as recollection of infantile memories or the depth of intellectual insight. In cases when, during interruptions or reductions in frequency, feelings of yearning for the analyst become more intense upon returning to the analysis or upon increasing the frequency of the interviews, the patient may be able now to verbalize those feelings and thus gain greater insight into the nature of his dependent strivings. It is insight based on emotional experience, especially with regard to the transference, that is the aim of these stratagems. (Selesnick, 1967, p. 201)

Alexander (1956) believed that interruptions in treatment may have therapeutic value insofar as they show the degree of the patient's dependence on the analyst. By increasing or decreasing the number of sessions per week, the analyst may intensify or dilute the transference, according to the emotional needs of the patient and the treatment strategy.

Corrective experience cannot be simply a replica of childhood, nor should it be a mere recollection and reconstruction of the past. Alexander and French (1946) stressed the importance of the here-and-now, real-life situation of the patient. What's the use of digging out the past if the patient still fails to adjust to her or his present life conditions? Discovery of the past should be geared toward an understanding of the current situation. The unraveling of childhood experiences offers clues to the present; interpretation of the past is not a goal in itself, but a means toward the goal, and the goal is rational adjustment to mature adult life. The present situation is, to some extent, enacted in the analyst's office. Here, patients have the opportunity to learn about themselves and their own behavioral patterns.

Alexander (1950) did not approve of the passive attitude of the analyst. The analyst must convey to the patient her or his own self-confidence and faith in the success of the treatment. A passive attention of the analyst who refrains from expressing her or his feelings may be of little therapeutic value. Alexander believed that the patient must *feel* the difference between the primitive, unstable, and rejecting parents and the present relationship with a friendly and mature analyst. This new relationship is the bedrock of a corrective and healing experience.

The main task of psychoanalytic therapy is to help the ego to assume its adaptive functions and to relate in a rational way to the tasks and challenges of adult life. This approach is also applied to the treatment of psychosomatic problems.

Treatment of Ulcers

According to Alexander and Flagg (1965), in *peptic ulcer,* the first therapeutic consideration must be treatment of the local condition with antacids or antispasmodics or by surgery. Suction of the vagus nerve to the stomach is a useful technique in the therapy of peptic ulcer because it decreases continuous acid secretion. However, psychotherapy is the only treatment that can alter the patient's psychic conflict, which constitutes the primary disturbance in the chain of events causing the ulcer.

According to Alexander and Flagg (1965) psychoanalytically oriented psychotherapy directed at the patient's specific emotional conflict may produce marked symptomatic improvement as well as a marked personality change toward maturity.

Treatment of Colitis

Mucous colitis is a disorder of functions of the colon resulting from a parasympathetic nervous system that is overactive because of neurotic conflicts. Overconscientiousness, dependency, sensitivity, anxiety, guilt, and resentment are the emotional traits most commonly found in patients suffering from mucous as well as other forms of colitis. Patients with chronic diarrhea and spastic or mucous colitis reveal a conflict centering on their strong demanding (oral aggressive and receptive) wishes, for which they try to compensate by activity and by substituting bowel movements for real accomplishment. They worry and fret about their duties and obligations and appear overconscientious, but they harbor great reluctance to exert themselves. Thus, an essential difference is seen between the patient with colitis and the peptic ulcer patient, who also overcompensates for dependency, but who does so by actual exertion and accomplishment in his or her external activities (Alexander & Flagg, 1965).

Alexithymia

Sifneos (1972) coined the term *alexithymia* to denote the psychosomatic disorder of patients who display a particular difficulty in describing their feelings and who experience a severe decline in their fantasies. Alexithymic patients may not be able to distinguish between their emotional states and their bodily sensations: "They seem to have a defect in the ability to be in touch with their inner feelings" (Taylor, 1987, p. 80).

The psychoanalytic treatment of alexithymic patients is a controversial issue. Some psychoanalysts suggest that the analyst should encourage these patients to observe their own cognitive-affective disturbances. Other psychoanalysts recommend a sort of therapeutic guidance that should enable psychosomatic patients to interpret and organize their own feelings. It seems:

> . . . that the interoceptive confusion of alexithymic patients is best treated by assisting these patients to identify accurately their affective states rather than telling them what they are *really* thinking or feeling. Alexithymic patients may readily comply with interpretations of symbolic meaning or redefinitions of their experiences, and psychotherapists must avoid repeating previous interactions in which others have appeared to know the patient's feelings better than they do themselves. Instead of attempting to identify and interpret unconscious conflicts, therapists need to increase patients' awareness of the inaccessibility of their unconscious minds. It is probable that only patients with mild and secondary types of alexithymia will be able to use psychoanalytic psychotherapy even with modified techniques. However, some psychoanalysts are experimenting with more adventuresome techniques in an attempt to reverse the psychosomatic process in patients who are more severely alexithymic. (Taylor, 1987, p. 113)

REFERENCES

Alexander, F. *Psychoanalysis and psychotherapy*. New York: Norton, 1956.

Alexander, F., & Flagg, T. The psychoanalytic approach. In B. B. Wolman (Ed.), *Handbook of clinical psychology*. New York: McGraw-Hill, 1965.

Alexander, F., & French, T. *Psychoanalytic psychotherapy*. New York: Ronold Press, 1946.

Blank, G., & Blank, R. *Ego psychology*. New York: Columbia University Press, 1974.

Breuer, J., & Freud, S. Studies on hysteria. *Standard Edition* (Vol. 2). London: Hogarth Press, 1955. (Originally published, 1895.)

Fenichel, O. *The psychoanalytic theory of neurosis*. New York: Norton, 1945.

Freud, S. The ego and the id. *Standard Edition* (Vol. 19). London: Hogarth Press, 1962. (Originally published, 1923.)

Freud, S. New introductory lectures on psychoanalysis. *Standard Edition* (Vol. 22). London: Hogarth Press, 1962. (Originally published, 1933.)

Garfinkel, P. E., & Garner, D. M. *Anorexia nervosa: A multidimensional perspective*. New York: Brunner/Mazel, 1982.

Glover, E. *The technique of psychoanalysis*. New York: International Universities Press, 1958.

Greenson, R. R. *The technique and practice of psychoanalysis*. New York: Hallmark Press, 1967.

Menninger, K. *Theory of psychoanalytic technique*. New York: Basic Books, 1958.

Selesnick, S. The technique of psychoanalysis developed by Franz Alexander and Thomas French. In B. B. Wolman (Ed.), *Psychoanalytic technique: A handbook for the practicing psychoanalyst*. New York: Basic Books, 1967.

Sifneos, P. *Short-term psychotherapy and emotional crisis*. Cambridge: Harvard University Press, 1972.

Sulloway, F. J. *Freud: Biologist of the mind.* New York: Basic Books, 1983.

Taylor, G. J. *Psychosomatic medicine and contemporary psychoanalysis.* Madison, CN: International Universities Press, 1987.

Wolman, B. B. (Ed.). *Psychoanalytic technique.* New York: Basic Books, 1967.

Wolman, B. B. *The unconscious mind: The meaning of Freudian psychology.* Englewood Cliffs, NJ: Prentice-Hall, 1968.

26

Behavior Therapy

Behavior therapy includes a number of diverse techniques for treating a wide range of psychosomatic disorders. In behavior therapy for psychosomatic disorders, the therapist draws on the general principles and procedures of behavior therapy in adjusting the therapy to the individual's specific problems. These behavioral principles and procedures are derived from experimental research in psychology; they originated in the classical and operant conditioning described in Part II of this volume. A brief summary of a few of these methods is followed by a description of their application to particular psychosomatic disorders (Davidson, 1976; Lazarus, 1981; Turner, 1984; Wilson & Lazarus, 1983; Wolpe, 1980).

The basic assumption behind *desensitization* techniques is that the fear evoked by subjectively threatening situations can be reduced by a graded and progressive exposure to a hierarchy of anxiety-generating situations. The patient is taught to use various "antianxiety" responses (e.g., deep muscle relaxation, pleasant imagery, or rational self-assurance) and thereby to systematically extinguish each level of anxiety.

Data from animal and human studies have indicated that the necessary condition for the successful desensitization of fear and avoidance behavior is nonreinforced exposure to the fear-producing situation. In actual clinical practice, desensitization involves important attitudinal and expectancy components, demand characteristics. and cognitive labeling.

Role-playing and *role-reversal* procedures are important components of behavior rehearsal. The therapist assumes the role of significant people in the client's life, and progressive series of important encounters are enacted. Feedback from videotapes or tape recordings is often useful in monitoring the client's mode of expression, verbal content, inflection, and tone of voice and resonance, and in removing needless apologies, hesitations, or querulous overtones. Nonverbal behavior, such as posture, facial expression, gait, and eye contact, is also shaped. Behavior rehearsal, unlike

other forms of role playing, focuses primarily on modifying current maladaptive behavior patterns rather than on "working through" symbolic
conflicts.

The most frequent application of behavior rehearsal is within the context of *assertion training*, that is, in overcoming situations in which patients
complain that they are exploited by others, inhibited, or unable to express
love, affection, and other positive feelings. The use of modeling and behavior rehearsal is often referred to as *social skills training*.

Aversion conditioning has been used to eliminate or control unwanted
or undesirable behavior, such as alcoholism, drug abuse, and sexual disorders. The undesirable response is repeatedly paired with an aversive
event, such as a painful electric shock or a chemically induced nausea.
Aversion conditioning has always been controversial, and erroneous beliefs about its effects abound.

Behavioral conceptions of self-control range from the extreme operant
position, which maintains that *self-control* refers to certain forms of the
environmental control of behavior, to cognitive approaches, in which self-
regulatory mechanisms are said to mediate overt behavior. *Self-monitoring*
refers to the systematic observation of one's own behavior (e.g., the
number of calories consumed daily). The person then self-evaluates his or
her behavior, that is, judges the adequacy of his or her performance in
terms of some standard or comparison criterion. Depending on whether
the behavior matches the standard or not, the person then either applies
self-reinforcement or self-punishment.

TOKEN ECONOMY PROGRAMS

One of the most impressive applications of operant conditioning principles has been the modification of entire groups of individuals through the
use of token economy programs. Token economies have been instituted for
a wide range of different behaviors in diverse populations, including psychiatric inpatients and outpatients, retarded and autistic children, delinquent youths, normal and disturbed children in classroom settings, and
patients with psychosomatic disorders.

The token is a compound discriminative and secondary reinforcer that
stands for the backup reinforcers. The advantages of using tokens as reinforcers are that they bridge the gap between the target behavior and the
backup reinforcers, they permit the reinforcement of any response at any
time, and they provide the same reward for patients who have different
preferences in backup reinforcers. The token may be a tangible item, such
as a poker chip or a plastic card, or it may be a check mark on a piece of
paper. Token economy procedures incorporate many social-influence processes, including operant and classical conditioning, social reinforcement,

modeling, and expectancy of success. Within this general social-influence context, the specific token-reinforcement contingencies play the decisive role in regulating behavior change.

In the token economy method, the therapist functions as a consultant who knows how to formulate and plan behavior change programs. These plans are then implemented by the *mediators*, those people who have the closest contact with the *target* (anyone who has a problem to be modified). The mediators may be parents, teachers, peers, nurses, attendants, or employers—in fact, anyone who is in a position to control the reinforcement contingencies in the target's environment (Wilson & Lazarus, 1983).

Goal-Directed Behavior

As already mentioned, psychosomatic disorders are acquired through an interaction between behavioral patterns and the nervous system; thus, modifying the patient's patterns of behavior is the most logical method to be used in the prevention and treatment of psychosomatic disorders. In classical behavior therapy (Wolpe, 1980), the therapy attempts to alter the morbid conditioned response and other behavior. The therapy methods condition the patient to replace the conditioned morbid responses with healthy reactions. For instance, presenting the anxiety-producing stimulus when the patient is in a relaxed state undoes its impact and enables the patient to become conditioned to an anxiety-free response. Behavior modification methods are often used in preventive ways to reduce the individual's reactivity to stress (English & Baker, 1983).

The main idea in the treatment of psychosomatic symptoms is to help patients to use rational methods, instead of psychosomatic symptoms, to attain their goals.

Systematic desensitization discrimination training, and behavioral skill learning are behavioral methods frequently used in the treatment of psychosomatic disorders. Their common aim is to enable the patient to cope with anxiety and depression not by psychosomatic symptoms, but by realistic goal-directed behavior.

Systematic Desensitization in the Treatment of Psychosomatic Disorders

The systematic desensitization often applied in the treatment of psychosomatic diseases is a primary technique derived from classical conditioning and is used to desensitize an individual who is reacting to an anxiety-inducing situation. The patient is placed in a state of relaxation through progressive relaxation exercises, a series of structured muscle-relaxation exercises involving the small and large muscle groups through-out the body. In the relaxed state, the patient is instructed to imagine the anxiety-inducing stimuli or situations, beginning with mildly anxiety-inducing situations and gradually extending to more provocative imaginings.

Many psychosomatic disorders are situation- or stimulus-specific, often becoming exacerbated under the stimulus of a particular stressor. Systematic desensitization can often help to alleviate the anxiety evoked in such situations, particularly when the situations do not currently threaten the individual as much as they did previously. *Asthma* is one example. To treat asthma, Moore (1965) used desensitization along three hierarchies: one based on the progression of an asthmatic attack; one based on an allergic or infective situation; and one based on a psychologically stressful situation. All were directed toward the anxiety-provoking situation present at the beginning of an attack. Moore found significant objective and subjective improvement in her patients. Two-year follow-up studies demonstrated the lasting effects of such types of intervention (Garrick & Kimball, 1983, p. 521).

DISCRIMINATION TRAINING IN EXACERBATED PSYCHOSOMATIC CASES

The discrimination-training method is a derivative of the operant behavioral model. It identifies the discriminative stimuli that occasion specific behaviors leading to specific consequences. An analysis of the relationship between the discriminative stimulus, the behavior, and its consequences is the foundation of several behavior therapies. This approach is used in the behavioral analysis of exacerbations of psychosomatic disorders.

Consultation is often requested when the medical workup fails to identify the presence of somatic disease. The consultee wishes to know if the symptom is a somatic expression of psychological distress. A behavioral approach, in which characteristic patterns of the onset of symptoms are identified, often contributes to both an explanation of the behavior and the formulation of a method of therapeutic intervention. For example, for patients with complaints of debilitating abdominal pain and diarrhea, consultations are frequently requested by the gastrointestinal service. The extensive medical workup has been negative, and management has been frustrating. A careful exploration of the circumstances surrounding daily episodes of symptoms identifies recurrent stress situations that are connected with the development of the symptoms. A careful behavioral analysis may be aided by the patient's filling out extensive daily diaries that record his or her activities, thoughts, and feelings, together with a record of his or her experience of the symptoms. The repeated concurrence of the symptoms and anxiety-inducing situations noted in the records could be striking to both patient and therapist (Garrick & Kimball, 1983; Lazarus, 1981).

BEHAVIORAL SKILLS TRAINING

This strategy is used when the behavioral analysis or other diagnostic procedures suggest that the patient's disorder is due, in part, to poor interactional skills, that is, when the patient uses illness behavior rather than more direct techniques, to adapt to his or her environment. The therapy focuses on helping the patient to learn a more adaptive repertoire. Skills training has often been used in the treatment of psychosomatic disorders.

Asthmatic attacks in a child may serve to attenuate upsetting marital discord in the family. Another child in the same family may develop a different maladaptive behavior that also results in decreasing the marital discord. Both behaviors, although topographically different, may produce the same beneficial outcome for each of these children (Skinner, 1974). A third child may react with altered eating behavior, headaches, anxiety attacks, or psychosis. Behavioral treatment may be directed toward teaching the patient and/or the family means of decreasing discord without the use of somatic symptom formation. A behavioral management program is based on identifying the situations and the associated outcomes in which physiological behaviors develop. An example of this approach might include patients with irritable bowel syndrome whose symptoms are concurrent with inadequate coping skills, along with feelings of frustration and anger, who are taught to use assertiveness to replace episodes of anger, frustration, and gastrointestinal symptoms (Garrick, 1981; Wolpe & Reigna, 1976).

Following is an unusual case application of such a treatment approach:

> Mr. A is a 33-year-old man who was seen by the psychiatric consultant to evaluate paroxysmal atrial tachycardia (P.A.T.) of four years' duration. Propranolol (120 mg/day) was helping to maintain his heart rate below 160 beats per minute. However, the patient continued to have attacks in which anxiety was prominent. The patient had been given Valium early in the course of his illness and was unable to decrease his daily 40 mg dose without precipitating P.A.T. and/or anxiety and/or withdrawal.
>
> Mr. A was a successful businessman, from which he gained most of his pleasure. He was married four years before for the second time and felt this present marriage to be difficult. He identified his propensity for extramarital affairs. Neither he nor his wife was able to decide to divorce. He was the youngest of two boys of a distant father who was disliked by the patient for as long as he could remember. He felt his mother to be intensely controlling, such

that the patient could barely spend one day with her before needing to escape. The patient was thrown out of school at 15 years of age and had hustled his way since.

Behavioral analysis revealed two significant findings. First, he demonstrated such poor writing and communication skills (in the face of clearly above average intelligence) that understanding him was difficult. Second, nearly all attacks of P.A.T. occurred when the patient was on his way to meet his wife. Therapy focused on pointing out the correlation between symptoms and intended behaviors and on teaching the patient new skills to more effectively communicate with his wife. These skills included paying attention to subtle processes of verbal and nonverbal interactions.

Within three months of weekly therapy, the P.A.T. resolved, allowing cessation of the propranolol. The patient, at one year of treatment, was treating his anxiety attacks with planning and organized action. One year following treatment, the patient was also free of symptoms of P.A.T. (Garrick & Kimball, 1983, p. 523)

BEHAVIORAL TREATMENT OF ANOREXIA

Operant conditioning was applied to 65 hospitalized anorexic patients by Toyouz, Beaumont, and Glaun (1985). The researchers reported that rewarding weight gains had been more successful than stressing eating behavior. One group of 31 patients was treated in a strict bed-rest program, whereas the other group (34 patients) was requested to stay in bed for 1 week, after which the patients were allowed to move around freely, provided they complied with the agreed-upon 1.5-mg weight gain per week. The patients who took part in the more lenient program were more cooperative than the patients who took part in the strict program. Ultimately, the patients on the more lenient and rewarding program showed greater progress.

BEHAVIORAL TREATMENT OF OBESITY

Among the best-known self-control methods for regulating problem behaviors are those that are used for treating obesity. These methods have been extended to a variety of problems, including cigarette smoking, alcoholism, and study habits. In the weight reduction program, patients are taught to keep records of eating and exercise. The patients are instructed to narrow the number of stimuli associated with the act of eating (e.g., not eating while engaging in any other activity, such as watching TV or reading). Procedures are introduced to disrupt and control the actual process of eating (e.g., eating utensils have to be placed on the table between bites, and all food has to be chewed slowly and completely swallowed before the next bite). Weight loss has been maintained at 1-year follow-ups, although little further weight loss has occurred after the end of the formal treatment (Wolman, 1982).

Self-monitoring and self-evaluation strategies have been implicit in virtually all forms of behavior therapy and are increasingly being investigated as important behavior-change methods in and of themselves. Most behavioral techniques are being viewed within the context of the self-management of behavior. According to Bandura (1969) and Wilson and Lazarus (1983), the aversion therapies are best construed as self-control methods in which the patient cognitively re-creates the aversive consequences in order to control undesirable behavior.

BEHAVIORAL TREATMENT OF SEXUAL DISORDERS

The behavioral treatment of sexual disorders is quite different from the Freudian treatment methods:

1. The behavioral methods are concerned with the maintenance rather than with the origin of the sexual disorder. Origin and history become important only as they reveal what the person does to perpetuate the very things she or he wants to change.

2. The identification of very specific target behaviors (including such covert behaviors as fantasies, feelings, and desires) that maintain the disturbing condition is the core of the behavioral diagnostic and evaluative procedure. Deliberate and systematic efforts to modify these target behaviors are the core of the treatment. The measurement of change in the target behaviors and of disturbed behaviors in the life situation is also an integral part of the therapeutic procedures.

3. Modification of the problem-maintaining behaviors is a sufficient goal for treatment, and an exploration of intrapsychic dynamics is not necessary for successful and permanent change. As the target behaviors change, there is a feedback into the person's psychological organization that brings about a "healthier" alignment of the intrapsychic forces (Fensterheim & Kantor, 1980, pp. 314–315).

Premature ejaculation appears to be one such behaviors. As long as it is treated as a counterhabit of ejaculatory control, good results are obtained in treatment in majority of patients (Waggoner, 1980).

Although the irrelevance of intrapsychic considerations to the treatment of habitual disturbed sexual behaviors is clear, the same behavioral perspective may be applied to all sexual disturbances. Many behavioral therapists take any sexual problem, break it down into its component behaviors, and systematically change each behavior in turn. With this approach, they have achieved some excellent results.

A classical conditioning method known as *fading* has been used to establish heterosexual arousal, and aversive methods have been used to decrease homosexual arousal. Through the successful modification of these component behaviors, the patients change from desiring sex-transformation surgery toward a behavior that leads to a full heterosexual life. The success and limits of such a behavioral approach to complex sexual problems have not yet been fully tested, but this approach does have great promise (Wolman & Money, 1980).

A Case Description

A man complained of intermittent impotency. Periodically he was able to attain and maintain an erection but under those conditions, was usually disappointed in sex. At other times, he was unable either to attain or to maintain an erection. At these times he was aware of feelings of irritability and resentment, and often there were sharp words and fighting between the couple. Closer examination revealed that the more actively the wife behaved in the sexual situation, the more apt the husband was to be impotent. Although such a pattern is usually associated with a fear of premature ejaculation, this did not seem to be true in this instance. Rather, the husband interpreted the wife's level of activity as demands being placed on him, and he responded to these "demands" with resentment. Further examination showed a similar, although a much lower, response to demands in nonsexual situations.

The first treatment attempt was assertiveness training. His rights and his wife's rights were discussed with him. He practiced saying "no" to demands in life situations as well as in role-playing situations with the therapist. He also practiced responses to possible "put-downs" by his wife if he did not meet her expectations. These procedures yielded only a slight and transitory change in the problem area. (Fensterheim & Kantor, 1980, p. 317)

It has been demonstrated that an automatic sexual response can be conditioned to pictures of boots. If this is so, certain of the sexual variants may be treated by phobic reduction techniques. Two examples follow:

1. A nineteen-year-old woman had a sexual response to chewing gum. Whenever she was in the presence of anyone chewing gum (the stimulus could be visual or auditory) her sexual response was so strong that she would have to rush to the nearest bathroom to masturbate. She herself traced this reaction to her early adolescence when she had trained her dog to masturbate her by licking her clitoris. The sexual response, however, was limited to the middle range of the phobic stimuli. At a lower level, pictures of a chewing gum pack would set off slight but definite anxiety. At higher levels, the sight of a dog or cat licking itself would set off panic.

This sexual response responded to a phobic reduction approach. Actually, systematic desensitization both to imagined situations and to the therapist chewing gum in her presence had no effect. She did respond to in-viv-flooding with response prevention (Marks). She exposed herself to situations in which people were chewing gum and remained in that situation while actively inhibiting the sexual response and practicing deliberate muscle relaxation. In a telephone contact six months after termination of treatment, the patient stated that despite repeated exposure to chewing gum situations, only once was there any sign of sexual response.

2. A twenty-eight-year-old man was a fetishistic transvestite. At age thirteen

he became attracted to his mother's lingerie, particularly to the tactile sensations, and he would masturbate with the lingerie as a stimulus. At age nineteen
he performed his first cross-dressing with the intent of heightening the tactile
sensations. Over time he became more enamored of the visual impact of his
appearance, although his greatest thrill was when walking in the street cross-
dressed, someone would brush against his clothing. He would always cross-
dress alone, never in the presence of his girlfriend with whom there was a
normal pattern of heterosexual behavior.

He was treated with phobic reduction methods. A desensitization tape was
prepared for him to play at home. With this tape, he first relaxed, then he
imagined a transvestite or fetishistic scene. Upon the first feelings of any sexual
arousal, he would relax again. . . .

At the present time he reports a complete cessation of all transvestite
thoughts or feelings. This in itself is not conclusive, for on a number of occasions
these have spontaneously disappeared for periods of up to two-and-a-half
months. This time, however, he reports that there is a different feeling; he has a
feeling of being in control. Further follow-up is of course necessary to determine
if the phobic reduction method really did work. (Fensterheim & Kantor, 1980,
pp. 317–318)

Treatment of Coronary Heart Disease

Coronary heart disease is the primary cause of premature death in the
United States (Feuerstein, Labbe, & Kuczmierczyk, 1986). Research has
identified a set of risk factors associated with coronary heart disease, such
as smoking, obesity, age, sex, elevated serum cholesterol, and family history. However, there is an additional risk factor that outweighs all the others.

The *Type A* person—time-urgent, impatient, hard-driving, ambitious,
and competitive—has been found to be *particularly susceptible* to coronary
heart disease (CHD). Therefore, the treatment of CHD is mainly directed
toward modifying the Type A personality. *Progressive muscular relaxation,
rational emotive therapy, training in improving communication and problem-solv-
ing skills,* and *stress innoculation* have been helpful in controlling coronary-
prone Type A behavior.

In progressive muscular relaxation, the goal is for the participant to
learn to monitor and reduce stress and tension. Rational emotive therapy
helps the Type A person to control negative emotions, such as hostility,
anxiety, and depression. The improvement of communication and prob-
lem-solving skills helps the individual to send and receive clearer messages, which focus on the problem rather than attacking the other person.
Finally, stress innoculation helps the participant to recognize the physical
and mental cues of stress.

There are also various other methods for controlling Type A behavior.
Psychotherapy treatment focuses on modifying the individual's need for mas-
tery and control over his or her environment. *Cardiac-stress-management*

training (Suinn, 1982) starts with a recognition that Western culture admires and rewards Type A behavior. Type A individuals internalize these values and impose these stresses on themselves. This program seeks to associate reward values with other types of behavior.

Other systems are *anxiety management training,* in which individuals are taught to identify their own stress responses and to try to reduce them through relaxation, and *visuomotor behavior rehearsal,* in which individuals begin to use other types of behavior, such as taking coffee breaks. *Physical fitness programs* have also been beneficial in modifying coronary-prone behavior (Feuerstein *et al.,* 1986; Millon, Green, & Meagher, 1982).

Treatment of Pain

Pain is a multidimensional phenomenon; therefore, it is difficult to pinpoint whether it is a sensation, a reaction, or an emotion. An increasing number of psychological treatments are available for the treatment and management of chronic pain (Feuerstein *et al.,* 1986).

Operant therapy attempts to change pain behavior, which includes avoidance of physical activity, medication use, and verbal pain complaints. The goal of operant therapy is to reduce pain behavior while increasing well behavior, such as physical exercise, the pursuit of hobbies, and work.

Biofeedback training brings patients' physiological functions into awareness. The patient receives feedback about his or her pain response through such methods as meter readings of skin temperature and auditory signals. This feedback allows the patient to become aware of the voluntary physiological processes associated with pain, with the eventual goal of controlling them (White & Tursky, 1982).

Another method of pain management is *relaxation training.* The goal here is for the patient to be able to discriminate between tensed and relaxed muscles, and then to relax those muscle groups that contribute to the health problem when tensed.

Hypnosis is also used to modify pain. Hypnosis may alter the patient's negative perception of the pain, may enhance positive self-statements, and may instill feelings of deep relaxation that do not normally occur with certain pain behaviors. Hypnosis can also help to direct the patient's attention away from the pain and toward hobbies, activities, and non-pain-related thoughts.

The goal of the *cognitive-behavioral* approach to pain innoculation is to help the patient develop more adaptive mental and behavioral responses to the physical problem. The individual is taught to recognize negative pain-thoughts and then to substitute healthier thoughts. The individual is also taught to use relaxation, distraction, and imagery to reduce his or her suffering (Meagher, 1982).

TREATMENT OF IRRITABLE BOWEL SYNDROME

Irritable bowel syndrome (IBS) is a common gastrointestinal disorder defined by abdominal pain and diarrhea and/or constipation, without a corresponding physical cause. Treatment of this abnormality may be successful for a short time, but the symptoms tend to return. Other non-gastrointestinal symptoms are often found in these patients, including fatigue, muscle pains, insomnia, dizziness, and headaches, and the patients have also been found to have similar psychological characteristics, such as anxiety, depression, and neurosis.

The approach to the treatment of IBS is usually comprehensive, using such methods as *education, symptom management, stress management,* and *contingency management.* Education involves explaining to the patient the responsiveness of the gastrointestinal tract to stressful events and emotions. Symptom management concurrently relieves the short-term symptoms while other long-term work goes on. Stress management tries to control stress in reaction to specific situations, such as criticism or disapproval. In contingency management, the treatment involves making positive reinforcing events contingent on more adaptive behavior by the patient (Feuerstein *et al.*, 1986).

TREATMENT OF DERMATOLOGICAL DISORDERS

Emotional and psychological factors powerfully affect the human skin, and the treatment of dermatological disorders often requires a psychotherapeutic approach (Engels, 1985). However, psychosomatic patients with dermatological disorders are typically not good candidates for intensive psychotherapy, as they frequently have difficulty discussing their emotions.

If psychotherapeutic treatment is to succeed, the referring physician and the psychotherapist must cooperate, the physician treating the visible somatic symptoms and the psychotherapist uncovering the origins of the disorder.

REFERENCES

Agras, W. S. The behavioral treatment of somatic disorders. In W. D. Gentry (Ed.), *Behavioral medicine: A new research paradigm* (pp. 479–530). New York: Guilford Press, 1984.

Bandura, A. *Principles of behavior modification.* New York: Holt, Rinehart & Winston, 1969.

Davidson, P. (Ed.). *The behavioral management of anxiety, depression and pain.* New York: Brunner/Mazel, 1976.

Engels, W. D. Dermatologic disorders, In W. Dorfman & L. Cristofar (Eds.), *Psychosomatic illness review* (pp. 146–161). New York: Macmillan, 1985.

English, E. H., & Baker, T. B. Relaxation training and cardiovascular response to experimental stressors. *Health Psychology*, 1983, *2*, 239–259.

Fensterheim, H., & Kantor, J. S. The behavioral approach to sexual disorders. In B. B. Wolman & J. Money (Eds.), *Handbook of human sexuality* (pp. 313–328). Englewood Cliffs, NJ: Prentice-Hall, 1980.

Feuerstein, M., Labbé, E. E., and Kuczmierczyk, A. R. *Health psychology: A psychobiological perspective*. New York: Plenum Press, 1986.

Garrick, T. R. Behavior therapy for irritable bowel syndrome. *General Hospital Psychiatry*, 1981, *3*, 48–51.

Garrick, T. R., & Kimball, C. P. Recent developments in psychosomatic disorders. In B. B. Wolman (Ed.), *The therapist's handbook* (2nd ed.. pp. 514–528). New York: Van Nostrand Reinhold, 1983.

Lazarus, A. A. *The practice of multimodal therapy*. New York: McGraw-Hill, 1981.

Meagher, R. B., Jr. Cognitive behavior therapy in health psychology. In T. Millon, C. Green, & R. Meagher (Eds.), *Handbook of clinical health psychology* (pp. 499–520). New York: Plenum Press, 1982.

Millon, T., Green, C., & Meagher, R. (Eds.), *Handbook of clinical health psychology*. New York: Plenum Press, 1982.

Moore, N. Behavior therapy in bronchial asthma: A controlled study. *Journal of Psychosomatic Research*, 1965, *9*, 257–262.

Skinner, B. F. *About behaviorism*. New York: Knopf, 1974.

Suinn, R. M. Intervention with Type A behaviors. *Journal of Consulting and Clinical Psychology*, 1982, *50*, 797–803.

Toyouz, S. W., Beaumont, P. J., & Glaun, D. Refeeding patients with anorexia nervosa. In P. Pichot, P. Berner, R. Wolf, & K. Thau (Eds.), *Psychiatry: The state of the art: Vol. 4. Psychotherapy and psychosomatic medicine* (pp. 423–428). New York: Plenum Press, 1985.

Turner, S. M. (Ed.). *Behavioral theories and treatment of anxiety*. New York: Plenum Press, 1984.

Waggoner, R. W. A brief description of the Masters and Johnson treatment of sexual dysfunction. In B. B. Wolman & J. Money (Eds.), *Handbook of human sexuality* (pp. 325–328). Englewood Cliffs, NJ: Prentice-Hall, 1980.

White, L., & Tursky, B. (Eds.). *Clinical biofeedback: Efficacy and mechanisms*. New York: Guilford Press, 1982.

Wilson, G. T., & Lazarus, A. A. Behavior modification and therapy. In B. B. Wolman (Ed.), *The therapist's handbook* (2nd ed., pp. 121–154). New York: Van Nostrand Reinhold, 1983.

Wolman, B. B. (Ed.). *Psychological aspects of obesity: A handbook*. New York: Van Nostrand-Reinhold, 1982.

Wolman, B. B., & Money, J. (Eds.). *Handbook of human sexuality*. Englewood Cliffs, NJ: Prentice-Hall, 1986.

Wolpe, J. Behavior therapy for psychosomatic disorders. *Psychosomatics*, 1980, *21*, 379.

Wolpe, J., & Reigna, I. J. (Eds.). *Behavior therapy for psychosomatic disorders*. New York: Pergamon Press, 1976.

27

Interactional Psychotherapy

Human behavior can affect physical health in three ways: (1) in etiology, when behavior directly causes psychosomatic disorders; (2) in prevention, when one develops unhealthy life styles and self-destructive habits that reduce one's chances of a healthy life; and (3) in rehabilitation, through appropriate or inappropriate reactions to one's illness, one's sick role, and one's lack of cooperation with treatment (Strupp, 1978).

No human being acts in a vacuum, and a considerable part of human behavior is interaction with other people. How one interacts with others plays a highly significant role in one's physical and mental health. In a way, psychotherapy is a psychosomatic interaction, for the therapist's friendly and understanding attitude can produce physiological changes in the patient. Psychosomatic patients need a great deal of reassurance. Psychotherapy is always a process of interaction. From a sociological point of view, there are two partners: one who seeks help and one who is supposed to offer that help. One partner (the patient) feels that his or her life has gone wrong and needs some kind of adjustment, and the other (the therapist) believes that he or she can help. The person who asks for help believes this, too. Without faith in psychotherapy, without the belief of patients that they can be helped, they will never come to us, at least not willingly (Sifneos, 1972).

The process of psychotherapy is actually a split-level or two-level process. On one level, it is an interaction of two adults. One of them has an office, calls herself or himself an M.D. or a Ph.D., has passed some examinations, has got a license or certification, and is approved by society for the job she or he is doing. The other can be a lawyer, a teacher, an accountant, a housewife, or a garbage collector who feels disturbed and is perplexed by being disturbed. There is little chance of helping somebody unless he or she feels perplexed by being disturbed. On the other level, psychotherapy is the *interaction* of two adults that resembles the type of interaction that takes place between parents and their offspring with the possibility of a great many irrational positive and negative feelings directed toward the therapist (Wolman, 1983). Our patients may be great scholars, brilliant writers, or famous singers. In the therapeutic situation, they look up to us. Outside the therapeutic situation, the relationship may be reversed, and we may look up to them.

TRANSFERENCE

The interaction that takes place between a psychotherapist and the patient transcends the usual one-to-one relationship. Psychotherapists deal with the emotional problems of people, and a particular phenomenon called *transference* takes place (Wolman, 1967).

Any kind of human relation, called by Freud an "object relation," is a cathexis or an investment of one's emotions in the other person. However, whereas Freud stressed the point of view of the person who cathects, I have developed an additional concept that takes into consideration the person who is at the receiving end of cathexis. Thus, instead of using the term *cathexis* as described in classic psychoanalysis, I deal with the concept of *interindividual cathexis,* which represents the emotional load that is *directed* by one person toward another and that is *received* by the other. In other words, if a mother loves a child, the mother is cathecting her sublimated or neutralized libido in the child, and the child is at the receiving end. How the child feels about it, how the child perceives the mother's love, is a highly important factor in his or her emotional balance and personality development (Wolman, 1984).

The cathectic situation in any kind of psychotherapy is also a two-way process. The patient cathects his or her emotions in the therapist, but the therapist cannot be totally unaware of the fact that the patient has invested some of his or her emotions, positive or negative, in the therapist. A psychoanalyst or a psychoanalytically oriented psychotherapist need not assume that she/he has the right always to deal with these cathected processes in transference in the same way, no matter who the patient is. Alexander and French (1946) introduced the concept of *intentional manipulation of transference* by decreasing the number of sessions. I go further than Alexander and French: I maintain that whether the therapist is aware of it or not, his or her behavior influences the patient's transference; thus, I suggest making a more efficient use of transference (Wolman, 1967).

In the treatment of psychosomatic disorders, one can expect a great deal of resistance and negative transference. The therapist is often perceived as a person who tries to take away the escapist psychosomatic symptoms.

Courage and Wisdom: The Purposes of Interactional Psychotherapy

Psychotherapeutic interaction should be divided into three phases. The first phase is *analytic,* which implies overcoming whatever irrationalities one has developed during one's lifetime. It involves the removal of infantile inhibitions and a resolution of the infantile conflicts that cripple the personality and prevent adult individuals from behaving maturely. The resolution of past conflicts is the first phase of interactional therapy.

As soon as the psychotherapy helps to resolve past conflicts and the patient is liberated from past handicaps and able to put his or her intelligence and energy to productive use, the psychotherapy moves toward two higher phases, which I call the *search for identity* and *becoming,* or *self-realization* (Wolman, 1984).

In order to be able to find oneself (that is, in order to be able to become a mature adult), one has to go through the analytic phase, in which one acquires a good sense of reality, emotional balance, and social adjustment.

The *sense of reality* is a necessary prerequisite for any adjustment to life and any chance of finding oneself in life. The sense of reality makes the patient aware of the irrational aims of psychosomatic symptoms.

Emotional balance includes four factors:

1. The emotional reaction must be *appropriate* to the situation. We react with sorrow to defeat and with joy to success. Disturbed people react in a paradoxical way, enjoying their defeat and finding success unacceptable.
2. Well-balanced emotionality is also *proportionate.* Disturbed individuals overreact or underreact to success and failure.
3. The third factor in emotional balance is *self-control.* Infants and disturbed people are unable to control their emotions and to react in a way that will serve their purposes and help them in attaining their goals.
4. The fourth factor in emotional balance is *adjustability.* No matter how deep the sorrow is or how great the joy, life goes on and one cannot live in a dream world. Psychosomatic symptoms are a maladjustive reaction.

The third achievement in the analytic phase should be *social adjustment.* People who have undergone psychotherapy should be able to develop a meaningful relationship with one or more individuals and should be able to form with others rational give-and-take relationships, devoid of psychosomatic symptoms, which reflect the need for attention and sympathy.

The analytic phase enables the individual to think clearly and to act in a realistic way, but it does not solve the problem of a direction in life. What one is going to do with oneself, what life should mean to one, and what one's goal in life is—these are the problems dealt with in the second phase of interactional psychotherapy, called the *search for identity*.

Awareness of oneself is not necessarily acceptance of one's faults and errors and shortcomings. Awareness of oneself is an awareness that these are the cards that one has received from heredity and experience. One must play these cards the best one can. The individual does not necessarily accept all the aspects of his or her personality, nor does he or she necessarily subscribe to all the possibilities. People may make a choice between various ways of life and find fulfillment in what is the most important aspect in their lives; then, they will no longer need to escape into a psychosomatic illness.

BECOMING: SELF-REALIZATION

One can distinguish three attitudes toward other people. The first attitude is *instrumental*, that is, using people for the satisfaction of one's own needs. This narcissistic attitude is typical of infants because they need to be supported. As children grow, they learn that one cannot get unless one gives, and they gradually develop a *mutual* attitude based on giving and receiving. This attitude is typical of friendship, sexual relations, and marriage: Each party tries to please the other and expects the same in return. The third type of attitude is giving without expecting anything in return. This *vectorial* attitude is typical of a rational parent–child relationship (Wolman, 1970). It can also be directed toward one's social, religious, and other ideals.

A balanced individual should be able to function at all three levels: to be instrumental in bread-winning functions, mutual in friendship and in marriage, and vectorial with regard to one's children and/or one's beliefs and ideals. Unfortunately, a great many individuals never outgrow the first level, that is, taking care of themselves and disregarding others. Living that kind of life may give a person a feeling of futility.

In the third phase of interactional psychotherapy, one helps the patient to develop worthwhile goals. To be a fully developed individual, one cannot remain at the instrumental level. Not only should one be capable of mutual relationships (marriage, sexual relations, and friendship), but one must also be able to develop the ability and the desire to give. Getting is limited; giving is unlimited.

The third phase of interactional psychotherapy should enable individuals to decide in which direction to utilize their energy as well as their intellectual and emotional resources. In this phase, patients find out the meaning of their lives. They discover that they can create something and add something to life. Creating is the sign and symbol of power, and being a giver and a creator is the highest level of personality development.

PSYCHOSOMATIC DISORDERS

I have applied the above-described method to the treatment of psychosomatic disorders (Wolman, 1982). Over the years of my psychotherapeutic practice, I have treated several obese people. The tendency to gain weight is related to a great many factors, most of them of a psychological nature. However, even the psychosomatic origin of obesity is not homogeneous, and one must not put all obese people into one clinical category. Scientific literature is full of contradictory empirical data and diverse theoretical explanations, and there is no reason to ascribe uniformity to obesity.

The complexity of the problem and the diversity of the clinical pictures militate against simplicity and uniformity in the treatment of obesity. A careful differential diagnosis of every single case, as well as flexibility in treatment techniques, is imperative. The following paragraphs describe one of the possible approaches, with adequate room for individualization.

All the patients I have treated for obesity have been compulsive eaters. Overeating resembles other types of addiction, such as the addictions to alcohol or drugs. In the treatment of addictions, I have avoided a head-on confrontation with well-entrenched compulsive drinking or, even worse, drug addiction. I do not believe that one can expect good results with a direct attack on overt pathological behavioral patterns. Usually, I have assumed that the need to take drugs or alcohol is rooted in the unconscious, for consciously, all of my patients have agreed that it is very bad to be addicted. Their addictions were *symptoms* of deep, underlying emotional problems, and the removal of the symptoms would not have lasted long if the underlying causes had been left untouched.

I compare the symptoms to the branches of a tree that blocks the light. Cutting the branches does not solve the problem, for sooner or later, new branches grow. In order to solve the problem, one must dig out the roots, for no tree can grow without roots. As soon as the roots are out, the tree falls, and the problem is solved. And in fact, whenever I have dug out and cut away the roots of addiction, the addicts have been cured. I believe that the first task of psychotherapy is to dig out and remove the roots of the patient's emotional problems, and the following sections briefly describe the technique that I have been using.

Hypochondriasis

My patient Mrs. L. had rich psychosomatic experiences greatly supported by her hypochondriasis.

As mentioned above, my psychotherapeutic strategy has three phases. During the first phase, the 40-year-old Mrs. L. was calling her "mommy" every day to give detailed reports of what she had eaten for breakfast, lunch, and dinner and how much money she had spent on groceries and fake jewelry.

After several affairs, Mrs. L. had married a poor but impressive man who somewhat represented a father image to her. Mrs. L. demanded affectionate approval from her surrogate daddy. She was constantly sick, mostly with imaginary and grave diseases, and expected a continuous supply of affection for herself, the "sick girl." Mrs. L. demanded from her husband that he be seductive and sexually aggressive, but at the same time, she avoided any opportunity for sexual encounters. Her best friend, whom she invited on every vacation, was a 40-year-old infantile homosexual. Traveling in trio prevented possible advances from her husband. Moreover, she was quite eloquent when describing her "illnesses" to her acquaintance.

The psychotherapy was directed toward building her self-esteem and guiding her toward a more active life.

Another hypochondriac, Mrs. H., complained about "excruciating pains" and a variety of physical diseases—preferably very grave ones and, if possible, lethal. In treatment, I had her check with a competent physician of *my choice*, whom I could trust and with whom I could communicate. Then, Mrs. H. embarked on the three phases of interactional psychotherapy.

Cardiovascular Symptoms

Following the hypothesis that psychosomatic disorders are goal-directed, I have been quite successful in their treatment, with the exception of cases of long duration when the emotional conflicts have already caused significant physical harm. I have persistently refused to treat patients who had bleeding ulcers or properly diagnosed cardiovascular diseases.

There is not much new in my approach. Feldman (1981) put it succinctly:

> The most common focus of rehabilitation, of living as full a life as possible or achieving the highest level of functioning, is to help the individual with chronic illness to enter or re-enter the world of work. . . . It is through work that many persons establish their social connections with others. Work has long been regarded as a restorative activity and it is in the workplace that the worker comes face to face with forces and values of the larger society; these forces, in turn, act directly on the individual's social relationships, value orientations, and emotional well-being. (p. 142)

REFERENCES

Alexander, F., & French, T. M. *Psychoanalytic psychotherapy.* New York: Ronald Press, 1946.

Feldman, L. F. Teaching of psychosocial and human issues: Rehabilitation and humanistic issues. *Proceedings of the American Cancer Society 3rd National Conference on Human Values and Cancer.* Washington, DC: American Cancer Society, 1981.

Sifneos, P. E. *Short-term psychotherapy and emotional crisis.* Cambridge: Harvard University Press, 1972.

Strupp, H. H. *Psychotherapy: Clinical research and clinical issues.* New York: Macmillan, 1978.

Wolman, B. B. *The unconscious mind: The meaning of Freudian psychology.* Englewood Cliffs, NJ: Prentice-Hall, 1967.

Wolman, B. B. Interactional psychotherapy of obesity. In B. B. Wolman (Ed.), *Psychological aspects of obesity: A handbook.* New York: Van Nostrand Reinhold, 1982.

Wolman, B. B. The patient–doctor relationship. In B. B. Wolman (Ed.), *The therapist's handbook* (pp. 3–21). New York: Van Nostrand Reinhold, 1983.

Wolman, B. B. *Interactional psychotherapy.* New York: Van Nostrand Reinhold, 1984.

28

Biofeedback, Autogenic Therapy, Meditation, and Hypnosis

BIOFEEDBACK

Biofeedback is a feedback of biological information. It represents a flow of information displayed to an individual concerning his or her internal physiological processes, such as heart beat, brain rhythm, and muscular tension (Olton & Noonberg, 1980; Yates, 1980).

There are several different approaches to what biofeedback implies. Biofeedback is often defined as a self-regulation process, somewhat related to the paradigm of the operant conditioning of autonomic responses. Such a definition points to the temporal contiguity between the stimulus and the response.

Another highly optimistic definition of biofeedback is related to the fact:

> . . . that changes in physiological responses and related emotional responses may be the consequences of changes in life style, which may be fostered by a greater awareness of the psychophysiological consequences of alternative response styles. In practices, biofeedback may be the only technique within a multimodal treatment package. (White & Tursky, 1982, p. 445)

A somewhat different definition was given by Green and Green (1986) in Wolman and Ullman's *Handbook of States of Consciousness* (1986):

> Biofeedback is the feedback of biological information to a person. It is the continuous monitoring, amplifying, and displaying to a person (usually by a needle on a meter, or by a light or a tone) of an ongoing internal physiological process, such as muscle tension, temperature, heart behavior, or brain rhythm. (p. 553)

Biofeedback Therapy

Biofeedback therapy is a technique of self-control of the physiological elements of stress, which may otherwise lead to the formation of morbid symptoms. Biofeedback therapy stimulates conscious and voluntary acts of psychological control over physiological phenomena.

The biofeedback therapy method has been used in the treatment of migraine headaches, asthma, essential hypertension, incontinence, and other psychosomatic disorders. Biofeedback seems to be particularly successful in the treatment of severely character-disordered psychosomatic patients (Garrick & Kimball, 1983, p. 524).

The rationale of using biofeedback therapy in the treatment of psychosomatic disorders is the belief that lasting improvement in a psychosomatic disorder is made possible only if the patient is made aware of the connection between his or her attitudes and ways of thinking and the pathological functions of the body. Biofeedback is believed to produce such an awareness by making psychosomatic patients change their thoughts and attitudes and become sensitive to the body signals that indicate a physiological dysfunction.

Biofeedback therapists use a variety of instruments. One of the most used is the *electromyographic instrument,* (the EMG), which enables the patient to become aware of his or her muscles and their activity. The EMG is often used in the treatment of muscular tension in various parts of the body.

Clinical Biofeedback Training

According to Green and Green (1986), so-called clinical biofeedback training is a therapeutic method based on self-regulation training. Self-regulation training involves an increased awareness of one's own body, passive volition processes, and visualization. In biofeedback training, the cortex becomes aware of what the biofeedback device "says" and then knows what that means with respect to the body:

> This knowing, when accompanied by appropriate visualization, is *followed* by the development of direct physiological awareness, the internal feedback. Finally, skill in self-regulation of the CNS is achieved, without machines, including large or small sections of the system, formerly thought to be completely autonomous and unconscious. (Green & Green, 1986, p. 562)

Biofeedback training can be a useful tool in visualization training because it is of great help in developing a simultaneous awareness of physiological and psychological processes; thus, it contributes to psychosomatic self-regulation, which is believed to be of therapeutic value (Newell, 1977).

Biofeedback and Psychosomatic Disorders

Biofeedback is a frequently used to treat psychosomatic disorders. Instrumentation is used to display to patients specific physiological signals related to their symptoms. Using the feedback as an immediate consequence, the patient learns to alter and control the physiological variable. Biofeedback has been used to train individuals with both tension and migraine headaches to alter these disorders; to train patients with asthma to decrease airway resistance; to train patients with incontinence to use autonomically innervated sphincters to regain continence; and to train patients with hypertension to decrease their systolic and diastolic blood pressure. When combined with behavioral analysis, biofeedback techniques can become a powerful therapeutic adjunct and can be particularly useful in the treatment of severely character-disordered psychosomatic patients. The active involvement in self-regulation supports a sense of positive self-esteem, and ego strength can help stabilize people with these disorders (Garrick & Kimball, 1983).

Miller (1983) maintained that one of the main advantages of biofeedback is that its measuring instruments provide the therapists with better information than they can secure from their own sense organs. After initial training, the patient is able to use this information to guide his or her own practice, thus relieving the therapist of constant vigilance. The patient may eventually learn to discriminate the sensations indicating the correctness of his or her responses and may therefore no longer need the help of the measuring instrument. For example, when a child must exercise a certain muscle group, he or she may be motivated to comply by equipment that keeps a cartoon show turned on as long as he or she is performing satisfactorily. Ingenious uses of rapid advances in chip and microprocessor technology will allow such applications to be radically extended. They could greatly increase the cost effectiveness of behavioral therapies, allowing patients to be given longer periods of practice and, in certain cases, to continue that practice in life situation, thus solving the problem of transfer from the clinic to everyday life.

Tension Headaches, Bruxism, and Asthma

Miller (1978) described the use of biofeedback therapy for tension headaches, migraine headaches, bruxism, asthma, and other psychosomatic disorders. According to Miller, tension headaches are produced by muscle tension in the forehead and neck. EMG electrodes have been used as a source of feedback, with rapid clicks indicating greater tension. This type of treatment may effect a reduction in headaches in the majority of patients who continue with home practice in relaxation. Headaches are notoriously subject to placebo effects, but some studies on relatively small numbers of patients suggest that the effects of biofeedback are greater than those of a placebo pill.

Bruxism is a tendency to clench and grind the teeth. Some preliminary case studies indicate that it and related conditions may be relieved by use of the EMG to train relaxation of the jaw muscles. Some patients with bruxism describe a tension around the jaws that can be relieved by clenching the teeth, and using the EMG to correct this misperception is a key step in their treatment. On the other hand, the myofascial pain dysfunction (MPD) syndrome does respond to placebo treatment.

It seems that training in relaxation can increase peak expiratory flow rates in asthmatic children. In one study in which children were given contingent feedback for relaxation recorded from frontalis leads, the children showed greater relaxation and improvement in flow rate than those who were given noncontingent feedback or who were not trained.

Miller (1978,1982) described several studies on migraine headaches. In a study of 32 migraine patients on whom pretraining data were available, 29 were rated as improved on the basis of a global assessment after having been given training in warming their hands first in the laboratory and then at home by the use of a biofeedback temperature trainer and a series of autogenic-type phrases that they repeated to themselves in order to help them to relax. In another study, out of 110 headache sufferers originally entering the migraine study, 74 completed 270 days of training and follow-up and 36 dropped out. Of the total of 110 participants, 60% were judged to show moderate to very good improvement at the time of completion or dropout, and 40% were judged to show only slight or no improvement. In a follow-up 3–4 years later, 68 of the patients were located. Of these, 10% were worse than at the end of training, and 90% were as good or better; 14% had tried other forms of treatment during this interval.

Gastrointestinal Symptoms

According to Miller (1978), the most impressive results of biofeedback training have been seen in the rare but extremely troublesome symptom of fecal incontinence. Patients were provided with feedback on how their internal and external sphincters responded to increased pressure, produced by the inflation of a balloon in the lower colon. Out of 40 patients, 28 were either cured or virtually so; 20 of these showing the maximal improvement after one session. For a number of these patients, the length of the previous history of unsuccessful treatment and of follow-up with successful results is impressive.

Three quite different cases of ruminative vomiting have been treated by use of the EMG to detect the first evidence of the muscular activity involved in emesis; this activity was then immediately punished by uncomfortable electric shock. Four patients with severe functional diarrhea were trained to alternatively increase and decrease their bowel sounds, which were recorded by an electronic stethescope and heard over a loudspeaker. Marked improvement was recorded for some patients with longstanding severe conditions. Also, patients with irritable bowel syndrome can be trained to suppress the spastic response to the inflation of a balloon in the rectosigmoid colon (Miller, 1978).

Cardiovascular Symptoms

Miller (1978) described 34 hypertensive patients who were randomly assigned to one of two treatments given twice a week for 6 weeks. Their blood pressure was taken by a nurse before and after the treatment. An experimental group was trained in progressive relaxation, rhythmic breathing, and a type of transcendental meditation while receiving feedback from a tone whose pitch fell as the patient relaxed, as determined first by an increase in skin resistance and later by a reduced EMG reading. They were also encouraged to practice relaxation and meditation twice a day at home.

Green and Green (1986) reported the following:

> Our own work in the field of hypertension uses a variety of self-regulation techniques including thermal biofeedback (emphasizing increased blood flow in the feet), striate muscular relaxation, breathing exercises, and autogenic training, which includes visualization. We stress self-awareness, blood flow control, blood pressure reduction, and medication reduction. In the first series of patients, 6 out of 7 who had been using prescription medications for hypertension control (from 6 months to 20 years) were able to self-regulate their blood pressures and at the same time reduce their medication levels to zero. Later, additional hypertensive patients were trained, many in groups, with similar positive results.
>
> Our medication-free patients attributed maintenance of their success over a long period of time (the longest follow-up was ten years) to being able to maintain the self-awareness and self-control that developed during their original training. An important feature of their success was freedom from the generally deleterious side-effects of their medications. The pleasure expressed by these patients at having well-functioning bodies made it obvious that the physical state of consciousness is a part of mental health.
>
> The biofeedback literature now includes several thousand research and clinical reports. The list of syndromes includes anorexia, bradycardia, blepherospasm, cancer, colitis, diabetes, epilepsy, esophageal spasm, fecal incontinence, foot drop, fibrillation, glaucoma, hypertension, insomnia, migraine, multiple sclerosis, nystagmous, oculomotor spasm, pain of various types, psoriasis, Paynaud's disease, strabismus, tachycardia, tension headache, tinnitus, and more.
>
> It is significant, in considering states of consciousness, that most of the above syndromes can be temporarily ameliorated by the use of placebos (medically innocuous procedures, or "sugar pills"); and it is this wide range of syndromes responding to biofeedback training that originally led many psychologists and physicians to classify biofeedback training as a placebo—not realizing that placebo effect is unconscious self-regulation, whereas biofeedback training is conscious self-regulation. Originally it had been thought (erroneously) by many researchers and clinicians that the placebo effect was imaginary. Nothing could be further from the truth. When a placebo slows the heart rate, that is real.

When it changes gastric secretions, that is real. And now it has been shown that when the placebo "controls" pain, it does so through the release of endorphins, the endogenous morphine-like substances of the body. (p. 563)

However, biofeedback used as a conditioning tool has had consistently negative clinical results. According to Green and Green (1986), "fifteen of the first sixteen published research studies using biofeedback for control of hypertension either failed completely or had statistically significant results that were *clinically* insignificant" (p. 562).

AUTOGENIC THERAPY

Autogenic therapy is a self-generating method of therapy. It applies a self-induced psychophysiological shift to the autogenic state that facilitates self-directed and self-regulatory processes. The standard exercises always use the concept of passive concentration. The six standard exercises require passive concentration on heaviness and warmth in the extremities and the torso, cardiac and respiratory regulation, and cooling of the forehead—form the core of autogenic training. The exercises are first performed in the therapist's office, and the patient then continues the exercises at home. The sessions at home are usually practiced daily after lunch, after dinner, and before going to sleep.

There are individual differences in the time required for training, ranging from a couple of days to several weeks or months. Individual indications are taken into consideration, and the six standard exercises are not applied in all cases. The exercises of heaviness and warmth are most frequently applied, with subsequently induced muscle relaxation and vasodilation. The regular practice of autogenic exercises is associated with functional changes that are opposed to the effects of stress.

Meditative exercises in the framework of autogenic therapy include the experience of static uniform colors, the experience of selected colors, the visualization of concrete and/or abstract objects, the experience of a selected state of feeling, the visualization of other persons and answers from the unconscious, and experiences related to the psychodynamic constellation of the patient.

Autogenic therapy aims at the modification of mental functions (neutralizing, reinforcing, abstinence, paradoxical, and supporting). These exercises have to be carefully chosen and adapted to the needs of the individual.

The autogenic neutralization methods are different from those of autogenic modification because they promote the "brain-directed" release of some psychosomatically disturbing material. As autogenic discharges seem to have a therapeutic importance, different techniques have been elaborated to facilitate these discharges.

The psychotherapeutic applications of the autogenic approach include the domain of psychosomatic medicine: disorders of the gastrointestinal tract, of the cardiovascular system, of the respiratory tract, of the endocrine and metabolic functions, and of the skin. Autogenic therapy has been successfully applied in neurotic disorders and also in disorders of motor function (e.g., writer's cramp and stuttering), the perception of and reaction to pain, and sleep disorders (Jus & Jus, 1977, pp. 250–251).

Autogenic therapy puts patients into an "autogenic shift" that resembles a hypnotic state. In this state, the body, the emotions, and the mind are all quiet at the same time. The body approaches sleep, and the emotions are deeply quiet, but a volitionally stilled receptive mind is still alert, and not wandering aimlessly or daydreaming (Green & Green, 1986, p. 570). The state of autogenic shift is reachable through autogenic training, through meditation, and through biofeedback.

If a person can easily slip into the state of autogenic shift, biofeedback training may not be needed for getting information from the unconscious, but for most unsophisticated persons, the most productive approach is first to learn to use thermal and EMG training, which is followed by brain-wave (EEG) training.

In autogenic training, two of the psychophysiological conditions needed for autogenic shift are warmth in the peripheral parts of the body and an overall sensation of heaviness (or lightness, in some cases). In biofeedback, thermal training accomplishes the warmth condition, and EMG training accomplishes the heaviness condition. The feeling of warmth corresponds with quiet emotions, and the physical feeling of heaviness, which is quiet in the striate nervous system, corresponds with deep relaxation (English & Baker, 1983).

When the voluntary turn-down of sympathetic firing is established through biofeedback-aided visualization training, and when the limbic brain is involved in making the appropriate changes in the hypothalamic circuits, the psychological result is emotional quietness. The autogenic shift requires "getting answers" from the unconscious. The mind must be alert but not active. It is useful to consider the difference between the voluntary production of alpha rhythm and theta rhythm (Green & Green, 1986).

States of Consciousness

For most people, conscious alpha production means relaxing in their usual way, with their eyes closed. Of the human population, 90% normally produce some occipital alpha under these conditions, whether daydreaming or not. Interestingly, it is quite easy to learn in a few brain-wave training sessions, using auditory feedback, to produce occipital alpha with the eyes open but unfocused. According to Green and Green (1986), conscious theta production, on the other hand, is much more difficult (they base this judgment on their own experience, on research experience with college students and others, and on clinical experience in their Biofeedback Center since the mid-1970s).

Many people cannot succeed in causing the theta tone to sound in an EEG feedback machine unless they are almost asleep. Then, when the tone sounds, they return to their "alpha or beta attention" so quickly that the theta state is eradicated. The task is to develop alert internal attention without eliminating the theta rhythm. The trainee must learn to "hear" the theta feedback tone without changing the state of consciousness toward "normal," and thus causing the theta state to disappear. It is necessary to learn to remain alert in the so-called twilight state of consciousness (Wolman & Ullman, 1986).

A Case Report

An excellent example of "interrogating the unconscious" with the aid of theta training occurred in our lab when a biofeedback technician (at a Topeka hospital), himself skilled in EMG and blood flow control, and successful in training others, began to suffer from what seemed to be a form of colitis associated with "spontaneous" anxiety. Marty (an assigned name) had mentioned this problem to us, but not until he said that it was not responding to sympathetic quieting did we begin to suspect deeper causes than normal life stress. He obtained medical opinions from two physicians, following a "work up" of the GI tract, but no physical causes could be found, and he was advised to talk to a psychotherapist. (Green & Green, 1986, pp. 571–572)

MEDITATION

Meditation has often been used as a psychotherapeutic method in the treatment of various mental and psychosomatic disorders (Wolman & Ullman, 1986). This approach suggests a certain parallelism with a concept in modern physics that conceives of the universe as looking, in the words of Sir James Jeans (1937), "more like a great thought than a great machine." At present, however, we still have to view this concept as belonging to the realm of metaphysics rather than to the spheres of physics and biology; its relationship to scientific inquiry remains, as yet, no more than a speculative one.

In meditation, the organism shifts gears from the active to the receptive mode; from a state of ego dominance to a state where the ego is subordinate and can be partially dispensed with; from a state of automatization to one of deautomatization.

Carrington (1986) maintained that there is a similarity between what occurs during a meditation session and what occurs during the systematic desensitization used in behavior therapy. During the latter, increasing amounts of anxiety (prepared in a graded hierarchy) are systematically "counterconditioned" by being paired with an induced state of deep relaxation. In meditation, the meditative focus becomes a signal for turning one's attention inward and bringing about a state of deep relaxation. The patients maintain a permissive attitude with respect to the thoughts, images, or sensations experienced during meditation. They neither reject nor unduly hold onto them; they merely let these impressions flow through their minds, either simultaneously with their focus of meditation or alternating with it.

Meditation sets up a subjective state in which the deep relaxation brought about by attention to the meditative focus is paired with a rapid, self-initiated review of an exceedingly wide variety of mental concepts and tension areas. As thoughts, images, sensations, and amorphous impressions drift by during meditation, the meditative focus seems to neutralize their effects; the patients believe that they emerge from meditation with the "charge" taken off their current concerns or problems, and that this result enables them to cope with these problems more effectively (Carrington & Ephron, 1977).

In systematic desensitization, the therapist and the patient identify together specific areas of anxiety and then proceed to deal with a series of single, isolated problems in a step-by-step, organized way. In meditation, the areas of anxiety to be "desensitized" are selected automatically by the responding organism, that is, the meditating person. The brain of the meditator appears to behave during meditation as though it were a computer programmed to run relevant material through "demagnetizing" circuits, handling large amounts of data at one time. We might conceptualize subsystems within the brain as scanning vast memory stores at lightning speed with the aim of selecting those contents of the mind that are: first, most pressing emotionally; second, most likely to be tolerated without undue anxiety; and third, best capable of being handled currently. The decision to surface certain mental contents rather than others for "demagnetizing" is presumably made automatically, in the course of weighing such considerations as those just described and arriving at an optimal compromise (Carrington, 1986, p. 519).

According to Carrington (1986), studies of the effects of meditation on anxiety:

> . . . have shown marked reduction in anxiety levels in meditators versus non-medical controls, even as soon as a few weeks following the commencement of meditation. This has been a consistent finding whether physiological measurements were taken or the researchers relied upon self-reports or standardized tests of anxiety to determine the extent of the changes. Evidence also suggests that meditators may actually develop some immunity to stress. (p. 497)

The same applies to psychosomatic symptoms produced by stress, anxiety, and depression. Whether the therapeutic effects of meditation are lasting is still an open question.

HYPNOSIS

Hypnosis has been tried with some success in a number of psychosomatic complaints. Hypnosis has been found to affect blood glucose, both positively and negatively, and has been successful in the treatment of anorexia and bulimia. In lab situations, there has been some link between hypnosis and pain reduction; however, changes in heart rate or blood pressure generally have not been affected (Barber, 1982; Hilgand, 1975).

According to Barber (1982), about 90% of back problems resolve themselves within a few weeks or months regardless of the type of treatment received. The small percentage of back problems that persist and become chronic may be due to one or more of a large number of causes, such as diseases of the spinal cord, neoplasms, arthritis, referred visceral or somatic pain, and compression and irritation of spinal nerves and the spinal nerve roots, as well as muscle problems.

Barger (1982) cited a 1979 report by Crasilneck:

> Crasilneck showed how hypnosuggestions can be used successfully for the control of back pain. He worked with a very difficult-to-treat population of patients with chronic back pain: 29 referrals who were addicted to or dependent on pain medication and who had had at least one unsuccessful surgical operation for their back pain. Crasilneck was unable to work with 5 of 29 because they had a negative attitude toward the initial treatment, were deeply depressed, or were extremely masochistic. Of the remaining 24 patients, 16 reported an average of 80% relief from pain at least by the fourth session and 20 of the 24 reported an average of 70% relief by the sixth session. Of the 20 successful patients, 15 voluntarily discontinued pain medication and the remaining 5 were withdrawn from the medication by their physicians. The 20 patients who were markedly relieved of back pain resumed work at a realistic level.
>
> Crasilneck's (1979) excellent results were associated with the following treatment. In the first session rapport was established, hypnosuggestive therapy was discussed, and—after it was evident that the patient had positive attitudes toward the treatment—Crasilneck suggested eye heaviness and eye closure. He then gave the patient a series of test suggestions (e.g., inability to open the eyes, numbness of a finger, and smelling a spicy aroma). The patient was told that the ability to experience what was suggested demonstrated the "power of your unconscious mind" and the "control of your mind over your body." Next, the patient was told, "Now, I give you the suggestion that as you blocked pain in your finger a few minutes ago, you can block the pain in your back. Nothing is beyond the power of your unconscious mind. You are going to block most of the pain. Most of the pain will come under control." Crasilneck stated that additional suggestions were given to control the pain, to reduce the need for medication, and to stimulate the desire to get well. During the second session, each patient was taught to give himself or herself suggestions of relaxation and suggestions for pain relief (self-hypnosis) and was encouraged to use the self-suggestions as frequently as necessary. The patients were seen for hypnosuggestive treatment daily during the first week, every other day during the second week, every third day during the third and fourth weeks, and then once a week for about two more months. Following this, the patients were seen whenever they wished. The patients were seen an average of 31 sessions over a period of

about 9 months. During these many sessions, discussions at times focused on the psychodynamic meaning of pain, the understanding of secondary gains, and the handling of life problems. (pp. 526, 527)

The hypnotic method has frequently been used in the treatment of a variety of psychosomatic disorders, among them tension and migraine headaches (Burrows & Donnerstein, 1980).

References

Barber, T. X. Hypnosuggestive procedures in the treatment of pain. In T. Millon, C. Green, & R. Meagher (Eds.), *Handbook of clinical health psychology* (pp. 521–560). New York: Plenum Press, 1982.

Burrows, G., & Donnerstein, L. *Handbook of hypnosis and psychosomatic medicine.* New York: Elsevier, 1980.

Carrington, P. Meditation as an access to altered states of consciousness. In B. B. Wolman & M. Ullman (Eds.), *States of consciousness* (pp. 487–523). New York: Van Nostrand Reinhold, 1986.

Carrington, P., & Ephron, H. S. Meditation as a therapeutic agent. In B. B. Wolman (Ed.), *International encyclopedia of psychiatry, psychology, psychoanalysis and neurology* (Vol. 7, pp. 67–71). New York: Aesculapius Publishers, 1977.

English, E. H., & Baker, T. B. Relaxation training and cardiovascular response to experimental stressors. *Health Psychology,* 1983, 2, 239–259.

Garrick, T. R., & Kimball, C. P. Recent developments in psychosomatic disorders. In B. B. Wolman (Ed.), *The therapist's handbook* (2nd ed. pp. 514–528). New York: Van Nostrand Reinhold, 1983.

Green, E. E., and Green, A. M. Biofeedback and states of consciousness. In B. B. Wolman & M. Ullman (Eds.), *Handbook of states of consciousness* (pp. 552–589). New York: Van Nostrand Reinhold, 1986.

Hilgard, E. R. Hypnosis. In M. R. Rosenzweig & L. W. Porter (Eds.), *Annual Review of Psychology,* 1975, 26, 19–44.

Jeans, J. *The new background of science.* Ann Arbor: University of Michigan Press, 1937.

Jus, A., & Jus, K. Autogenic therapy. In B. B. Wolman (Ed.), *International encyclopedia of psychiatry, psychology. psychoanalysis and neurology* (Vol. 2, pp. 249–252). New York: Aesculapius Publishers, 1977.

Miller, N. E. Clinical and experimental research on biofeedback. In L. White & B. Turshy (Eds.) *Clinical biofeedback: Efficacy and mechanisms.* New York: Guilford, 1982.

Miller, N. E. Biofeedback and visceral learning. *Annual Review of Psychology,* 1983, 29, 373–404.

Newell, K. M. Knowledge of results and feedback. In B. B. Wolman (Ed.), *International encyclopedia of psychiatry, psychology, psychoanalysis and neurology* (Vol. 6, pp. 305–310). New York: Aesculapius Publishers, 1977.

Olton, D. S., & Noonberg, A. R. *Biofeedback: Clinical applications in behavioral medicine.* Englewood Cliffs, NJ: Prentice-Hall, 1980.

White, L., & Tursky, B. (Eds.). *Clinical biofeedback: Efficacy and mechanisms.* New York: Guilford Press, 1982.

Wolman, B. B., & Ullman, M. (Eds.). *Handbook of states of consciousness.* New York: Van Nostrand Reinhold, 1986.

Yates, A. J. *Biofeedback and the modification of behavior.* New York: Plenum Press, 1980.

29

Coping

DEFINING COPING

Coping is perhaps the most important method of dealing with psychosomatic disorders. As has been repeatedly stated in this volume, psychosomatic disorders represent an array of escape routes from painful, stressful, frightening, or embarrassing situations. In nearly all instances, psychosomatic symptoms resemble jumping from the proverbial frying pan into the fire, as the various psychosomatic disorders are more harmful to the individual than the situations that he or she is trying to run away from. Quite understandably, all treatment methods aim at helping the patient *to cope* with his or her problems instead of escaping into illness. In other words, all treatment methods are intended to show patients ways of dealing with their difficulties instead of creating the much worse and more harmful psychosomatic symptoms (Coelho, Hamburg, & Adams, 1978).

The key word is *coping,* that is, a process of managing the external and internal demands that are perceived by the individual as taxing or exceeding his or her resources. The task of coping is to tolerate or adjust to adverse events and situations and to reduce the harmful environmental conditions. Coping helps the individual to maintain a positive self-image and maintain emotional balance, and to continue satisfying relationships with others (Lazarus & Folkman, 1984).

Many people are unable to cope with adversities. They tend to evade hardships instead of seeking remedies. As described in Part II of this volume, some individuals are genetically predisposed to hide from rather than to stand up to adversity. Some individuals' immune systems are biogenetically and psychogenetically weak. In many instances, the hammer-and-anvil scenario unfolds: Stressful conditions, the hammer, hit on a genetically weak somatopsychic background, the anvil.

It is imperative that therapists, no matter what their preferences are, try to encourage, foster, and guide coping behavior. The success of such guidance depends on the patient's condition and cooperation, as well as on the skill of the therapist.

Lazarus and Folkman (1984) drew a distinction between problem-focused and emotion-focused coping. *Problem-focused coping* comprises efforts directed at doing something constructive about external conditions, thereby eliminating, or at least reducing, the source of stress. An overweight patient may remove all weight-adding food from the refrigerator, and an alcoholic may destroy the available alcoholic supply. According to Moos and Billings (1982), problem-focused coping includes seeking information about the situation and asking for guidance from an authority figure. This type of coping implies an action directed toward the solution of the problem, as well as a search for rewards that will replace the morbid ones.

Emotion-focused coping describes efforts directed at regulating the emotion itself, whether the focus is the total behavior, verbal or nonverbal expressions, physiological disturbance, subjective distress, or a combination of these. Emotion-focused coping leads to affective regulation, resigned acceptance, and emotional discharge. Quite often, psychosomatic patients practice affective regulation that implies self-control and disregard of sickness wishes. They harbor hypochondriachal fears, but they refuse to pay attention to them and act as if they did not have them. People under stress tend to use both problem-focused and emotion-focused coping.

The coping process is what the person actually does in a particular encounter, and how what is done changes as the encounter or encounters unfold. Coping is a reaction to being in a stressful relationship with the environment (Coyne & Holroyd, 1982).

COGNITIVE APPRAISAL

When a person is in a psychologically stressful relationship, he or she makes conscious appraisals of the relationship. This evaluative process has been called *cognitive appraisal* (Lazarus & Folkman, 1984). There are three kinds of appraisals, and they all affect how a person copes: an appraisal of *harm* indicates that damage has already been done; *threat* points to a potential for harm; and *challenge* shows a potential for significant gain under difficult odds. The degree of stress depends on an appraisal of the power of the environment to do harm and the power of the individual to prevent this harm, along with an appraisal of how much is at stake.

Coping behavior is influenced by situational requirements, or *situational factors*. Not all situations can be easily evaluated as harmful, threatening, or challenging. Many social contexts are ambiguous. When a situation is ambiguous, a person must consider the possibilities of interpretation and must be able to rank them in some kind of logical order. It is possible, therefore, that coping effectiveness depend on the ability to resolve ambiguity.

The coping process also depends on *person factors*, or on an individual's personality traits. A Type A person, one who is aggressive and heavily committed to achievement, may display greater stress reactions than a Type B person in a situation that threatens successful achievement. However, a Type B person, one who is oriented toward maintaining friendly social relationships, may show greater stress than a Type A person in a situation threatening rejection by others.

Moos and Billings (1982) similarly described these two coping processes as appraisal-focused coping and situation-specific measures of coping. *Appraisal-focused coping* implies a logical analysis of the situation, a cognitive redefinition and a careful planning of the relevant remedies. In dealing with psychosomatic symptoms, the *situation-specific measures of coping* may, for instance, analyze the role of a marital interaction in a variety of psychosomatic symptoms, such as nausea, throwing up, impotence, and other symptoms that I have observed in my patients.

OUTCOMES OF COPING

Coping behavior affects our lives in at least three ways: it affects our *morale*, or how we feel about ourselves; it influences our *social functioning*, that is, our ability to achieve happiness in work, friendship, and marriage; and it affects our *somatic health*. Lazarus and Folkman (1984) suggested that negative emotions can result in damaging hormonal secretion patterns, whereas positive emotions, such as love and joy, may produce biochemical substances that protect tissues, ward off disease, and speed recovery. Whatever the final results of coping, it is clear that the coping process is inextricably linked to the emotional and physical maintenance of health (Pichot, Berner, Wolf, & Thau, 1985).

PREVENTION OF PSYCHOSOMATIC DISORDERS

Psychosomatic disorders are usually a product of a difficult life situation and of morbid efforts to escape from it. Therefore, it seems logical for preventive efforts to tackle both causes. There are several predisposing and eliciting factors, but the most relevant factors are probably related to *intrafamilial relationships* in childhood. There is a substantial body of evidence to prove that many children under stress escape from stressful situations into psychosomatic symptoms.

Ackerman (1958) suggested the following prevention program:

> Were we able to build a program of prevention, what would it be? A maximum effort would entail a huge job in social engineering; it would produce nothing less than a social revolution, a fundamental transformation of the values and

forms of family and community. A maximum program toward prevention would require family-life education, social therapy, and psychotherapy of parents and the family group. (p. 143)

REFERENCES

Ackerman, N. *The psychodynamics of family life.* New York: Basic Books, 1958.

Coelho, G. V., Hamburg, D. A., & Adams, J. G. (Eds.). *Coping and adaptation.* New York: Basic Books, 1978.

Coyne, J., & Holroyd, K. Stress coping and illness: A transactional perspective. In T. Millon, C. Green, & R. Meagher (Eds.), *Handbook of clinical health psychology* (pp. 103–128). New York: Plenum Press, 1982.

Lazarus, R. S., & Folkman, S. Coping and adaptation. In W. D. Gentry (Ed.), *Handbook of behavioral medicine* (pp. 282–325). New York: Guilford Press, 1984.

Moos, R. H., & Billings, A. G. Conceptualizing and measuring coping resources and processes. In L. Goldberger & S. Breznitz (Eds.), *Handbook of stress* (pp. 212–230). New York: Macmillan–Free Press, 1982.

Pichot, P., Berner, P., Wolf, R., & Thau, K. (Eds.). *Psychiatry: The state of the art: Vol. 4. Psychotherapy and psychosomatic medicine.* New York: Plenum Press, 1985.

Author Index

Subject Index